DATE			

FRIENDS BUT NO ALLIES

The Political Economy of International Change
John Ruggie and Helen Milner, General Editors

THE POLITICAL ECONOMY OF INTERNATIONAL CHANGE

John Gerard Ruggie and Helen Milner, General Editors

Friends But No Allies

Economic Liberalism and the Law of Nations

STEPHEN C. NEFF

COLUMBIA UNIVERSITY PRESS *New York*

Columbia University Press
New York   Oxford
Copyright © 1990 Columbia University Press
All rights reserved

Library of Congress Cataloging-in-Publicaiton Data

Neff, Stephen C.
Friends but no allies : economic liberalism and the law of nations
/ Stephen C. Neff.
p.   cm.—(The Political economy of international change)
Includes bibliographical references (p.   ) and index.
ISBN 0-231-07142-6 (alk. paper)
1. Free trade.   2. Free enterprise.   3. Commerce.
4. International relations.   I. Title.   II. Series.
HF1713.N44   1990
380′.3—dc20   90-2119
                                                                  CIP

Printed in the United States of America
c 10 9 8 7 6 5 4 3 2 1

To my father and mother

Contents

Preface

Book-writing (or producing?) is a collective art, notwithstanding the deceptive attributions on dust jackets and title pages to single authors. Behind the apparently solitary labors of scholars is a veritable empire of librarians, archivists, assistants, translators, editors, publishers, and assorted inspirers and comforters (not to mention prior researchers in the field). In the present instance, the aforementioned have been present in full force and effect, to the immense gratitude of the author.

To the following research institutions, much thanks is due: the Universities of Edinburgh, Cambridge, and London, and Columbia University; the British Library; the British Public Record Office; the Library of Congress; and (above all) the National Library of Scotland. Valuable assistance in translation was generously provided by Dr. Axel Tiemann.

In the preparation of the manuscript for publication, I have been singularly fortunate to have had the assistance of Anne Drummond and Glynis Kilpatrick. For their aid as proofreaders, editors, and general literary critics, no measure of thanks is adequate. The typing was done (more than once) by Mrs. May Norquay, who can amply attest that the "new technology" leaves ample scope for old-fashioned drudgery.

Particular thanks is due to the United Nations Institute for Training and Research (UNITAR), thanks to whose generosity the early stages of the research were undertaken. The author had the good fortune to hold the UNITAR Fellowship in Public International Law at Christ's College, Cambridge University, from 1981 to 1983. To the support of UNITAR, and the stimulating intellectual environment of Christ's College, an immense debt is owed.

Professor Richard B. Lillich, of the University of Virginia School of Law, is also due especial thanks, for his work as overseer of this opus during its first incarnation as a dissertation for the degree of S.J.D. at that institution. It was a labor which, I fear, taxed his patience rather more than his wisdom.

Finally—though very far from least—I wish to thank the persons who have so generously offered accommodation and hospitality to a wandering scholar on his researches. Special thanks are due to Mr. and Mrs. Jeremy Mathis, to Ms. Jane Mann, and to Mr. and Mrs. John Cousins. This book, alas, is but a paltry reward.

FRIENDS BUT NO ALLIES

INTRODUCTION
The Idea of an "Economic" World Order

Speaking very broadly, it may be said that there are two basic forms of international cooperation. One is between *states;* the other, between *peoples*. Intercourse between states is a matter of diplomacy and treaty-making, regulated by the rules of public international law (appropriately termed the "law of nations" in slightly old-fashioned parlance). In old international-law treatises, the law relating to "commerce" between states referred to the law of diplomatic relations and of treaties. "Commerce" between peoples, on the other hand, is of a quite different character. It may consist of cultural or family links; but, most commonly, it takes an economic form, such as international trade or investment. It is, accordingly, governed primarily by private-law rules of property and contract.

These two basic forms of cooperation correspond to two quite different conceptions of international order. A system of world order based upon cooperation between states may be said to be "political" in nature, in that it is brought about through negotiation between governments acting on the basis of their respective national interests. By contrast, a system of international order based upon the direct cooperation of the peoples of the world may be termed "economic," in the sense that it comes about through the development of an ever-tightening web of economic transactions which gradually bind the world into a single community. A system of "political" order is concerned essentially with power and security, with the ever-delicate balancing of rival state interests. A system of "economic" order, in contrast, is concerned with the unification of the peoples of the world and the promotion of their prosperity.

This history is the story of the idea of an "economic" (as opposed to "political") system of world order, and of the attempt—or rather, of the several attempts—to bring it to fruition. It is the story of one of the boldest and most ambitious social experiments in the history of the human race: the attempt to fashion the disparate peoples of the entire world into a single society. There have been various systems of thought which have posited the essential unity of the human race. The Christian and Islamic religions are two of the most obvious examples. Our concern, however, will be with the attempt to bring about the unity of the human race by material means—through the promotion of freedom of trade and ever-greater economic interdependence amongst the far-flung peoples of the earth. The ultimate goal of this experiment is the fundamental transformation of the very nature of the international community—from its present state as a welter of jealous and quarrelsome nation-states, into a single integrated world society.

Clear glimmerings of such an idea can be traced back through the Middle Ages to ancient times. But it was only in the eighteenth century that a comprehensive and coherent theory of an "economic" world order emerged, at the hands of the *philosophes* of the European Enlightenment and, most particularly, of the French physiocrats. They spoke in terms of "economic" policies in the broadest sense of that term, meaning policies designed to advance the welfare of the common people of the world generally. The Marquis de Mirabeau typified the exuberant (if somewhat naive) idealism of that heady age by proclaiming himself the "Friend of Mankind." His son, the French Revolution figure, echoed his views by looking forward to the complete disappearance of political alliances between nations and their replacement by the peaceful and productive activity of commerce. In that enlightened time, Mirabeau *fils* averred, nations would have "friends and no allies"; and the whole world would bask in peace and prosperity.

In sorriest contrast to this dream of an "economic" world order was the "political" reality that the *philosophes* saw about them—the petty jealousies of corrupt, decadent and repressive oligarchies; the deceits of diplomats; the ravages of soldiers and tax-gatherers; the frauds and extortions of monopolists; and the parasitism of ecclesiastics and lawyers. It is small wonder that the radicals, the humanitarians, the idealists who championed the idea of an "economic" order regarded the very term "politics" as a byword of contempt. Thomas Paine, one of the eighteenth century's foremost radical idealists, summed up the contrast between the benighted "political" ways of old and the enlightened "economic" vision of the future in the following terms:

> Nothing can appear more contradictory [he asserted] than the principles on which all governments began, and the condition to which society, civilization, and commerce are capable of carrying mankind. Government on the old system, is an assumption of power, for the aggrandizement of itself; on the new, a delegation of power, for the common benefit of society. The former supports itself by keeping up a system of war; the latter supports a system of peace, as the true means of enriching a nation. The one encourages national prejudices; the other promotes universal society, as the means of universal commerce. The one measures its prosperity, by the quantity of revenue it exacts; the other proves its excellence, by the small quantity of taxes it requires.[1]

This sharp contrast between "economic" and "political" policies is rooted, ultimately, in similarly contrasting rival frames of mind, which manifest themselves on a variety of planes. The concern in this history will be with the struggle between these two rival mentalities in the field of international law. The earliest notions of international law, based upon the law of nature of the later Roman jurists and the medieval schoolmen, were distinctly cosmopolitan in character, reflecting a vision of mankind living in a unified world community, governed by universalistic norms of conduct. The classical law of nations which emerged in the seventeenth and eighteenth centuries, however, was strikingly different. It was thoroughly "political" in character, in that it was based firmly on the safeguarding of the sovereign rights and prerogatives of the various separate and independent nation-states as corporate entities. The source of international law, on this view, did not lie (as in natural-law theories) in general ideas about right and wrong conduct. Instead, the rules of international law sprang entirely from the freely expressed will of the nations themselves. This classical, or traditional, international law was, in other words, strongly *positivist* in character. This positivist outlook was aptly encapsulated by an American professor in the 1980s, who described international law as "nothing more or less than a system of mutual restraints and reciprocal concessions that nations accept because it serves their interests to do so."[2] International law, on this view, is based upon a perception of international relations as essentially competitive in nature. Each nation-state has its own set of interests, and the function of international law is to provide the basic "rules of the game" for the perpetual jockeying and rivalry that this entails.

A system of "economic" world order is based on a diametrically opposite view of the nature and role of states—and, perforce, of the nature and role of international law. To the physiocrats and the liberal political economists of the eighteenth and nineteenth centuries, the nation-state was essentially an arbitrary and irrational impediment to economic freedom. There was no reason that the free flow of goods, capital and persons should stop at national frontiers—on the contrary, there was every reason that it should not. The reason was that the basic driving force of the liberal capitalist system which the classical economists advocated was the principle of the division of labor. All persons were to be set free to produce whatever they happened to be best at making; and the products of all of these individual efforts were to be distributed by means of an unimpeded system of free trade. In such a world, the only way to attain maximum efficiency of production and distribution was for the entire earth to become integrated into a single gigantic "mercantile republick." In a system of this kind, the role of states is not to promote their own respective national interests—for these can scarcely even be said to exist, on the liberal view—but rather to cooperate with one another to advance the common interest of the whole of mankind, by establishing the basic conditions in which free markets can function most effectively. Immanuel Kant characterized such a legal regime as a "cosmopolitical" one, in which nation-states would not be the exclusive subjects and makers of the law, but instead would function as mere "constituent parts of the great state of the human race."[3] States, in short, would become the servants of the people of the world, rather than the masters. The vision of an "economic" world order, therefore, extends far beyond economics in the narrow sense of that term. Ultimately, an "economic" world order is concerned with our perception of the nature of international society and of the laws that govern it. The real transformation which it seeks is in the minds of persons rather than in their pocketbooks.

Even if the vision of an "economic" world order is not fundamentally material in character, the fact remains that the sphere of international economic relations is the main field of battle. It was in economic terms that the basic arguments for an integrated world society were first put in a rigorous and scientific way, by the physiocrats and the classical liberal economists who followed them. And it is in the field of economic relations that the most immediate and urgent battle has been fought: the struggle against economic nationalism. The continuous, and constantly shifting, duel between freedom of trade, on the one hand, and economic nationalism, on the other, constitutes a kind of microcosm of the broader struggle between cosmopolitan and nationalistic conceptions of international relations. Traditional positivist international law is clearly on the side of the economic nationalists. Indeed, the classical law of nations assumed its modern form during one of the most rabidly economic nationalist periods of human history, the age of mercantilism. The relationship between mercantilism and positivist international law was, in fact, so close that the two were, for all intents and purposes, the economic and juridical counterparts of one another. The idea of an "economic" world order is just as clearly cosmopolitan in character, since it looks to the unification of the entire world into a single economic system. Much of our study will, accordingly, concentrate upon this central conflict between freedom of trade and economic nationalism. But it should always be borne in mind that this contest is essentially a surrogate for the broader and deeper struggle between the "economic" and the "political" mentalities in the most general sense.

There have been—so far—three major attempts to put the idea of an "economic" world order into practice. The first was during the nineteenth century, reaching its high-water mark in approximately 1850–1875. In material terms, this first experiment may have been the most successful of all. Its achievements with regard to freedom of movement of goods, persons and capital were astonishing. The attempt to overturn the traditional positivist foundations of international law, however, did not succeed. Nor did even the free-trade movement prove durable. In the face of the economic depression of

1870–90, and of the increased political tensions of the late nineteenth century, this first experiment in "economic" world order went discouragingly into reverse. The second attempt, this time under the guidance of the United States, came during the 1920s, in the wake of the carnage of the Great War. In certain ways, this experiment was the most interesting of the three, in the way that it attempted to apply technocratic and scientific expertise to the major problems of international relations, and in the way that it sought to coordinate the forces of governments and of private industry for the promotion of world order and prosperity. In the event, however, this second experiment proved the most transitory of the three, as it ignominiously collapsed in the face of the Great Depression of the 1930s and the virulent resurgence of economic nationalism that accompanied it.

The third attempt at instituting a system of "economic" world order began in the aftermath of the Second World War and is still in progress. It has, accordingly, already proved itself the most durable of the three attempts. It is also, by a considerable margin, the most thoroughly institutionalized of the three experiments, in that it is centered upon three formal international arrangements: the General Agreement on Tariffs and Trade (GATT), for the advancement of freedom of trade; the World Bank, for the promotion of economic development by means of foreign investment; and the International Monetary Fund (IMF), for provision of a framework of monetary stability for the international commercial world. A whole sub-discipline of international law, known as "international economic law," has even grown up to deal with the legal issues raised by the operation of these, and other, mechanisms of international economic relations.

If this third experiment is the most long-lasting and the most firmly based, however, it is also the most cautious and conservative of the three. It has achieved much, but only at the cost of postponing, apparently indefinitely, some of the most ambitious elements of the program of an "economic" world order. In particular, the prospect of a root-and-branch reform of international law has been quietly laid aside, in favor of a campaign concentrating more sharply, if also more narrowly, on the specific phenomenon of economic nationalism. What happened at this crucial juncture was that the post-1945 world was organized into two parallel systems of international relations: one of political relations, centered upon the United Nations and governed by a combination of traditional international law and the UN Charter; and the other of economic relations, governed by the norms of international economic law as set forth in various treaties. What this meant was that the pursuit of the vision of an "economic" world order was now to be confined, at least for the time being, to the economic sphere in the narrow sense of that term. The GATT, the World Bank and the IMF were carefully designed to promote and safeguard freedom of trade and investment—but not to reform the law of nations per se. That task is, presumably, to come later.

The struggle against economic nationalism, to be sure, remains far from easy. In certain respects, however, impressive progress has been made. Most notably, it may be said that general international law is coming, gradually, to look with increasing disfavor upon the most extreme and negative form of economic nationalism: waging of economic warfare. In the years since the Second World War, it is possible to discern an increasing tendency to restrict the traditional right of states to impose boycotts against one another for political purposes. In addition, the norms of the GATT and of the IMF impose severe restrictions upon the more important weapons of economic warfare, boycotts and freezes of financial assets.

The broader campaign against economic warfare, however, has gone less smoothly. The principal reason is that it has fallen foul of the developmental ambitions of the third-world countries. The liberal capitalist system of economics, with its orientation toward the needs of individual (and corporate) entrepreneurs, has always been relatively unsympathetic toward programs of national economic development which, by their very nature, tend to be economic nationalist in character. That has been the case ever since the nineteenth century. But since World War II, the discontent of the developing states with the various restrictions of classical liberal economics has become particularly apparent—most vividly in the turmoil of the "IMF riots" of the 1970s and 1980s. More generally, it may be said that the depth of economic nationalist feeling in the third world—together with the passionate attachment of the developing countries to the traditional positivist dogmas of state sovereignty—provide a revealing indication of the extent of the opposition to the ideal of an "economic" world order. The developing states have even gone so far as to advance a program of world order of their own, rooted in nineteenth-century economic nationalism and oriented toward the transferring of real resources from wealthy nations to poor ones in the name of development. This proposed "new international economic order" stands little chance of being implemented in anything like the form in which it has been set forth. But it reveals the extent to which the dream of an "economic" world order based upon classical liberal economic theories remains, even now, largely confined to the developed industrial states.

In the face of all of the opposition, however, the ambition of creating a single global "mercantile republick" has made impressive strides, at least in the material sense. The phenomena of the rootless multinational company and, even more notably, of the international banks and the evolution of the Euro-currency markets provide vivid illustrations of the extent to which individual entrepreneurs have been able to liberate themselves from the confines of individual nation-states. More to the point, the manifold transnational vested interests of these new cosmopolitans have so criss-crossed the major political and ideological boundaries of the world as actually to inhibit the ability of statesmen fully to vent their hostilities upon one another. To that extent, the dream of an "economic" world order might indeed be inching toward reality.

For all of the natural interest that we take in this third attempt at an "economic" world order, and for all of its achievements, the fact remains that the basic ideas underlying the system remain remarkably unchanged from the time of their original formulation. They have undergone no significant change since the heyday of the British and French classical political economists of the early nineteenth century. Similarly, the most important hurdles remain quite recognizably the same as those of a century and a half ago: the practice of economic nationalism by states and the positivist conception of international law which underlies it. It is therefore perhaps best not to say that there have been three attempts to implement the vision of an "economic" world order, but rather that there has been but one, punctuated on two occasions—so far—by serious relapses. The great social experiment in "economic" world order, then, has been more or less continuously under way for some two centuries, with remarkably little fundamental change over the years. We shall, accordingly, trace it from its very beginnings and follow its progress to the present day.

ONE

FROM POLIS *TO* KOSMOS:
Expanding Horizons of International
Political Economy

The idea of a unified human family living as a single society, bound together by the material ties of economic relations, arose relatively late in history. It would not assume a systematic and rigorous form until the eighteenth and nineteenth centuries. Throughout most of human history, the prospect of relying upon the "outside world" for one's daily bread has inspired thoughts far more of nervous dread than of brotherly love. The predominant feeling—by no means absent in the late twentieth century—has been that self-sufficiency is an important hallmark of a secure society. When governments did take an interest in international trade, the concern was to ensure the presence within the territory of adequate supplies of essential goods —i.e., to restrict the exporting of necessities and, correspondingly, to secure inflows of goods (especially foodstuffs) from abroad. In this kind of world, international trade could be a brutally competitive business, particularly in times of general famine. Small wonder, then, that states placed such a high premium on autarky, that the craving for foreign luxuries was condemned, that international trade was carefully policed by governments in the national interest—in short, that economic nationalism has been the prevailing tendency through most of human history.

Even in the ancient and medieval worlds, however, economic nationalism did not hold undisputed sway. On the material plane, it was recognized that some kinds of international trade were beneficial. And in the conceptual sphere, there were various philosophical, religious and legal schools of thought which readily acknowledged the essential unity of the human race. These two tendencies, between them, resulted, by the end of the European Middle Ages, in a natural-law doctrine of freedom of trade. The classical law of nations, however, as it emerged during the seventeenth and eighteenth centuries, powerfully reinforced the dominant economic nationalist view. The principal international-law writers during that period increasingly insisted upon the right—and indeed the duty—of each state to regulate economic activity with a view to promoting its own collective welfare or interest. International law became, in other words, increasingly positivist in its outlook.[1] Its state-centered and collectivist ethos matched up perfectly with the then-dominant practice of mercantilism, with its elaborate state regulation, and manipulation, of the economy in the general national interest. So perfectly did these two systems match up, in fact, that they be seen merely as different aspects of the same basic world-view.

This dominant economic-cum-juridical ethos could only be replaced when a fundamental change of attitude toward international trade had taken shape. It was necessary for the idea to take hold that international trade in general was, by its very nature, beneficial to the entire body of mankind. Only in the eighteenth century, a time of relative prosperity, could such an idea become important. Some of the major writers of the Enlightenment, with their strongly universalist outlook, began to insist with increasing force that the international economy was itself fundamentally cosmopolitan and transnational in character, and that individual freedom of trade would best promote the interests of the mass of humanity as a whole. With this important development, the concept of an economic world order would receive its first systematic exposition, at the hands of the French physiocrats.

10

NATURAL LAW AND THE EVOLUTION OF THE "LAW OF TRADE"

In ancient and medieval times, people tended to be strongly local in outlook, and not just in economic matters. Even religion was a local and tribal affair. There was, to be sure, a very general sense in which all human beings were seen to share certain characteristics. Aristotle identified rationality as the distinctive trait of human beings. At the same time, however, the Hellenic sage showed himself to be most reluctant to rely upon his fellow rational beings for anything of importance. On the contrary, the mark of the superior man, to Aristotle, was *autarkeia* ("self-rule"), total independence from his fellow creatures. The same consideration applied on the political plane as on the personal one: the ideal *polis* (or city-state) was one which was completely independent of the outside world for all of its wants.[2]

Plato's views on this subject were, characteristically, rather more extreme and doctrinaire, to the point that he may fairly be regarded as the patron saint of economic nationalism. Plato made an explicit link between foreign intercourse and the moral degeneracy of a society. "In the nature of the case," he cautioned sternly, "contact between state and state produces a medley of all sorts of characters, because the unfamiliar customs of the visitors rub off on to their hosts —and this, in a healthy society living under sound laws, is an absolute disaster."[3] In the interest of preventing such defilement, Plato believed that city-states should ideally be situated far from seacoasts and that foreign travel by persons under the impressionable age of forty should be severely restricted. To make foreign trade as difficult as possible, the ideal state should also adopt an inconvertible currency, valid for domestic transactions but not for international ones.[4]

Plato and Aristotle lived in a world in which, to a very great extent, these precepts were actually practiced. An extreme example was the city-state of Sparta, which clearly provided much of the inspiration for Plato. Sparta was an agrarian community with a strongly provincial and isolationist outlook, even to the point of maintaining an inconvertible currency, in the form of its famous iron money.

More commonly, however, it was recognized, for example by Aristotle, that complete self-sufficiency, even if ideal in theory, was not possible in reality. Most city-states would require at least some supplies from abroad. It must be emphasized that the concern here was with *imports* and not with exports. The reason is obvious: the ancient world was haunted by the fear of shortages. Most feared of all were, of course, food shortages. The purpose of international trade, accordingly, was to acquire imports of materials from the outside world. The idea of promoting exports as a matter of deliberate and consistent policy would have seemed outlandish. Exporting was seen purely in instrumental terms, as a means of acquiring necessary imports.[5]

It is hardly surprising that, in a world such as this, there was a widespread suspicion of private merchants. The fear was that such persons, being concerned only with personal profit, would all too happily see one state—even their home country—starve if another would pay higher prices. More generally, there was a great reluctance to allow an unregulated market system to operate. No state could tolerate with equanimity the prospect of its own scarce supplies being drained away in a famine to some other country where prices happened to be higher. The tendency, on the contrary, was for governments to manipulate trade and markets with a view to maximizing the flow of essential imports—the kind of program to which the label "policy of provision" would later be attached. One common practice was to employ professional purchasers abroad (known as *sitonai*), to acquire supplies in time of emergency—and, in the process, to forestall potential rival buyers—for shipment back home.

Harsher methods were also used. In Athens, for example, it was a capital offense to export grain. Sometimes, very elaborate arrangements were devised, most notably by Athens and Rome—the two city-states of the classical world—which, quite exceptionally, did rely upon foreign sources even for their normal food supplies. Athens entered into long-term arrangements with the local rulers of the Crimea, its chief source of supply.[6] Rome, some centuries later, devised a state-supervised supply apparatus of great sophistication to guarantee the alimentary component of its regimen of "bread and circuses."[7]

The implications of this state of affairs for international economic relations are easily seen. In a system in which states are competing against one another, particularly in time of famine, for imports, foreign economic relations must inevitably assume an intrinsically competitive character. Other nations are seen automatically as rival scramblers for scarce resources. Freedom of trade for individual merchants cannot be contemplated, since the result obviously would be to drain supplies out of the poorer nations and into the richer ones.

From this kind of system emerged the basic characteristics of economic nationalism, a rich and coherent blend of beliefs and practices which remains in vigorous health to the present day (and no doubt far into the future). We may identify three particularly outstanding, and interrelated, aspects as its characteristic features. First is the tendency to see the outside world as fundamentally threatening and, consequently, to see international economic relations as intrinsically competitive, rather than cooperative, in character. A direct consequence of this tendency is the placing of a high premium on self-sufficiency, or autarky, in the way that Plato and Aristotle did. Economic nationalism, then, is essentially defensive in ethos. It has about it a general aura of wariness and suspicion. It is strongly provincial, looking sharply askance at rootless cosmopolitan types (such as merchants). It promotes love of country far more than love of humanity. A second key attribute of economic nationalism is its collectivist, as opposed to individualist, outlook. It values the social solidarity and welfare of the community above that of the person. Economic nationalism, accordingly, is most characteristic of tight-knit, relatively egalitarian societies, such as ancient Sparta. It is small wonder, then, that Plato looked with such unconcealed distaste upon seaport communities, teeming with transients and sundry riffraff. Finally, we should note the austerely moralistic strain of economic nationalism. The economic nationalist denounces greed and selfishness (the characteristics of merchants) as the basest of human vices. In times of shortage, the ethic of altruism is urgently required. Cold-hearted, rational self-interest is clearly anti-social. Economic nationalism is, in sum, a remarkably comprehensive system, embracing the full range of human belief and conduct from the level of international relations to that of personal ethics. Its single most outstanding unifying factor is easily identified: the ever-present fear of shortage. Even today (as we shall see), whenever such fear is present, this complex of ideas and practices reasserts itself in quite recognizable form.

Since the fear of shortage was by no means unique to the Hellenistic world, it is hardly surprising to find the same basic economic nationalist outlook prevailing in other ancient societies as well. In China, for example, Taoist and Legalist thought, much like that of Plato and Aristotle, posited the ideal society as a network of independent, self-sufficient agrarian villages. As the *Tao Te Ching* stated, with approval: "Though adjoining states are within sight of one another, and the sound of dogs barking and cocks crowing in one state can be heard in another, yet the people of one state will grow old and die without having had any dealings with those of another."[8] When trade was necessary, the Chinese tendency, like the Greek, was to stress the value of importing and the abhorrence of exporting. *The Book of Lord*

Shang, a collection of sayings from the Legalist school, explicitly taught that "a state that imports products is strong and one that exports products is weak."[9] After the unification of the Chinese Empire in the late third century B.C., the general suspicion of foreign economic intercourse assumed the concrete institutional form of the famous "tribute system." In essence, the tribute system was a means of controlling trade with the barbarian outside world, by restricting it to the official and ritualistic exchange of "tribute" (from the barbarian rulers) and "gifts" (from the Chinese government).[10]

In ancient India, much the same autarkist mentality prevailed. The Hindu concept of *swaraj* is even a virtually precise counterpart of the Greek *autarkeia* in its meaning of "self-rule." Like the Greek concept, the Hindu one operated on many levels from the political to the personal. It referred to political independence from foreign rule, and also to the personal ethical virtues of moderation, self-discipline and self-control.[11]

If the economic nationalist mentality was widespread among the civilizations of the ancient world, it should not be thought that, even then, it held universal sway. Around the turn of the Christian Era, the seeds of a very different outlook were being planted. The Stoics, for example, began to express the view that all of mankind constituted in reality a single "universal city-state," or *kosmopolis.*[12] From its first century, Christianity propounded similar ideas, from a theistic rather than a philosophical base. Far nearer in spirit to the later concept of an economic world order was the natural-law thinking of the classical Roman jurists. They posited the existence of a universal *jus gentium,* described by Gaius in his *Institutes of the Civil Law* as "the law that natural reason establishes among all mankind [and that] is followed by all peoples alike."[13] This *jus gentium* differed from the thinking of the Stoics and the Christians in being rooted firmly in human nature and in human relationships as they were thought to be in the real world. It was therefore practical and empirical and materialistic in spirit, as contrasted with the distinctly otherworldly ethos of Stoicism or Christianity. It may furthermore be noted that the *jus gentium* was not—at least at its inception in late Roman times—a law of *nations,* but rather a law of *peoples.* It was concerned with universal principles governing private-law relations between ordinary persons the world over.

At this same time, during the later Roman imperial era, there also arose the foreshadowings of a more positive attitude toward economic interdependence than had generally prevailed in the ancient world. It was stimulated by the way in which the *pax Romana* enabled faraway persons to exchange goods with one another in comparative safety and thereby to distribute the fruits of the earth more evenly among the various peoples. A certain Libanius, a rhetorician from Antioch in the Fourth Century A.D., commenting upon this phenomenon, maintained that foreign economic contact, far from being a source of danger and corruption, as it had been for Plato and Aristotle, was actually a blessing from God because it served "to incline men to social relations by the need of mutual assistance." God, he averred, "has disclosed the avenues of trade, with the intent to bring all mankind the common enjoyment of those things which are produced only among a few."[14]

During the Middle Ages, these two fundamental mentalities—the nationalist and the cosmopolitan—continued to coexist uneasily. There is no doubt that economic nationalism had the upper hand. The fading away of the Western Roman Empire, and the consequent political fragmentation and economic relapse that accompanied it, meant that medieval Western Europe bore, in many respects, a strong resemblance to the Greek city-state world of old. It is hardly surprising, then, that the Christian Aristotle, Thomas Aquinas, clearly echoed his classical forbear in his autarkist outlook. The angelic doctor, when advising the king of Cyprus during the thirteenth century on the art of statesmanship, cautioned that it was far better to rely on one's own resources for essential food supplies than on foreign trade. Following Plato, Aquinas even cautioned about the corruption of local customs that would accompany an influx of foreign traders.[15]

In one important respect, the medieval city-states were actually in a more precarious state than their ancient Hellenic counterparts. They were far more sharply cut off juridically from their immediate hinterlands, to the point that their legal universes frequently stopped right at the town walls. Effective policies therefore had to be devised to secure "imports" from fields sometimes located a mere stone's throw away from the urban markets. The typical "policy of provision" (as some historians have termed it) that the medieval towns devised for dealing with this problem provides an instructive insight into both the conceptual and the material worlds of medieval civilization.

The basic purpose of such policies was quite clear: to ensure that the maximum quantity of foodstuffs was available to the general public, at a reasonable price, in a free (i.e., unmanipulated) market. The policy necessarily operated on a number of levels, from the economic to the moral to the legal. The entire process of provisioning was subjected to the most careful supervision, to discourage various forms of anti-social behavior. One important task was to curb excessive consumption. The various religious fasts were of some material assistance in that regard. So were the laws against "regrating" (i.e., hoarding). Markets were carefully policed and regulated. For example, there were rules against "forestalling," i.e., approaching sellers while they were en route to the market, with a view to buying their wares and thereby reducing the flow of supplies to the general public. Attempts were also made to stop the practice of "engrossing," i.e., cornering a market in some commodity.[16] Laws of this kind, it might be noted, endured well beyond the Middle Ages proper. In the 1760s, in England, Blackstone was still presenting them as living law, under the rubric of "offenses against public trade."[17]

The medieval Catholic Church played a crucially ambivalent role in the economic process. On the one hand, it brought its moral authority to bear in firm support of "policies of provision." It denounced the vice of greed, particularly in its most extreme form of price-gouging during times of famine.[18] At the same time, however, the church never condemned the activity of trading per se, for it well realized that certain forms of commerce were positively beneficial to the community at large. From this realization sprang the ecclesiastical doctrine of "laudable" (*laudabilis*) commerce. The most obvious example of laudable commerce was the importing of foodstuffs to relieve a famine. For such services to the community at large, merchants were to be entitled to a fair profit commensurate with a reasonable wage for the labor expended.[19]

One consequence of the doctrine of laudable commerce was that *international* trade came to be looked upon in quite a different light from the local trade with which the normal "policy of provision" commonly concerned itself. In the context of purely *local* trade, any gain made by unscrupulous manipulators was *ipso facto* a loss inflicted onto other people. But it was otherwise in the case of long-range trading. If a merchant came to town with a cargo of goods from far away, that could only be for the benefit of the community in general. Of course, the goods had to have come from somewhere. But (assuming that the merchant did not steal them) they must have come from a place where there was a surplus, perhaps from a region which specialized in production for export. The conclusion seemed inescapable that trade of this nature could only be unambiguously for the benefit of all.[20]

It was to facilitate laudable commerce of this kind that theologians

16

and jurists in the Middle Ages began increasingly to condemn unreasonable restraints on international trade, such as the levying of burdensome tolls. As early as the twelfth century, the church was excommunicating and anathematizing persons engaging in such practices.[21] During the same period, the canon law of the church was beginning to provide for the exemption of travelling merchants—together with other categories of persons such as women, children and agricultural laborers—from exposure to measures of war (such as plundering by rival belligerents).[22]

Secular rulers sometimes adopted similar policies. A notable illustration is Article 41 of the English Magna Carta of 1215, which provided for the security of foreign merchants traveling to and within the realm, and for their freedom from "all evil tolls." It even went so far as to afford safety to foreign merchants of nations with which England was at war, provided that the enemy country reciprocated.[23] The noted French jurist of the same century, Philippe de Beaumanoir, added his authority to this general policy by urging local lords to cater to the needs of travelling merchants.[24] During the following centuries, the general trend continued toward removing barriers to international trade, as rulers began to conclude treaties with one another providing for restraint in the issuing of letters of reprisal against foreign merchants.[25]

Other, more elaborate, ways of providing legal protection to transnational enterprise were also devised. The major trading cities of the Byzantine and Islamic worlds, for example, often had communities of Western (chiefly Italian) merchants permanently settled in them. Sometimes, the conditions of their settlement, including various legal privileges and immunities, were set out in formal charters or treaties. There was a certain amount of competition among the rival foreign merchant communities to secure the most favorable arrangements from the host states. Some French and Spanish cities obtained commitments from Arab rulers to treat their nationals on a par with Italians. Herein lay the earliest developments of what, many centuries later, would be an international network of most-favored-nation agreements.[26]

In the course of time, merchants increasingly came to constitute a kind of transnational community of their own, largely divorced from the jurisdiction of any particular territorial ruler. Perhaps the archetypal institution of this transnational "mercantile republick" (to borrow a term later used by Adam Smith) was the fair, which was an emporium for the sale of goods of all kinds, and also a financial market, for the purchase and sale of foreign exchange and the settlement and clearing of debts. The essentially transnational character of the fairs was evident from the array of legal arrangements that surrounded them, to ensure their exemption from the regular law of the territorial state in which they were held. Persons traveling to and from these gatherings were protected by a "franchise" from reprisals for alleged crimes committed or debts contracted outside the fair. The fair itself was under the jurisdiction of special guards (*custodes nundinarum*). While it was in progress, lawsuits and executions relating to outside matters were suspended. Also—and most importantly for the financial component of the fair—the normal medieval prohibition against usury was typically relaxed.[27] The law which governed transactions within the fair—and, more generally, in international commercial affairs at large—was the so-called "law merchant," which was an informal body of commercial law and practice that gradually evolved within the merchant community.[28]

At these fairs, money changers traditionally plied their trade at a table or bench (*banc*). In the course of time, the *banc*, or "bank," became a permanent institution, sometimes with established branches in many countries. The first true international banking network, in the twelfth century, was run by the Knights Templar, the militant monastic order established during the Crusades. In the following century (and even before their suppression in the early 1300s), they were superseded by the Italians. The earliest of the great "Lombard" banking houses was the Buonsignori family of Sienna, who became bankers to the Papacy in the mid-thirteenth century. The fourteenth century became the age of many of the great banking enterprises of Sienna and Florence—the Salimbene, Frescobaldi, Peruzzi and Bardi. The Florentine house of Acciajuoli, in the 1340s, had no fewer than forty-one "factors" located in other cities, from as far away as London, Nicosia and Tunis. The Peruzzi had an even more far-flung network of some 150 factors spread through Europe, Africa and the Middle East. Medieval enterprise, however, was hazardous even at these exalted heights. The Buonsignori house, for example, failed spectacularly in 1307. So did both the Bardi and the Peruzzi in the 1340s, when King Edward III of England defaulted on debts contracted from them. More arose in their place, however. By the sixteenth century, Germans had become prominent in international finance, with the rise of such families as the Welsers, Hochstetters and (most famously) the Fuggers of Augsburg.[29]

During the fifteenth and sixteenth centuries, the institution of the exchange arose, which was basically a permanent financial fair. The earliest exchanges were probably organized in the Mediterranean world around 1400. The most famous, though, became that of Antwerp which, during the sixteenth century, became the financial capital of Europe, a "home common to all nations."[30] The Antwerp exchange was a rough-and-tumble affair, with wild gyrations of currencies and feverish attempts at manipulation of various kinds. It was also an important source of financing for the various monarchs of Europe. In this brutally rational world, the niceties of religion and politics meant nothing. Credit ratings meant everything. The most financially virtuous country of Europe at this time was England, which was duly rewarded with the lowest interest rate. Antwerp's golden age ended in an instructive manner: it fell victim to the brutalities of warfare, suffering a sack in 1576 in the course of the Dutch war of independence against Spain. The business, in contrast, underwent migration rather than destruction—to Amsterdam and London, which succeeded to the frenzied greatness of Antwerp.[31]

Notwithstanding the prevailing defensive economic-nationalist mentality of the medieval city-states, there was, then, a clear picture, both conceptually and in practice, of a very different kind of economic life—one that was transnational and individualistic in character. The natural lawyers and theologians of the period were not unaware of these developments. They had occasion to consider them, in the context of the debate over whether rulers had a right, under the natural law, to prohibit international trade. In answering this question in the negative, the Spanish Dominican scholar Francisco de Vitoria of the University of Salamanca articulated, in the sixteenth century, a *general* concept of freedom of trade which was individualistic and libertarian in character. The particular issue was whether or not the native rulers of the various kingdoms in the New World had the right to exclude Spanish traders from their dominions. He concluded that they did not. "[F]riendship among men exists by natural law," Vitoria maintained, "and it is against nature to shun the society of harmless folk," holding also that it was "contrary to natural law for one man to dissociate himself from another without good reason."[32] His conclusion was that individual merchants had a natural-law right to ply their trade freely in foreign countries and that the rulers of those countries had a corresponding natural-law duty not to interfere with them, in the absence of compelling reasons.

At the same time, Vitoria recognized that the Indians, being "timid by nature" and also unlearned in the ways of the wider world, might fail to perceive their duties under the natural law. In such an event, this theologian did not flinch from advocating drastic measures. As a first step, he said, it was the duty of the Spaniards to reason with them and attempt to instruct them. If that should fail, however, the Spaniards would be fully entitled to enforce their rights by the sword, making war on the Indians and exercising the full range of belligerent rights against them—e.g., despoiling their goods, deposing their rulers and reducing the population to captivity.[33]

This medieval "law of trade," as it was sometimes termed, attracted support from some noted political writers. It formed part of the scheme for world peace advanced by Éméric de Crucé in 1623, for example.[34] It also featured in the contemporary "Grand Design" of the Duc de Sully for the reconstitution of the political map of Europe.[35] At the hands of the professional lawyers, however, the doctrine fared significantly less well. It died a gradual death by suffocation, under a steady accretion of exceptions and qualifications. A "law of trade" of Vitoria's type, with its focus on the rights of traders and its corresponding restrictions on the regulatory power of states, became increasingly obsolete with the rise of the powerful nation-state—and of the important change in the nature of international law which accompanied it.

THE AGE OF MERCANTILISM: ECONOMIC NATIONALISM AND THE CLASSICAL LAW OF NATIONS

Vitoria's libertarian doctrine of freedom of trade may be seen, in retrospect, as the culmination of an older line of thinking, the theologically based natural-law cosmopolitanism of the Middle Ages. The future—or at least the immediate future—lay in a very different direction. The emergence of increasingly centralized and bureaucratic nation-states (notably France, England and Spain) during the sixteenth and seventeenth centuries formed, for the first time, the basis for policies of economic nationalism of a recognizably modern kind. The basic ingredients, however, were substantially unchanged from the age of Plato and Aristotle. New was that the policies of the ancient and medieval city-states could now be applied on the scale of the modern nation-state—and with an aggressive thoroughness that was quite alien to the ancient and medieval worlds. In short, the age of "mercantilism" was at hand.

Mercantilism was never a systematic body of doctrines. Rather, it was a set of more or less similar practices followed by the major economic powers during the seventeenth and eighteenth centuries. Inevitably, the phenomenon differed somewhat from country to country. Nevertheless, it is possible to isolate its most important characteristics.[36] Above all else, mercantilism was economic nationalism of the most forthright and aggressive sort. One modern scholar has described it as a "militaristic coordination of state and economy."[37] It was premised on the assumption that the world's economic product was basically fixed in quantity and that, accordingly, one nation's gain could only come at the expense of some other's loss. This assumption was not an unreasonable one in the context of the seventeenth century, which was a period of general economic depression. As we shall see in due course, there has been, throughout history, a general association between times of economic recession, and flowerings of economic nationalism. The age of mercantilism provides the first clear indication of such a link. The result, not surprisingly, was that mercantilism was suffused with a brutally competitive ethos. There was no room in this kind of system for even the conception of a truly *international* economy, or of the nations of the world constituting a true international community, in any meaningful sense of that term. There were only rival *national* economies, locked in permanent and desperate competition, with the devil hungrily waiting to devour the hindmost.

Mercantilist policies were, most emphatically, *state*-directed practices designed to enhance the wealth of the nation as a collective entity. In its general collectivist outlook, mercantilism was squarely within the tradition of economic nationalism. The grim determination with which this basic policy was pursued, and the way in which the activities of private individuals were enlisted in carrying it out, imparted something of a fascist-style aura to mercantilism. Characteristic of this period was the close alliance between the states and the great trading companies, such as the British and Dutch East India Companies, the Hudson's Bay Company and the infamous South Sea Company. Armed with elaborate privileges and monopolies—and sometimes with weapons of a more ballistic nature—they performed a vital, if often unofficial, role in the advancement of their respective national interests in faraway climes.

Mercantilism was also highly manipulative in character. National economies, for the first time in history, were coming to be seen as more or less coherent systems which a ruler of sufficient skill and determination could mold to his advantage. It is no accident, then, that the heyday of mercantilism, the seventeenth century, was also the period when state administrative apparatuses were becoming more sophisticated than before and when a rigorous science of state-craft—the "cameralism" taught in the newer German universities—was developing. The most famous of the manipulators was the French controller-general of finances, Jean-Baptiste Colbert, who was a tire-less promoter—and protector—of French industry.

Superficially, mercantilism might seem to have been the very an-tithesis of ancient and medieval "policies of provision," in that ex-ports played a critically central role. Such a conclusion is deceptive. Mercantilism was, in fact, itself a "policy of provision" of a more ruthlessly single-minded character than any that had preceded it. The difference was that the key "provision" now was not foodstuffs but precious metal, that most useful commodity of all.[38] Unless a country happened to possess gold- or silver-bearing lands (as Spain did), the principal way to ensure an inflow of specie was to run a balance-of-trade surplus. The way to achieve that goal, in turn, was to export as many goods as possible. To that end, it was necessary to under-sell one's competitors, by reducing one's own costs of production below theirs. There were various ways of managing this. Tariffs on raw materials were kept low, for example, in the interest of reducing the cost of inputs. Tariffs on the finished goods of one's competitors, on the other hand, naturally tended to be high. Colonies could be a useful source of raw materials which could, at the same time, be denied to one's rivals. Nor were the mercantilists disposed to let humanitarian concerns stand in the way of cost reduction. They typically advocated low wages for laborers and the liberal use of (cheaper) female and child labor.[39]

This kind of system clearly fostered a rather ambivalent attitude toward international trade. In a certain sense, foreign trade must be a good thing, for how else could the desired inflow of specie come about? Domestic trade was of no value in this regard, because it could only redistribute the country's existing stock of precious metal, not add to it.[40] At the same time, though, a country had to manage its trade with the greatest care. Foreign trade was not seen as a good thing per se. It was "beneficial" if, but only if, it brought an influx of wealth into the country. Otherwise, it was "ruinous." The essential art of the mercantilist statesman was to promote "beneficial" trade as aggressively as possible, while at the same time taking equal care to minimize the "ruinous" variety.

This mercantilist idea that foreign trade should be carefully managed by the government in the general national interest clearly left little room for a libertarian "law of trade" of the kind that Vitoria had propounded. Indeed, in the course of the seventeenth and eighteenth centuries, international-law writers gradually abandoned Vitoria's natural-law conception of freedom of trade, in favor of a state-centered and regulatory approach more in harmony with mercantilism. Where Vitoria had emphasized the *duty* of rulers to allow individuals to trade, the newer tendency was to stress the *right* of states to decide the matter for themselves, on the basis of the national interest.

This change in attitude toward international trade was part and parcel of a much broader tendency within international law: the shift from natural law to positivism as the foundation of the law of nations. By positivism in international law is meant, in essence, the thesis that the basis of the law of nations is the will of the states themselves, rather than some external body of moral (or natural-law) principles. International law, in the positivist conception, is therefore a law *between* nations, consciously and voluntarily crafted by the states themselves, and not a transcendental law *above* nations. In perhaps no other area of international life was this profound shift so clearly illustrated as in that of foreign commerce. It is true that international-law writers, throughout the seventeenth and eighteenth centuries (and even the nineteenth) continued to pay lip service to the old natural-law principle that states have a general duty to trade with one another, for the benefit of their respective peoples. In reality, however, this doctrine came increasingly to be reduced to a mere empty shell. In its place was substituted the principle that freedom of trade meant the right of each state to decide for itself, in good mercantilist fashion, to what extent it would permit foreign commerce.

This evolution of legal doctrine began with the writings of the Italian scholar (based at Oxford) Alberico Gentili. Writing in 1598, he conceded the validity in principle of Vitoria's "law of trade," but then proceeded to add some quite significant qualifications to it. It was permissible, in Gentili's eyes, for a state to restrict foreign traders to certain designated portions of its territory. It was not required to let them roam as they wished. Also, it was permissible for a state to restrict the exporting of certain commodities of particular importance, such as precious metals.[41] In addition, Gentili made it clear that considerations of national security overrode the natural-law rights of individual traders. He presented a vigorous and eloquent argument, for example, in favor of the legality of the English government's interference with the activities of neutral traders in the course of its wars against Spain.[42]

Hugo Grotius, writing in the early seventeenth century, took this line of thought a decisive step further. He considered the question of freedom of trade in the context of the debate over whether the Portuguese had the right to enforce their claim to a trading monopoly in the Indian Ocean against Dutch interlopers. Grotius, a patriotic Dutchman (in the employ of the Dutch East India Company) and a staunch Protestant, concluded that they did not. Freedom of trade, in his view, meant the right of states—in this case, the Netherlands and the Asian states—to choose for themselves whether or not they wished to trade with one another. If they did so choose, as in this case, then no outside party had the right to interfere. Fundamental to the Grotius view, though, was the idea that the decision on whether or not to trade was within the sovereign right of each individual *state*.[43]

The position of modern international law on the subject of freedom of trade was substantially laid down by the German natural-law scholar Samuel Pufendorf, writing in 1672. Like Gentili, he confirmed the existence, in principle, of a natural-law duty on the part of states to trade with one another. But this was only an "imperfect" obligation, he argued, i.e., one which no *other* state had the right to enforce against it. The duty to trade could be transformed from an "imperfect" obligation into a "perfect" one by means of a trade agreement. But, in the absence of such an agreement, states had no *enforceable* duty to trade with one another. Pufendorf also explicitly denied Vitoria's contention that states were obliged to admit foreign traders into their realms. Rulers, he objected, were like property owners, possessing an unfettered right to decide whom to admit into their domains.[44] Here was the effective death-knell of the medieval libertarian "law of trade."

This state-centered, positivist approach reached its full maturity in the following century, in the writings of Pufendorf's fellow countryman Christian Wolff. In a magisterial treatise on the law of nations written in 1749, Wolff set forth the basic conceptual foundations of classical positivist international law substantially as they remain to this day. As the cornerstone of the law of nations, he posited the principle of the sovereign equality of states, in recognizably modern form. He stressed that the law of nations springs from the will of the states themselves, and that their consent, freely given, is the basis of the binding force of international law.[45] His strong insistence on the rights of states was reflected in the first section of his treatise, entitled

"Of the Duties of Nations to Themselves and the Rights Arising There-from." He expressly held that a state's duties to itself take precedence over its duties to other nations.[46] Foremost among these is the duty of a state to "perfect" itself, i.e., to develop its social and political system in accordance with its own traditions and inclinations.[47] Economic considerations, of a quite distinctly mercantilist sort, had a role to play in this "perfection." Wolff defined a nation's wealth as the sum total of the stocks of money held by all of the individuals within it, immediately drawing the obvious conclusion that a favorable balance of trade increases the wealth of a state, while an unfavorable one reduces it. (Redistribution within the nation, of course, has no effect on the national wealth.)[48]

The only surprising thing in Wolff's treatment of the subject of international trade is that he bothered even to pay lip service to the existence of a general duty of a state to engage in commerce. He certainly did no more than that, for everything in his system points to a state's having a totally unfettered right to decide for itself whether or not to enter into economic relations with other states. "Commerce between nations," he contended, "is . . . naturally, a right of pure power, consequently acts pertaining to it are acts of pure will."[49] As a concrete illustration, Wolff pointed to the case of China, which, as part of its quest for "perfection," had decided to disallow foreign trade. He staunchly defended its legal right to adopt this policy of isolationism (or "non-intercourse," as it was sometimes termed).[50]

In the following decade, the Swiss jurist Emmerich de Vattel vir-tually reproduced these conclusions. Like Wolff, he devoted the first section of his treatise on *The Law of Nations* (1758) to the duties that a state owes to itself. Like Wolff, he assigned them precedence over the duties to the community at large.[51] Unlike Wolff, he was actually rather fulsome in his praise of foreign commerce, urging states to take active steps to promote it.[52] He clearly had in mind their doing so in a purely mercantilist framework. Like the mercantilists (and like the majority of economic nationalists throughout history) he denounced "the pest of luxury," which was likely to lead to the importing of expensive trifles to the detriment of the nation's balance of trade.[53] Also in accordance with mercantilist doctrine, he held foreign com-merce to be more advantageous to a state than domestic.[54] And he expressly cautioned rulers to show skill in the management of foreign trade, and specifically to be "carefully on the watch to encourage such trade as is beneficial to the people and suppress or restrict what is hurtful. . . ."[55]

He was thoroughly of the positivist mentality in defining freedom of trade as the right of *states* to choose whether to engage in trade or not. A state, Vattel contended, "may accept or refuse an offer of trade from foreign Nations without their being able to accuse it of injustice or to ask reasons. . . . It is free to carry on its affairs as it pleases, and is not accountable to anyone."[56] Like Wolff, he cited China as an example of a state that was availing itself of that right, in the interest of preserving its own civilization and culture.[57]

This effectively absolute right of states to decide whether or not to engage in foreign trade had two particularly interesting consequences. One was that, as just observed, it permitted policies of economic non-intercourse, like that of China. Rather more interestingly, it also permitted policies of economic warfare, in the form of a refusal on the part of one state (or group of states) to trade with another on political grounds. The relationship between these two phenomena is obvious. If a state has an absolute right to refuse to trade with *any* other country, must it not have a right to refuse to trade with some *particular* state? The general consensus was that it did. Furthermore, it was generally accepted that such a refusal could be motivated by purely political factors. After all, what was to prevent a given trade from being deemed "ruinous" on political as well as economic grounds? Was not a policy of non-importation simply an extreme form of a protective tariff or quota system, which were universally recognized as being within the sovereign right of states?

This conclusion was illustrated in concrete form—and on the grandest of scales—during the Napoleonic Wars in the early years of the nineteenth century. Napoleon's "Continental System" consisted basically of a continent-wide policy of non-importation directed explicitly against Great Britain. It was nothing more, nor less, than mercantilism of a particularly baroque sort, since the intention was to continue sending exports *to* Britain, in order to drain it of specie.[58] Not even Napoleon's mortal enemies contended that such a policy was illegal in and of itself. As Lord Stanley asked rhetorically in the British House of Commons, of the Continental System: "What was it . . . but adopting a principle of policy, and enforcing it with more than ordinary vigor, which every state had an inherent right to adopt, as a principle of mere municipal regulation?"[59] Similarly, there was no suggestion that the various non-importation and non-intercourse policies directed by the United States against Britain and France between 1806 and 1812 were illegal.[60]

The position was similar regarding non-exportation policies—i.e., embargoes, using this term in a loose and extended sense to mean the refusal to export goods to another country. As a matter of state sovereignty, nations were free to engage in such policies. Wolff, in fact, gave an embargo of this sort as an illustration of the legal concept of "retorsion," which is an unfriendly, but lawful, act directed by one state against another, as a response to some prior unfriendly act by the target country.[61]

Things were somewhat different, however, regarding embargoes in the original and strict sense of the term, i.e., the detention of ships within the territory of the embargoing state. No difficulty was posed by measures affecting only the state's own vessels. Such a measure (known as a civil embargo) was merely a piece of municipal legislation of no legal concern to other countries. An embargo affecting foreign vessels, however, was different. It was lawful provided that it was imposed impartially against *all* foreign vessels—typically as an emergency measure of some kind. For example, an embargo might be imposed to stop news from spreading outside the country. A discriminatory embargo, on the other hand, was regarded as a hostile act, or even as a *de facto* declaration of war.[62]

It is certainly no accident that classical international law, as it had evolved by the middle of the eighteenth century, was so tolerant of the practice of economic warfare. Given the strongly state-centered, or positivist, character of international law, and the extent to which it shared the general ethos of mercantilism, it could hardly have been otherwise. Indeed, for all intents and purposes, mercantilism and classical positivist international law were the economic and juridical equivalents of each other. They had their roots in the same basic world-view. Both systems were clearly nationalistic in outlook, in their stress on the right—and indeed the duty—of states to pursue their own national interests first and foremost. Both systems lacked any real sense that the nations of the world might be embarked upon some kind of common enterprise. On the contrary, international life, in their perception, was a grimly competitive struggle between rival national interests.

The cosmopolitan spirit of the medieval theologians and natural lawyers therefore wilted in the face of the aggressive economic nationalism of the mercantilists, and the positivist legal doctrines which so clearly supported it. The cosmopolitan ethos, however, was soon to be revived, although with one very significant difference. It would henceforth be rooted not in theology or natural law, as in the past, but rather in the new science of economics, which would be as thoroughly secular and materialistic as mercantilism itself. That crucial change would lay the foundation for a systematic and scientific theory of economic world order.

COMMERCE AND CIVILIZATION:
THE DAWN OF THE "ECONOMIC" AGE

In both the material and the intellectual spheres, forces were at work in the eighteenth century which were to undermine and challenge, if not actually to extirpate, mercantilism and all its works. On the material side, it was an age of economic growth, in striking contrast to the preceding period of stagnation. The effect was to erode one of the key foundations of the mercantilist outlook: the belief that the global economic product was static and that, consequently, any one state's advance could come only at the expense of another. In the realm of ideas, it was the age of Enlightenment, when there was a burning optimism that humanity, through the determined application of human reason, now had it within its power to fashion a more humane, rational and prosperous world than had ever been known before. Both of these characteristics of the eighteenth-century scene were to have their impact on the evolution of the law of nations. A few observations on each are therefore in order.

The economic growth of the eighteenth century was not merely quantitative in nature. It was qualitative as well. Trading networks were becoming ever more far-flung, and ever more effective at shunting the products of the world all over the globe with impressive dependability. It was becoming progressively easier to see the world economy as a single wide-ranging social mechanism operating according to laws peculiar to itself. On the one hand, this system was ubiquitous. Its fruits were everywhere to be seen. Voltaire, for example, found in the products on his daily breakfast table confirmation, if any were needed, of how far the exotic goods of the world— coffee, tea, sugar, tobacco, spices—traveled to their final destinations.[63] On the other hand, however, this system was nowhere. It was decentralized. It had no government, no sovereign. But at the same time, it was far from anarchic or random.[64]

It is small wonder that this system of international commerce, together with people's thoughts about it, would have important political (and legal) implications. It could hardly escape the notice of the more perceptive observers that this global network of production and exchange stood in the sharpest contrast to traditional political ways of organizing the world. Commerce satisfied the material wants of ordinary people and improved standards of living. What did governments do, on the other hand, except engage in repression and war? What was diplomacy, but the systematic practice of deception and scheming? What was the balance of power but a murderous see-sawing between peace and war for the cruel amusement of princes? What, indeed, was the whole practice of international relations but (in the words of Thomas Paine) "a continual system of war and extortion"?[65] Merchants and artisans, in striking contrast to princes and generals, were peaceful folk. They were also thrifty, hard-working and productive, in clearest opposition to feudal landlords, churchmen and lawyers, who were idle and parasitic. The social status of merchants accordingly began to rise considerably during this period. The Scottish writer David Hume, for example, hailed them as "one of the most useful races of men" in society.[66] More generally, the *philosophes* of the age came to sing the praises of what they called *le douceur de commerce* ("the sweetness of commerce"), which united the disparate people of the world in the great peaceful enterprise of material prosperity.[67]

Examples abounded of this new kind of thinking, so alien to the crabbed and suspicious mentality of mercantilism. The French political philosopher Baron de Montesquieu, for example, hailed commerce as a vital force making for peace and understanding between peoples. "Commerce," he wrote in his famous treatise on *The Spirit of the Laws* in 1748, "is a cure for the most destructive prejudices; for it is almost a general rule, that wherever we find agreeable manners, there commerce flourishes; and that wherever there is commerce, there we meet with agreeable manners."[68] He went on to hold it to be "a true maxim that one nation should never exclude another from trading with it, except for very great reasons."[69] Immanual Kant contended, in his work on *Perpetual Peace* (1795), that what he called the "trading spirit" could not co-exist with war.[70] Hume shared this view, strongly attacking mercantilism's single-minded obsession with the impoverishing of rival nations. On the contrary, he argued, any country should be pleased to see its neighbors growing in prosperity, because it would thereby be assured of a larger market in which to sell its own goods. Far from being a source of rivalry and divisiveness, as in the mercantilist view, commerce should be a powerful engine of peace, prosperity and harmony among nations.[71] Thomas Paine, in *The Rights of Man* (1792), hailed commerce as "a pacific system, operating to cordialize mankind, by rendering nations, as well as individuals, useful to each other."[72] In general, the *philosophes* and their sympathizers looked forward to the dawning of a new age when rulers of the world would concern themselves exclusively with what became known during this period as "economic," or "true," policies—i.e., policies designed to promote the general welfare of the human race—to the exclusion of "political," or "false," ones such as the waging of senseless and destructive wars.[73]

The foremost advocates of the refashioning of international relations along "economic," rather than "political," lines were the group of French thinkers known to us by the label of "physiocrats." They were the first to propose a comprehensive and systematic vision of an economic world order based upon the principle of freedom of trade. Significantly, one of the designations by which they were sometimes known in their own time was the "economic" school—in the sense in which that term was used during the eighteenth century. That is, they favored policies designed to promote the material well-being of the common people of the world as a whole, rather than to advance the political interests of any particular nation-state. The physiocratic theories were to undergo some significant modification at the hands of the later liberal political economists. Nevertheless, many of their basic ideas survive to the present day.[74]

Physiocracy means, literally, "rule of nature." It was an appropriate name, because much of the thinking had its roots in natural-law jurisprudence, as well as in what we would now recognize as the science of economics. The leading thinker of the school, François Quesnay, was trained as a physician rather than as a lawyer; but he was keenly interested in jurisprudential thought. The physiocratic conception of natural law, however, differed in a quite fundamental way from previous thinking in that tradition. In keeping with the general spirit of Enlightenment thought—if not, indeed, as almost a caricature of it—the physiocratic natural law was rigorously secular, scientific and mechanistic in character, in marked contrast to the theological and ethical cast of previous natural-law theories. Just as, in this enlightened age, the world of nature was steadily revealing itself to be governed by the rule of law, so would the same be said of the social realm. The physiocrats conceived the economic system to work on the basis of principles as thoroughly mechanistic as the celestial one. To this social world, Quesnay and his followers would be the Newtons. The principles of operation of the economic world were triumphantly set forth before the world in 1758—the same year that Vattel published *The Law of Nations*—in the form of the famous *tableau économique*. The purpose of the *tableau* was to demonstrate how the "net product" of the economic system was generated (exclusively by agriculture, to the physiocrats) and how it was then distributed.[75]

The supreme task, in the eyes of the physiocrats, was to *understand* the nature of the economic mechanism. There could be no question of substituting a man-made order for it. It could not be improved upon or even changed in any fundamental way. But it could be clogged up, interfered with and sabotaged by policy-makers ignorant of its secrets, just as any machine can be ruined when entrusted to the care of unskilled hands. One of the central planks in the physiocratic program, then, was to educate peoples (particularly policymakers) in the secrets of the machine which held such promise for material prosperity, if only it were properly tended.

A great deal had to be done to bring the physiocratic vision to reality, for the machine had been in ignorant hands for a very long time. Irrational practices and artificial impediments had to be swept ruthlessly away. In this regard, the physiocrats were the boldest of reformers. They favored firm, even despotic, central government, because only a forceful hand on the levers of power would be strong enough to sweep away the artificial encrustations from the past. But their despotism was of a very special kind: it had to be what was called a *legal* despotism. So insistent were they on this point that the phrase "legal despotism" became one of the most prominent of their many slogans. Their intention was certainly not to place absolute arbitrary power into the hands of some ruler. Instead, the despot was to be rather in the image of the emperor of China, a country whose social system fascinated the physiocrats. The Chinese emperor was a despot in the sense that there were no man-made constitutional restrictions upon his power. His actual function, though, was not to do whatever he liked, but rather to perform the various ceremonies to ensure the favor of the gods and the continuation of the "mandate of heaven." In these activities, he was to be carefully advised by the Confucian literati, who were the real custodians of the secrets of social harmony. The *real* despot, then, was the economic mechanism itself— with the physiocrats as the Confucian literati who were learned in its mysteries. (So powerful was the image of China on the physiocrats that Quesnay was nicknamed "the Confucius of the West.")

A central aim of these economic literati was to uproot the host of restraints upon trade imposed by sundry vested interests—from priv-

ileged corporations with their monopolies, to petty territorial mag-
nates with their "evil tolls," to provinces and states with their old-
style "policies of provision" or newer-style mercantilist manipulations. They favored, in short, a return to the older libertarian "law of
trade" of Vitoria—though in a far more thorough-going way than
Vitoria himself had applied it. One of their thirty "general maxims of
economic government" was that individuals should be free to decide
what to cultivate, with no dictation by feudal lords or government
officials. Another of the maxims was a ringing endorsement of the
general principle of freedom of commerce. Another specifically called
for the freeing of the trade in grain—in effect, a call to renounce
traditional "policies of provision" and instead to give free scope to
market forces.[76] In general, physiocracy was strongly individualistic
in outlook, in contrast to the collectivist and corporate ethos of mercantilism and of economic nationalism generally. The physiocrats
looked to the emancipation of individuals from subservience to traditional feudal, aristocratic and theological hierarchies. Economic
transactions should take place between individuals freely across provincial and national frontiers. Crucial to the effectiveness of such a
system, though, was the ability of those individuals to know and
define their legal rights clearly. Systems of feudal property rights,
with their morass of multiple and intergenerational and customary
interests, were anathema to the physiocrats. They advocated instead
a regime of absolute rights of private property for individuals, together with an effective mechanism for the making and enforcing of
contracts.[77] In short, the physiocrats readily perceived that a viable
regime of free trade had to be underpinned by an effective system of
private law which rigorously guaranteed rights of property and of
contract.

One of the most striking things about the physiocrats was their
universalistic outlook. They were the cosmopolitans *par excellence* of
the eighteenth century. One of the principal evangelists of the movement, the Marquis de Mirabeau, brashly proclaimed himself to be the
"Friend of Mankind" in a book of that title published in 1757.[78] The
physiocrats looked forward to nothing less than the eventual reorder-
ing of the entire world on "economic" principles. They foresaw the
time when treaties of political alliance between states would be obsolete and when nations, in the words of Mirabeau's revolutionary son
and namesake, would have "friends and no allies."[79] Only commercial
treaties would bind countries together; and, as trade became progressively more free, even they would become superfluous. Since the uni-

versal truths of nature did not stop at the arbitrary boundaries of states, neither should trade. *"Laissez-faire, laissez-passez"* was, of course, the most famous of all physiocratic slogans. The physiocrats looked forward to nothing less than the transformation of the whole world into one giant "mercantile republick." Nothing could have been in sharper contrast to the orthodox positivist, state-centered outlook which international lawyers like Wolff and Vattel were propounding at the same time. The physiocrats were concerned to perfect not each individual state singly, but rather (ultimately at least) the whole human race as one society dwelling under the dictates of natural law.

Ideas of this general nature found a certain reflection in the practice of states and even in some marginal areas of international law itself. It became common during the eighteenth century, for the first time, to separate questions of international political and economic relations, by concluding treaties of commerce separately from treaties of political and military alliance. Such treaties of "amity and commerce" were designed to facilitate economic contact, by providing guarantees of fair treatment of traders from each state while in the territory of the other. They typically provided for access by the merchants of each to the ports of the other and for their general protection on an equal basis with nationals. They also commonly set out the rights that merchants of the one country would have in the event that the other one went to war with some third state. Another increasingly standard feature was a most-favored-nation clause, whereby each state promised to grant the other whatever benefits it might accord in the future to any third country.[80] Here were sown the seeds of what would later be the principle of nondiscrimination in international economic relations generally.

Also during the late seventeenth and, more especially, the eighteenth centuries, there was an increasing tendency for states to safeguard the flow of international commerce from the ravages of war. The most notable development was the evolution of the law of neutrality, which was designed to permit neutral parties to continue their economic relations with either, or even both, belligerent sides without fear of interruption (save in certain more or less agreed respects, such as the carriage of contraband and the running of blockades). The formative age for this body of international law was approximately the period from 1650 to 1750.[81] Belligerent states even began to tolerate a degree of free economic intercourse between their nationals and those of the enemy. Britain, for example, permitted its insurance industry (not without controversy) to offer coverage to enemy vessels risking capture by Britain itself and its allies. The continental European countries even adopted a general practice that, contrary to the traditional view, the outbreak of a war would not automatically make trading with enemy nationals unlawful.[82] Britain and France, in a treaty of 1786, provided that, in the event of war between them, the nationals of each who resided in the territory of the other would be permitted to remain and dwell in peace.[83] States were becoming so willing to modify the traditional rules about warfare in this direction that the conservative Dutch judge Cornelius Bynkershoek was led to remark in 1737 (not altogether approvingly) that "the interests of the mercantile class and the mutual needs of peoples have almost annulled the laws of war relating to commerce."[84] Thomas Paine confidently asserted that "[i]t is impossible to engross commerce by dominion," that the interests of the transnational trading system had become too strong for the rulers of mere nation-states to confine or harness.[85]

These new ideas and practices were also finding expression in more general terms. For example, the Danish diplomat and international-law scholar Martin Hübner, writing in 1759, posited the emergence of a principle of "sociability" among nations, according to which the rights of those at peace would be accorded a general preference over the rights of those at war.[86] Kant went further, in advancing the idea of a whole new category of law to deal with transnational contacts (primarily economic) between peoples, as opposed to states. In addition to the familiar *jus gentium*, as expounded by Wolff and Vattel, which regulated "the relations of nations among each other," Kant set forth the idea of a *jus cosmopoliticum* ("cosmopolitical law"), in which "men, or states, are considered as influencing one another, in quality of constituent parts of the great state of the human race."[87] He condemned the principle of "the reciprocal independence of neighboring and separate states"—i.e., the foundation of the positivist view of international law—as "itself a state of war."[88] The law of nations as expounded by Wolff and Vattel was, in Kant's view, merely a preliminary historical stage in the evolution "toward a public right of men in general and toward a perpetual peace."[89]

Two countries went especially far in molding their policies to this new enlightened way of thinking. One was the Netherlands, which, during the eighteenth century, consciously abandoned its ambitions as a great political power to concentrate on the more profitable, if hum-drum, business of making money. The Netherlands became the foremost practitioner of neutrality.[90] This policy duly made the Dutch the most prosperous people in Europe. It did not, however, make them the most popular. They were constantly accused of mercenarism of the lowest order, of being little more than professional war profiteers, appropriating and then retaining the trade of other countries as it was interrupted during wartime. It is not difficult, however, to detect liberal tinges of envy mixed with this resentment.

The other country which went furthest in applying the enlightened thinking was the newly independent United States. As early as 1776, during the struggle for independence from Britain, the Continental Congress of the rebellious colonies had occasion to consider the relative merits of economic and political ties to other nations. The immediate question at hand was how best to enlist the aid of France in the conflict. John Adams proposed that the colonies offer nothing more to France than a commercial treaty, granting it such special favours as most-favoured-nation status. The prospect of the economic benefits of close commercial ties with the United States, Adams maintained, should provide France with an ample incentive to take the American side. A political alliance should be avoided, lest it suck the virtuous republic into the moral cesspool of European power politics. In the event, Adams's advice was not followed. In 1778, the two countries simultaneously concluded two treaties, one of amity and commerce, and the other of political alliance.[91] Adams's fears, however, were well founded. When France became embroiled in European wars in the 1790s, the United States duly found the political alliance to be acutely inconvenient. Only in 1800, after an undeclared naval war with France, was it able to break free of the political tie.[92]

In the meantime, American diplomats had been active on other fronts in the cause of freedom of commerce. In 1776, as it was debating the French alliance, the Continental Congress drafted a "Plan of Treaties," or model treaty of commerce which it would seek to conclude with as many nations as possible. Its outstanding feature was the liberality of the provisions on neutral trading in time of war.[93] The Treaty of Amity and Commerce with France in 1778 was modelled on the plan, as were commercial agreements with the Netherlands in 1782[94] and Sweden in 1783.[95] In a treaty with Prussia in 1785, the United States took the further step of providing for a right sometimes known as "belligerent commerce," i.e., a right on the part of nationals of the two countries, even in the event of war, to carry on their normal economic relations with one another.[96] The practical value of this provision was distinctly limited, as the chances of war between the United States and Prussia were slender in the extreme.

All the same, the American negotiators were pleased at being able to present, in John Adams's words, a "Platonic lesson" to the world at large in the conducting of foreign relations according to the precepts of reason.[97]

These precepts were summarized by President George Washington in 1796 in his famous Farewell Address, in words that could have come from Mirabeau. Washington cautioned his fellow countrymen to avoid political entanglements with foreign nations, whether in the form of alliance or of hostility—while, at the very same time, taking care to increase the country's economic ties with the world at large impartially. "A passionate attachment of one nation for another," he warned, "produces a variety of evils," the chief of which was the dragging of allied states into wars in which they have no genuine interest.[98]

> Nothing is more essential [Washington insisted] than that permanent, inveterate antipathies against particular nations and passionate attachments for others should be excluded, and that in place of them just and amicable feelings toward all should be cultivated. The nation which indulges toward another an habitual hatred or an habitual fondness is in some degree a slave. It is a slave to its animosity or to its affection, either of which is sufficient to lead it astray from its duty and its interest.[99]

The conclusion was clear. "The great rule of conduct for us in regard to foreign nations," said Washington, "is, in extending our commercial relations, to have with them as little political connection as possible."[100] The Farewell Address is often, but misleadingly, depicted as the cornerstone of American isolationism. It is often forgotten that Washington favoured a most active involvement with the outside world on the economic plane.

Despite these myriad ways in which the new thinking of the eighteenth century influenced the practice of statecraft and the development of the law of nations, it cannot be said that a truly thoroughgoing attempt was made during this period to institute a system of economic world order of the kind that the physiocrats had set forth. There remained a very wide residuum of suspicion about the physiocratic programme, for a variety of reasons. For one thing, physiocracy seemed too doctrinaire, too mechanistic, too academic to inspire the confidence of practical statesmen. Moralists were suspicious of its libertarianism and its frank acceptance of the vice of human greed as the mainspring of economic progress. Conservatives and vested interests of all sorts saw it as threatening, because of its aggressive insistence on extirpating old ways and old power structures.

Most concretely, however, the fully fledged physiocratic system was seen as highly dangerous on one outstanding count: its insistence upon free trade in grain, even to the point of permitting free exporting during times of famine. Such advice, of course, flew squarely in the face of centuries (even millennia) of received wisdom and amounted to nothing less than the outright abandonment of traditional "policies of provision." Even in the relatively prosperous eighteenth century, it was a bold ruler who would attempt such a thing. It meant opening the doors to profiteering by speculators in times of famine, when the obvious natural tendency was to do just the opposite—to impose export embargoes to conserve supplies, and to regulate prices to prevent food rioting.

In the event, the few bold attempts that were made to institute the physiocratic programme foundered on just this age-old rock. In France, Spain and Tuscany, rulers briefly flirted with physiocratic policies, only to withdraw them quickly in the face of public panics in periods of dearth.[101] It was the first sign—there would be many more—that the success of an experiment in economic liberalism was crucially dependent upon general conditions of prosperity and abundance. The dream of an economic system of world order, in other words, would prove far more feasible in an age of Industrial Revolution than it had in an age of Enlightenment.

TWO

FREE TRADE IS THE INTERNATIONAL LAW OF GOD: A First Experiment in Economic World Order

The various piecemeal attempts to implement the physiocratic program failed for one overwhelming reason. In a world beset by shortages, the natural tendency of states, as of individuals, is to hoard scarce materials. In an anarchic, free-market system, no state could be certain that its supplies would not be voraciously sucked away from it by some more prosperous (or more desperate) neighbor. A truly thorough-going experiment in economic world order, therefore, was only feasible in conditions of abundance rather than of dearth; when competition was for export markets for surpluses, rather than for imports of precious foodstuffs or glittering metals. In sum, the vision of an economic world order based upon the libertarian principle of freedom of trade for individuals became a serious possibility only in the wake of the Industrial Revolution.

Beginning around the middle of the nineteenth century, the world embarked upon its first systematic experiment in economic world order. A starting date is impossible to fix with any certainty because the experiment was a highly informal affair. It was not officially launched at any international conference or embodied in any international convention. Instead, it gradually grew up in an empirical and incremental fashion. It was, however, rooted very firmly in a highly coherent set of theoretical ideas: the writings of the classical liberal economists who followed in the wake of Adam Smith (and, less directly, of the physiocrats). These writers showed, even more rigorously and systematically than Quesnay and his followers, that the world as a whole would prosper best if *all* barriers to economic contact between peoples would be removed and the whole world united into a single integrated "mercantile republick."[1] To an impressive extent, the program of the liberal economists actually was implemented, most notably in the period from about 1850 to 1870, when the tide in favor of free trade ran strongest.

These doctrines of the liberal political economists produced an effect upon international lawyers—or at least upon some of them. It was obvious that the traditional positivist emphasis on state sovereignty was incompatible with the new economic thinking. From the standpoint of liberal capitalism, the role of the states of the world was to cooperate with one another in removing the fetters upon individual economic freedom. They were to provide a general stable framework within which the forces of free enterprise could play themselves out, on a global scale, without interference. In this kind of system, states could not be allowed unlimited rights to hamper free trade in their parochial national interests. Some international lawyers readily saw the implications of these economic principles and proceeded to argue for a new international law based upon the "solidarity" of peoples and nations, rather than upon the sovereignty and independence of individual states.

As the nineteenth century progressed, however, it became apparent that the liberal program was less solidly founded than its more voluble supporters realized. It was liable to slip into reverse in times of economic depression. It also provoked opposition because of its impatience with the traditional rights of sovereign states, which revealed that they had no intention of being stripped of their immense legal prerogatives. Most of all, this first attempt to institute a liberal world economic order fell victim to a renascent economic nationalism. The "new" economic nationalism of the nineteenth century was animated by the urge to economic development on the part of the non-industrialized states—which meant, during this period, virtually all countries save Great Britain. As the forces of nationalism gathered strength in the late nineteenth century, there was a growing tendency for states to enlist and subordinate their economic interests to furtherance of political ends. In the face of such pressures, and of world economic depression in the late nineteenth century, the ideal of an economic world order was driven into sullen retreat.

COSMOPOLITANISM BECOMES SCIENTIFIC

The classical liberal tradition in political economy began with the seminal work of Adam Smith, *An Inquiry into the Nature and Causes of the Wealth of Nations,* of 1776, and reached its first maturity in the course of the first half of the nineteenth century, with the writings, in Britain, of Thomas Malthus, James Mill, David Ricardo, John Ramsay McCullough, Nassau Senior and John Stuart Mill.[2] In France, the most prominent early exponent of the new science was Jean-Baptiste Say, followed a generation later by Frédéric Bastiat. In its essentials, the new science of classical liberal economics bore a great resemblance to physiocracy. Adam Smith, for example, knew and admired the work of the physiocrats. There were, however, some differences. One was that Smith and his followers discarded the physiocratic obsession with agriculture and its condemnation of manufacturing and commerce as "sterile" activities. The liberal system, accordingly, was to prove far more suited to the world of the Industrial Revolution. The liberal economists also rejected the relentlessly deterministic and mechanistic character of physiocracy, in favor of a more radically libertarian, individualistic, and competitive ethos.[3]

The New Science of Liberal Political Economy

The fundamental driving force of economic progress, in the eyes of the liberal economists, was the division of labor—a principle that lent itself with the utmost ease to application on, literally, a global scale. Smith himself, with his characteristically common touch, illustrated the concept in terms of life at the village level. Did it not make sense, he asked, for each villager to specialize in what he himself did best, and then to trade his products for those of others, rather than for each and every person to produce the entire range of things that he needed?[4] And if this made sense within a single village, did it not also make sense within a region, or within a whole nation? And why not, indeed, over the entire world? As James Mill pointed out in 1807:

> The commerce of one country with another is merely an extension of that division of labor by which so many benefits are conferred on the human race. As the same country is rendered richer by the trade of one province with another; as its labor becomes thus infinitely more divided and more productive than it could otherwise have been; and as the mutual interchange of all those commodities which one province has and another wants, multiplies the accommodations and comforts of the whole, and the country becomes thus in a wonderful degree more opulent and happy; so the same beautiful train of consequences is observable in the world at large, that vast empire of which the different kingdoms may be regarded as the provinces.[5]

The implication of this kind of thinking was clear. The best way—indeed the *only* way—to attain the maximum possible efficiency in the world economy as a whole was for the entire earth to become, literally, one single integrated market—a single gigantic "mercantile republick." In the words of the French economist Frédéric Passy, one of the most fervent of the free-trade evangelists, the time must surely come when "mankind, constantly united by continuous transactions, will form just one workshop, one market, and one family."[6] One obvious implication of this holistic, radically cosmopolitan pattern of thinking was that it could make no sense even to think in terms of *national* economic development, because the nation-state, from this perspective, was simply not a "natural" economic unit.[7]

The cardinal importance of the principle of freedom of trade was another obvious consequence of this line of thought. If every region specialized, as the theory said that it should, in whatever it could produce most cheaply (i.e., if the principle of comparative advantage were applied), then it would be necessary that the products in question be traded with as complete a freedom as possible back and forth between the regions. There was nothing dramatically new about this insight. Aristotle and Libanius, as well as the medieval natural-law theorists, had readily perceived it. What was new with the classical political economists was their strong insistence that the different regions *must*, as a matter of conscious policy, specialize in production, in the interest of promoting the maximum material output of the entire system.[8]

It should be emphasized that the new science of classical political

economy promised more than mere prosperity to the world. It promised peace between nations as well. In the light of the principle of the
world-wide division of labor, it was now easier than it had ever been
before to see just how and why warfare was so pernicious. To the
extent that it disrupted the free flow of goods, services and capital
around the world, it prevented the full application of the international division of labor, thereby reducing the efficiency and productiv-
ity of the global "mercantile republick" as a whole. As Thomas Paine
put it:

> Every kind of destruction or embarrassment of commerce serves
> to lessen the total quantity, and it matters but little in what part
> of the commercial world the reduction begins. Like blood it
> cannot be taken from any of the parts without being taken from
> the whole mass in circulation, and all partake of the loss.[9]

It was fitting, then, that a number of the liberal political economists should have become active participants in the peace movement,
armed as they now were with clear "scientific" proof that *any* armed
conflict was of general international concern because it caused economic injury to the entire human community. One of the most active
economists in the peace movement was the French writer Frédéric
Bastiat. In Britain, the most prominent figure to unite the causes of
free trade and world peace was the crusading liberal Richard Cobden,
who had no hesitation in proclaiming that "[f]ree trade is the international law of God."[10] Passy likewise (and in characteristically ex-
travagant terms) paid solemn homage to what he called "the gran-
deur, the truth, the nobility, I might almost say the holiness of the
free-trade doctrine; by the prosaic but effective pressure of [material]
interest it tends to make justice and harmony prevail in the world."[11]
Here, verily, was laudable commerce of the most exalted kind. Even
some of the more restrained and judicious writers, such as John
Stuart Mill, were of this general view. In his *Principles of Political
Economy* of 1848, Mill candidly admitted that the moral and intellectual benefits to be derived from free trade exceeded the merely material ones.[12] The sociologist Herbert Spencer expressed much the same
idea when he posited the category of an "industrial" society as the
polar opposite of a "militaristic" one.[13]

There were, to be sure, some peace crusaders who had misgivings
about linking their cause with the naked materialism of liberal capitalism. The suspicion of the moralist toward the selfishly rational
utility-maximizer is doubtless a permanent feature of human history.

The mid-nineteenth century, however, may have been the period in which this suspicion, though certainly still present, was at its lowest ebb. It is easy to see why. The impact of the new science of political economy was so exhilarating, its degree of certainty so high, its basic principles so clear and simple, its benefits to the whole human race so manifold—who but the most dour and reactionary of puritans could speak out against a body of scientific truth that would make man not only free, but prosperous and peaceful as well? If the world would only learn to heed the teachings of the new science—if it could become thoroughly imbued with what was sometimes called the "industrial spirit"—then a millennium that was simultaneously moral and material could be at hand. It would be no exaggeration, therefore, to characterize liberal capitalism, as expounded by the nineteenth-century political economists, as one of the foremost missionary faiths of world history. The message borne was one of joy and liberation. And—perhaps more to the point—the message could not be realized to its fullest extent unless the whole world took heed.[14]

It was obvious that, in order for the millennium to be realized, significant changes in the policies of governments would be required. Some of these were negative in character, involving the removal of irrational impediments to the free functioning of the global economic system. Most obviously, of course, tariff barriers would have to be dismantled. So would all other barriers to the free movement of goods, such as quotas and other quantitative controls. In addition, the free movement of capital should be promoted, so that finance could readily migrate to wherever it could earn the highest return. Labor too should be free to roam the face of the earth in search of the highest wages. To that end, states should remove controls on both emigration and immigration. They should also refrain from any discrimination in favor of their own nationals over foreigners (something that the classical international lawyers explicitly permitted).

In addition, governments would have to undertake a number of important tasks of a more affirmative nature. Broadly speaking, the states of the world were expected to provide the essential economic, juridical and even psychological infrastructure of the liberal capitalist system. They were to ensure the existence of a general atmosphere of stability and predictability, so that business could be transacted across large expanses of space and time without undue risk. One such task was to ensure the existence of a stable system of exchange rates, so that currency gyrations would not unreasonably disrupt transnational business activities. Another was to provide effective protection for the crucial private-law rights of property and of contract, so as to provide adequate security for trade and foreign investments. Perhaps the most definitive short summation of the liberal program, in almost credal form, was by Thomas Macaulay in 1830:

> Our rulers [he averred] will best promote the improvement of the nation by confining themselves strictly to their legitimate duties, by leaving capital to find its most lucrative course, commodities their fair price, industry and intelligence their natural reward, idleness and folly their natural punishment, by maintaining peace, by defending property, by diminishing the price of law and by observing strict economy in every department of state. Let the government do this, the people will do the rest.[15]

Implementing the Liberal Program

To a significant extent, the nations of the world actually did go far toward putting the program of the liberal political economists into practice in the course of the nineteenth century—so far, in fact, that we may characterize the high tide of the nineteenth-century free-trade era, from approximately 1850 to 1875, as the world's first systematic attempt to institute a system of economic world order. Political policies, in the contemptuous eighteenth-century sense of that term, did not, of course, fall into disuse. Nor, as we shall see presently, was economic nationalism by any means dead. Nevertheless, states did, for the first time in history, begin to take conscious steps to promote the evolution of a single integrated world economy.

One particularly outstanding characteristic of this nineteenth-century "mercantile republick" should be stressed: its radically de-centralized nature. Among the political liberal economists, there was a strong hostility to the very idea of establishing governmental or political institutions at the international level.[16] The prevailing opinion was that the "industrial spirit" of the times would gradually infuse the governments of the various individual states, which would then voluntarily and unilaterally bend their policies in the proper direction. From this standpoint, one of the quintessential "institutions" of the nineteenth-century liberal system was the international gold standard. It had no formal institutional or legal structure, but instead was simply a *modus vivendi*, a set of parallel practices adopted gradually by the principal economic powers on their own, beginning with Great Britain in 1819.[17] In general, most of the legal initiatives that underpinned the nineteenth-century "mercantile republick" were matters either of unilateral state action or of bilateral treaty practice.

The promotion of the free movement of goods during the mid-nineteenth century illustrates this point. With the repeal of its famous "corn laws" in 1846, Britain unilaterally forswore the imposition of protective tariffs. (It continued to levy modest duties for revenue-raising purposes.) For a time, it looked as if other leading economic powers might follow suit. France, during the early 1850s, began to move in that direction. The German *Zollverein*, the customs union formed in 1839 among the various German states, also inclined toward a free-trade policy, as did the German Empire after its formation in 1871. In the event, however, no other state followed Britain's lead. Instead, the preferred policy was to liberalize trade by the more cautious method of bilateral agreements between trading partners. Two types of treaty were used for this purpose. One was the commercial treaty—an agreement regulating the conditions of trade in specified categories of goods. Treaties of this type were, accordingly, of a detailed and technical character. The most famous one was the Cobden-Chevalier Treaty of 1860, between Britain and France.[18] (The two eponymous negotiators of this agreement between traditional political rivals were, significantly, both prominent in the international peace movement.) During the decade of the 1860s alone—the high tide of the nineteenth-century free-trade movement—Italy concluded some twenty-four such agreements; Belgium and France, nineteen each; Germany, eighteen; Austria-Hungary, fourteen; and Britain, eight. (The figure for Britain was low because its unilateral free-trade policy made it less reliant upon such treaties.)[19] Of a more general nature were treaties of friendship, commerce and navigation (FCN treaties, in lawyers' parlance), which commonly included most-favored-nation clauses. As the name implies, these arrangements obliged each contracting party to grant to the other any benefits which it granted to a third state.[20] Neither commercial treaties nor FCN agreements were an innovation of the nineteenth century. But both came into significantly greater use then than ever before.

The effect of this ever-thickening network of commercial treaties and most-favored-nation agreements was the gradual implementation of a general practice of freedom of trade.[21] These arrangements increasingly constrained the ability of states to make use of their general legal right to manipulate their economies at will in the national interest. Most-favored-nation agreements, in particular, precluded them from discriminating amongst their trading partners in

the granting or withholding of favors of various kinds. In the phrase-
ology of the traditional international lawyer, what was happening
was that states were, as a matter of practice and free choice, transforming the general—and rather notional—duty to engage in commerce from an "imperfect" obligation into a "perfect" one, through
the conclusion of treaties.

There was some multilateral treaty activity as well for the promotion of the free movement of goods. In the field of transport, a determined attack was made during the nineteenth century on the age-old
practice of "evil tolls" on the principal commercial waterways of the
world. The most ambitious such arrangement was the first one, dating
from 1815, concerning the Rhine. A Rhine Commission was set up
with a variety of legislative and judicial powers, directed toward the
promotion of freedom of navigation.[22] A similar regime was created
for the Danube in 1865. Other international commissions, albeit with
lesser powers, were instituted for the Elbe (1821), Douro (1835), Po
(1949) and Pruth (1866) Rivers.[23] In 1884–85, the Berlin West Africa
Conference provided for freedom of navigation for all states on the
Congo and Niger Rivers.[24] In 1888, the Constantinople Convention
guaranteed freedom of navigation through the Suez Canal even by
belligerent states in time of war.[25]

The free movement of persons, another important element of the
liberal program, became one of the most striking features of the
history of the nineteenth century. This was made possible, in large
part, by the simple absence of significant restrictions on immigration
and emigration in the major states. Countries even discontinued their
traditional practices of requiring aliens to have passports in order to
enter their territories. Bilateral FCN treaties, however, also had a role
to play in this process. One of their most important features was a
kind of charter of rights for the nationals of the contracting states
when settled in one another's territories. These catalogues of rights
became so standard that FCN treaties between entirely different
countries sometimes had virtually identical wording in this area. In
general, the nationals of the two contracting states, when settled in
the territory of the other, were protected from discrimination on the
ground of foreign nationality. Equality of treatment with nationals
was guaranteed over a range of economic matters, such as taxation,
the right to ownership and protection of property and the right of
access to courts. One common provision of such treaties was the
reciprocal protection of nationals of the two states from discriminatory embargoes.[26]

The achievements of the nineteenth-century free-trade period were staggering. In many ways, they exceeded anything that the world has been able to achieve since that time. On the material level alone, the results were striking. The free movement of goods, for example, made enormous advances, both in absolute terms and in relation to total world output. As a proportion of global production, trade climbed steadily from a mere 3 percent in 1800 to more than 33 percent by 1913. (For 1980, the comparable figure was 15 percent.) Even more impressive was the record with respect to the free movement of persons, as the nineteenth century became the greatest period in world history for voluntary mass migration, primarily from the crowded countries of Europe to the wide-open lands of the New World and the South Pacific. Never before or since have the borders of states been so open as they were in the generation preceding the First World War.[27] Figures on the movement of capital are scarcely less impressive. Britain was the leading state in this area, investing something between 25 and 40 percent of its entire national savings in foreign countries (inside and outside its empire) during the period from 1870 to 1914. The income from these investments represented some 5 to 8 percent of its gross national product—far higher than the comparable figures for the United States after World War II.[28]

By the middle of the nineteenth century, it was clear to even moderately careful observers that the world was being drawn closer and closer, almost daily, into a single economic unit. Even those who had little sympathy for the wondrous new science of liberal political economy had no trouble seeing what was happening. Karl Marx and Friedrich Engels, for example, who looked upon world economic developments in 1848 with a fascinating blend of wonder and horror, summed up the scene in the following terms:

> The bourgeoisie [they concluded] has through its exploitation of the world-market given a cosmopolitan character to production and consumption in every country. To the chagrin of the Reactionists, it has drawn from under the feet of industry the national ground on which it stood. All old-fashioned national industries have been destroyed or are daily being destroyed. They are dislodged by new industries . . . that no longer work up indigenous raw material, but raw material drawn from the remotest zones; industries whose products are consumed, not only at home, but in every quarter of the globe. In place of the old wants, satisfied by the productions of the country, we find new

wants, requiring for their satisfaction the products of distant lands and climes. In place of the old local and national seclusion and self-sufficiency, we have intercourse in every direction, universal inter-dependence of nations.[29]

Our concern is not primarily with these material achievements, impressive though they were. Rather, it is with the way in which international lawyers sought to make use of these developments to fashion a comprehensive system of economic world order in place of the traditional positivist law of nations inherited from the previous century. In this area, progress was far more modest.

The "Industrial Spirit" and the Law of Nations: Toward an International Law of "Solidarity"

It is, apparently, more difficult to change the minds of people—certainly of international lawyers—than to transform the economy of the world. If international lawyers had absorbed and applied the lessons of the liberal political economists, then the result would have been nothing less than a fundamental transformation of the positivist foundations of international law. In particular, it would have meant the overturning of the basic principle, inherited from Wolff and Vattel, that a state's duties to itself take precedence over its duties to the world community at large. The thinking of the liberal economists was to precisely the opposite effect. In their opinion, the basic duty of states was to take the sorts of steps just outlined to advance the material, and also the moral, well-being of humanity generally. States were to be transformed, in effect, into agencies for the service of the human community as a whole.

Such a radical revolution at the core of international law did not take place, either in the nineteenth century or afterwards. The basic positivist core of international law, as laid down in the previous century by Wolff and Vattel, remained intact. International lawyers continued to nod in the direction of the old natural-law duty of states to engage in commerce, but the majority were unwilling to concede it the status of a "perfect" (i.e., legally enforceable) right.[30] As in the previous century, however, a number of specific areas of international law did evolve in the direction pointed by the classical political economists. We shall look very briefly at five of these: state immunity from suit by private parties; armed conflict; the status of aliens; economic warfare; and economic isolationism. It will then be possible to distill the fundamental tenets of an emerging "common law" (as it might be termed) of a liberal system of international economic order. (Later generations would know it, as we shall see, under the term "international economic law.")

The subject of state immunity is instructive, because it touches so intimately upon the basic principle of sovereignty. The traditional rule of international law was that all states were immune from suit by private parties in the domestic courts of other countries. The rationale was the doctrine of the sovereign equality of states, that conceptual foundation stone of positivist international law. Because all states were juridically equal to one another, no country was entitled to subject another to the judgment of its domestic courts. In the late nineteenth century, however, doubts began to arise as to whether this principle should be applied in cases where states were engaging in commercial activity. Since humdrum buying and selling were not governmental functions, it began to be argued that when states were involved in such activities they were not actually functioning as sovereigns. On this argument, the traditional immunity from suit by private parties ought not to apply in such cases. This restrictive view of state immunity, as it is known, was accepted by Italian courts in the 1880s and 1890s, and by Belgian ones in 1903.[31] The significance of this state-immunity question lies in the way that it highlights the basic incompatibility, in the economic sphere, between the traditional prerogatives of sovereigns and the smooth functioning of a liberal economic system. If a liberal economic regime is to work effectively, then the private-law rights of property and contract must receive adequate protection. They do not, if one party possesses the crucial advantage of immunity from suit. The evolution of the restrictive theory of state immunity, then, was a sign that the norms of a liberal international economic order were making some inroads into the customary prerogatives of states.

A second area of international law in which the "industrial spirit" of liberal political economy manifested itself was armed conflict. During the nineteenth century, several steps were taken toward the greater protection of commerce from the blows of belligerents. For example, this period witnessed the gradual abandonment of the principle that the outbreak of a war automatically terminates treaties of commerce between belligerents. The newer rule came to be that it was up to the belligerents to take specific steps to terminate them if they so wished.[32] In addition, it came to be recognized that various categories of private property were exempt from seizure by belligerents. As a matter of practice, if not of strict law, debts came to be so regarded.[33] More generally, *all* private property was, in principle, recognized as immune from seizure by enemy forces in the law of land warfare.[34] At sea, things were somewhat more perilous. But an important step in the direction of moderation was the definitive acceptance by the major European powers that the goods of one belligerent were immune from seizure by the other, if they were carried in a neutral vessel— i.e., "free ships make free goods," in the snappy popular parlance. The decisive event here was the acceptance of the principle by Britain, traditionally its firmest opponent, in the Declaration of Paris of 1856.[35]

In addition, there was considerable agitation for other changes in the laws of war, which, although not generally accepted, indicate the general liberal atmosphere of the times. There was a campaign, led by the United States, to prohibit the practice of commercial blockade during wartime. A commercial blockade is a blockade of a commercial port that is not being invested simultaneously by land. The idea of directing a blockade purely against trade per se, without any connection to a military operation, was, in the words of American Secretary of State Lewis Cass, "difficult to reconcile with reason or with the opinions of modern times."[36] In the second half of the nineteenth century, the United States also spearheaded a campaign for a significant extension of the Declaration of Paris. Its proposal was to exempt *all* private property from seizure at sea during wartime, even if it was being carried on belligerent vessels. This idea was not accepted, but it gained a strong body of adherents (including, for a time, Lord Palmerston in Britain).[37] Finally, some lawyers favored the incorporation of the principle of "belligerent commerce" into the body of general customary international law. The influential Swiss writer Johann Kaspar Bluntschli, for example, expressed the view that, even during wartime, the principle of freedom of trade between private parties should remain in force (as the Prussian–U.S. treaty of 1785 had provided).[38] Although these proposals were not adopted, they indicate the kind of ideas that were abroad at the time, even in the conservative discipline of public international law.

A third area of international law in which the teachings of the political economists had an obvious impact concerned the rights of aliens. This is the sphere in which the new ideas had their greatest effect, even if only subconsciously. It has already been pointed out that one important purpose of FCN treaties was to ensure that nationals from each of the contracting states could settle and do business in the other without undue fear of discriminatory treatment. These treaty provisions, however, were only binding on the particular states that were parties to them. In the realm of customary international law, the more general idea gradually emerged that *all* aliens were legally entitled to a certain minimum standard of treatment.[39] It is easy to see that this general customary-law rule served essentially the same function as the FCN treaty norms. A standard of treatment for aliens that was applicable throughout the world would facilitate freedom of movement. This principle, it might be noted, was a sort of juridical equivalent of the international gold standard, in that it fixed a universal standard of a highly de-centralized character, since there were no international courts or world police forces to enforce it. As in the case of the gold standard, each state was expected to apply itself to the task.

The other two areas in which the ideas of the classical liberal economists had an impact—economic warfare, and economic isolationism—were closely related to each other. In fact, they were simply different forms of a single, more general phenomenon: a refusal on the part of some state to participate fully in the activities of the global "mercantile republick." It cannot be said that rules of international law evolved during the nineteenth century forbidding either of these practices. There were, however, some arguments advanced to that effect. These two subject areas merit attention primarily because those arguments were rooted so directly in the teachings of the liberal political economists. The subject of economic warfare, in particular, has continued to function, right up to the present day, as a juridical touchstone, indicating the extent to which the ideal of an economic system of world order has insinuated itself into general international law.

The late nineteenth and early twentieth centuries witnessed the development of the two principal weapons of economic warfare in international relations: the capital embargo and the trade boycott. (Two other important economic weapons—the freezing of financial assets and the nationalization of property—were, as will be seen, developments of the twentieth century.) Capital embargoes (i.e., refusals to lend funds or to permit investments) would appear to have attracted no adverse comment from international lawyers. Boycotting —formerly "non-intercourse"—was a different matter. The term owes its origin to the misadventures of a certain Captain Charles Cunningham Boycott, an oppressive agent in County Mayo, Ireland for an absentee English landowner. During the early 1880s, angry tenants decided to wage a campaign to ostracise him (perhaps inspired by the ecclesiastical practice of excommunication). Laborers and tenants refused to gather in his crops. Shopkeepers refused to sell him supplies. Even the postmen refused to deliver his mail. The campaign was effective, as the hapless captain was driven from the country in despair.[40]

In terms of international relations, a boycott may be defined simply as a refusal either to export to, or to import from, a target country. A boycott, then, is essentially a combination of an embargo (in the extended sense of a refusal to export) and a non-importation policy of the sort exemplified by the Napoleonic Continental System.[41] As a form of political hostility on the international scene, boycotting made its first major appearance in China in 1905, when the Chinese population, against the wishes of their government, instituted a boycott of American goods, in protest against restrictive immigration legislation in the United States affecting orientals.[42] (Over the next twenty-five years or so, the Chinese proved themselves to be the world's most adept boycotters, with Japan as their most frequent target.)[43] The other notable political boycott of the pre-World War I era was by the subjects of the Ottoman Empire against Austria in 1908–09, in response to the Austrian annexation of Bosnia-Herzogovina.[44] In both of these cases, the boycotters succeeded in inflicting measurable, if hardly crippling, economic injury onto their intended targets.

International lawyers had some difficulty in deciding how to react to this new form of hostility.[45] On the basis of traditional law, however, there was no real room for doubt. If, as Wolff and Vattel had insisted, states were entitled to refuse to have economic dealings with one another on any grounds whatever, then how could boycotting be said to be unlawful? Some international lawyers, such as Thomas Baty, forthrightly took this view:

> It is indeed difficult [he ruminated] to understand the objections brought against the . . . principle of the boycott. That persons who strongly disapprove of the character and acts of another should bind themselves to have no intercourse with him, and to unite others with them in that course, seems the most natural thing in the world.[46]

From the standpoint of the liberal political economists, precisely the opposite conclusion emerged. The reason is readily apparent. From the standpoint of their holistic view of the world economy, *any* trade disruption would prevent the principle of the division of labor from operating to its fullest extent, and would therefore reduce the efficiency of the overall system. Consequently, any act of economic warfare which interrupted the "natural" flow of the world economy was the concern, not simply of the parties involved, but of the entire transnational "mercantile republick."

A hardy minority of international lawyers followed this line of reasoning and accordingly argued against the orthodox positivist position. The Austrian writer Franz von Liszt, for example, echoed the views of Hübner from the previous century in positing the existence of a set of rules of "sociability" of states. One of these rules was that states should refrain from interfering unreasonably with trade and that they should, as much as possible, keep economic matters separate from political ones.[47] On this view, of course, boycotts instituted on political grounds would be unlawful. The writer Styrios P. Séfériadès probably went to the furthest extreme. He contended that states had a positive duty to suppress boycott movements undertaken by their nationals, even if they involved no specific unlawful acts (such as violence or property destruction). In his view boycotting was "a sort of war between nationals of different states," which ought not to be permitted by international law.[48]

The final specific area in which the "industrial spirit" of the liberal economists impinged upon international law, economic isolationism, involved essentially the same issues as boycotting. Both were non-intercourse policies, with the one targeted against a particular state or states, and the other operating more generally. Séfériadès readily recognized this affinity between the two practices when he condemned the isolationist policy of China as a "colossal and monstrous boycott" of the international commercial world in general.[49] The question of China in fact posed the problem of general economic non-intercourse in its most acute form, since Wolff and Vattel had both turned their attention specifically to the matter and firmly pronounced China to be within its sovereign rights. (China, incidentally, took this particular nugget of Western teaching readily to heart. The earliest writings on international law to be translated from Western languages into Chinese were the passages of Vattel affirming the right of states to regulate imports and exports as they saw fit.[50] Significantly, the so-called "Opium War" of 1839–42 was not, strictly speaking, fought because of China's refusal to allow the importing of opium. Britain readily recognized that such a prohibition was within China's legal rights. The actual *casus belli* was the mistreatment of British nationals, in the course of some over-zealous enforcement of the opium ban.)

The international lawyers who were attuned to the ideas of the political economists naturally disputed China's right to wall itself off from the world at large. Von Liszt, as part of his concept of the "sociability" of states, held that an isolationist country like China, even if it was not actually acting illegally, strictly speaking, was at least relegating itself to a second-class citizenship in the international community.[51] A similar concept of a new international law of "solidarity" was advanced at the turn of the twentieth century by the French writer Albert de Geouffre de La Pradelle. This new international law of "solidarity," in the eyes of La Pradelle, was concerned not so much with the political relations between states as with the "economic and social relations ... between people and people."[52] Where the old law of nations had concerned power, the new law of "solidarity" concerned commerce. China was offending against this new law of "solidarity," La Pradelle contended, by obstinately withholding its vast natural-resource wealth from the stream of world commerce, where it rightly belonged. Anticipating Séfériadès, he accused China of deliberately and maliciously inflicting an economic injury upon the world at large. It is true that La Pradelle and Séfériadès found few international lawyers to support their views. But it is also clear that the arguments which they advanced were the direct and logical consequence of the teachings of the liberal political economists.

We are now in a position to sum up the basic legal foundations of a system of liberal economic world order, as they had emerged by the end of the nineteenth century—and as they remain, essentially intact, to the present day. These basic "common-law" principles (as they have sometimes been termed)[53] could be formulated in various ways. For present purposes, two fundamental, and closely related, concepts may be said to form their core.

One is the principle that the duty of states, at least in the sphere of economic relations, is not the single-minded pursuit of their own individual national interests, but rather the promotion of the welfare of the human race as a whole. The dominant ethos of the system of international relations should therefore be one of cooperation rather than of competition. Over the longer term, the goal of international law, and of the individual states, should be the progressive integration of the entire world into a single economic system operating on the basis of the international division of labor. In the interest of promoting the maximum efficiency and harmony of the global economic system, state policies of economic isolationism and economic warfare cannot be allowed. The concept of a liberal economic world order is, accordingly, distinctly holistic and universalistic in character.

The other basic tenet of this liberal vision of an economic world order is closely related to this first one: there should be maximum opportunity for individuals (and by extension, corporations) to range over the entire face of the earth in their quest for utility maximization. There should be not only complete freedom of trade, but also full mobility of capital and of labor. All barriers to trade and to foreign investment should be demolished, the currencies of the various countries stabilized, the private-law rights of property and of contract safeguarded, and the rights of migrants (i.e., of aliens) protected. In this area, the strongly individualistic nature of the liberal vision of economic world order is particularly apparent.

Two general comments may be offered about these principles. One is that the concept of a liberal economic world order operates simultaneously at two levels: that of the individual, and that of the global "mercantile republick" at large. The system is strongly individualistic in its stress on free enterprise and competition between individuals, as well as on the rights of individual freedom of trade, investment and migration. In this regard, the liberal vision is a restatement, now in strictly materialistic terms, of Vitoria's libertarian "law of trade" from the Middle Ages. At the very same time, the cosmopolitanism of the system is apparent in its stress on safeguarding the efficiency of the overall global economy, primarily by permitting the principle of the division of labor to play itself out to the fullest extent possible. In between these two levels is, of course, the nation-state. The state, it may now be seen, is essentially an alien entity to classical liberal thought. Or rather, it would be more accurate to say that the traditional *sovereign rights* of states are alien to it—the very rights upon which positivists in the tradition of Wolff and Vattel insist so strongly. States do have a part to play in the liberal scheme of things. But it is a strictly subordinate, service-oriented role of the kind outlined by Macaulay. States are not, on this view, allowed to pursue their selfish national interests to the point of undermining the norms of the liberal system itself.

The second general comment is closely related to the first one. It should be stressed that these basic principles of an economic world order are not, ultimately, economic in character—at least not in the sense in which that term is ordinarily used. In the final analysis, the concept of an economic system of world order is a juridical one, because its most significant and fundamental element is the overturning of the basic positivist principle that the sovereignty and independence of each individual state is the cornerstone of international relations. Only when this idea is replaced by the *general* principle that the primary duty of states is to advance the welfare of humanity as a whole can a new law of "solidarity" or a system of economic world order be said truly to have arrived.

For all of the significant progress made during the nineteenth century in the implementation of the liberal program,[54] it cannot be concluded that this critical step was taken. On the contrary, as the century progressed, it became increasingly clear that there were many daunting obstacles to the implementation of an effective economic world order. For one thing, liberalism had some weaknesses which its early proponents either failed to observe or deliberately downplayed. In addition, there were rival schools of economic thought in the field, of which two were especially important: the "socialism" of the St.-Simonians and, more significantly, a resurgent economic nationalism which gradually gained the upper hand over liberalism. We shall look at each of these developments.

WEAKNESSES OF LIBERALISM: THE HAZARDS OF ABUNDANCE

For all of the claims of its most fervent apostles to universal validity, classical liberal economics, like any other social system, was a product of historical circumstances. We have observed that a free-market, libertarian economic system is not viable in a general atmosphere of shortage and privation. More generally, free trade and liberal capitalism have been strongly associated, in effect if not in strict theory, with *industrial* production. It is easy to see why. Technological advances and capital investment make long production runs possible. But they also make them necessary, if unit costs are to be kept low. Therefore, the industrial mass-producer is crucially dependent upon the widest possible access to markets. He is, in other words, a natural advocate of free trade—provided, of course, that he is the lowest-cost producer of his goods. This crucial connection between free trade and industrial production has had—and continues to have—two outstanding consequences. The first is that a liberal capitalist system tends to be biased toward the interests of advanced industrialized economies and therefore to relegate primary-producing countries to an inferior status. The second is that liberalism is dangerously vulnerable to conditions of hardship caused by overproduction, when protectionist tendencies are likely to assert themselves. Some comment on each of these matters is in order.

First, on the bias of liberalism toward the interests of industrialized states. The evidence for this proposition is clear from the historical record. It is no accident that the most prominent free-trading state during the nineteenth century was Britain, the pioneer industrial economy. It was particularly well placed to reap the benefits of a free-trade regime. As the leading industrial country, it had, for a long time, no fear of undue competition from foreign imports of industrial products and, accordingly, no incentive to impose protective tariffs against them. As for raw-material inputs (such as cotton for the textile industry), it was obviously to Britain's advantage to obtain these as cheaply as possible and therefore to maintain low, or even non-existent, tariffs on them. (Even the mercantilists, it will be recalled, favored low tariffs on raw materials for this same reason.) Britain, therefore, had no interest in protectionist policies and could well afford to dispense with them unilaterally.

No other country had so strong a stake in the new order. Other industrializing states, for example, found it difficult to emulate Britain without resorting to protective tariffs, if only to shelter "infant industries" from British competition. The two major industrial powers of the nineteenth century, after Great Britain—the United States and Germany—both achieved that status with the assistance of high-tariff policies.[55] More particularly, raw-material producers stood to gain relatively little from the free-trade system, because tariffs on their exports were already relatively low. Furthermore, there was the danger—as the developing countries themselves saw it—that primary producers would be relegated to that status more or less permanently. After all, the concern of the liberals was with the development of the economy of the *world*, and not of any particular state. As a result, liberals tended to see no need to promote industrialization within the arbitrary political boundaries of the various nations.

Liberalism, therefore, has always tended to be unsympathetic to aspirations of *national* economic development. More generally, its sweepingly universalistic ethos has made it unsympathetic to *any* form of economic unorthodoxy—i.e., to any interference with the world-wide division of labor and with the open-door regime of trade and investment which follows from it. The cosmopolitanism of liberal capitalism, accordingly, has always had a menacing underside to it, a dictatorial and interventionist streak. The case of China in the nineteenth century furnishes the outstanding illustration. That country was, in effect, forcibly conscripted into the citizenry of the global "mercantile republick" by strength of arms. The international lawyers most imbued with the teachings of the liberal economists lent a certain general support, even if not outright endorsement, to this coercive conduct by the major capitalist states. La Pradelle, for example, in his concern for the interests of the world community at large, gave those of China very short shrift. He brusquely dismissed Chinese culture and civilization as "no longer necessary."[56] Although he opposed the use of military force against the Chinese, he did advocate, rather darkly, "expelling their egoism from them, . . . expropriating them of their routine, . . . dispossessing them of their inertia."[57]

The principal, and most controversial, use of military force to uphold the principles of liberal orthodoxy was in support of the rights and interests of aliens—aliens, that is, from the advanced industrialized states when they were being mistreated by weaker and underdeveloped powers. We have noted the emergence, during the nineteenth century, of the thesis that a general international minimum standard exists for the treatment of aliens—including the upholding of the economic rights of property and contract. Any country that transgressed this standard was likely to be met with a formal diplomatic protest. Small and weak states ran the additional risk of a visitation by gunboats. As there was no world government or centralized law-enforcement agency for the global "mercantile republick," each state took it upon itself to enforce the rules on behalf of its nationals.

Latin America was frequently the scene of these self-commissioned enforcement measures. France, for example, sent a naval force to Haiti in 1825 to compel the government to agree to indemnify the descendants of French planters of the colonial period for losses suffered. As a flamboyant means of collecting payment from Mexico for French claimants, it bombarded the port of Vera Cruz in 1838. It blockaded Argentina in 1838–40 and again in 1845–50 (this time in conjunction with Britain) for similar purposes and forcibly intervened in Venezuela on a number of occasions in the second half of the nineteenth century.

Spain landed a military force in Tampico, Mexico in 1829. The United States sent its marines to Uruguay and its navy to Paraguay to redress various grievances. It also dispatched military forces to the Isthmus of Panama to protect a railway financed by American investors. In 1862, Britain mounted a blockade of Rio de Janeiro in response to the plundering of a wrecked British merchantman. One of the most notable of these Latin American interventions was the blockading of Venezuela, in 1902, by Britain, Germany and Italy, to compel the payment of various unsatisfied claims.

Such practices took place in other parts of the world too. The "Opium War" of 1839–42, as we have seen, was undertaken in response to alleged Chinese mistreatment of British nationals. Perhaps the single most famous of all the incidents of "gunboat diplomacy" was the Don Pacifico affair of 1850, in which Britain blockaded the coast of Greece and captured several Greek vessels in a dispute over the indemnification of one of its nationals for losses caused by mob action.[58]

Only slightly less striking was the spectacle of governments going bankrupt and being, in effect, delivered up into the hands of their private capitalist creditors, like common paupers being hauled into debtors' prison. The first country to suffer this humiliating fate was Egypt in the 1870s, which was compelled to experiment with a variety of different arrangements with its creditor banks. By the end of the century Evelyn Baring (Lord Cromer), of Baring Brothers Bank, was the virtual ruler of the country.[59] Other states that similarly had to surrender important sovereign functions to private banks included Greece, Tunisia, Morocco, the Ottoman Empire and various small countries in the Caribbean and Central America.[60]

It is hardly surprising, then, that the loyalty of the small, weak and underdeveloped nations to this liberal system of international economic order has never been strong. To the extent that such countries are raw-material producers, rather than industrial states, they occupy a marginal position economically in the system. They can do little more than hope that general world prosperity will "trickle down" to them. Furthermore, their political and military weakness has left them particularly vulnerable to the practitioners of "gunboat diplomacy." For these reasons, the developing countries have always tended to be more *in* the global "mercantile republick" than *of* it. Their real loyalty has been to policies of economic nationalism rather than of liberal capitalism, with ramifications that will be explored in due course.

The other major consequence of the connection between classical liberal economics and industrialization is the vulnerability of a liberal capitalist system to the dangers of excessive production.[61] Virtually from its inception, classical political economy has been haunted by the fear—and sometimes the reality—of underconsumption, i.e., of excessive production, unsold goods, falling prices and rising unemployment. Where ancient and medieval populations feared shortfalls of essential supplies, modern industrial people fear the loss of markets for their produce. Marx and Engels, ever fascinated by the workings of capitalism, looked forward to the day when the liberal system would relapse into barbarism from "too much civilization, too much means of subsistence, too much industry, too much commerce."[62] Britain, as the leading industrial state, was the first to experience this modern-style hardship of abundance. During the Napoleonic Wars, there was serious distress in the industrial areas, caused partly by the loss of two important export markets: the European one (by virtue of Napoleon's Continental System) and the American one (by virtue of various non-intercourse policies of the United States).

Not until the period from approximately 1870 to 1890, however, did the world in general suffer its first great modern-style depression caused by conditions of glut rather than dearth. The result was a discouraging retreat from free trade, which took the form, naturally, of measures that were the very opposite of old-style "policies of provision," which had been designed to deal with shortages. Instead of sending out *sitonai* to scour the world markets for imports, states erected tariff barriers to protect their home markets from foreign penetration. The closing decades of the nineteenth century became a great age of tariff wars, as states became locked into cycles of retaliation and counter-retaliation. The single most damaging one economically was probably between France and Italy between 1888 and 1898. Other major tariff duels took place between Germany and Russia between 1890 and 1894, and between Austria-Hungary and Serbia from 1906 to 1909.[63] States also began to compete ever more intensively during this period for increasingly saturated export markets. Allegations of unfair practices began to fly, especially accusations that governments were subsidising their national enterprises, to the prejudice of lower-cost foreign competitors. Germany was the foremost target of these claims.[64] (In particular, German subsidies to its beet sugar industry were alleged to have caused hardship among traditional producers in the West Indies.) Britain continued to adhere to its unilateral free-trade policy, but there was increasing domestic pressure to modify it. Around the turn of the century, support began to grow for a policy of "fair trade," which would entail retaliating against countries (such as Germany) that were found to be taking undue advantage of Britain's liberalism by flooding it with goods while themselves huddling behind tariff walls. This "fair trade" campaign did not succeed, but it was a clear sign that the halcyon days of liberalism were over by the end of the nineteenth century.[65]

The world depression of 1870 to 1890, then, was a vivid and dispiriting demonstration of how easy it was for the free-trade trend to slip into reverse. It showed, too, the dangers posed by the highly decentralized nature of the global "mercantile republick." The lack of any means of ensuring an equilibration of supply and demand meant that the system was vulnerable to crises of overproduction. In addition, the lack of a formal legal framework for the liberal order meant that, when such crises arose, there was nothing to prevent states from relapsing into protectionist ways and adopting beggar-my-neighbor policies to safeguard their domestic markets at the expense of foreigners.

In addition to these various weaknesses in the liberal international economic order itself, there were also challenges in the field to classical liberal economics, in the form of proposals for a "socialist" (or planned-economy) system; and also, far more significantly, there arose a revived and invigorated economic nationalism.

AN ALTERNATIVE ON THE "LEFT": ST.-SIMONIAN SOCIALISM

The St.-Simonian system, named for the imaginative and eccentric French nobleman Count Henri de St.-Simon, is sometimes described as socialist. It was, in the sense that it favored subjecting the economic activity of society to comprehensive regulation and direction, instead of leaving it to the free play of market forces. (St.-Simon himself, incidentally, coined the word "socialism" with this meaning in mind.) The St.-Simonian system was, and remains, the most thorough-going and ambitious program for an economic system of world order that has ever been devised. Since it was even more radically cosmopolitan in character than the liberal one, it is best seen as an extreme variant of it, rather than as a fully-fledged alternative. It is therefore only necessary to outline some of the more salient points in which St.-Simonianism differed from liberalism.[66]

The single most outstanding difference between the two was that the St.-Simonian program, in marked contrast to the liberal one, was essentially *dirigiste* and technocratic in character, rather than libertarian and individualistic. To the St.-Simonians, unbridled competition between individual entrepreneurs was destructive, wasteful and irrational. The powerful forces of the new industrial age should not be the playthings of private interests, but instead should be harnessed rationally and systematically for the maximum benefit of all mankind. Economic progress, in the St.-Simonian view, should proceed on the basis of cooperation and planning and should be under the direction of persons with the appropriate technical skills—worthy successors, in certain ways, to Quesnay's Confucian literati. Where Quesnay's system had had deep roots in natural-law jurisprudence, however, St.-Simon's was firmly based upon the new science of economics. It was also firmly industrial rather than agricultural in outlook, to the point that the members of this new skilled elite were dubbed *industriels*.

These *industriels* were seen as a technocratic elite, which would supplant the older, obsolete ruling groups—the aristocrats, the warriors, the ecclesiastics and the lawyers. Old political policies such as territorial aggrandizement and the balance of power were outmoded and irrelevant. The supreme task of the human community was economic development on a truly global scale. Engineers, naturally, were to be one of the most important sub-groups of *industriels*, since one of the centerpieces of the St.-Simonian vision was a massive program of public works, particularly in the transport field. St.-Simon himself had been a canal enthusiast. His followers duly became ardent advocates of railroad construction. The captains of industry would also be among the *industriels*, since the new forces of the Industrial Revolution were to be systematically put to work for the benefit of mankind. Not least, the major financiers would be in this group, since vast amounts of capital would clearly be required for the grandiose schemes that were envisaged.

In the fully fledged St.-Simonian ideal, all of the problems of the world would be relentlessly reduced to technical issues, upon which the skill and expertise of the ruling *industriels* could be brought to bear. One should actually say "administering" *industriels*, since the very concept of political power as it had traditionally been known was to be superceded in the new age. Governments were not to be educated, as in the liberal system, but actually abolished, since they served no useful purpose. The whole of Europe was to be reorganized as a federal system under a single head. St.-Simon's proposal to this effect is sometimes hailed as a precursor of the later League of Nations, but in fact its spirit was quite different. He had no use for an association of states in which the members would retain their traditional sovereign rights.

The St.-Simonian program has obviously never been implemented in anything like its comprehensive form; but it has continued to exert some influence down to the present day. Bureaucratic or "scientific" socialist thinking, for example, owes it an obvious debt. The Marxist idea of the state "withering away" in favor of a wholly administrative system is a distinctly St.-Simonian conception.[67] In actual practice, it may be said that the various European river commissions mentioned earlier were applications, on a very humble scale, of St.-Simonian ideas, since they entailed the substitution of rational administrative skills for traditional legal prerogatives.

Only in the twentieth century, however, would ideas of this kind really come into their own first (as will be seen) in certain aspects of the "associationalist" system of the 1920s and then, after 1945, in the creation of a galaxy of functional economic organizations. During the late nineteenth and early twentieth centuries, the real opposition to the liberal vision of an economic world order came from quite a different quarter: from a resurgent economic nationalism, elaborately decked out in the latest scientific garb of the time.

CHALLENGE FROM THE "RIGHT": ECONOMIC NATIONALISM AND THE ART OF DEVELOPMENT

In its essentials, economic nationalism retained in the nineteenth century (as in the twentieth) the basic traits apparent since the age of Plato and Aristotle. Various developments of the period served to reinforce it, by enabling it to pursue its traditional ends in a more thorough-going and scientific fashion than ever before. By the end of the century, it was clearly in the ascendency, and liberalism just as clearly on the wane.

Characteristics of the New Economic Nationalism

Since the basic principles of economic nationalist thinking are already familiar, the new developments of the nineteenth century can be noted with reasonable brevity. The principal innovation may be summed up quite simply: nineteenth (and, as we shall see, twentieth) century economic nationalism was *developmental* in character. The "perfection" of states now came to be seen in terms of the evolution of the nation-state into a balanced economic unit in its own right,

often with considerable governmental guidance. In immediate concrete terms, that meant (and has continued to mean) one thing: industrialization.

An early intellectual pioneer of economic nationalism in this modern sense was the Scottish political economist James Steuart, whose
Inquiry into the Principles of Political Economy (1767) stressed the
importance of government action in ensuring a proper equilibrium
within a country between production and consumption.[68] Jean-Jacques
Rousseau manifested much the same concern in his plans for the
governments of Poland and Corsica.[69] In the United States, a similar
program was proposed by Alexander Hamilton in his *Report on Manufactures* of 1791, which has been regarded as a sort of Magna Carta
of economic nationalism. His basic plan was straightforward enough.
He proposed to knit the newly independent United States into a true
nation in the economic sense, by ensuring that the various regions
produced for the mutual benefit of one another rather than of the
outside world. Part of his program was a scheme of protective tariffs
for the nurturing of manufactures.[70] The same basic idea reappeared
in the 1820s as the "American system" of Henry Clay. As Clay envisaged it, the northeastern part of the country would become the center
of manufacturing, under the secure protection of high tariff barriers.
The federal government would then use the tariff revenues to finance
"internal improvements" (such as roads and canals) in the developing
frontier areas.[71]

Ideas of this sort were having a fruitful reception on the continent
of Europe at the same time, where it became apparent just how far
such notions could be taken. The nineteenth century's most worthy
successor to Plato as an economic nationalist was the German philosopher Gottlieb Fichte. Fichte's extraordinary work *The Closed Commercial State* (1800) must surely have the doubtful distinction of being
the most radical economic nationalist program in human history.
Like Plato, he proposed the abolition of convertible currencies (*Welt-
geld*, or "world money"), in favor of purely national money systems
(*Landesgeld*). Each state, in his system, would rigorously eschew trade
with any other. All economic rivalry would thereby be totally removed from the world scene. He also echoed Plato in his view that
even foreign travel by individuals should be sharply restricted. Every
society would then be free to develop its own "spirit" along its own
"natural" lines, with no fear of disruption from the outside.[72]

The economic nationalism which gained increasing force on the
continent of Europe in the course of the nineteenth century was of a

rather more moderate stripe than this. The most influential single figure, the German economist Friedrich List, was decidedly more of the Hamiltonian than the Fichtean persuasion. In fact, List lived in the United States for a number of years, was quite familiar with the ideas of Hamilton and was a personal friend of Clay. It is hardly surprising, then, that ideas very similar to theirs found their way into his major work, *The National System of Political Economy* (1841). This work is the great classic of modern economic nationalism, as Smith's *Wealth of Nations* is of liberalism.[73]

List was a moderate by temperament and a historicist by intellectual inclination. While accepting that free trade was, as an ideal, the best possible system, he went on to point out that the historical times were not yet ripe for it. He realized that, under the circumstances then prevailing in the world, a free-trade system was particularly tailored to the interests of the single leading industrial country, Britain. List also perceived that the needs of primary-producing countries were not adequately met by a free-trade system. He was one of the first thinkers firmly to equate agricultural production with economic backwardness, and industrial production with progress. In this respect, he is the father of much of twentieth-century development economics. His program was essentially that of Hamilton and Clay. States should employ protective tariffs in order to diversify their economies (i.e., to foster industry). Only *after* the Industrial Revolution had thus spread to the various countries of the world should the tariff barriers then be dismantled and the ideal free-trade system brought into being.

List had a particularly clear idea of the kinds of international regimes that were appropriate to his own program, and to that of the liberals. He labeled his own as a "national" system, contrasting it with the "cosmopolitan" one of the liberals. He described the role of the state under his national system in language strikingly reminiscent of that of Wolff and Vattel: it is "to preserve and develop its prosperity, culture, nationality, language, and freedom—in short, its entire social and political position in the world."[74] In the cosmopolitan conception, in contrast, the duty of the state is "to join with other countries in the task of promoting the welfare and prosperity of the whole world."[75] Each of these two viewpoints corresponded to a particular science of economics in the narrower sense. Corresponding to the national system was what List called true "political" economy, which taught "how a given *nation* in the present state of the world and its own special national relations can maintain and improve its economical conditions. . . ." Associated with the cosmopolitan system was what he called (echoing Kant) the science of "cosmopolitical" economy, which was rooted "in the assumption that nations of the earth form but one society living in a perpetual state of peace."[76]

List's thinking was an important influence on the writings of the historical school of political economists which arose in the next generation in Germany. Its prominent figures included Gustav Schmoller, Wilhelm Roscher, Lujo Brentano, Karl Knies and Werner Sombart.[77] Their historical investigations concentrated on the evolution of nation-states as collective economic units. Schmoller inaugurated an important historical reassessment of mercantilism, doing much to rehabilitate it from the scorn to which Smith and his followers had subjected it.[78] Alongside the historical school of economists—and often strongly influenced by them—were social scientists such as Ferdinand Lassalle and Max Weber, who sought to harness the insights of the new science of sociology to bring about a systematic improvement in the socioeconomic health of the German nation. Perhaps the most significant figure in this tradition was Lassalle, who combined into a single coherent program the working-class socialism of Marx with the economic nationalism of List. Like Marx, he heaped scorn upon liberalism as a tawdry materialistic creed based upon pettiness and greed. But where Marx's working-class socialism had been, at least in principle, cosmopolitan, Lassalle's was clearly nationalist. The workers of *Germany*, rather than of the whole world, were to unite. Furthermore, they were to unite not simply with one another, but with the other elements of German society, under the stern and careful helmsmanship of the government, whose task was to synchronize the interests of all classes in the forging of a cohesive and unified German nation.[79]

Much the same kind of program was advocated in France by the adherents of the philosophy of "solidarism," which, in essence, was the application of the basic concept of La Pradelle's idea of "solidarity" at the level of the nation-state, rather than of international relations. The French solidarists were concerned to promote programs of voluntary cooperation and mutual assistance among the French people, with a view to creating a French nation-state in the fullest sense of the term—in which all citizens would have a stake, both material and moral. The most durable intellectual monument of this movement was Emile Durkheim's treatise on *The Division of Labor in Society*, published in 1893.[80]

To a significant extent, the program of the economic nationalists was implemented. The nineteenth century proved to be a great age of economic nation-building. A seminal event in this regard was the French Revolution, one of the most striking and enduring legacies of which had been the abrupt sweeping away of the myriad internal obstructions to trade (something which the physiocrats had sought in vain). As other nations followed suit, it became the norm, for the first time in history, for the political boundaries of states to coincide with economic ones. By the same token, it now became possible, also for the first time in history, for states to have truly *national* economic policies in the full sense of the term. The mercantilists, it is true, had been diligent, even ruthless, manipulators of "beneficial" and "ruinous" trade. But they had never attempted the sort of thorough-going social engineering that their nineteenth-century successors envisaged.

Tariff policies played a particularly critical role in the socioeconomic nation-building of the nineteenth century.[81] This period saw the birth of (appropriately enough) the "scientific tariff"—a tariff carefully designed to promote the maximum possible degree of social solidarity within the country in question. The pioneer practitioner of this art was the Australian colony of Victoria in the 1860s, which devised a tariff policy to promote the transition from a gold-mining to a handicraft-based economy.[82] The "Méline" tariff of France in the 1890s was of this same general type. This measure of agricultural protection was designed to help ensure the stability of French society by keeping a prosperous (or at least solvent) peasantry on the land.[83] The most thorough-going of these programs was, characteristically, the German one. Beginning in 1879, Chancellor Otto von Bismarck began to implement what was, for all intents and purposes, the program of social welfare-and-protectionism advocated by Lassalle and other historical-school writers. Agriculture and industry both duly received the protection of high tariff barriers, while the working classes became the beneficiaries of the world's most advanced (if somewhat paternalistic) system of government-sponsored social welfare.[84] It should be noted, in this connection, that it would be a very great error to equate the new scientific economic nationalism of this period with mere conservatism. This solidarist and social-welfare ethos of the economic nationalists contrasted very strongly with the atomistic and social Darwinist flavour of liberalism.

If governments were showing increasing concern for the economic and social health of their people during this period, they were also expecting some favors in return. Economic interests were expected to do their share for the advancement of national causes—as perceived, naturally, by the governments concerned. With the steady heating up of political rivalries in the course of the late nineteenth century, there came to be an increasing tendency on the part of all of the major states to conscript their economic interests for the service of national ends. "Cosmopolitan" increasingly came to be a pejorative term, signifying someone whose patriotism was suspect. Sometimes, it was a thinly-veiled anti-semitic epithet.[85]

Governments accordingly began to take an increasing interest in the activities of financial forces within their jurisdiction. This attention assumed a variety of forms. One was a measure of informal cooperation with the creditor banks that controlled various aspects of state administrations (such as those of Egypt, the Ottoman Empire and other countries mentioned earlier). Evelyn Baring, for example, had a dual capacity in Egypt, as both the head of the committee of bankers administering Egyptian finances and, simultaneously, as British consul-general in Cairo. In general, bankers were expected to give due regard to the foreign policies of their home states while discharging their own duties as creditors. Governments of capital-exporting countries also became interested in influencing bank lending with a view to maximizing political, rather than economic, returns. In the United States and France, the governments, by various forms of pressure and persuasion, induced bankers to steer their loans in politically productive directions—in the case of France, to the economic cementing of the Russian alliance of 1894; and in the case of the United States, to the pursuit of "dollar diplomacy" in the Caribbean and Central America in the early 1900s.[86]

Such government influence sometimes took the negative form of capital embargoes directed against states deemed to be politically hostile. In France and Germany, the governments had formal powers to veto flotations of loans to foreign countries, if they considered them to be contrary to the national interest. Britain was exceptional in relying only upon informal controls: in appropriate cases, word would be passed discreetly to the financial interests that certain loans should not be made.[87] These countries exercised their powers on a number of occasions during the late nineteenth and early twentieth centuries. The French were the most active, although their degree of success was (at best) modest. The barring of Italy from the French capital markets in the 1880s, for example, served only to compel that country to rely more heavily than before on Germany, thereby providing some economic underpinning to the growing political alliance between the two states.[88] Germany had a similar experience when, also in the 1880s, it barred Russia from access to its capital markets. The result was to drive Russia economically into the hands of the French, as a prelude to the political alliance of the 1890s.[89]

In the late nineteenth and early twentieth centuries, then, there was a general tendency in international relations for economic rivalries and alliances to align themselves with political ones. This development was to have a variety of implications; but the one that is of concern here is the impact of the new economic nationalism on international law.

Economic Nationalism and International Law: Looking Backward and Forward

The resurgent economic nationalism of the late nineteenth century did not, on the whole, produce any radical changes in international law. It did not need to, for the simple reason that international law, in its orthodox positivist version, was already quite consonant with economic nationalism. To some extent, however, international lawyers of a traditionalist stripe did strike out against some of the innovations which had begun to creep into the law in the wake of the new science of liberal political economy.

In the 1860s, the Argentinian diplomat and writer Carlos Calvo spearheaded an attack on the concept of the international minimum standard for the protection of aliens. The Calvo doctrine, as it became known, was essentially a straightforward reassertion of the basic sovereign rights of nations. Calvo contended that the principle of the international minimum standard was unacceptable, because it restricted the sovereign right of states to conduct their affairs as they wished within their territories. He certainly did not suggest that states should have a licence to treat aliens as they wished. What he did insist was that each state should have the unfettered right to determine for itself what its general standard of justice would be. Once that basic domestic-law decision had been made, the state's only international-law obligation was to apply its rules even-handedly to nationals and aliens alike. The Calvo doctrine had two important implications. One was that the standard of treatment which aliens could expect in foreign countries would not be a universal one, but instead would vary from state to state. The other consequence was that, once a state accorded equality of treatment to aliens and nationals, its international-law duties were discharged—regardless of what that standard actually was. In such a case, there was no scope for any diplomatic protest by other countries about the standard of treatment—and, *a fortiori*, no right to dispatch the gunboats.[90]

The validity of the Calvo doctrine has been a subject of vigorous dispute among international lawyers up to the present day. From the time of its inception, it has been championed by the developing countries, and opposed by the developed ones. The most vigorous opponents have been the capital-exporting states concerned about the protection of the rights of property and contract and the safeguarding of foreign investments. In the early twentieth century, the Latin American states succeeded in incorporating the Calvo doctrine into a regional convention on the rights of aliens.[91] But no broad consensus has ever emerged as to its general validity.

More interesting than the Calvo doctrine, because less forthrightly traditionalist in character, was the thesis that a new kind of economic world order was beginning to supercede the liberal capitalist one. Certain writers of the German historical school were major figures here. Werner Sombart, for example, propounded the existence of what he called a "law of declining exports." This law was to the effect that, as more and more countries around the world followed Britain's lead and became industrialized, they would thereby become more and more self-sufficient economically. International trade in raw materials would continue, but trade in manufactured goods would decline. As a result, the countries of the world would increasingly tailor their economic production to the consumption needs of the home market.[92]

Friedrich Naumann, a prominent publicist who typified the solidarist-cum-economic nationalist outlook of the period, spoke of the impact that trends of this kind would have on the nature of international relations generally. He contended that a new type of "international idea" was in the making. The earliest form of cosmopolitan thinking, he pointed out, had been religious and philosophical in character. The second type, he contended, had been "commercial" in nature, spearheaded by Britain and its leadership in the free-trade movement. That particular type of cosmopolitanism had performed marvels in its time, Naumann readily conceded. But its time was drawing to a close, because the next stage—the "social democratic" one, as he called it—was about to begin. It would be based, he predicted, on production rather than exchange, i.e., upon a high degree of regimentation of economic life by governments. It would not necessarily be universal in character as the "commercial" age had been. It would more likely be based on closed colonial systems, in which the colonies had the task of feeding raw materials to the industries of the mother countries. (Naumann himself was a notable advocate of the German colonization movement.) It would also be based on the formation of regional trading blocs dominated by local hegemonic powers (as in central Europe, where Germany naturally would lead).[93]

It is hardly surprising that some observers, like Naumann, believed that the vision of a liberal system of economic world order was one whose time had come and gone. The effects of the world depression of 1870–90, in combination with the new scientific economic nationalism of the nineteenth century, had very clearly pushed liberalism into a steady retreat. Then, in August 1914, the liberal program became wholly irrelevant. But a vision so powerful in its appeal, so simple in its basic premises and so scientific in its methods was not lightly to be written off. On the contrary, once the carnage of the Great War was over, a second attempt would be made to implement a liberal economic world order.

THREE

BUSINESS, NOT POLITICS:
The Interwar Experience

If the nineteenth-century experiment in economic world order was visibly fading in the face of the resurgent economic nationalism of the post-1875 period, then it was definitively terminated by the Great War of 1914–18. The "industrial spirit" was one of the casualties of the conflict, as the world received a horrifying lesson in the slaughter and destruction that international political rivalry could bring. As a result of the conflict, the basic legal and economic infrastructure of the nineteenth-century free-trade system lay in ruins. The network of commercial agreements and of treaties of friendship, commerce and navigation (FCN) was largely destroyed. Agreements between the Allied states and Germany were severed. France even went so far as to terminate *all* of its treaties containing most-favored-nation clauses. Its minister of commerce, Étienne Clémentel, vowed that the clause would never again "poison" French tariff policy.[1] From the ashes of the former empires of Central and Eastern Europe arose a host of new countries whose distinguishing economic feature was a virulent economic nationalism and an almost superstitious reverence for autarky.[2] Further east, the picture was worse yet, as Russia fell under the control of Bolsheviks, who aggressively flouted all of the norms of civilized economic conduct by repudiating the debts of the predecessor regime and nationalizing property without compensation. The dream of the mutual cooperation of states in the cause of advancing human prosperity seemed as far as it had ever been from realization.

Despite these daunting obstacles, the vision of an economic system of world order did not die out. Alongside the better known attempt to institute a political system of international order, in the form of the League of Nations, a parallel attempt was made on the economic side. This second experiment in economic world order bore significant resemblances to its predecessor effort of the nineteenth century. Like the free-trade movement of that period, this new initiative was based squarely on the teachings of the classical liberal economists. It saw private enterprise as the basic mechanism of economic growth, with states providing the necessary structural framework. In addition, however, there was something new about this second experiment in economic world order. Its proponents were more willing than their forbears had been to equip the global "mercantile republick" with a certain degree of guidance from above. This post-war system, then, had less of the spirit of Cobden, and more of St.-Simon, than its nineteenth-century predecessor.

The experiment in economic world order of the 1920s consisted basically of two components. The first was a straightforward campaign against economic nationalism. The second—and more significant—component was the technocratic one: the attempt to provide a degree of scientific management of international economic affairs. The basic philosophy of this effort was that the proper organization of international economic relations should be entrusted to trained experts—certainly not to clumsy and vindictive politicians—who would bring to the task a neutral scientific expertise and sound business judgment. This aspect of the experiment in economic world order was more in the spirit of the physiocrats or of the St.-Simonians than of the classical liberal free traders. Perhaps its single most noteworthy feature was a close coordination between government and private enterprise—a feature that has led to application of the label "associationalist" to describe it (a term that will be applied here).

We shall look at each of these two major strands of the interwar experiment in economic world order, together with their implications for the development of international law, and then proceed to see why they proved unable to prevent the surge of economic nationalism that accompanied the Great Depression of the 1930s.

ECONOMIC WORLD ORDER IN THE 1920S

There was a school of thought, particularly prominent in the United States, which held that economic rivalry had been one of the principal causes of the Great War.[3] At the root of the problem, on this view, was the tendency to regard economic forces in purely *national*, as opposed to international, terms. As a result, states had set about manipulating the international economic system with a view to gaining advantages for "their" enterprises and thereby (so it was thought) enhancing their national power. The inevitable result had been a proliferation of unfair and discriminatory practices. At the very least, policies of this kind would lead to economic fragmentation and the loss of any clear sense of the world as a single, integrated economic unit. At worst, the ill-will and "jealousy of trade" (in Hume's words) spawned by such conduct could lead to outright war. As Arthur Salter, one of the most prominent crusaders against economic nationalism, bluntly put it, "too close an identification of the foreign trade of a country with its political power constitutes a danger to peace."[4]

The Crusade for "Economic Disarmament"

One prominent figure who was of this general persuasion was President Woodrow Wilson of the United States, whose economic outlook was that of a free-trade liberal of the classic nineteenth-century kind.[5] Among the five "Bases of Peace" which he proposed to the belligerent parties before the U.S. entry into the conflict was a provision for a "[m]utual guarantee against ... economic warfare."[6] His famous Fourteen Points of January 1918 included a call for "the removal, so far as possible, of all economic barriers and the establishment of an equality of trade conditions."[7] His five Additional Points of September 1918, in this same general vein, contained a proposal that "there should be no selfish economic combinations or any form of economic coercion ... , except as a meansof preventing aggression."[8] In keeping with these general ideas, two international lawyers attached to the American delegation to the Paris Peace Conference, David Hunter

Miller and James Brown Scott, drew up a draft Declaration on Equality of Trade for adoption by the gathering.[9]

In the event, the "industrial spirit" of economic liberalism proved to be little in evidence at the Paris conference. The concentration, instead, was overwhelmingly on political issues. There was, for example, the task of applying the principle of self-determination of peoples and creating a battery of new nation-states—and, perforce, new national economic units—out of the ruins of the Central and Eastern European empires. In addition, penalties were to be inflicted onto Germany, in the form of the notorious "war-guilt clause" of the Treaty of Versailles, together with a variety of economic disabilities, of which the most notable was the obligation to pay reparations to the triumphant ex-Allied states.[10] Finally, the conference applied itself to the creation, for the first time in history, of a system of world political order, inthe form of the League of Nations.[11] The League was clearly a political, as opposed to economic, system of international order, in that its purpose was to forge an alliance of sovereign nation-states against aggression, rather than to create a single integrated world society. The Covenant of the League contained only two provisions relating to the promotion of freedom of trade. One was Article 22(5), requiring states administering League of Nations mandates to "secure equal opportunities for the trade and commerce of other Members of the League" in the mandated territories.[12] The other was Article 23(e), which urged—but did not actually require—League members to "make provision to secure and maintain freedom of communications and of transit and equitable treatment for the commerce" of other member states.[13] (The most famous provision on economic relations was, of course, Article 16, dealing with concerted economic sanctions against states violating the Covenant. This, however, was purely a law-enforcement measure and not a device for promoting freedom of trade.)

Throughout the 1920s, there were pleas for a set of international norms, and even for an international organization, to govern the economic conduct of states in the way that the Covenant of the League governed their political activity. One of the most prominent pleaders was the American economic specialist William S. Culbertson, who combined the technical expertise of a trained economist with the moral fervor of a Wilsonian internationalist. He became a tireless campaigner for "economic disarmament" and for "a conscious international direction of the great forces of international trade and finance in the interests of a better and more peaceful world."[14] To this end, he proposed the formation of an International Tariff Commission and also the regulation of international finance by a body under the auspices of the League of Nations.[15] In addition, he favored "an international code for the regulation of the economic relationships of nations," together with an international commission for the settlement of economic disputes.[16]

> Trade between nations must be made fairer [he insisted] by the elimination of unfair trade practices and transportation discriminations. Such practices as export bounties, . . . preferential shipping rates, and predatory price-cutting must go. The economic resources of the world must be developed not . . . in the interests of classes in particular nations that happen to control them, but in the interests of social welfare throughout the world. It is of international concern that the resources of the world are made available on equal terms for all. The principle of the open door and of unconditional most-favored-nation treatment are an essential basis in solving the problems of tariff discriminations and colonial development. The wide problems of financial control, investments, and concessions are also international problems which need and must have the regulating influence of international machinery.[17]

The noted political economist Jacob Viner was of a like mind. He too looked forward to the evolution of "an international code of economic relations," together with an international organization to administer it.[18] The economist Stephen Bailey, in 1931, made a ringing call for "the renunciation of economic sovereignty by the . . . states of the world and the general acceptance of the principle of international control."[19]

As compared to these grand ideals, concrete progress in the interwar period was discouragingly meager. The principal achievement was the drafting of several multilateral conventions in the fields of transport and communications. The League sponsored two such conventions in 1921, one on freedom of international transit[20] and the other on a regime of navigable waterways of international concern[21] (both of which took effect the following year). In 1923 came two further conventions, one on an international regime of maritime ports[22] and the other on a regime for railways[23] (both of which entered into force in 1926). These various agreements embodied the general principle of non-discrimination on the basis of nationality among the contracting parties.

Against these humble achievements must be set some important failures. The League considered the drafting of an international convention to implement the Covenant's principle of "equitable treatment" of commerce. In 1922, however, the Provisional Economic and Financial Committee decided that such a project was too ambitious.[24] Later in the decade, in 1927, the League sponsored an Internatioinal Convention on Export and Import Prohibitions and Restrictions, designed to regulate quantitative restrictions on trade (such as quotas).[25] This agreement, however, failed (though just barely) to attract enough ratifications to enter into force. In the face of the Great Depression of the 1930s, and the protectionist pressures that it brought, the League made a valiant, but ultimately pathetic, attempt to stem the tide of protectionism. The so-called "tariff truce" which it sponsored in 1930 was actually nothing more than an agreement on the part of states parties to refrain, for a mere one year, from denouncing commercial treaties. Even so, it failed to attract sufficient ratifications to take effect.[26]

On the whole, then, efforts during the interwar period to restore the free-trade system of the mid-nineteenth century were a discouraging failure. Rather more successful—at least for a time—was the other component of the interwar system of economic world order. Although it ultimately failed, it provided the world with some invaluable experience in the fine art of managing an international economic system.

The Associationalist System

The associationalist aspect of the interwar experiment in economic world order was an attempt to channel and direct the powerful economic forces of the time—meaning, principally, those of private enterprise—to ensure that they would do the most good for society. Essential to the associationalist system, and fully in tune with the general campaign against economic nationalism, was the thesis that economic policymaking should be carefully insulated from the rivalries of traditional power politics. The critical economic issues of the time needed to be removed from the clutches of ham-fisted politicians and entrusted instead to financiers, business executives and central bankers—i.e., to persons who could be depended upon to bring dispassionate, neutral, scientific expertise to bear on the problems of the world. To this extent, the associationalist scheme was essentially St.-Simonian in character.[27] It was fitting, then, that its dominant figure, the American Secretary of Commerce (and later President) Herbert

Hoover, should have been an engineer by training—and hence a charter member of the elite of *industriels*—with a deep distrust of traditional politicians.[28]

In its style of operation, the associationalist system was marked by the sober professionalism of the banker rather than the glowing fervor of the evangelist. It therefore did not lend itself to the promulgation of sweeping, universalistic principles. It never possessed either a formal organizational structure or a written constitution, in the way that the League of Nations did. Nor were its labors undertaken in open forums such as tribunals or international conferences. It also never produced an important body of literature. It had no Mirabeau or Cobden or List, or even a latter-day St.-Simon, to expound its virtues to the world at large. Instead, the associationalist system had a rather ad hoc and empirical flavor. It consisted of a series of policies which were gradually assembled on a piecemeal basis into the rudiments of a governmental apparatus for the global "mercantile republick." From a perspective of some decades, the efforts of Hoover and his associates appear rude and primitive in the extreme. They should be seen, however, in the context of their time, as pioneering departures from the more purely laissez-faire ways of the nineteenth century.

The dominant power in this associationalist system was, without any doubt, the United States. Abruptly transformed by (literally) the fortunes of war into the world's foremost creditor nation, it was the principal source of capital for the reconstruction of war-shattered Europe and, more generally, for the growth of the world economy. There could be no question of its withdrawing from international economic affairs, as it did from political ones when it declined to join the League of Nations. Seldom, if ever, in their history have Americans so faithfully followed Washington's advice in the Farewell Address as they did during the 1920s, when they coupled political isolationism with the most active involvement in the economic affairs of the wider world.[29]

That involvement took a variety of forms. For one thing, the United States now became a foreign investor on a large, and constantly growing, scale. A postwar fear of a resource shortage in the United States, most notably of oil, led American industry, with the vigorous support of Hoover, far afield into raw-material investments the world over. The 1920s, for example, was the period when American oil companies first became international enterprises on a significant scale, as they invested heavily in overseas production in Latin America and, to a lesser extent, the Middle East. Natural rubber was another important need of modern industry, leading American rubber companies to invest on a significant scale in Southeast Asia and Liberia. All of these ventures had energetic U.S. government support, in the larger national interest of securing adequate supplies of essential raw materials.[30]

The U.S. government also perceived it to be in the national interest to have American private enterprise underwrite the stability of the international economic system. Hoover had an instinctively internationalist outlook—although, at the same time, a watchful eye for the particular interests of the United States.[31] He was, accordingly, concerned to restore international economic order by stabilizing the various major currencies, arranging for the funding of international indebtedness (most of it, coincidentally, owed to the United States by its ex-partners in conflict) and resuscitating Germany. In all of these goals, the active, if informal, cooperation of American private financial interests was essential.

The first major step, as circumstances dictated, was placing the payment of German reparations onto a much-needed sound business footing.[32] The unsatisfactory state of the reparations problem became spectacularly apparent in December 1922, when the Germans defaulted in their payments, sparking the military occupation of the Ruhr valley by France and Belgium the following month. The result was economic chaos, as the German people embarked on a ruinous campaign of economic passive resistance. The loss of the industries of the Ruhr, together with the disruption of coal supplies from that area, led to falling industrial production and mounting unemployment. In addition, a desperate and reckless resort to the printing press by the government led in short order to history's single most famous case of runaway inflation.[33]

The task of sorting out the reparations wreckage fell upon a committee of private experts, headed by the American banker Charles G. Dawes. The Dawes Plan (as the committee's solution was dubbed) became the economic centerpiece of the associationalist system. In its report of April 1924, the committee stressed that its members had acted strictly as individual experts and not as representatives of any governments, and that they had approached their assigned task "as business men anxious to obtain effective results."[34] The committee went on to emphasise that the plan which it had devised was "economic and not political" in nature.[35]

The basic thrust of the Dawes Plan may be stated quite simply. It was to transform the German reparations process from an engine of impoverishment and austerity into one of economic growth and prosperity. The proposal, in essence, was that German reparations be discharged through the expansion of the German economy, rather than, as hitherto, through the deflation of German domestic demand. The fuel for this expansion would be foreign lending from, inevitably, private banks in the United States. American banks would be encouraged to lend half of the initial $200 million required to launch the plan, after which the schedule of reparations payments would be indexed to the growth of the German economy as a whole. In the early stages, therefore, the payments would be relatively modest. They would then rise automatically over the course of time *pari passu* with the growth of the German economy and with Germany's capacity to pay. The need for agonizing renegotiations of the payment schedule would thus be avoided. In general, then, the Dawes Plan constituted a technical economic solution to what had formerly been a divisive political issue. The steady and single-minded application of neutral scientific expertise, entailing the exclusion of traditional political jockeying, was seen as a model approach to the world's outstanding problems. "Business, Not Politics" was, appropriately enough, the slogan of the Dawes Plan.[36]

There were, to be sure, some nervous doubts as to whether the desired collaboration would actually materialize, i.e., whether the private American banks would really be willing to lend to Germany on the scale called for. Such worries were soon seen to be unnecessary, as the initial Dawes Plan loan, in September 1924, was oversubscribed ninefold. This loan, accordingly, proved to be only the beginning of a torrent of U.S. private loan capital which poured into Germany over the next five years, fueling an enormous economic boom, just as the experts had intended. The only misgivings about the arrangement were, ironically, that it had succeeded only too well—that the private banks were lending too profligately and that the boom was not sustainable. Hoover was one who, correctly, as it turned out, was concerned about rash lending to Germany.[37]

In all events, the Dawes Plan formed the economic mainspring of the program for postwar European economic recovery. This recovery program basically consisted of a three-step circular flow of private capital from a fount on Wall Street. The three central actors in the drama were the United States, Germany and the European ex-Allied states. The first stage was the massive transfer of capital from the United States to Germany, in the form of private loans spearheaded by Dawes-Plan lending. The second step was the transferring of funds from Germany to the European ex-Allied states, now in the form of reparations payments. Finally, there was the transfer from the European countries to the United States government, this time in the form of repayments of inter-governmental war debts. This three-step financial flow served the purpose of knitting together the principal economic powers of the world into a single system—with the whole arrangement underpinned by capital from U.S. private banks, prodded and nudged by the American government into appropriately constructive channels.[38]

The Dawes Plan represented the positive form of this prodding and nudging. Associationalism had a negative and punitive side as well, however, in the form of a capital-embargo program comparable to those practiced by the major European financial powers during the previous century. The method used was an informal loan-supervision arrangement, whereby the United States Department of State exercised a de facto veto over proposed flotations of bonds by foreign parties—including foreign governments—on the United States market. This program, which was instituted in full form in 1922, entailed an informal commitment on the part of private banks to notify the Department of State when plans were afoot for foreign bond flotations. The department would then inform the banks in due course whether it had any objections to the proposed transaction. If it did, then the banks would "voluntarily" refrain from proceeding.[39] The U.S. status as the principal source of capital for the world economy would (it was hoped) guarantee the effectiveness of the program as a disciplinary tool against would-be borrowers.

In the event, the loan-supervision program proved not to be very successful as a means of coercing other states into behaving cooperatively. In cases where the Department of State disapproved of lending, the borrowers often did have alternate means of obtaining finance. Privately placed loans in the United States were one possibility, since the loan-supervision program covered only publicly floated bonds (save in the one case of the Soviet Union, in which privately placed loans were stopped as well). Another possibility was to borrow in a foreign market, so that the stopping of an American flotation often meant nothing more than a loss of business for U.S. banks. On the whole, then, the loan-supervision policy was of little material effect.[40]

The overall program to provide a stable general framework for the international economy was, however, making visible progress during the 1920s. One major achievement was the gradual resolution of one

81

of the most divisive issues: inter-governmental war debts. The main concern of the U.S. on this question was not so much with the actual payment of the debts as with the point of principle involved. It resolutely opposed any suggestion that the debtor states had a right to scale down their obligations unilaterally (to say nothing of repudiating them altogether). Such a flagrant violation of elementary principles of the law of contract would (the United States feared) hinder the arduous task of restoring confidence and stability in international economic relations generally. In the event, a workable compromise was reached. The United States and the various debtor states proceeded to conclude, one by one, a series of bilateral debt funding agreements. The first was reached in 1923 with the United Kingdom,[41] followed by twelve others over the next four years. Generally speaking, these arrangements entailed a reduction from the original level of indebtedness of approximately 15 percent. The United States therefore succeeded in staving off the threat of unilateral action, while the debtor countries in turn managed to obtain some measure of relief.[42]

Another major achievement of the 1920s was the eventual stabilization of the major currencies (i.e., the restoration of the prewar international gold standard). Progress here, as in the area of debt funding, was piecemeal, but steady. One major step was the stabilization of the German currency after the hyper-inflation of 1923 which had accompanied the Ruhr crisis. Another important achievement was the return of the United Kingdom to the gold standard in 1925, with the pound set at its full prewar value. The Austrian and Hungarian currencies were stabilized with the assistance of loans arranged by the League of Nations. Other states gradually stabilized their currencies (although seldom at the prewar value), until, by 1928, the process was substantially complete.[43]

By the mid-1920s, therefore, the three principal problems of international economic relations among the developed countries—German reparations, inter-Allied war debts, and the stabilization of currencies—were well on the way to resolution, thanks to the patient efforts of financial experts public and private. And thanks also to the lubrication of the whole system by American private capital, in discreet collaboration with the American government. By the late 1920s, it looked very much as if the rancor and bitterness of the immediate postwar years were fading into history; that Germany was being reintegrated into the larger family of nations; that a general atmosphere of confidence and stability—indeed, even of prosperity—was returning, after the nightmare of the Great War. The world, it appeared, was steadily learning the virtues of stability and patient cooperation in the sphere of economic relations.[44]

THE IMPACT ON INTERNATIONAL LAW

In certain respects, it would appear as if these post-World War I developments in the international economic sphere had no effect upon international law. The newly established World Court, for example, found occasion to describe the general nature of international law and of international society in terms that could have come directly from Wolff or Vattel:

> International law [the Court pronounced in 1927] governs relations between independent States. The rules of law binding upon States therefore emanate from their own free will . . . in order to regulate the relations between these co-existing independent communities. . . . Restrictions upon the independence of States cannot therefore be presumed.[45]

As in the nineteenth century, there was some dissent from this orthodox position. One source was, not surprisingly, the advocates of an international law of "solidarity," the intellectual followers of La Pradelle. A prominent bearer of the "solidarity" banner during the interwar period was the French lawyer Robert Redslob. He strongly criticized the orientation of traditional international law toward the autonomy of states, together with the self-centered utilitarian "pseudo-morality" to which it gave rise. Redslob's version of the concept of "solidarity" had two basic aspects: a duty of mutual aid on the part of states, and a duty of states to facilitate the exchange of goods. In place of the old international law, with its isolationist and utilitarian ethos, would come a new law based upon "devotion to the human collectivity." The emphasis on the *right* of states to promote their own welfare must give way, in Redslob's view, to a stress on the *duty* of states to promote the general welfare of the human community.[46] Of similar view was the American lawyer Ellery C. Stowell. He explicitly advocated the discarding of the traditional doctrine of absolute sovereignty of states, on the ground that the purpose of international law should be not merely the negative one of keeping the peace but also the positive one of facilitating mutually beneficial commercial intercourse.[47]

In addition to this straightforward dissent from the basic orthodox doctrines of international law, there were also some indications that the specific developments of the period were having a greater impact on the policies of states and the minds of statesmen than most lawyers allowed. There was a general awareness, during this period, of a blurring of traditional boundaries between the public and the private spheres, as well as between the domestic and the international. It was coming to be appreciated that the actual functions that entities performed were of greater importance than their nominal status as "public" or "private" bodies.[48] For example, acceptance of the restrictive theory of state immunity gained ground during this period. In this view, states were to be denied their traditional sovereign prerogative of immunity from suit when they were undertaking a commercial (as opposed to governmental) activity.[49] Conversely, private parties, such as banks, were coming, under the associationalist system, to play an important role in international affairs. It was therefore proper that a certain degree of public oversight of their activities take place. On this ground, the American lawyer Charles Cheney Hyde voiced his support of his government's loan-supervision policy, pointing out that it was simply a reflection of "the international and essentially public character" of foreign bond flotations, even when they were undertaken by nominally "private" parties.[50] In much the same vein, Culbertson expressed a general approval of the policy on the ground that bankers had a responsibility not simply to themselves and their shareholders, but also to governments and the public at large.[51]

Similarly, states, in the formulation of what had traditionally been their "own" policies, were increasingly aware that larger international issues were at stake. Here again, attitudes toward the American loan-supervision policy are instructive. We have observed that, when capital-embargo policies were deployed by states on political grounds during the nineteenth century, they gave rise to no legal misgivings. Now, however, there were rumblings of protest, if not about the legality of such policies strictly speaking, then at least about their employment in pursuit of unduly parochial ends. John Foster Dulles was one who urged caution on this score.[52] So did the educator James Angell, who contended that there was a general presumption against the employment of capital embargoes for narrow national purposes. Their use should be confined, he urged, to the pursuit of genuinely international goals, such as the promotion of world peace.[53]

Attitudes of this kind were apparent even in connection with the formation of state tariff policies, which traditionally had been within the unrestricted sovereignty of states. During the nineteenth century, "scientific" and "bargaining" tariffs had been used exclusively to promote the interests of the states enacting them. The American tariff of 1922, however, was a "scientific" tariff of (theoretically at least) a different kind. It was intended to be used not for the promotion of the parochial interests of the United States, but rather for the policing of the rules of the international economic system as a whole. It was designed to be a flexible retaliatory weapon against unfair trading practices. For example, if a state was gaining an unfair edge over its competitors by using "sweated" labor policies to reduce costs of production, then the American tariff rate could be adjusted upward by precisely the amount necessary to counteract the effect of the unfair policy. The necessary element of technical expertise required to decide that fine point would be the province of the Tariff Commission, a panel of neutral experts in international trade matters.[54]

These general attitudes received some expression in rather more general and philosophical terms. The French lawyer Georges Scelle, for example, put forward a theory of what he called a *dédoublement fonctionnel* ("functional dualism"), which postulated that state officials actually acted in a dual capacity in the fulfillment of their duties —as officials of their states, and also as upholders of the norms of the international legal system.[55] Hans Kelsen's theory of "monism" was broadly to this same effect. Kelsen rejected the idea that domestic law and international law were entirely different legal regimes, contending instead that they formed part of a single grand structure of norms of conduct.[56] Neither of these theories was specifically economic in character. But, in their general rejection of narrow, traditional views of state sovereignty, they were very much in keeping with the ideas of a liberal economic world order.

As in the pre-World I period (and also, as will be seen, after 1945), there was one single issue which highlighted the distinction between the traditional positivist ways of thinking about international law, and the newer attitudes more attuned to the thinking of liberal political economy: economic warfare. The attitude of the international community toward the waging of boycotts on political grounds provides the best insight into the direction in which the minds of statesmen—and lawyers—were drifting.[57] There were two major boycotting incidents in the interwar period. One was a Chinese boycott against Japan following the invasion of Manchuria in 1931. The other was a boycott by Britain against the Soviet Union in 1933, in response to that country's arrest of some British nationals.

The British boycott lasted only a brief time (less than three months) before the incident was resolved. It has the minor distinction, however, of being the first open, official boycott in international history by one state against another (outside of the context of armed conflict).[58] Short-lived as it was, this British boycott stimulated a protest by the French writer Édouard Lambert, who condemned it as contrary to what he called "the common law . . . of our societies," with its ethic of free economic intercourse between peoples.[59] Echoing the earlier views of Séfériadès, he feared that boycotting constituted a step toward armed conflict and accordingly called upon the jurists of the world to take a firm stand against the practice.[60]

The earlier incident, involving China and Japan, is of rather more interest, since it came to the official attention of the League of Nations. What is noteworthy about the debate at the League is that it was conducted, by both sides, almost entirely on the tacit assumption that boycotting, as an act of hostility, should be regarded as wrongful in principle. The Japanese delegate denounced it as "a form of hostility" and demanded to know why it should not be condemned by the international community in the way that warfare was.[61] More interesting is the Chinese response (put by Wellington Koo, a future judge of the World Court). China did not justify the boycott on the ground that boycotting was within its sovereign rights as a state. Instead, it defended it on the alternate grounds of self-defense and retaliation.[62] On either of these bases, the position would be that boycotting was unlawful *in principle*—though permitted in this particular case as a response to Japan's prior aggression. In its final conclusion on the matter in 1933, the League of Nations Assembly endorsed this view by holding that the boycott fell into the category of reprisal.[63]

This finding by the League of Nations Assembly was a political decision and not a legal judgment. Even if it is not a precedent in the strict legal sense, however, it is a revealing indication of the way in which the general consensus of the international community was drifting on the question of economic warfare. Boycotting appears, from this incident, to be in a curious juridical limbo—not, strictly speaking, unlawful (at least not according to traditional positivist views of international law); but not exactly lawful either. There would appear to have been a general consensus at the League that a policy of boycotting was far enough outside the range of "normal" state conduct to call for a specific justification.

The interwar experiment in economic world order, therefore, gave rise to a number of interesting developments in the legal sphere.

Some of them, as will be seen in due course, proved permanent. The wider acceptance of the restrictive view of state immunity, for example, as well as the increasingly ambivalent attitude toward economic warfare, would both be features of the post-1945 legal world. The associationalist system itself, however, proved rather less durable. Like the free-trade regime of the nineteenth century, it was handicapped by a number of flaws which, in the face of hard economic times, led to its undoing.

THE FLAWS IN THE ASSOCIATIONALIST SYSTEM

It is clear in retrospect that the associationalist system of the 1920s had several grave weaknesses. From the institutional standpoint, it was weak because of its lack of firm safeguards to prevent resurgences of economic nationalism. From the material standpoint, it was dangerously fragile because of its critical dependence on the continuing flow of private American capital to underpin it. Like its free-trade predecessor of the nineteenth century, the associationalist system was crucially dependent upon an atmosphere of general economic prosperity. Finally, it may be said that the system was weak because of an excessive domination by, and dependence upon, a single hegemonic country, the United States. All of these points are closely interconnected.

Consider first the overall structure of the system. As pointed out above, it was centered upon a closed loop of capital flows initiated by the Dawes Plan: of private American lending to Germany, of German reparations payments to the European ex-Allied states and then of Allied debt repayments to the United States government. Crucial to the effective functioning of this rather fragile system was the continuation of capital flows from private U.S. sources, and also the productive use of those loans. The loans had to contribute to economic recovery in Germany, so that the growing German economy could repay them—and, at the same time, discharge its reparations obligations. If the American loans were used improvidently, such as for current consumption or for mere "show" projects, then the whole mechanism was simply storing up trouble for the future, in the form of impending defaults. Hoover, realizing the dangers, urged the use of the loan-supervision program to prevent the private banks from lending for purposes that were not "reproductive" (i.e., did not add to the capital stock of the debtor country). Hoover's views were not adopted, but his fears were justified. Of the American private capital that gushed into Germany in the wake of the Dawes Plan, all too little of it went for the support of economically viable investments. With the halt in American lending in 1929, therefore, and the consequent onset of depression in Germany, the American loans went rapidly into default, as did reparations payments. The loop was fatally ruptured.

Even when the system functioned effectively, it should be noted that large portions of the world were left outside of the three-cornered central mechanism. The developing countries, in particular, played an obviously subservient part. As observed in the previous chapter, an international system based upon liberal capitalist principles is, in effect if not in theory, biased toward the interests of industrialized countries. Its central concern with efficiency and the division of labor gives it an orientation toward long production lines and the exploitation of economies of scale, a concern for large and open export markets and an obvious and vital interest in free trade. One element of this general concern for efficiency is the reduction of production costs —i.e., the acquisition of raw-material inputs as cheaply as possible. Just as obviously, however, it is to the advantage of primary-producing countries to raise raw-material prices as much as possible.

The efforts of the developing countries to raise the prices of their exports during the interwar period sometimes took the form of government-directed schemes of market intervention, such as production restrictions or price-support programs. Against such un-liberal practices, the United States assumed the role of self-appointed market policeman of the global "mercantile republick." A principal use of the loan-supervision program was to defeat such arrangements. The Department of State adopted a policy of disapproving foreign bond flotations for the financing of government-sponsored raw-material monopolies and cartels, or of government price-support schemes. Hoover was a particularly energetic crusader against these practices, bringing to the campaign some of the zeal of the medieval theologians with their denunciations of wicked monopolists and price-gougers. He saw to it, for example, that a French-German potash syndicate was barred from floating bonds in the United States, and that the Brazilian state of Saõ Paolo, which sought financing for price-support schemes for coffee, was similarly excluded from the American capital market.[64] The capital-embargo policy appears, however, to have been of little effect, since the rejected borrowers often obtained capital elsewhere. It is true, though, that, throughout the 1920s, raw-material prices on the world markets were relatively low, with the result that the developing countries did not, for the most part, share in the prosperity enjoyed by the industrialized states.[65]

Another country that did not participate fully in the affairs of the global "mercantile republic" was the Soviet Union. It is interesting to note that there had been plans to coax the Soviets into the wider economic world, by organizing a Dawes-Plan-style arrangement for them. The plan, whose chief sponsor was the British Prime Minister David Lloyd George, envisaged massive lending by Western interests to the Soviet Union for the economic development of the country, in return for which the Soviets would provide appropriate compensation for the defaulted debts and nationalized property, and also would guarantee raw-material flows to the lending countries in repayment. Repayments to German interests involved would go to the reparations account. It was an intriguing plan, but the refusal of the United States to participate meant that it was not possible to raise the necessary capital.[66]

The United States followed, instead, a plan of economic isolation of the Soviet Union (although not of total boycott). It did not forbid either trade with or investment in the Soviet Union, although the lack of diplomatic relations (until 1933) meant that diplomatic and consular services were not available to persons dealing with the Bolsheviks. In addition, the United States Federal Reserve maintained a "gold boycott" against the Soviet Union, refusing to accept Russian-origin gold for deposit, thereby inhibiting the country's ability to import goods from the United States. Finally, the Department of State applied the loan-supervision program against the Soviet Union with special strictness, taking steps to prevent even private placements of loans to Russia, as well as public bond flotations.[67] All of these measures in combination appear, however, to have had little real impact. American traders and investors seldom hesitated to do business with Russia when appropriate opportunities beckoned. During the period 1924–31, in fact, the United States was one of the country's principal trading partners, even in the absence of formal recognition.[68]

In the meantime, the Soviet Union was busily gaining at least a legal *entrée* into the wider economic world, through the conclusion of bilateral trade agreements with as many countries as possible. One element of many of these treaties was an explicit mutual forswearing of boycotting and similar practices. The first significant step was an agreement with Britain in March 1921 (even before the United Kingdom's recognition of the Bolshevik government), in which the two states agreed "not to impose or maintain any form of blockade against each other" and "not to exercise any discrimination" against each other's trade, as compared with their treatment of third states.[69] During the next several years, the Soviet Union concluded a series of bilateral treaties containing commitments on the part of the parties to refrain from participating in boycotts against one another mounted by third states. Agreements of this kind were reached with Turkey (1925),[70] Germany (1926),[71] Lithuania (1926),[72] Persia (1927),[73] Afghanistan (1931),[74] Estonia (1932)[75] and Latvia (1933).[76] In addition, agreements with Germany (1925)[77] and Latvia (1926)[78] included provisions that the commercial relations between the parties were to be governed solely by economic considerations. (More conventional provisions for most-favored-nation status were negotiated with Denmark (1923),[79] Japan (1925),[80] Norway (1925),[81] Estonia (1929)[82] and Turkey (1931).)[83] On the whole, therefore, the marginal economic status of the Soviet Union in the 1920s was probably more the result of poverty on its part than of systematic discrimination by the capitalist countries.

The associationalist system of the 1920s was not only strongly centered upon Western Europe and the United States. It was also particularly American-dominated. Nor was it long before suspicions began to grow that the United States had its own interests more at heart than those of the wider "mercantile republick." The strict U.S. stand on the repayment of the war debts was one of the most important issues leading to widespread resentment. Another was its tariff policy. In striking contrast to Britain during its period of leadership in the previous century, the United States did not either endorse or practice free trade in the true sense of forswearing the use of protective tariffs. Instead, it supported the lesser, "halfway" principle of non-discrimination in trade relations. Under this policy, states are left to fix their tariff rates at whatever level they wish, so long as they treat all of their trading partners on a par (apart from retaliation against unfair trade practices). Not only did the United States not eliminate its protective tariffs; it actually raised them in 1922 and proceeded—to the dismay of the rest of the world—to run balance-of-trade surpluses throughout the decade. These surpluses made it all the more difficult for the rest of the world to obtain hard currency for the payment of reparations and war debts. Nor did the tariff's retaliatory feature actually do much to combat unfair trade practices, since the United States failed to make serious use of it.[84]

Even when the United States's trading policies were more in accordance with general global interests and practice, its own concerns were often rather nearer to the surface. A good example is the United States's change of policy, during the 1920s, from the use of the conditional most-favored-nation clause, to the use of the more common unconditional variety. Under the conditional form of the clause, the parties grant one another only the *opportunity* to obtain benefits accorded to third states. In order actually to receive the benefits, the parties must duplicate whatever concession the third state gave to receive its favor. Under the unconditional version, in contrast, each party automatically grants to the other whatever it gives to a third state. The United States's endorsement of the unconditional form of the clause in the 1920s placed it in line with other major trading states; but it clearly made the change in its own national interest. It concluded, upon rational assessment, that, as a major exporting state, it now stood to benefit from the use of the unconditional most-favored-nation clause.[85]

In other respects as well, the U.S. national interest tended to assume a higher profile than the concerns of the international community at large. In conducting the loan-supervision program, for example, the United States yielded to the temptation, despite the warnings of Dulles and Angell, to pursue narrow interests. The Department of State adopted a policy of not approving loans for enterprises which would compete with American ones in foreign markets.[86] It also disapproved of loans to governments not recognized by the United States (as Greece discovered to its discomfort).[87] It even struck a minor blow for the American policy of prohibition of alcohol by disapproving a loan for the financing of a brewery in Czechoslovakia.[88] Even Hoover's campaign against government-sponsored monopolies and price-fixing schemes was motivated primarily by the desire to protect the interests of American manufacturers and consumers. It is small wonder, then, that suspicions began to grow that the United States, far from assuming the responsible leadership of a campaign against economic nationalism, was actually guilty of the practice itself on the grandest of scales. Hoover may have shared the general outlook of St.-Simon, but many of his policies were those of Colbert.[89]

In certain respects, then, the charges of "economic imperialism" leveled against Hoover had some foundation.[90] He certainly was an energetic user of American economic strength in the United States's interest. More to the point, however, such accusations indicated the need (pointed out by Culbertson and Viner) for a truly disinterested agency or set of general norms to guide the economic conduct of states

and to enforce the rules of the system. In the absence of such institutions, it was inevitable that the individual states would take on a role
as enforcers. And equally inevitable that, in the process, they would
pursue their own interests as well as—or even in preference to—
those of the wider community.

Just how completely dependent the entire interwar economic system was on the policies—and the economic health—of this one dominant state became vividly apparent in 1929, when the Wall Street
stock-market crash sent the United States sliding into recession. Germany, deprived of American lending, shortly followed it, demonstrat-
ing the unsoundness of much of the American lending by defaulting
on both its private loans and its reparations payments. With the
general international banking crisis of 1931 the depression spread
further. The developing states were affected, as the fall in purchasing
by the developed economies sent raw-material prices plunging. Latin
American states in large numbers consequently defaulted on their
debts. A proposal by President Hoover (as he now was) for a one-year
moratorium on intergovernmental debt repayments, in an attempt to
shore up the international economy, was hopelessly inadequate. The
interwar system of economic order lay in ruins.

THE GREAT DEPRESSION:
ECONOMIC NATIONALISM TRIUMPHANT

The Great Depression of the 1930s, like its predecessor of the 1870s
to the 1890s, was a post-Industrial Revolution crisis of abundance. A
devastating shrinking of the money supply in the United States and
elsewhere led to falling prices (by some 6 percent per year in the wake
of the Wall Street crash) and to the piling up of unsold goods. With
the reduction in overall demand, output inevitably declined—the
aggregate gross domestic product of the industrialized world fell by
some 17 percent in 1929–32—and unemployment rose.[91]

The fundamental problem faced by governments around the world
was to find ways to bolster demand, i.e., to raise prices, thereby
stimulating production and reducing unemployment. There were,
broadly speaking, two possible strategies for achieving this end: the
internationalist and the nationalist. The internationalist solution was
to reduce tariff rates and generally to sweep away trade barriers, so
as to ensure that producers had as wide a market as possible for the
sale of their wares. The nationalist solution was the opposite: to raise

trade barriers and exclude foreign goods, with a view to reserving home markets for home producers. There was certainly no shortage of pleas for the internationalist approach.[92] But it had one critical disadvantage: it required concerted action, continuous discipline and heroic self-restraint on the part of countries. It required the states to refrain from discriminating against foreign goods in favor of domestic ones at a time of catastrophic surplus.

Any such feelings of altruism or community-mindedness melted rapidly away in the face of crisis. In the absence of any international legal constraints, international economic relations degenerated into an orgy of economic nationalism. Beggar-my-neighbor policies of various sorts proliferated with sickening rapidity. The most obvious strategy was the simple raising of tariff barriers so as to close out unwelcome competition. Here, the leading state was the United States, which in 1930 discarded its "scientific" tariff of 1922 in favor of the notoriously protectionist Hawley-Smoot Tariff. This measure promptly sparked retaliation from countries all around the world, as world trade spiralled downwards, diminishing by approximately 60 percent (in gold dollar terms) between 1929 and 1932.[93] A particularly momentous step was taken in 1932, when Britain, the world's foremost free-trade champion for nearly a century, abandoned the policy in favor of a rather unsystematic series of British Empire-preference arrangements devised at an imperial conference in Ottawa that year.[94]

Manipulative currency practices could, and did, perform the same protectionist function as increased tariffs. By devaluing its currency, a state could make its own exports cheaper in foreign markets and so steal a march on its competitors—provided, that is, that the competitors did not follow suit. To a large extent, however, they did. The 1930s became a period of "competitive devaluation" of currencies.[95] (A notable exception to this practice was Germany, which deliberately *over*-valued its currency. The reason was that, in contrast to other countries, it followed what was in effect a "policy of provision" in the field of armaments, i.e., it sought to promote imports rather than exports, in the manner of the ancient and medieval city-states.)[96]

Another way of dealing with the "crisis of markets" of the 1930s was by "dumping" goods abroad at extremely low prices in order to obtain any amount of foreign exchange, however small, at the expense of producers in the markets concerned. The Soviet Union was the principal practitioner of this art.[97] Other countries, such as France, took retaliatory action against it. The Soviets responded by proposing, at the League of Nations in 1931 (before their entry into the organization), a draft Protocol on Economic Non-aggression, to which other countries paid scant attention.[98]

One of the most common ways of dealing with the Depression was through the set of practices which falls under the general rubric of bilateralization of trade. A typical practice of this kind would involve a barter agreement between two countries, which had the virtue of conserving scarce foreign exchange. It also had the obvious vice, from the standpoint of a liberal free-market economist, of conducting trade according to the dictates of government administrators rather than of impersonal market forces. Trade that was forced into pre-determined channels in this way was removed from the larger arena of the "mercantile republick" as a whole, with the consequent distortion of the world trading system generally.[99]

Bilateralization could be applied in the monetary field as well, by means of clearing agreements, i.e., arrangements between states to fix the relative values of their currencies bilaterally, sometimes for the exchange of pre-determined quantities of goods. This practice was objectionable too from the standpoint of advocates of a multilateral, open-door system. It allowed states, in effect, to juggle the values of their currencies and even to have a variety of different currency values according to the number of different clearing arrangements in force. The result, here also, was to channel trade away from the open markets of the world and into administratively dictated paths.[100] In the course of the decade, these agreements proliferated. Germany was the principal employer of this device, entering into no fewer than nineteen such arrangements. Dark suspicions arose that it was using these clearing agreements with its Central European neighbors to build an economic empire for itself, although it now appears that the policy was more one of desperation than of intention. Because of the policy of over-valuing its currency in order to promote imports for its armaments industry, Germany had to take particular care to prevent a balance-of-payments crisis from arising. The clearing-agreement "system," then, was basically a defensive measure aimed at the conservation of scarce foreign exchange.[101]

Economic nationalism on the various domestic fronts took a host of different forms during this period. Without doubt, the most radical policy was that of Stalin in the Soviet Union. To a large extent, his policy of "socialism in one country" was forced upon him, by the catastrophic fall in prices of the traditional Russian raw-material exports (timber, grain and oil). Be that as it may, Stalin made good use of the opportunity to embark, with murderous thoroughness, on

the creation of a new society. This consisted in part of a crash industrialization program, designed to make the country virtually entirely
self-sufficient. He succeeded. By the late 1930s, the Soviet Union had
been transformed into a virtual hermit kingdom, with foreign trade
amounting to well under 1 percent of its output—an achievement
surely without parallel in modern times.[102]

Another of Stalin's many accomplishments was to provide a vivid
illustration of the intimate link between economic nationalism and
the running of a centrally planned economy. The connection is readily
apparent. Planners work on the basis of issuing instructions, which
they can only do to persons under their control. Excessive reliance
upon foreign trade, either for imports or exports, introduces uncertainty. Foreigners cannot be compelled to accept shoddy goods. They
also have a distressing habit of charging world market prices for
things which they sell, and of expecting payment in hard currency.
The instinct of the planner, therefore, is to set about equilibrating
production and consumption within his jurisdiction. Ever since this
experience of the 1930s, it has been clear that socialism of the Stalinist variety is economic nationalism of the most thorough-going sort—
complete with an inconvertible currency, an ideology of egalitarian-
ism and fierce patriotism, an intense cultivation of the virtues associated with austerity and privation, an ethical stress on the creation of
a "new Soviet man" and a notoriously defensive attitude toward the
outside world. It is a wonder that statues of Fichte are not as common
in the socialist world as those of Lenin.[103]

No other country went so far down the road of economic nationalism. But virtually all went at least part way. In the United States, for
example, the New Deal of President Franklin Roosevelt was frankly
nationalist in outlook. Roosevelt candidly stated in his first inaugural
address in 1933 that he favored putting "first things first" and concentrating on the recovery of the American economy before turning his
mind to the international scene.[104] Gone was the concern of Hoover
with such matters as the stabilization of currencies or the resolution
of the international debt problem. Roosevelt casually took the United
States off the gold standard. In a message to the delegates of the
London Economic Conference of 1933, he brusquely consigned the
policy of currency stabilization to the ranks of "old fetishes of so-
called international bankers" and (in an unconscious echo of Plato
and Fichte) blithely asserted that the development of "national currencies" was the answer to the economic crisis.[105]

Britain's policy was to withdraw within its natural sub-kingdom of the global "mercantile republick," the British Empire. In the aftermath of Roosevelt's torpedoing of the London Economic Conference, it organized its own currency bloc, known as the Sterling Area (including certain non-empire countries with which it had long-standing commercial ties, such as Iran). The intention was to institute a multilateral trading system on a reduced scale, with the use of sterling, rather than gold or the dollar as the leading currency. The United Kingdom also, as observed above, abandoned free trade in favor of a policy of tariff preferences for the empire.

Economic nationalism took more menacing forms as well. In Germany, Hitler talked volubly of the autarkic potential of a politically united Europe—under, of course, German rule. In Japan, the distress brought on by the collapse of American purchases of Japanese silk exports was a factor in bringing a military dictatorship into power. The soldiers favored gaining access to essential raw materials by means of a "territorial" rather than a "commercial" policy—i.e., by conquest. Beginning with the invasion of Manchuria in 1931, the Japanese military machine began its inexorable expansion, first into China and then into Southeast Asia toward Singapore and the Netherlands East Indies.[106]

This Japanese expansion posed a particularly cruel dilemma for those who associated free trade with peace. The United States was the principal source of exports to Japan—including crucial war materials such as scrap iron and oil. There naturally was pressure to impose embargoes on these materials. The worry, however, was that Japan would only be stimulated to expand yet further afield to make up for these supply reductions. The experience of the League of Nations certainly offered little scope for optimism. The League imposed economic sanctions against Italy in 1935–36, in response to its aggression against Ethiopia, but to no avail. The sanctions did have some effect, notably on Italy's balance of payments; but they conspicuously failed to halt the conquest of Ethiopia.[107] In the event, the United States imposed various economic measures against Japan bit by bit. An early step was a "moral" (i.e., non-legally binding) embargo on the sale of aircraft and related parts. In 1939, the United States prepared for further measures by denouncing its 1911 FCN treaty with Japan.[108] An embargo of iron and steel scrap followed Japan's occupation of northern Indochina and its alliance with Germany and Italy in 1940. Then, after the occupation of southern Indochina in 1941 came the most serious measures: an oil embargo and a freezing of Japanese assets in U.S. banks. As the pessimists had feared, the climax of this growing hostility was the attack on Pearl Harbor by Japan in December 1941.[109]

The dispiriting decade of the 1930s ended, then, all too appropriately, in the outbreak of war both in Europe and the Pacific—an effective, if sanguinary, means of overcoming the Great Depression. Those years held many bitter lessons for policy-makers. One of the most important was that, if a third experiment in economic world order were ever to be undertaken, it would have to be fashioned from far sturdier materials than either of the first two had been.

FOUR

PROSPERITY, PEACE AND
WORLD ORDER: A New Beginning

During the 1940s, the nations of the world commenced their third and, so far, most concerted effort to fashion a regime of economic world order. The result was the system under which we continue to live. Its basic principles are those of the nineteenth-century liberal economists, with scarcely a single significant modification. The immediate historical model was the associationalist system of the 1920s which had proved so fragile in the face of the Great Depression of the 1930s. The innovation of the post-World War II period lay not in the realm of basic ideas, but rather in the means of implementation. In sharpest contrast to their predecessors of the nineteenth century and of the interwar period, the founders of the post-World War II "mercantile republick" were mighty drafters of codes and builders of institutions. Their strategy was to create a network of formal legal and

institutional constraints to prevent a resurgence of the economic nationalist atavism of the Depression.

In certain respects, then, this third attempt at a system of economic
world order was far more ambitious and thorough-going than its two
predecessors had been. In other ways, however, it was more conservative and restrained. The founders of the post-1945 economic order, for
example, may have shared the beliefs and ultimate ambitions of their
nineteenth-century forbears; but they lacked their vibrant evangelism
and boundless optimism. The lyrical idealism of Cobden or Bastiat or
Passy was not their style. These figures of the 1940s were, for the most
part, hard-headed diplomats and lawyers, seasoned negotiators, and
skilled draftsmen. Their main task, as they saw it, was to devise a
system that actually *worked.* They showed no interest in the high-
flown abstractions of a new international law of "solidarity" or of a
dédoublement fonctionnel. On the contrary, they simply accepted classical, positivist international law as they found it—as a law between
states only, emanating from the will of the states themselves. In its
juridical underpinnings, therefore, the post-World War II system of
international economic order was thoroughly traditional. The arrangements governing it were strictly intergovernmental in character, consisting of treaties made by sovereign states with one another.
The founders of the postwar "mercantile republick," in short, were
reformers of international economic relations, but not of international
law per se.

The post-World War II arrangements were also more modest than
their predecessors in that they were self-consciously designed to be,
so to speak, only one-half of a system of economic world order. We
have observed that the more radical dreamers of the cosmopolitan
dream—from Mirabeau and St.-Simon, to Cobden and Bastiat, to La
Pradelle and Redslob—had hoped for the total replacement of old
political ways by new economic ones. The statesmen of the 1940s
were more modest and realistic. They harboured no illusions that
politics, with all that it implied, could be wholly banished from the
world in their lifetimes, if ever. Instead, they contented themselves
with creating a dualistic system of world order. Political and economic relations would *both* be catered for—but carefully kept apart
from each other. There were now to be, accordingly, two separate and
coexisting systems of international relations, one political and the
other economic. Each, in its own distinctive fashion, would be an
important component of the overall quest for world peace. Political
relations were to be governed by the Charter of the United Nations,

which was designed to promote the peaceful settlement of disputes, to outlaw the use of force, and to provide for collective enforcement action in cases of dire emergency. This was peace in the narrow and rather negative sense of preventing war. Peace in the larger and fuller sense—i.e., continuous cooperation by the nations of the world to improve the conditions of the human race—was the task of the system of economic relations.

This consciously dualistic strategy of political and economic world order was by no means the self-evidently obvious solution to the world's problems in the wake of the Second World War. Its implementation required a degree of steady persuasion, and even of pressure, on the part of its chief promoter, the United States. There were many obstacles in its path, some of which proved to be insuperable. On the whole, however, the founders of this post-World War II avatar of the liberal "mercantile republick" achieved an impressive degree of success.

LAYING THE FOUNDATIONS

The chief architect—indeed, the patron saint—of this post-1945 installment of the experiment in economic world order was Cordell Hull, who served as U.S. Secretary of State from 1933 to 1944. He was as worthy a descendant of Cobden or Passy as has ever held high office in a major economic power. In his tireless devotion to the twin causes of free trade and world peace—and in his firm insistence that the two were indissolubly linked—he was a figure straight out of the halcyon days of mid-nineteenth-century liberalism.[1] Under his direction, the United States became, for the first time in its history, a champion of free trade in the true sense of the word, in place of the more limited principle of nondiscrimination in trade relations, as in the interwar period. Hull and his principal lieutenants in the United States Department of State—Dean Acheson, William Clayton, Willard Thorp, and Robert Lovett—led a sustained crusade to institute a postwar era of world peace rooted in economic cooperation and material prosperity. The liberal political economists had long since shown the way to this material-cum-moral millennium of peace and free trade. It was now high time that the statesmen of the world got on with the task.

The most immediate and obvious chore was the slaying of the demon of economic nationalism. President Roosevelt's basic lack of interest in this strategy for combating the Great Depression meant that Hull's campaign could only begin with modest steps. His major initiative of the pre-war period was the inauguration of the reciprocal trade agreements program in 1934, for the negotiation of bilateral tariff-reduction agreements with as many states as possible. The immediate intention was to open export markets for American goods, as an anti-Depression measure. The broader goal was to initiate a world-wide trend toward freedom of trade. By 1939, twenty-one bilateral agreements had been concluded, covering some 60 percent of American trade. The program did succeed in boosting American exports; but the larger goal of spearheading a global trend toward free trade proved elusive. Average world tariff rates remained very high; and the agreements had no appreciable effect on the vast array of non-tariff trade barriers, such as subsidies, dumping, and bilateralization generally.[2]

Hull's great opportunity came with the Second World War. Even before the United States entered the conflict, it began to lay the foundations for an open-door, multilateral postwar economy. The Atlantic Charter agreement of August 1941 between Britain and the United States confirmed that the two countries would

> endeavor, with due respect for their existing obligations, to further the enjoyment by all States, great or small, victor or vanquished, of access, on equal terms, to the trade and to the raw materials of the world which are needed for their economic prosperity.[3]

This provision reflected the difficulties that lay ahead, as much as the opportunities. Hull was disappointed that the commitment had not been stronger. But the British resisted committing themselves to anything too far-reaching—in particular, to the dismantling of the imperial-preference arrangements devised at the Ottawa conference of 1932. For this reason, they had doggedly insisted on expressly preserving "due respect for . . . existing obligations."[4]

After the United States entered the war, it was in a position to press its views rather more vigorously. Its role as the dominant economic power and paymaster-in-chief of the Allied side enabled it to extract certain commitments from its co-belligerents concerning the shape of the postwar world. The chief vehicle was the lend-lease program, which was implemented by a series of bilateral wartime assistance agreements between the United States and its allies. Most of these agreements included an identically worded provision, known as "common Article 7," committing the two parties (i.e., the United

States and the assisted state) to future negotiations about ways to promote expansionary economic policies in general and, in particular, to eliminate "all forms of discriminatory treatment in international commerce, and . . . [to reduce] tariffs and other trade barriers."[5] The common Article 7 effort, then, was a continuation and intensification of the reciprocal trade agreements program of the 1930s.

Hull and his lieutenants, however, entertained far more grandiose plans for the postwar world. They envisaged nothing short of a grand alliance of nations, on literally a world-wide scale, for a permanent collective crusade against the menace of economic nationalism.[6] Before such an ambitious project could be realized, some careful missionary work would clearly be required. The nations of the world would have to be persuaded, or cajoled, into subscribing to the ideals in question. In particular, three categories of countries would have to be persuaded: the Western European Allies, the Soviet Union (soon to be joined in a socialist bloc by a belt of countries in Central Europe) and the developing states (concentrated, at that time, in Latin America).

In certain important respects, the atmosphere was propitious for grand designs of the kind that the Americans had in mind. There was considerable optimism, for example, that the Soviet Union would be willing to enlist. Both at first blush, and with hindsight, such an idea appears far-fetched. The Stalinist regime of the 1930s, after all, had been the world's most radical (and ruthless) practitioner of economic nationalism. In some ways, however, the Soviets were thinking along very similar lines to the Americans. For example, both believed that the ending of the war might well entail the resumption of the Great Depression of the 1930s. The socialist doctrine of the long-term "cheapening of commodities" (i.e., of manufactured goods), together with the belief that the Great Depression represented the death-throes of the capitalist system, inclined the Soviets to think in these terms. Furthermore, the Soviets, during the interwar period, had protested against "capitalist encirclement" and "economic aggression" and had pressed for the principle of nondiscrimination in international economic relations. Ideas of this kind were, at least in general, quite comfortably in line with American thinking.

More concretely, the material interests of the two superpowers-in-the-making appeared to complement one another very neatly. American business interests, with their fear of an impending redescent into recession, were anxious to find new foreign markets. Many, therefore, were intrigued by the potential of the giant socialist hermit kingdom to the East. Stalin was happy to play upon these hopes (which he surely knew to be illusory) by dangling before American business leaders the prospect of dazzling new markets. Much more to the point, Stalin was hoping for a substantial postwar reconstruction loan from the United States government. To keep that prospect alive, he needed to maintain a generally positive and cooperative attitude toward the American postwar economic plans.[7]

The developing countries (chiefly Latin American) presented rather more of a problem. In one respect, though, the Latin American states and the United States were at one: both anticipated that the ending of the war would result in a significant glut of raw materials on the world markets. They parted company in their plans for dealing with the problem. The Latin American countries favored the concluding of international commodity agreements designed, in essence, to bolster raw-material prices above the levels that free-market forces, operating on their own, would sustain. The United States favored a free-market solution. Keeping prices artificially high, in its view, would only encourage the further production of materials that were already in surplus. Furthermore, such a policy would harm industrial countries, by needlessly raising the prices of their raw-material inputs, to the ultimate detriment of consumers generally, who would suffer higher prices. It was much better, in the American view, to permit raw-material prices to decline to their free-market levels and thereby to encourage (or perhaps drive) primary producers to shift their efforts out of sectors that were in surplus and into more fruitful areas of production. International commodity agreements could be justified as devices for smoothing this transition process, but not as mechanisms for permanently maintaining prices at non-market levels.[8]

This debate had clear, and disturbing, implications. If the free-market strategy was adopted, then the economic well-being of the primary-producing countries would depend wholly on the level of purchases by the rest of the world, i.e., on forces beyond their own control. Furthermore, the "rest of the world," in the immediate aftermath of the war, was, for all intents and purposes, the United States alone. As a virtual monopoly purchaser of raw materials from the Latin American countries, the colossus of the North clearly had an effective economic stranglehold over its southern neighbors. There were, accordingly, attempts on the part of the Latin American states to place constraints on the use of this power. For example, at an Inter-American Conference on Problems of War and Peace, held in Mexico City in 1945, the Latin American states sponsored an American Economic Charter, which called for an "orderly transition" from wartime to peacetime conditions, i.e., for the United States to refrain from an excessively abrupt cut-back in its purchases.[9] At the same time, the Latin American countries were attempting to impose legal restrictions on the ability of the United States to use its economic might for interventionist purposes (as the next chapter will discuss in more detail). The seeds of future disaffection on the part of the developing states were clearly present; but in the short term, they had little choice but to go along with the American plans.

Ironically, the American planners of the postwar international economic system anticipated the greatest resistance to their plans from the Western European countries. In retrospect, this appears odd; but, at the time, the fears were well grounded, for Europe was rife with dangerous economic heresies (from the liberal standpoint). The British, for example, were thinking of the postwar world in terms not of surplus but of shortage, and were therefore disturbingly (to the Americans) receptive to ideas about government-administered rationing systems.[10] The French were entertaining similar ideas. At the San Francisco conference of 1945, which drafted the UN Charter, they suggested that the various wartime Allied allocation boards be retained and continued in peacetime under UN auspices.[11] There were also ambitious schemes being mooted for the "monetization" of commodities (which Americans opposed on the ground that such plans would produce burdensome surpluses).[12] Finally, ideas of economic nationalism were by no means dead. The Americans were particularly dismayed to find that John Maynard Keynes was thinking, in terms somewhat akin to those of Friedrich Naumann earlier in the century, of a postwar system of regional or imperial economic blocs which might be relatively liberal internally, but largely autarkic vis-à-vis one another.[13]

The United States, as the chief custodian of the vision of a multilateral, open-door economic system, was determined to defeat these various heresies and to organize the nations into ranks for a permanent battle against the scourge of economic nationalism. In order to accomplish this feat, it realized that it would need to make use of its economic muscle to induce other states to cooperate. Mention has already been made of the use of the lend-lease program in this way. After the war, a similar opportunity presented itself when the United Kingdom, in a state of desperation, sought a massive postwar loan (of $3.75 billion) from the United States. The Truman administration agreed to grant the loan in December 1945, but only on some rather stringent conditions. In general, the United Kingdom was required to subscribe to the American position on postwar international economic policy. More specifically, it undertook to make its currency fully convertible by the end of 1947 and to dismantle the Sterling Area. In addition, all quantitative controls on imports from the United States were to be lifted.[14]

A similar policy was followed during the implementation of the Marshall Plan in 1948–1952. The United States insisted that, as a condition of the assistance, the European recipients remove restrictions on imports from the United States and dismantle trade barriers between one another. Here, too, the power of the aid purse proved effective. The recipient countries formed a body called the Organization for European Economic Co-operation to coordinate the aid program at their end. They also adopted, in 1950, a Code of Trade Liberalization. The results were impressive. Throughout the 1950s, the proportion of intra-European trade conducted on a nondiscriminatory basis, and free of various quantitative restrictions, steadily rose.[15] By the end of the decade, the Western European states were organizing themselves into a European Economic Community (EEC) and a European Free Trade Area (EFTA).

In the meantime, the United States was also sponsoring an ambitious project for an international organization which would be to the sphere of economic relations what the UN was to political affairs. In March 1948, fifty-three states signed the Havana Charter (named for the city in which the conference adopting it took place), which was to establish a body known as the International Trade Organization (ITO).[16] The ITO—which, as will be seen, never came into existence—was designed to be a permanent mobilization of the nations of the world against the evil of economic nationalism, just as the UN was a permanent mobilization against aggression and armed conflict. The UN, therefore, would have the task of keeping the peace in the narrow and negative sense of the term, i.e., of preventing outbreaks of violence and uses of armed force. The ITO would promote peace in a broader and more positive sense, by promoting international economic cooperation for the material welfare of humankind as a whole. The one organization would have the task of promoting political world order; the other, of promoting economic world order.

The ITO, as the main organ of government of the post-World War II "mercantile republick," was to have been a kind of economic mirror image of the UN. The Havana Charter, like its UN counterpart, was to set out the basic norms of state conduct and also to establish a multilateral mechanism for their enforcement. Just as the individual states members of the UN agreed to forgo the unilateral use of military force (subject to some exceptions), so the states members of the ITO agreed (in Article 92 of the Havana Charter) that they "will not have recourse to unilateral economic measures of any kind contrary to the provisions of the Charter." Claims of unfair trading practices and the like were therefore to be dealt with exclusively through the multilateral machinery of the ITO. The organization was also to parallel the UN in having a conference of the entire membership (analogous to the UN General Assembly), to set the general policy of the organization, together with a smaller Executive Board to oversee the implementation. There would also be various specialized commissions, plus a dispute-settlement mechanism. Here, at last, was to be the realization of the dream of Culbertson and Viner and other crusaders against economic nationalism of the interwar period.

The normative provisions of the Havana Charter constituted, in effect, a codification of the principles of international "solidarity" as expounded in previous generations by La Pradelle and Redslob and their sympathizers. The purposes of the organization, as set forth in Article 1 of the charter, constituted a veritable litany of the ideals of the liberal political economists. The states pledged to "further the enjoyment by all countries, on equal terms, of access to the markets, products and productive facilities which are needed for their economic prosperity and development." They were also to "promote on a reciprocal and mutually advantageous basis the reduction of tariffs and other barriers to trade and the elimination of discriminatory treatment in international commerce." Success in these goals would "enable countries, by increasing the opportunities for their trade and economic development, to abstain from measures which would disrupt world commerce, reduce productive employment or retard economic progress." Article 1 also contained a frank recognition of the importance of a generally healthy and expanding world economy for the realization of these various goals. In a clear reference to the painful memories of the 1930s—and to the fear of their repetition— the first of the ITO's stated purposes was "[t]o assure a large and steadily growing volume of real income and effective demand, to increase the production, consumption and exchange of goods, and thus to contribute to a balanced and expanding world economy."

The charter went on to deal with a host of specific issues in the sphere of international economic relations, in the manner favored by the American postwar planners. International trade was to operate on a fully multilateral, nondiscriminatory basis. Unfair trading practices such as dumping and subsidizing were to be eliminated, as were quantitative restrictions on traded goods. Steps were to be taken against restrictive business practices. International commodity agreements were permissible, provided that their purpose was to ease the transition away from the production of materials in surplus toward those in short supply. State trading was permitted, so long as the state-trading entities in question conducted their purchasing "solely in accordance with commercial considerations" and not in the furtherance of political ends.[17]

The principal important respect in which liberal capitalist principles were compromised by the Havana Charter was in the area of foreign investment. Here, the developing countries successfully opposed a sweeping commitment to an open-door regime. Article 12 of the charter expressly allowed countries the freedom to decide whether foreign investment would be allowed into their territories at all. Host countries could also take "appropriate safeguards" to ensure that foreign investment was not used for interference in their internal affairs. They were permitted to set the terms of ownership of such investment "on just terms" and to prescribe other "reasonable requirements" for the conduct of foreign investors. On the other hand, host countries were required to provide "adequate security" for existing and future foreign investments and also to refrain from any discrimination between foreign investors. This initial disagreement on the subject of foreign investment was only the tiniest prelude to the difficulties that would arise in this area in future years.[18]

The ITO was to be supplemented by a number of other international bodies of a functional kind, which were to deal with special areas of international economic relations. For aviation, there was the International Civil Aviation Organization (ICAO); for employment-related matters, the International Labor Organization (ILO), a carry-over from the age of the League of Nations; for agricultural affairs, the Food and Agriculture Organization (FAO); for postwar reconstruction and general economic development, the World Bank (International Bank for Reconstruction and Development, or IBRD); and for monetary relations, the International Monetary Fund (IMF).

These were bold and far-reaching plans. Their implementation, however, proved to be less than complete. In particular, the plans went awry in two major respects: the failure of the ITO to materialize, and the effective secession-cum-expulsion of the socialist countries from the system as a result of Cold-War rivalries.

What doomed the ITO, ironically, was the build-up of opposition by vested interests in the United States, its chief sponsor. As alarmist cries of an "economic Munich" began to well up, and as the Truman administration became steadily weaker politically, it became apparent that the necessary two-thirds support in the United States Senate could not be mustered for the ITO.[19] Without U.S. membership, it was plain that the project was simply not viable. As a result, the Havana Charter failed to attract even a single ratification.[20]

A kind of consolation prize, however, was available. The charter's provisions relating to trade had been embodied, in advance of the completed document, into a preliminary General Agreement on Tariffs and Trade (GATT) in October 1947.[21] Twenty-three countries signed this agreement, at the same time that they agreed upon history's first major multilateral tariff reduction (encompassing some 45,000 tariff concessions and about $10 billion in trade). The intention had been that the GATT would self-destruct and merge into the larger ITO machinery. The stillbirth of that organization meant that, perforce, the GATT would be left on its own.

The other major blow to the vision of a global system of economic order was the onset of the Cold War. The rancor which it engendered poisoned the general postwar atmosphere and meant that an important part of the world's population would be left outside the boundaries of the transnational "mercantile republick." Trouble began even during the war, when the Americans were dismayed to find that assistance from the United Nations Relief and Rehabilitation Administration (UNRRA), which was largely financed by the United States, was going to pro-Soviet groups in Eastern Europe which were showing a disturbing hostility to pro-democratic and pro-Western elements. After concluding that it was not possible to reorient UNRRA's policies to prevent such developments, the United States, in 1946, took the more drastic step of bringing the organization to a complete end by the simple expedient of withdrawing its support and shifting its postwar assistance program onto to a bilateral basis.[22]

In the meantime, the United States had humiliated the Soviet Union itself with the abrupt termination, in May 1945, of lend-lease assistance to it.[23] It was also becoming clear that there would be no postwar reconstruction loan to the Soviet Union. The Soviets responded by refusing to participate in the arrangements for the postwar international economic system, which they began to denounce as a vehicle of American economic imperialism. They declined to join either the World Bank or the IMF (even though they had participated in the Bretton Woods Conference which did the planning for them). The Soviet Union also refused to participate in the Marshall Plan or to permit its new socialist allies of Eastern Europe to do so. It heaped scorn on the ITO, refused to sign the GATT and, in general, showed an open hostility to the very idea of a multilateral international trade system.[24]

During this same period, U.S. vision of prosperity as the key to world peace was undergoing a subtle, but significant, change. It was becoming increasingly security-oriented. Material prosperity was now being seen less in Cobdenite terms as a means of promoting world peace, and more in Cold-War terms as a means of preventing the spread of Communism.[25] It therefore became a matter of urgent priority to concentrate economic assistance on the areas most vulnerable to the advance of Communism. That meant Western Europe. In its assistance efforts to Italy and France in particular, the United States took some care to time its aid shipments for maximum effect in bolstering pro-Western elements at the expense of the local Communist parties.[26] The Marshall Plan as well was designed in part to minimize the risk that Western Europe, out of frustration or desperation, would turn toward Communism. (The United States was, accordingly, no doubt relieved that the socialist countries, at Moscow's insistence, turned down its invitation to participate in the program.)

Considering the general atmosphere of this early Cold-War period, it is hardly surprising that the United States succumbed to the temptation to use its influence in the World Bank to prevent lending to the socialist countries. So great was the pressure, in fact, that the first president of the Bank, Eugene Meyer (a U.S. national), abruptly resigned his post in disillusionment after only a few months on the job. The most notable American intervention involved undermining a loan application by Poland, submitted to the Bank in 1946 for the financing of mining equipment. By 1948, negotiations between Poland and the Bank had progressed to the point that the Bank could not refuse the loan without risking unwelcome embarrassment. At the same time, Meyer's successor as president, John J. McCloy, was willing (indeed, anxious) to accommodate the United States Department of State. A workable solution was soon devised. Word would be put about that the loan would not be well received on Wall Street (where the actual funds would be raised by the Bank), because of Poland's recalcitrance regarding compensation for nationalized property and settlement of lend-lease debts. The story was untrue, but it sufficed to torpedo the Polish loan.[27]

The socialist countries responded by criticizing the World Bank as an American-dominated institution doing U.S. political bidding behind a fraudulent guise of neutrality.[28] Nor were the socialist states alone in their concern. The British were distinctly unhappy about American political influence on World Bank activities. So was Harry Dexter White of the United States Department of the Treasury, who was one of the most prominent founding fathers of the IMF and the World Bank. He lamented that U.S. domination of these two bodies "resembles much too closely the operation of power politics rather than of international co-operation."[29] In all events, the United States succeeded in preventing assistance from these bodies from going to socialist countries. Poland withdrew in an angry huff from the World Bank and the IMF in 1950, denouncing the IMF in particular as "a submissive instrument of the Government of the United States."[30] Czechoslovakia lingered until 1954, when it was effectively expelled from the IMF for devaluing its currency without the required consultation with the Fund, and from the World Bank, for failing to pay its subscription.[31] (Czechoslovakia, however, remained a party to the GATT—the sole important element of socialist participation in the affairs of the liberal "mercantile republick" until the 1960s, when Yugoslavia and Poland adhered to the GATT.)

At this same time, during the late 1940s, the United States decided to stray still further from the ideals of Mirabeau and Cobden by embarking upon a campaign of systematic economic warfare against the socialist countries. The program did not—or not quite—amount to a total economic boycott, since the United States was aware that it would need to acquire materials from the socialist bloc from time to time (such as manganese from the Soviet Union). The real thrust of the campaign, however, was not the refusal to purchase goods from the socialist bloc, for the simple reason that those countries had little to sell on the world markets anyway. Their real need was to acquire goods from the Western world. The United States was determined to interfere with that effort. The heart of its economic-warfare campaign, therefore, was an embargo effort directed at the socialist countries. In its mature form, as instituted in 1948, it consisted of an export-licensing system, with government approval required before goods could be sent to the socialist bloc.

We shall see, in the next chapter, the legal and quasi-legal pitfalls that the United States encountered in implementing this program and inducing its European allies to join it. For the present, it need only be noted that, ironically, the embargo probably played into

Stalin's hands, because it enabled him to consolidate his grip, economically as well as politically and militarily, over Eastern Europe. As trade between the socialist states and the West dwindled to practically nothing by the early 1950s, it became increasingly apparent that the socialist countries were being grouped into a separate economic world of their own, into what one Soviet scholar has characterized as a "neo-Byzantine empire."[32] In 1952, Stalin forthrightly proclaimed "[t]he disintegration of the single, all embracing world market" and the evolution of "two parallel world markets . . . confronting one another."[33]

This combination of secession and expulsion of the socialist countries from the wider open-door "mercantile republick" was a grievous blow to the principle of universality. From the material standpoint, however, it had rather less significance. The socialist countries were so impoverished that they had little significance on the international economic scene in any event. It is true that, during the 1950s and early 1960s, there were occasional spasms of fear over a "Communist economic offensive"—i.e., a Soviet attempt either to ensnare Western countries economically by providing a market for their surplus goods, or else to disrupt the stability of world prices by maliciously dumping large stocks of goods (such as oil) onto the world markets. In retrospect, it is easy to see that such fears were a delusion. Regarding the purchasing of other countries' surpluses, the Soviet Union was capable of no more than the occasional opportunistic initiative (for example, acquiring rice from Burma and fish from Iceland). As for flooding the world markets with surpluses, such fears were little more than an excuse by American oil interests to plead for protection from general world surpluses, in the form of a quota on imports of foreign oil. For the most part, the socialist countries simply settled into the largely autarkist pattern pioneered by Stalin in the 1930s.[34] They had seceded from the wider "mercantile republick"; but they did not threaten it in any serious way.

Despite these two major shocks—the stillbirth of the ITO and the onset of the Cold War—the third experiment in economic world order was duly set on its course in the aftermath of the Second World War. We have already outlined its basic philosophy and features. We shall now glance in somewhat greater detail at the operations of its principal institutions.

THE GOVERNMENT OF THE "MERCANTILE REPUBLICK": THE GATT, THE WORLD BANK AND THE IMF

Of the array of functional institutions that were established to guide and oversee the post-1945 international economic system, the three most important, by a wide margin, were (and continue to be) the GATT, the World Bank and the IMF. Some particular attention to each is therefore in order.

At the outset, it is important to note a fundamental difference in character between the GATT, on the one hand, and the World Bank and the IMF, on the other. The GATT is not an organization, but merely a treaty. It is a code of laws, a set of norms, to which the states parties are expected to adhere. To some extent, the GATT parties (numbering ninety-six by the end of 1989) have given their system some institutional trappings. There is a small permanent GATT secretariat (located in Geneva), a council and a dispute-settlement mechanism. The GATT system, however, contains no institutional enforcement machinery, i.e., no organ possessing any form of coercive power over the states parties.

The World Bank and the IMF are significantly different, in that they are "operating bodies" (in UN parlance).[35] They are institutions in the true sense, with resources of their own which they lend to—or, as the case may be, withhold from—their member states. They possess, in short, the power of the purse. The funding for the purse comes, of course, ultimately from the member states themselves. In order to reflect the relative share of contributions made, these two bodies, uniquely in the UN family, possess weighted voting systems. In the immediate aftermath of the Second World War, these arrangements inevitably gave the United States an overwhelmingly dominant voice in both organizations—with over 35 percent of the voting power in each one.

The consequence of this crucial difference in the nature of these bodies is that the GATT is essentially legalistic in ethos, while the World Bank and the IMF are technocratic. In the GATT, there is (as just noted) no central body to take the initiative in bringing transgressors of the rules to brook. Instead, it is up to injured parties to protect their own interests by invoking the dispute-settlement mechanism. This procedure is essentially adversarial in nature, with all the trappings of a law-suit. Claims go before impartial ad hoc panels, which, in the manner of judicial tribunals, hear the submissions of both sides and then reach their decision on the basis of the GATT norms. The GATT, then, is a neutral arena in which the states parties can pit their rival interpretations of the rules against one another in an open contest.[36]

The World Bank and the IMF, in contrast, are decidedly more St.-Simonian in character. Instead of operating primarily on the basis of codes of conduct for the member states, they rely heavily upon the technical expertise and initiative of trained staffs. These latter-day *industriels* reach their decisions about the granting or withholding of funds on purely economic grounds. Unlike the GATT, then, these two bodies have no place for gladiatorial contests between the member states *inter se*. Instead, the staffs of the agencies themselves exercise a continuous policing power over the members (or rather, over such of their members as require their financial assistance).

With these preliminary remarks in mind, a few salient points may be made about the allotted role of each of these three bodies in the post-World War II system of economic world order. The basic function of the GATT is the easiest to grasp.[37] It is designed to promote the dismantling of the various barriers that impede free trade between private entrepreneurs the world over. Its basic purpose, then, is to enlist the cooperation of the states of the world in the establishment of a framework in which the forces of private enterprise can flourish most effectively. State trading is by no means excluded—but state traders are expected to conduct themselves in the way that private entrepreneurs would, i.e., to conduct their affairs solely on the basis of economic, and not political, factors.[38]

The legal cornerstone of the GATT is the principle of nondiscrimination in trade relations. Benefits granted to any one GATT party should be granted to all. The GATT, therefore, is also a multilateral most-favored-nation trade regime. On this same principle, any barriers to trade that do exist must not be targeted against particular states. International trade, therefore, is not to be used as a weapon of economic warfare (as the following chapter will discuss in more detail). The various practices of administered or bilateralized trade, so prevalent during the Great Depression, are banned. The GATT also contains legal prohibitions against specific unfair trade practices such as subsidizing exports and dumping. In principle, the *only* barrier to world trade permitted by the GATT is a nondiscriminatory tariff. And even tariff rates are to be reduced by means of the periodic multilateral negotiation by the GATT parties of "rounds" of tariff cuts. The first such round accompanied the drafting of the GATT itself in 1947. By 1979, six further ones had been completed, with a seventh launched in 1986. Overall, tariffs have been reduced by this means to about one-tenth of their immediate post-World War II levels.

Speaking more broadly, it may be said that the function of the GATT is to provide a legal foundation for the economic prosperity on which, as we have seen, the success of a system of economic world order depends so crucially. Bitter past experience had demonstrated how timid the "industrial spirit" could be in the face of an economic downturn. In the depressions of both the late nineteenth century and of the 1930s, states had panicked and resorted to protectionism and bilateralization. The vital function of the GATT is to place legal constraints on the ability of states to react to economic hard times in such a way. Recessions are now to be fought by tenaciously keeping world export markets open, not by closing them; by keeping tariff barriers low, not by raising them; by ensuring that trade flows remain fully multilateral, not by confining them into narrow bilateral channels.

It should be noted that the GATT was designed to deal with recessions of the type experienced in the 1930s and in the late nineteenth century: crises of abundance. It is therefore, in fact if not on its face, primarily oriented toward the problems faced by industrialized countries. That is not entirely the case. From its inception the GATT has contained a provision permitting states, with the consent of the contracting parties, to institute protective tariffs for infant industries.[39] In addition, as will be seen in due course, the GATT has been amended to take further account of the special problems and interests of developing countries. Even so, it remains the case that the third-world states have never played a prominent role in GATT. The principal forum for their initiatives in the trade area has been the UN Conference on Trade and Development (UNCTAD), set up in 1964, where they have pressed for preferential treatment for poor countries seeking to diversify their economies.

The role of the World Bank in the postwar economic system resembles that of the GATT in that it too was designed to facilitate the effective functioning of private enterprise—in this case, private foreign investment. During the nineteenth century and the interwar period, private investment had been seen as the basic engine of world economic growth. That was to be so in the post-1945 era as well. The experience of the 1920s and 1930s had taught, however, that private investment was in need of some guidance. Drastic fluctuations in the level of foreign investment by American banks had been an aggravating factor, if not actually a cause, of the Great Depression. There had been too much lending in the 1920s, when times seemed good, followed by a catastrophic falling-off, when times turned bad. What the world needed was some mechanism for moderating these de-stabilizing swings. Two things were therefore required. One was a means of dampening the excessive enthusiasm of private investors who were too ready to lend when conditions did not warrant it (as many American banks were prepared to do to Germany, in the wake of the Dawes Plan). Conversely, it would be desirable to have some kind of "swing" investor to step in and maintain lending levels in times of recession when private capital flows dried up. This would prevent economic recessions in the major capital-exporting countries from being automatically exported, as in the 1930s, to other states.

The Bank was not, therefore, designed to be a concessionary lending body. Rather, it was designed to be a benevolent disciplinarian-cum-stabilizer of the world of private investment. Admittedly, there was little that it could do directly to restrain lending by private banks which it believed to be excessive. It could, however, set an example to the private banks by conducting its own lending with the most rigorous rectitude. To this end, it adopted the practice of lending only for specific projects, and not for unspecified general purposes. Furthermore, the Bank's Articles of Agreement require it to take steps to ensure that the money lent is actually used for the purposes intended.[40] The Bank, in other words, was to be a more vigilant policeman over its borrowers than private lenders traditionally are.

In times of recession, the task of the World Bank would be not to restrain lending but rather to promote it. In its role as a "swing" investor, it would lend when private capital flows were insufficient. One suggestion made during the Bank's early period was that it could usefully draw up target figures for optimal amounts of foreign investment required for the world economy. When private capital fell short of the required sums, the Bank would step in and lend the balance. It would thereby constitute a bulwark against economic recession and help underpin the general expansionary atmosphere on which the success of a liberal economic world order so crucially depended.

One final useful function that the World Bank was designed to serve was to correct imperfections in the private capital markets in normal times. Because of the obligation of the Bank's member countries to supply it with extensive knowledge about their economies, the organization would possess more information about conditions in borrowing countries than private lenders would. It could thereby make a more accurate assessment of the risks involved. If a country which the Bank deemed to be an acceptable credit risk was unable, for any reason, to borrow on the private capital markets at the best commercial rates, then the Bank could step in and borrow the money itself, and then on-lend it to the state. Crucial to this process, of course, was the ability of the Bank *itself* to be able to borrow at the best commercial rates. Here is where its strictness with its own lenders would prove valuable. The conservatism of its own practices, plus the fact that it could call upon capital from its member states, meant that the Bank would have the highest possible credit rating on the private capital markets.[41]

The World Bank, in sum, was not designed to be a charitable body. Nor was it designed to be "socialistic," in the sense that it would regulate or displace private lenders. On the contrary, it was designed to function as the very pillar of financial orthodoxy and rectitude, and in general to promote, rather than supplant, private investment as the basic engine of world economic development. As will be seen in more detail in Chapter 6, the Bank's role was as an overseer, role model, stabilizer, "swing" lender and disciplinarian—all in the cause of the promotion of a *general* atmosphere of economic expansion and prosperity for the global "mercantile republick" at large.

Many of these same considerations are applicable to the Bank's sibling organization, the IMF. It too was designed essentially as a stabilizing mechanism for the international economic system as a whole, with a view to facilitating the efficient functioning of private enterprise. Also like the World Bank (and the GATT), it was designed with a close eye on the unedifying experience of the 1930s. An important part of its function was to guard against the recurrence of the damaging policies of currency manipulation, notably competitive devaluations and clearing arrangements, which had contributed so greatly to the bilateralizing of trade during the Depression period. The IMF's Articles of Agreement seek to preclude these evils by requiring the IMF member states, in Article 4(4)(a), "to promote exchange stability, to maintain orderly exchange arrangements with other members, and to avoid competitive exchange alterations."[42]

The strategy for achieving these desired ends was, in essence, the restoration of the nineteenth-century gold standard.[43] As in the case of the gold standard, the basic goal was the fostering of private enterprise, through the creation of a single world-wide currency area. To this end, the price of gold was fixed at the famous figure of $35 per ounce, with all other currencies then fixed to the dollar (and therefore indirectly to gold) at a stated, or par, value. Once the postwar conditions had settled into something like normality, currencies of IMF member states were to be made freely convertible into one another. So long as the par values were held constant—and that was the general intention—then the entire IMF membership would effectively constitute one single monetary system.

This new international currency regime was seen as possessing several virtues. One was the facilitation of private economic transactions across national boundaries. As in the case of the old gold standard, the risks associated with gyrating currencies were to be minimized, if not eliminated altogether. Another crucial virtue of the system was that there were now to be legal and institutional barriers in the way of currency manipulations, analogous to the rules of the GATT against manipulative trade practices. There was, accordingly, to be no resorting to competitive devaluation as an anti-recession device (or rather, as a device for shunting the effects of a recession onto one's trading partners). Under the old decentralized gold standard, each country had been on its own best behavior. Now, there was an element of policing. In the majority of cases, a country could only legally alter the par value of its currency in consultation with the *industriels* of the IMF staff.

A final key advantage of the IMF system was the way in which it was to promote currency stabilization in the framework of expansionary rather than deflationary domestic policies on the part of the adjusting state. In the absence of an arrangement like the IMF, a country which encountered balance-of-payments difficulties might well have no real choice but to embark upon deflationary policies to remedy them. Such a state had somehow to bring its imports into some reasonable balance with its exports. Ideally, it would expand its exports. It was all too likely, however, that that feat would be impossible to achieve on extremely short notice in the midst of a balance-of-payments crisis. If so, then the only alternative was to curtail imports. Such a strategy was deflationary, in that it reduced consumption within the country concerned. It also injured the country's trading partners by diminishing their export prospects.

One of the central purposes of the IMF was to rescue its member states from this dispiriting fate. So long as the balance-of-payments crisis was only transitory in nature, it was preferable that the deficit country borrow the hard currency necessary to tide it over. It could thereby keep its consumption up and avoid any harm to its trading partners. Countries could, of course, make *ad hoc* arrangements for borrowing foreign exchange as the necessity arose. The IMF was to function, though, as a standing loan mechanism. Each member state was assigned a quota to contribute to the Fund, 25 percent in gold and 75 percent in its own currency. The gold contribution constituted, in effect, a "nest egg" of foreign-exchange reserves deposited with the IMF for safe-keeping. A member state would be allowed to draw from the Fund the equivalent of this amount in foreign currency (i.e., hard currency) virtually at will. In addition, however, it would be possible for it to draw, in the general case, up to four further "tranches" (as they were called) of hard currency, each such tranche amounting to 25 percent of its own quota. The effect of this arrangement was that each state could borrow from other countries, via the IMF, a sum of hard currency equal to 125 percent of its own quota. There was, not surprisingly, a catch. As a country borrowed more and more tranches of foreign exchange from the Fund, the IMF staff would impose increasingly rigorous conditions upon it. We shall return in more detail to this contentious issue of "conditionality" in IMF policy in chapter 6.

For the present, it is only necessary to note that the IMF performed essentially the same kind of role for the monetary system that the World Bank did for private investment. It was designed not as a relief agency, but rather as an overseer and stabilizer of the system of international monetary relations as a whole. The IMF, like the World Bank, was a combination of a white knight and a policeman—all the time with a view to facilitating the most effective possible functioning of private enterprise in a general atmosphere of economic expansion and stability.

In the period since the establishment of these three institutions, together with the various other agencies of the international economic system, a whole subdiscipline of international law, known as "international economic law," has grown up to deal with their legal aspects.[44] International economic law might be defined, then, as the "house rules" of the international economic sphere. It is, broadly speaking, the law relating to economic cooperation between countries. In a certain sense, therefore, it is the modern equivalent of the international law of "solidarity" propounded by La Pradelle and Redslob. But there is, it should be noted, an important difference. The law of "solidarity" had its inspiration, and also its principal field of application, in the area of economic relations. But it was not, ultimately, an economic doctrine. What lay at its root was the juridical principle that the fundamental duty of the state, contrary to the teachings of the positivists, was to promote the welfare of the human community at large rather than its own national interest. The liberal political economists had given a rigorous demonstration of how this principle worked, why it was valid and what its advantages were. In the final analysis, though, the law of "solidarity" concerned the transformation of the law of nations itself.

The same cannot be said of present-day international economic law. This law is infinitely more detailed and definite than the rather wispy concept of "solidarity." But it is also different in spirit and narrower in outlook. It is essentially technical in character, "economic" in the narrow sense of that term. It is a subdiscipline of general international law, rather than a fundamental challenge to it. This point may be illustrated by contrasting the approach of these two bodies of law to that most central of problems to those who yearn for an economic world order: economic nationalism. La Pradelle and Redslob, of course, had been forthright opponents of economic nationalism. They saw it, however, not so much as a problem in its own right, but rather as merely the most obvious way in which traditional international law manifested its parochial and nationalistic nature. Economic nationalism would automatically become untenable as the law of "solidarity" became increasingly accepted.

In the period since World War II, the focus has been narrowed. The campaign launched by Hull and his followers was against economic warfare per se, and not against the positivist legal doctrines that underlay it. There was, accordingly, a crucial decoupling of the campaign against economic warfare from the broader campaign for international law reform with which it had previously been intimately linked. The founders of the postwar economic system may therefore be criticized for attacking only the symptoms of the disease rather than the underlying cause. But if they have narrowed their sights, they have also trained their weapons more accurately. La Pradelle and his followers may have dreamed much, but they achieved little.

Hull and his co-workers, then, may be said to have settled for the proverbial half-a-loaf in several respects. For one thing, as just pointed out, they largely divorced the campaign against economic nationalism from the broader vision which had once animated it, reducing it instead to a struggle on the technical plane of international economic law. The visionary had given way to the draftsman, the evangelist to the technician. In addition, the founders of the post-1945 "mercantile republick" frankly conceded that political relations between states, far from fading away, were here to stay, at least for as long as anyone can foresee. They even institutionalized political relations—while, it was hoped, making them less deadly—in the United Nations. Here again, however, if their vision was more limited than that of their forbears, their methods of construction were sounder. They may have had little confidence that international economic relations would ultimately displace political ones entirely. But they were determined at least to safeguard the autonomy of the economic sphere and to keep it safe from contamination by the poisoned fumes and acrid smoke of political rivalry. They did so by providing it with a range of legal protections which, in the aggregate, constitute a guarantee of the survival and independence of the "industrial spirit," if not of its eventual complete triumph.

THE JUDICIAL INDEPENDENCE OF THE "MERCANTILE REPUBLICK"

There are two ways in which the nonpolitical character of the principal international economic bodies can be legally safeguarded: by external and by internal means. Sometimes both are used simultaneously. External guarantees are rules that explicitly forbid political bodies from interfering in the affairs of the economic agency in question—that constitute a "fencing off," so to speak, of trespassers from the political wilderness outside. Both the World Bank and the IMF possess such external guarantees, in the bilateral agreements they concluded with the UN in 1947 when they entered the UN system as specialized agencies. Internal guarantees of nonpolitical status are limitations on the competence of the economic body itself—i.e., a deliberate withholding from the body, as a matter of its own internal law, of the *power* to act in a political fashion, even if it was disposed to do so.

The World Bank provides the clearest illustration of both of these devices. The external guarantee of its nonpolitical status is found in Article 4(3) of its specialized-agency agreement with the UN, which confirms that:

> the United Nations recognizes that the action to be taken by the Bank on any loan is a matter to be determined by the independent exercise of the Bank's own judgment in accordance with the Bank's Articles of Agreement. The United Nations recog-

nizes, therefore, that it would be sound policy to refrain from making recommendations to the Bank with respect to particular loans or with respect to terms or conditions of financing by the Bank.[45]

The Bank's internal guarantees of freedom from political considerations are found in its Articles of Agreement. Article 3(5)(b) stipulates that loan arrangements are to be made "with due attention to considerations of economy and efficiency and without regard to political or other non-economic influences or considerations." More explicit is Article 4(10), which provides that:

The Bank and its officers shall not interfere in the political affairs of any member; nor shall they be influenced in their decisions by the political character of the member or members concerned. Only economic considerations shall be relevant to their decision.[46]

The position of the IMF is broadly similar concerning the guarantee of its autonomy from the UN. It shares with the World Bank the distinction of being accorded, by means of its specialized-agency agreement, a higher degree of freedom from UN oversight than other economic agencies have. The arrangement between the Fund and the UN is to the effect that neither will present any formal recommendations to the other without prior consultation. Each institution is required to consider any such formal recommendations as soon as possible; but each also retains its freedom of action.[47] As for the internal law of the IMF, its Articles of Agreement contain no explicit provision forbidding the Fund managers from using political criteria in their lending decisions. Nevertheless, it has always been accepted that, as a matter of organizational practice, the Fund would rely exclusively upon economic considerations in its decision making.[48]

The GATT, not being an organization, is not a specialized agency of the UN and hence has no specialized-agency agreement. Nor does the text of the GATT itself explicitly forbid political considerations from playing a role, although that is clearly implied by the GATT's general principle of nondiscrimination. (It may also be noted that the Havana Charter, of which the GATT was originally to have constituted a portion, did have an explicit stipulation that the ITO "should not attempt to take action which would involve passing judgement in any way on essentially political matters.")[49]

Separating economics from politics in practice is far more difficult than stating general principles of the kind just given. In the case of the IMF and of GATT, there are (as we shall see in the next chapter) various means by which political factors are allowed, exceptionally, to play a role. For the present, it may simply be noted that "staying out of politics" can sometimes be as controversial as getting involved —if, indeed, it is really possible even to make a distinction between the two. The IMF, for example, has found itself at the center of controversy for providing support for that most notorious of pariah states, South Africa. In 1976, and again in 1982, the UN General Assembly made it clear that it disapproved of any lending to South Africa by the IMF.[50] By the terms of the specialized-agency agreement between the IMF and the UN, however, it was clear that the Fund was free to take its own decisions in the matter.

The World Bank had a rather more bruising encounter with the UN over southern African issues in the mid-1960s, when it provided assistance to both South Africa and Portugal (when that country was an African colonial power). These decisions also elicited critical resolutions from the UN General Assembly.[51] More importantly, they gave rise to a legal debate between the Bank and the UN secretariat about the meaning of key provisions of the Bank's Articles of Agreement. The general counsel for the Bank defended the lending decisions on the basis of Article 4(10).[52] The UN secretariat contended that this provision only prevented the Bank from interfering in the *internal* politics of its member states. *International* politics, in contrast—into which category South African *apartheid* and Portuguese colonialism were considered to fall—could and should be a factor in the Bank's lending policies.[53] The Bank, however, held its ground, insisting that its "technical and functional character" precluded *any* political involvement.[54]

It is surely inevitable that there will be occasional disputes, of the sort just described, about where economics ends and politics begins. That much is obvious enough. What is perhaps rather less obvious— though more interesting—is the slightly different, but related, point, that the frontier between the political and the economic is inherently unstable and liable to drift with the passage of time (rather like the distinction between "international" and "domestic" concerns). This drifting of the dividing line between economics and politics is of the utmost interest from the standpoint of the campaign for an economic world order. If the "industrial spirit" of the economic sphere were seen to be making inroads into what traditionally had been seen as the preserve of politics, then it might fairly be surmised that the ideal of an economic world order is at least inching toward realization. Conversely, if the nationalistic and states'-rights ethos of traditional international law were seen to be making headway in what was originally seen as the sphere of economics, then we might equally (and oppositely) surmise that the prospects for a system of economic world order are receding.

The main *situs* of the duel between politics and economics is, of course, the campaign against economic nationalism. It happens, however, that this struggle for *lebensraum* between politics and economics is fought in its most direct—and hence its most instructive—fashion in the very margins of the wider battle against economic nationalism. In particular, the struggle between the rival mentalities of politics and economics is seen at its most naked over the question of the legality of the most extreme and destructive of all forms of economic nationalism: economic warfare. We shall, accordingly, look first at that particular contest for some clues as to how the wider struggle for an economic world order has progressed since the 1940s. We will then turn our attention to the progress of the post-World War II campaign against economic nationalism generally.

FIVE

DISARMING CAPTAIN BOYCOTT:
The Evolution of Legal Restraints on Economic Warfare

Economic warfare is the most extreme and most negative form of economic nationalism. Where "normal" economic nationalist practices, such as protective tariffs, are designed to benefit the economy of the state adopting them, the purpose of economic-warfare measures is to injure some other state. Acts of economic hostility may be used in a wide variety of circumstances, such as disputes over alleged unfair trade practices. The term "economic warfare," however, is best reserved for cases in which a state (or group of states) inflicts economic injury on another in the course of a political dispute. The essence of economic warfare, therefore, is the use of economic power as a political weapon, rather than as a means for promoting the welfare of the human community as a whole.[1] Nothing could be more obviously contrary to the ideal of international "solidarity" or, more mundanely, to the general ideals of the founders of the post-1945 world, with its careful separation of economic from political relations. The phenomenon of economic warfare is, accordingly, of out-standing interest precisely because it is so sharply incompatible with the vision of an economic system of world order and, in particular, because it highlights so vividly the dualistic nature of the post-World War II transnational "mercantile republick."

As a matter of fact, the very *concept* of economic warfare as a distinct category of activity is so closely bound up with this dualistic framework as to have no meaning outside of it. Traditional positivist international law, for example, knew no such category. Nor would a fully fledged system of economic world order such as that envisaged by La Pradelle or Redslob. It is easy to see why, in each case.

According to traditional positivist international law, states are un-der a general duty to seek "perfection" according to their own lights. In furtherance of this exalted task, they are free to cooperate with other states in the economic sphere or not, as they themselves see fit (in the absence of a specific treaty commitment to the contrary, of course). Whatever choice they make in this regard is seen in terms of this duty to themselves, with no right of complaint by other countries about the outcome. Therefore, a refusal by one country to trade with another, whatever its purpose or motivation, cannot be regarded as illegal because it entails no violation of the legal rights of the state affected. At the very most, such a refusal could only be an act of retorsion, i.e., an unfriendly, but not unlawful, act. (Wolff, it may be recalled, gave an export embargo as an illustration of the phenome-non of retorsion.)[2]

Conversely, in a thoroughgoing system of economic world order, a distinct category of acts of economic warfare also would not exist. The reason is that *any* uncooperative behavior, whatever its motiva-tion, is seen as wrongful. From this standpoint, there can be no real distinction between a policy of general economic isolationism (such as that of China), on the one hand, and a boycott campaign waged against a political enemy, on the other. Both are distortions of the global system of free trade which ipso facto injure the world-wide "mercantile republick" as a whole. We have observed that legal writ-ers who were influenced by the ideas of the liberal political econo-mists, such as von Liszt, La Pradelle, Séfériadès and Redslob, readily perceived this point. Economic warfare, on this view, is therefore not a problem in its own right, calling for an autonomous rule of law specifically directed against it. Instead, it is a subcategory of the more general wrong of uncooperative economic conduct, against which the general rules of "solidarity" are directed.

These positions are faithfully replicated today *within* each of the two systems of international relations. The political sphere, governed by the rules of traditional customary law and also (since 1945) by the UN Charter, contains restrictions upon such conduct as aggression, intervention and the use of force—but not upon economic warfare per se. As far as this system of political relations is concerned, the law remains substantially as laid down in the eighteenth century by Wolff and Vattel. In the economic sphere, however, the opposite view prevails. There, the central concern, consistently with the principles of "solidarity," is to promote international economic cooperation generally. As a logical consequence of this broad concern, the rules of international economic law restrict such practices as boycotting and the freezing of foreign assets—not because they are politically motivated, but simply because they are inconsistent with the general liberal principle of freedom of trade.

Economic warfare is, therefore, already halfway unlawful, by virtue of its incompatibility with the rules of international economic law. In order for a *general* prohibition against economic warfare to emerge, however, it is necessary that the "industrial spirit" of the economic sphere make inroads into the political one. It is necessary, in other words, that a general ethos of cooperation displace the traditional positivist concern for the independence of states and the safeguarding of rival national interests. The debate over the legality or illegality of economic warfare is, therefore, a struggle between two rival frames of mind—the political, with its focus on the rights and interests of states; and the economic, with its concern for the promotion of the welfare of the human community as a whole. These are, of course, precisely the same rival frames of mind that underlie the debate between political and economic conceptions of world order generally.

Therein lies the true value of the puzzle of the legality of economic warfare.[3] It is not that the question is of great practical importance in international law. Rather, it provides the best possible litmus test for the contest between political and economic visions of international order. If the political mentality has been gaining the upper hand, then we would expect to see the ethos of the political system "spilling over" into the economic one. In particular, we might expect to see the evolution of a general "political exception" to the rules of international economic law, i.e., a principle allowing derogation from the norms of the GATT, the IMF and the World Bank in cases where political interests of states are at stake. Conversely, if the economic mentality has been gaining ground at the expense of the political one, then we would expect to see the opposite phenomenon: a spilling over of the spirit of cooperation and freedom of trade into the sphere of general public international law—in short, the evolution of a *general* legal prohibition against economic warfare.

We shall proceed to explore these matters. First, we will look at the basic internal rules of the two systems. Then we will proceed to the more important task of observing how the relations between them have evolved over the past four decades—first looking at the extent to which political considerations are able to play a disruptive role within the economic system; and then at the reverse position, i.e., at the extent to which the "industrial spirit" of the economic sphere has penetrated into the political world. At the slight risk of anticipating the conclusions to be reached, it will be observed that La Pradelle and Redslob and their intellectual *confrères* would have some reason to be pleased with the course that events in this area have taken since the Second World War. On the one hand, the economic system has managed, to an impressive extent, to defend itself successfully against intrusions from its political counterpart. While, on the other hand, the general cooperative spirit of the economic system has made itself felt in the sphere of political relations in a variety of ways, to the point that it may now be said that a law of "economic neutrality" has grown up, the function of which is to limit the effects (and, consequently, the effectiveness) of economic warfare, by safeguarding the interests of uninvolved third parties.

THE INTERNAL LAWS OF THE TWO SYSTEMS

The Political System: Economic Warfare under Customary International Law and the UN Charter

The basic position regarding the legality of economic warfare under customary international law remains essentially as laid down by Wolff and Vattel in the eighteenth century. The World Court so held in its judgment in 1986 in the case of *Nicaragua v. United States*,[4] when it considered the legality of three measures of economic hostility employed by the United States against Nicaragua during the 1980s: the withholding of foreign assistance; the drastic reduction (by some 90 percent) in the quota of sugar that Nicaragua was allowed to export for sale in the high-priced American domestic market; and a total trade boycott. The Court had little difficulty in holding that none of these measures was contrary to general customary international law. Its basic rationale was that, since there was no legal obligation on the part of the United States to grant any economic favors or to trade with Nicaragua, it could not be unlawful for it to withhold such favors or to refuse to trade. Since foreign aid is of a "unilateral and voluntary nature," a reduction could only be unlawful "in exceptional circumstances."[5] As for the trade boycott, the Court brusquely concluded, in language that could have come from Wolff or Vattel, that "[a] State is not bound to continue particular trade relations longer than it sees fit to do so, in the absence of a treaty commitment or other specific legal obligation."[6] It is clear from these statements that the most common forms of economic warfare in the modern world— boycotts, embargoes and aid reductions—are not violations of general customary international law. Furthermore, it may safely be assumed that *any* economic favor which is "unilateral and voluntary," in the way that foreign assistance is, may also be withheld on political grounds. Tariff preferences to developing countries are an obvious example, as is the granting or rescheduling of loans. (U.S. sugar-quota allocations are also in this category.)

Some countries—most notably the United States—have made great use of this latitude.[7] We observed earlier that, as part of the Cold-War struggle, the United States withdrew its support for UNRRA, curtailed aid to the countries of Eastern Europe and orchestrated its assistance to Italy and France in such a way as to give it maximum effect against domestic Communist parties in those states. It elevated this practice to a general principle in 1951, with the adoption of the Battle Act, which was a statutory policy (never actually invoked, however) of withholding foreign aid from countries that exported strategic goods to the socialist states.[8]

Since that time, the United States has made extensive use of foreign aid as a political bargaining tool.[9] Sometimes, aid reductions have been imposed on an *ad hoc* basis. An interesting example was the so-called "short tether" policy that the United States followed regarding food assistance to India during the famine periods of the mid-1960s. Largely in response to India's hostility to Pakistan (culminating in the war of 1965) and to its criticism of American "imperialism" in Southeast Asia, President Johnson refused to enter into long-term commitments for food aid to that country, and instead provided supplies only on a hand-to-mouth basis. The policy did not produce any significant change in India's political policies. But neither did it give rise to accusations of illegality on the part of the United States.[10]

Over the course of time, the United States has also adopted general policies of withholding or restricting assistance to states which engage in various forms of unseemly behavior. These include committing gross violations of human rights,[11] failing to cooperate in the war against narcotics,[12] supporting terrorism,[13] failing to participate in nuclear nonproliferation efforts[14] and nationalizing American-owned property without payment of adequate compensation.[15] On the whole, these reductions, like the Indian "short tether" policy, appear to have had little real effect on the policies of the states concerned. For present purposes, however, the point is merely that there is no serious doubt about their legality.[16]

The same may be said of terminations of treaty arrangements in the economic sphere (provided that the treaties themselves permit termination), or of refusals to enter into favorable treaty relations. In 1951, for example, the United States terminated all of its most-favored-nation agreements with socialist countries.[17] In the case of four of the states concerned (the Soviet Union, Poland, Hungary and Romania), the terminations were undertaken pursuant to provisions in the agreements. There was no suggestion that the United States was violating any overriding rule of customary law by ending these arrangements. (In the case of Czechoslovakia, the matter was somewhat more awkward, as will be noted presently, because of that country's status as a GATT party.) Similarly, in the period of detente during the 1970s, when some restoration of normal economic relations was undertaken, the United States imposed an important condition on the granting of most-favored-nation status to socialist countries: that the states concerned must permit freedom of emigration.[18] The wisdom of this measure has been the subject of some doubt, but not the legality.[19]

The basic principle, then, is that there is no rule in general customary international law forbidding the waging of economic warfare, nor any restriction on the most common specific forms that it takes. Several marginal points, however, should be mentioned. One is that, as the World Court pointed out, some "treaty commitment or other specific legal obligation" might exist in particular cases and thereby displace the general rules. That happened to be so in the *Nicaragua v. United States* case itself. After stating the general principles quoted above, the Court went on to hold the trade boycott unlawful as a violation of a bilateral treaty of friendship, commerce and navigation (FCN) between the two countries.[20] (For technical reasons, the Court did not have jurisdiction to consider the compatibility of the trade boycott with the GATT, to which the United States and Nicaragua were both parties. Nicaragua, as will be seen presently, complained separately in GATT against the sugar-quota reduction and the trade boycott, with some success.)

It should also be noted that, even if customary international law does not prohibit either economic warfare in general or the most common forms of it, certain specific categories of act are unlawful. For example, interfering with the freedom of trade of other countries by placing mines in their harbours is illegal, as the World Court confirmed in the *Nicaragua v. United States* case.[21] Also illegal are various forms of interference with the property either of foreign states or of foreign nationals. The two most notable, in the modern world, are the freezing of financial assets, and the nationalizing of property without payment of the compensation required by law. (The IMF, as will be seen presently, also imposes constraints on the practice of asset freezing.)

Acts in these categories will be lawful, if at all, only if they fall within the legal category of reprisal—i.e., if they are responses to prior unlawful acts on the part of the target country, designed to induce the target state to forsake its illegal ways.[22] Illustrations of this principle in action have been abundant. The first notable example of a retaliatory asset freeze was by the United States against Japan in 1941, in response to that country's expansionist policies in the Pacific and East Asia. After the war, the United States sometimes barred access to state bank deposits by socialist countries in response to their nationalizations of American-owned property (the accounts in question having originally been frozen during the war to keep them out of Nazi hands). The United Kingdom also began (and continues) to withhold Albania's gold supply because of that state's refusal to pay a World Court judgment (dating from 1949) in the United Kingdom's favor.[23] The United States, Britain and France all froze Egyptian assets in their respective territories in 1956 after that country's nationalization of the Suez Canal. The United States froze Iranian assets in 1979 in response to the taking of diplomatic hostages in Tehran;[24] Libyan ones in 1986 because of alleged Libyan support for terrorism;[25] and Panamanian ones in 1988 because of the refusal of that country's government to permit normal democratic activity.[26]

Developing countries, naturally, have resorted more frequently to nationalization than to asset freezing as a form of economic warfare. Here again, however, the governing principle is that of reprisal, assuming that the nationalization actually is unlawful in principle (i.e., is not followed by the legally required compensation). Illustrations of political nationalizations include the taking by Indonesia of Dutch-owned assets in 1958, because of the refusal of the Netherlands to cede West Irian to it; by Libya of British- and American-owned ones in the early 1970s, on the ground of undue toleration by the British government of Iranian expansionism, and of support for Israel by the American government; and by Nigeria of the assets of the oil company BP in 1979, in protest against the British government's policies toward South Africa. In all of these cases of asset freezes and nationalizations, the basic determinant of the legality of the action is the same. If—and only if—the precipitating act was in fact unlawful, then the economic measures invoked in response were justifiable as reprisals. Otherwise they were not.[27]

Finally, it should be noted that, even though economic warfare per se is not forbidden by customary international law in the general case, it might nonetheless be unlawful in particular instances where it is a functional equivalent of some act which *is* illegal, such as intervention or aggression or the use of force. A few remarks on each of these will illustrate the basic issues at stake.

The question of economic warfare as intervention is one which the Latin American countries advanced during the 1940s in the form of the Grau doctrine, named for President Ramón Grau San Martin of Cuba. As mentioned in the previous chapter, the Latin American countries were acutely aware during this period of their dependence on the purchasing power of the United States. They were accordingly anxious to have some kind of assurance that that economic leverage would not be misused. Cuba's interest in the question was particularly strong, since it was the victim of just such an attempt during the late 1940s, when the United States attempted to use its leverage as a purchaser of Cuban sugar to compel that state to conclude an FCN treaty with it.[28] The United States's effort did not succeed; but it did stimulate President Grau of Cuba to proclaim that the general international-law prohibition against intervention into the internal affairs of other states applied to intervention by economic, as well as by military, means.[29]

At the Rio de Janeiro conference of 1947, which drafted the Inter-American Treaty on Reciprocal Assistance, or Rio Treaty[30] (the Western Hemisphere's regional collective-security arrangement), the Cuban delegation unsuccessfully pressed for the inclusion of an express prohibition against "economic aggression."[31] It had more success the following year, with the drafting of the Charter of the Organization of American States (OAS) in Bogotá.[32] That document did incorporate the Grau doctrine, as Article 19 (as it is now numbered), forbidding "the use of coercive measures of an economic or political character in order to force the sovereign will of another State and obtain from it advantages of any kind." In 1965, the developing countries succeeded in having a formulation to this same basic effect included in a Declaration on Non-Intervention adopted by the UN General Assembly[33] (with this declaration, in turn, being incorporated into the General Assembly's Declaration on Friendly Relations between States of 1970).[34]

It is doubtful whether the Grau doctrine, or these various instruments which incorporate it, has much, if any, practical force in international affairs. The reason is that intervention in the legal sense is a rather narrower concept than in the popular usage. The World Court confirmed this fact in the *Nicaragua v. United States* case when it stated that intervention in the legal sense consists of coercive activity by the intervening state bearing on matters falling within the ambit of state sovereignty of the victim country. From the way that the Court applied the doctrine, it would appear that mere attempts to influence the policies of another state would not constitute intervention. The Court flatly stated that the three economic measures of which Nicaragua complained did not so qualify.[35] It would appear, then, that the Grau doctrine, even if valid in principle, has little relevance to the actual practice of economic warfare.

Attempts to subsume economic warfare under the categories of aggression and the use of force have met with even less success. From the time that the UN General Assembly began to consider adopting a definition of aggression, in the early 1950s, the developing countries sought to have acts of economic pressure included. They were given passive support in this effort by the socialist countries; but the Western states firmly, and successfully, resisted the idea.[36] The consensus definition of aggression that was finally adopted by the General Assembly in 1974, for this reason, concerned only the direct use of armed force.[37] Accusations of "economic aggression," to be sure, have surfaced from time to time in international affairs.[38] It is clear, however, that the expression is more a term of general opprobrium than a true legal claim.

The use of force is the other legal rubric under which the developing countries have attempted to bring economic warfare. Here also, the results have been meager in the extreme. The prevailing scholarly view is that the prohibition against the use of force by states in customary international law (as well as the explicit ban found in Article 2(4) of the UN Charter) applies, as a general principle, only to

the use of armed force.[39] Nor have the third-world countries succeeded in equating economic pressure with the use of force in other
contexts. Because of Western resistance, the UN General Assembly's
Declaration on Friendly Relations between States (of 1970) did not
deal with economic warfare in its section on the use of force. The most
that the developing countries have been able to achieve in this area
has been the adoption of a side declaration by the Vienna Conference
on the Law of Treaties in 1968–69, condemning the use of economic
pressure to coerce states into concluding treaties.[40] This declaration,
however, was little more than a consolation prize to the developing
countries, since the developed states successfully opposed including a
similar provision in the text of the Convention on the Law of Treaties
itself.[41]

One last remark will complete the survey of economic warfare
under customary international law. Even though, as we have just
seen, no convincing case can be made that legal prohibitions against
aggression or the use of force constitute *general* bans against economic
warfare, it seems reasonable to suppose that in specific, and highly
atypical, instances, the effect of measures of economic warfare might
be so severe as to be substantially equivalent to a use of armed force.
In such extreme cases, it should then be justifiable to condemn the
measures as unlawful.[42] In reality, however, it is virtually impossible
to find a single illustration of this proposition. Some might contend
that the Arab oil embargo of 1973–74 was such a case. In retrospect,
however, it is obvious that it was not. The material damage done by
the embargo to the target countries was actually minimal.[43] The real
impact was on the psychological, not the economic, plane. Unless one
seeks to equate the making of dramatic psychological gestures with
aggression and the use of force, no credible argument can be made
that the Arab oil embargo fell into either of these ominous-sounding
categories.[44]

Such, then, is the basic status of economic warfare in general
customary international law. In addition, a brief comment should be
made on the position under the UN Charter. At the drafting conference in San Francisco in 1945, Brazil proposed that what became
Article 2(4), prohibiting "the threat or use of force" by states against
one another, be amended to include a ban on the use of "economic
measures" incompatible with the purposes of the organization.[45] This
suggestion was overwhelmingly rejected (on a 26 to 2 vote), for reasons not very clear from the official records. It would appear, however, that the majority opposed the Brazilian amendment on the

ground that measures of economic pressure that are comparable in their effects to a use of armed force were already covered by the basic prohibition.[46] That would certainly appear to be the most reasonable interpretation of Article 2(4). In general, the article should be seen as prohibiting only the use of military force. Such is the view of the majority of international lawyers.[47] Exceptionally, however, as in the case of customary law, economic measures of particular severity should be held to be covered as well.[48] On this same line, it should be noted that the UN Security Council has the power (under Chapter VII of the Charter) to take action against any threat to the peace, breach of the peace or act of aggression. It is fully open to the Council to determine that an act of economic warfare falls into one or more of these categories. The Council, as yet, has never made such a finding; but the possibility always remains open to it.

In sum, no convincing case can be made that either general customary international law or the UN Charter contains any prohibition against the waging of economic warfare per se. Certain specific acts, however, such as asset freezes and nationalizations of property without lawful compensation, are in principle illegal and hence must be justified as reprisals. Third-world attempts to have economic warfare condemned as manifestations of intervention, aggression, and the use of force have achieved no significant success.

It should not be thought, however, that there are no significant legal restrictions on the resort to economic warfare. There are. It is simply that the realm of general customary international law and of the UN Charter—in short, the law governing the *political* relations of states—is not the place to look for them. The place to look is the law concerning the *economic* relations between states. Here, we find a markedly different picture from the one that we have just been considering.

The Economic System:
Economic Warfare Under the GATT and the IMF

International economic law (i.e., the internal law of the system of international economic relations) nowhere contains an explicit, general prohibition against economic warfare. Instead, it contains prohibitions—although not absolute ones—against its most significant forms: boycotting, embargoing and the freezing of financial assets. These restrictions are found in the GATT[49] and the Articles of Agreement of the IMF.[50]

The basic philosophy of the GATT is fundamentally antithetical to such practices as boycotting and embargoing, since one of the basic goals of the agreement is (in the words of the preamble) "the elimination of discriminatory treatment in international commerce." More specifically, Article 11 encompasses these practices in its general prohibition against quantitative restrictions. It provides, simply enough, that:

> No prohibitions or restrictions other than duties, taxes, or other charges, whether made effective through quotas, imports or export licenses or other measures, shall be instituted or maintained . . . on the importation of any product of . . . any other contracting party or on the exportation or sale for export of any product destined for the territory of any other contracting party.

States parties to the GATT are permitted to derogate from this norm only in certain defined circumstances. For example, a state party may obtain a waiver of this provision by a two-thirds vote of its fellow parties. Even in these exceptional cases, however, the general GATT principle of nondiscrimination must be adhered to. Article 13 provides that states imposing quotas must ensure that the adverse effects fall even-handedly onto their trading partners, i.e., that all potential exporters suffer the impact of the quota in proportion to their normal trade and that none be accorded special treatment (favorable or unfavorable).

Very few complaints have been made in GATT about measures of economic warfare. Even countries with potentially strong claims have sometimes refrained from bringing them. During the Arab oil embargo of 1973–74, for example, no effort was made by the target states to complain against Kuwait (the lone embargoing state which was a GATT party). Nor has Cuba made a serious effort to complain against the United States for its long-continuing trade boycott. South Africa has not objected to trade restrictions imposed against it. Poland likewise refrained from complaining against the United States for the revocation of its most-favored-nation (MFN) status in 1982, following the dissolution of the trade union Solidarity.[51] Before the 1980s, the only notable complaint in GATT about a politically motivated trade restriction was by Czechoslovakia against the United States in 1949, for the various export restrictions against it motivated by Cold-War hostility. The complaint had considerable merit, but it was rejected by a vote of the GATT parties.[52]

In the 1980s, several complaints of politically motivated boycotting arose in GATT.[53] In connection with the Falklands conflict of 1982, Argentina complained that several states (most notably Australia, New Zealand and the EEC states) adopted import restrictions against it, in sympathy with the United Kingdom.[54] In the event, however, this matter was not heard by a GATT dispute panel. But two complaints by Nicaragua against the United States were. The first one, decided in 1984, related to the drastic reduction by the United States of Nicaragua's sugar import quota.[55] The second, heard in 1986, concerned the trade boycott instituted by the United States the previous year.[56] For reasons to be explained presently, only the sugar-quota complaint was decided on its merits.

The sugar-quota complaint was relatively straightforward—to the point that the United States offered no defense on the technical issues raised. The U.S. system of allocating quotas of sugar imports to particular countries, although obviously contrary to the general GATT prohibition on quotas, was permitted by virtue of a waiver granted in 1967. The United States remained subject, however, to the Article 13 requirement that the burden of the quota fall impartially on its trading partners. The GATT dispute panel had little trouble deciding that, by singling Nicaragua out for special adverse treatment, the United States violated Article 13. This Nicaraguan sugar-quota claim is, so far, the only instance in which a GATT dispute panel has made a formal finding of illegality of an act of economic warfare. (Nicaragua's legal triumph, as it happens, did it little material good. The United States refused to restore its sugar quota, asserting that it would do so only in the framework of a general political settlement between the two countries.)[57]

In their general purpose, the Articles of Agreement of the IMF are as strongly incompatible with the waging of economic warfare as the GATT is. The general goal of the IMF—the promotion of a multilateral, open-door, nondiscriminatory monetary system—is clearly inconsistent in spirit with the pursuit of political vendettas. More specifically, the IMF's Articles of Agreement restrict the ability of states to wield one of the principal weapons of the modern economic warrior: the asset freeze. Such a practice is prohibited in general by Article 8(2)(a), which bans the imposition by IMF member states of "restrictions on the making of payments and transfers for current international transactions." (Since the IMF has no adversarial dispute settlement mechanism comparable to that of the GATT, there have been no state-to-state complaints arising from allegations of violation of this provision. The various asset freezes which have been imposed have been permitted under a de facto exception to Article 8(2)(a) which will be discussed in the following section.)

The basic internal rules of the political and the economic systems of international relations are, then, clear enough in outline. In a nutshell, the one system is permissive in the area of economic warfare, and the other restrictive. The political system is deeply rooted in a competitive model of international relations, in which economic methods are, as they have been for centuries, perfectly permissible tools of national rivalry. The spirit of the age of mercantilism lives on in the basic international-law rules on economic warfare. The other system, the economic one, is founded upon a spirit of cooperation, or "solidarity," in which states are expected to adopt economic policies that will benefit mankind as a whole. For such an ambition to be realized, it is essential that political rivalries be carefully excluded.

Having outlined the basic internal law of each of the two systems, we may now proceed to the more interesting question of the extent to which each has made inroads into the other. We shall look first at the role that political factors are able to play in the economic sphere, and then survey the ways in which the "industrial spirit" of the economic system has infiltrated the political world.

POLITICAL RIVALRY IN THE "MERCANTILE REPUBLICK": THE ART OF CONTAINMENT

The founders of the post-World War II "mercantile republick" never supposed that it would be possible (or perhaps even desirable) to bring about an absolute separation of economic from political relations. In several respects, they made explicit provision for the exceptional intrusion of political affairs into the economic domain. That is hardly surprising. It is scarcely to be expected that there should be an absolute guarantee of "business as usual" in the face of, say, serious threats to international peace or to the vital national-security interests of countries. There are, accordingly, legal rules which explicitly provide for derogation from the usual norms of international economic law in such cases.

A far more interesting question is a slightly different one: to what extent, if any, can it be said that there is a *general* "political exception" to the rules of the economic system, i.e., a general right on the part of states to derogate from the norms of economic cooperation when *any* political interests are at stake? The same question can be reformulated in slightly different terms: if a given act of economic warfare is motivated by political, rather than economic, considerations, can that act then be said to be political rather than economic in substance, and consequently to be outside the ambit of the rules of international economic law altogether? If so, then the prohibitions against boycotting and freezing assets would only apply in cases of economic, as opposed to political, rivalry. A state, for example, would not be allowed to redress an adverse balance of trade vis-à-vis another one by means of a boycott against it. Similarly, it would not be allowed to defend its exchange rate against speculative pressure by unilaterally freezing the accounts of would-be sellers of its currency. Entirely different (on this argument) would be measures of the same sort imposed on political grounds, because they are economic measures only in form, and not in substance.

The significance of this argument is obvious. If it is accepted, then the result is effectively to neutralize the provisions of the GATT and the IMF Articles of Agreement discussed above, so far as economic warfare for political purposes is concerned. It would permit unlimited trespassing by quarrelsome politicians into the territory of the transnational "mercantile republick." Our concern here, then, is to assess the validity (or otherwise) of this line of argument. We shall first survey the explicit provisions that allow the intrusion of political factors into the economic sphere, and then go on to consider this more important question of the existence (or otherwise) of a general "political exception" to the norms of international economic law.

The most obvious and important provision for the intrusion of political factors into the economic sphere is not found in any of the international economic instruments, but rather in the UN Charter. Enforcement action undertaken or ordered by the UN Security Council takes a clear precedence over any rules of international economic law. Once the Council makes a determination that a threat to the peace, a breach of the peace or an act of aggression has occurred, then it is empowered to issue binding orders to its member states to deal with the crisis. Article 41 of the Charter specifies that such orders can include the "complete or partial interruption of economic relations." In such an event, the commands of the Security Council automatically override any other legal obligations that the member states might have. As it happens, this power has been used only one time to institute a program of general economic sanctions: in 1966–1979, against Southern Rhodesia. Nevertheless, it remains the case that the Security Council's peacekeeping and enforcement power constitutes a clear, and potentially important, political exception to the normal rules of international economic law.[58]

In addition, both the GATT and the IMF themselves have provisions for emergency political exceptions. The GATT contains three principal "loopholes" that allow political factors to enter into the area of trade relations. The most sweeping of the three is the explicit national-security provision of Article 21, which allows a state party to take "any action which it considers necessary for the protection of its essential security interests . . . in time of war or other emergency in international relations." It may be noted that, according to the wording of the provision, each state is allowed to decide for itself when emergency action is "necessary" for the purpose stated. Such has been the interpretation over the years.[59] The provision has not been invoked with great frequency. The most notable occasion was in 1986, when the United States used it to ward off the second Nicaraguan complaint against it, concerning the legality of the trade boycott under the GATT. The "self-judging" nature of Article 21 enabled the United States to forestall a decision by the GATT dispute panel on either the merits of the Nicaraguan claim or the validity of its use of the national-security defense.[60] (The World Court, incidentally, did inquire into the justification of the boycott on national-security grounds, since the bilateral FCN treaty which it considered contained a national-security provision. The Court held that the boycott was not justified on that ground.)[61]

A second loophole in the GATT is Article 35. Under this provision, a state party is entitled, with complete freedom, to stipulate that the GATT will not enter into force as between it and a newly-acceding state. Conversely, any newly-acceding country is also entitled, again with complete freedom, to prevent the GATT from entering into force as between itself and some named existing party or parties. The original purpose of this article was quite clearly to permit a certain latitude for boycotting. It was included at the behest of India, to enable it lawfully to boycott South Africa (which it duly proceeded to do, at least on paper).[62] Other states have made use of Article 35 for similar purposes (although, rather curiously, seldom with South Africa as the target). Several states invoked it against Portugal, for example, at a time when it was an African colonial power. Egypt and Morocco made use of it against Israel, as did Pakistan against Bangladesh and the United States against Hungary and Romania. For the most part, however, Article 35 has been used for economic self-protection rather than for the waging of economic warfare. The most "popular" target, by a large margin, has been Japan, by countries fearful of being swamped by Japanese imports. (In due course, however, nearly all of the invocations against Japan have been withdrawn.)[63]

The third principal loophole in the GATT is the waiver provision of Article 25, which can be used for any purpose, including the imposing of trade restrictions on political grounds. A two-thirds vote of the GATT parties is required to obtain a waiver. On only one occasion has one been granted in a clearly political context. This was in 1951, when the United States adopted a policy of systematically depriving socialist countries of their most-favored-nation status. One of the affected states, Czechoslovakia, was a GATT party. The United States considered invoking the national-security exception but decided that such a claim would too obviously lack credibility.[64] It therefore set about mustering the necessary support for a waiver. It succeeded, but not without some intensive lobbying.[65]

The Articles of Agreement of the IMF contain no explicit national-security exception, although the organization adopted one in 1952 by decision of its executive board.[66] It is broadly in line with that of the GATT. An IMF member state is permitted to impose restrictions on currency transfers which, "in the judgment of the member, are solely related to the preservation of national or international security." The member state must notify the IMF of such measures before their imposition, if possible; otherwise, as soon afterwards as possible. If the state receives no objection from the Fund within thirty days of the notification, then it is entitled to assume that the measures are permitted. This provision has been used on a number of occasions by states, with the United States far in the lead. In the Suez crisis of 1956, France, Britain and the United States all invoked the procedure to impose freezes on Egyptian assets located in their respective territories. These freezes were lifted in 1957–59. The United States has employed this mechanism in connection with asset freezes against Cuba in 1963, North Vietnam in 1965, Laos and Cambodia in 1975, Iran in 1979 (lifted in 1981), Libya in 1986 and Panama in 1988. Both the United Kingdom and Argentina made use of it to impose freezes against one another in connection with the Falklands conflict of 1982 (both sets of measures being lifted later that year). On no occasion has the IMF objected to a currency restriction under this mechanism.[67]

These, then, are the principal explicit and specific political exceptions to the general rules of international economic law. It now remains to be seen whether it can be said that, in addition, intenational

economic law contains an implicit and general "political exception"
—i.e., whether there is a general right of derogation from the rules of
the GATT and the IMF whenever the derogation is motivated by
political, as opposed to economic, factors. It seems fairly clear that,
in each case, the answer is negative.

This issue first arose during the drafting of the GATT-cum-Havana
Charter in the late 1940s. India favored including in the GATT an
explicit *general* political exception of the kind just suggested. On that
view, *any* restrictive trade measure (i.e., a boycott of South Africa)
would have been permissible, provided only that it was imposed for a
political purpose rather than an economic one. This sweeping proposal was rejected, and the milder loophole of Article 35 (discussed
above) substituted for it.[68] (Article 35 is milder in that it allows
derogation from the general GATT rules on political grounds *only* at
the time of accession of new states parties.)

The basic principle that there is no general political exception to
the GATT has been reinforced during the 1980s. In 1982, the contracting parties issued a ministerial declaration which contained a statement that parties should "abstain from taking restrictive trade measures of a non-economic character, not consistent with the General
Agreement."[69] (This pronouncement was, in large part, a response to
Argentina's contention that the imposition of trade restrictions as
gestures of political solidarity, as some states had done during the
Falklands conflict, is not permitted by the GATT.)

The question arose more directly in the Nicaraguan sugar-quota
case of 1984, referred to above. The United States made no attempt to
argue that its reduction of Nicaragua's sugar import quota was consistent with either the letter or the spirit of the GATT itself. Instead,
it contended that, since the action in question was political in substance, the GATT was entirely inapplicable. The GATT dispute panel
firmly rejected this argument, holding, on the contrary, that the presence of a dominant political motivation was no defense.[70]

Even in the framework of the Article 21 national-security exception, the GATT parties have shown a wariness about the intrusion of
political considerations into the field of economic relations. This became apparent when the United States invoked Article 21 against
Nicaragua's complaint about the trade boycott of 1985. Although the
dispute panel was thereby precluded from passing on the merits of
the Nicaraguan claim, it did venture the general observation that
boycotts, even when they were justified under Article 21, "ran counter
to the basic aims of the GATT, namely to foster nondiscriminatory

and open trade policies, to further the development of the less-developed contracting parties and to reduce uncertainty in trade relations."[71]

In sum, GATT has consistently rejected any claims that a general "political exception" to its norms exists. It may be interesting to note that this is one of the factors that has led South Africa to maintain its adherence to the GATT. During the early 1970s, it considered withdrawing from the agreement so as to leave itself free to adopt a development strategy involving import quotas. One of the arguments in opposition was that withdrawal would leave the country without a legal remedy if other GATT parties imposed trade sanctions.[72] So far, South Africa has made no attempt to raise the question in GATT of trade restrictions against it. Should it do so at some point, an intriguing test will arise of the non-political nature of the GATT.

At the IMF, the question of a general "political exception" to the Articles of Agreement has arisen and (as in the case of the GATT) has been answered negatively. The issue arose in conjunction with the adoption of the national-security decision by the executive board in 1952. During the Korean War, the United States and Cuba imposed restrictions on the transfer of funds to mainland China and North Korea, contrary to the letter of Article 8(2)(a) of the Fund's Articles of Agreement. The United States contended (precisely as in the later Nicaraguan sugar-quota case in GATT) that, because the act was political in character, it was not covered by the IMF rules. The IMF executive board considered that contention and rejected it. The national-security decision of 1952 was designed not to undermine this holding but to reinforce it. The text of the decision conceded that the IMF is not "a suitable forum for the discussion of . . . political and military considerations." But it also expressly affirmed that, in principle, restrictions on the transfers of funds are unlawful, "irrespective of their motivation and the circumstances in which they are imposed."[73]

The position respecting the contamination of the system of economic relations by political rivalry may, accordingly, be summed up with the utmost brevity. Specific provisions do exist—in the UN Charter and in the internal law of both GATT and the IMF—for derogation from the normal rules of international economic "solidarity" on political grounds. The law and practice of those bodies, however, belies any claim of a *general* right to derogate from their normal rules for political purposes. The presence of a political motivation does not convert an act of economic hostility from an economic act into a political one. To this extent, then, the spill-over from the political sphere into the economic one has been limited. We shall now turn our attention to the flow in the opposite direction—i.e., the extent to which the rules of the economic sphere have intruded into the political one.

THE "INDUSTRIAL SPIRIT" IN THE POLITICAL SPHERE: TOWARD A LAW OF ECONOMIC NEUTRALITY

We have observed that the basic internal rules of the international political system—i.e., the rules of customary international law and of the UN Charter—allow a very wide degree of latitude to economic warriors. There is, however, one way in which rules restricting economic warfare can evolve: for the "industrial spirit" of the international economic sphere to infiltrate the world of political relations. Here, more than in any other single area of international life, is the real test of the evolution of a viable system of economic world order of the kind envisaged by the eighteenth-century *philosophes*, the physiocrats, the classical liberal economists and the proponents of a new international law of "solidarity."

There are some indications that the dream of an economic world order may be emerging after all, i.e., that the frontiers of the political sphere may be receding as those of the economic world expand. The clearest indication is the way in which, largely un-noticed, restrictions on the waging of economic warfare have begun quietly to creep into international law since the Second World War. In certain respects, the "restrictions" amount to little more than the vague feeling that acts of economic hostility are beneath the dignity of a civilized state, that they constitute, so to speak, an uncouth form of behavior. There are, however, some more concrete manifestations of this trend. The most important, as we shall see, is the emergence of what could arguably be called a law of "economic neutrality" protecting third parties from effects of economic warfare. Several illustrations will make these points clearer.

One of the most obvious indications that economic warfare is regarded, de facto if not de jure, as being rather in "bad form" in modern international life is the fact that states are generally reluctant to assert their legal prerogatives too forthrightly. In practice, states rarely justify measures such as boycotts and embargoes on the simple ground that they have an unfettered sovereign right to impose them. They nearly always justify acts of economic hostility on the basis of some prior wrongful act by the target country—human-rights violations, terrorism, aggression and so forth. This tendency dates from at least as far back as the 1930s, when China justified its boycott against Japan at the League of Nations as a reprisal, in response to Japanese aggression. Perhaps the best example of this tendency in the post–World War II period is the boycott of Israel by the Arab countries.[74] It has been equipped with an impressive array of justifications—as a measure of self-defense, as a belligerent right, as a means of promoting self-determination—but seldom as a simple sovereign prerogative of the boycotting states.[75] It would, admittedly, be unwise to make too much of this point. After all, states virtually never break diplomatic relations without alleging some form of misconduct on the part of the other country. But that does not mean that international law forbids diplomatic ruptures or requires the exchanging of ambassadors. Still, there does appear to be a certain consensus to the effect that it is the rule to engage in international economic relations, and the exception to disrupt them deliberately.

An excellent illustration of this general presumption in favor of "normal" economic relations is provided by the experience of the United States in its attempt to wage economic warfare against the socialist countries in the early years of the Cold War. It encountered difficulties in so doing, in large part because the policy was so embarrassingly contradictory to the principles of the global, open-door "mercantile republick" of which it was itself the chief sponsor. The economic-warfare effort, as it was gradually implemented during the late 1940s, therefore had to be creatively packaged.[76] In effect, it was disguised as an adjunct of the Marshall Plan. The official position was that essential materials of various kinds were in short supply and therefore had to be carefully rationed for optimum use in the cause of general postwar economic recovery, i.e., in the Marshall Plan.[77] In reality, the intention was to impose an embargo against the Soviet Union and its allies.

The socialist countries had little difficulty in perceiving what was actually happening. Czechoslovakia, as noted above, brought a complaint against the United States in GATT, albeit unsuccessfully. The socialist countries also fulminated against the American policy at the UN. At the 1948 session of the General Assembly, Poland condemned the United States policy as being motivated "not . . . by economic considerations but purely by political ones."[78] It proceeded to introduce a draft resolution that would have had the General Assembly declare that "any discrimination in trade or credit policy which is calculated to apply sanctions or to influence the domestic or foreign policy of any other country should be regarded as contrary to the principles of the [UN] Charter."[79] The draft resolution was rejected, in a vote on straight Cold-War political lines.

It soon became apparent that the Western European countries shared these misgivings about the American policy. To their annoyance, they were compulsorily brought into the campaign by virtue of the U.S. insistence, as a condition of Marshall-Plan aid, that they cooperate in the American embargo program.[80] (In 1951, with the enactment of the Battle Act, the United States extended this same policy to recipients of American aid generally.)[81] The European countries reacted to this pressure by taking the initiative in instituting a multilateral strategic-embargo effort, to be guided by an informal Coordinating Committee (CoCom, as it soon became known).

The Americans were pleased to have European support for their embargo program. This backing did not come without strings, however. Basically, the purpose of the European states in establishing CoCom was to moderate the severity of the American embargo, a concern most particularly of the French. The European countries were concerned over what they regarded as the fundamentally offensive character of the embargo effort.[82] For that reason, they insisted that the program be carefully tailored to the withholding of only military-related materials from the socialist countries, and that it not be a general economic-warfare campaign. Similarly, they insisted on CoCom's being kept carefully separate from the NATO alliance, which was being established at this same time. The fear was that the defensive nature of NATO might be undermined if the strategic-embargo program was too closely associated with it. The whole experience provides an interesting indication of the general aura of disrepute attaching to economic-warfare programs—to the point that a strategic-embargo program of this kind had to be carefully hidden away while, at the very same time, an outright military alliance could be entered into openly, in an age when the use of force was (supposedly) illegal.[83]

These various considerations continue to shape the Western strategic-embargo campaign to the present day. CoCom remains now, as at its inception, carefully set apart from NATO. It also remains to this day a relatively discreet arrangement. It has still never been embodied in a formal treaty, remaining instead at the legally subliminal level of a gentlemen's agreement or *modus vivendi*.[84] Also to the present day, the Western states firmly deny that they are engaged in a general campaign of economic warfare against the Soviet-bloc countries, a point reaffirmed as recently as 1984 by the Reagan administration.[85]

There are several instructive examples of the lengths to which states will go to deny that they are waging economic warfare even when it is patently obvious that they are and when justifications could credibly be claimed to exist. In the Tehran hostages crisis, for instance, the United States denied that its freezing of Iranian assets was a reprisal. Officially, it was a protective measure, designed to prevent chaos in the banking system which might result from precipitate withdrawals of funds by the Iranians.[86] Also, the U.S. withdrawal of most-favored-nation status from Poland in 1982, an obvious response to the dissolving of the trade union Solidarity, was justified on the technical ground that Poland had failed to honour commitments to purchase goods from other GATT parties.[87] In general, it may be said, then, that practices of economic warfare have a certain unsavoury reputation, even if there is no general international-law rule explicitly forbidding them. They "smell" of hostility.

The most concrete evidence so far of the general disrepute with which economic warfare is now regarded is the emergence—at least arguably—of what might be termed a law of economic neutrality, i.e., of a law protecting uninvolved third parties from the effects of economic-warfare campaigns. The comparison with the law of neutrality in armed conflict is obvious. The basic function of the traditional law of neutrality is to ensure that third parties may go freely about their normal lives—including trading in the normal way with either or both belligerents—without fear of disruption. Hostile measures should be directed exclusively by the belligerents against one another, and not against innocent outsiders.

Precisely this same consideration underlies the concern that has evolved since World War II over the practice of "secondary boycotting." A secondary boycott is directed not against the actual enemy itself, but rather against a third party trading with the enemy. The purpose is to make the main boycott effort (the primary boycott) as effective as possible, by discouraging third parties from trading with the target state. Those who do trade will be punished by being boycotted themselves. Secondary boycotting, then, is designed in effect to dragoon the world at large into the boycott campaign by exposing anyone who deals with the enemy to like treatment. Whoever is not with the secondary boycotter is against him.

From the standpoint of traditional international law, it is clear that there is no ground for a legal challenge to this practice. A secondary boycott, like a primary one, is simply an exercise by the boycotting state of its general right to refuse to trade with another country for any reason that it chooses (assuming, of course, the absence of a treaty commitment to the contrary). Since World War II, however, there has come to be an increasingly firm feeling that, notwithstanding the basic permissiveness of traditional international law in this area, secondary boycotting is a particularly reprehensible—and possibly outright illegal—practice.[88]

One of the earliest illustrations of an emerging consensus to this effect occurred in the context of the Arab boycott of Israel, and specifically of the Egyptian policy of forcing third states to stop trading with Israel. It did this by blacklisting ships carrying Israeli cargoes or calling at Israeli ports, and then denying those vessels passage through the Suez Canal.[89] The matter came before the UN Security Council in 1951, where the Western states, led by Britain and France, spoke up for the rights of third parties affected. (The United Kingdom, in particular, complained that it was being adversely affected by the interference with cargoes of crude oil bound for refining in Haifa.) Upon the initiative of these countries, the Security Council adopted a resolution noting

> that the restrictions on the passage of goods through the Suez Canal to Israel ports are denying to nations at no time connected with the conflict in Palestine valuable supplies required for their economic reconstruction, and that these restrictions together with sanctions applied by Egypt to certain ships which have visited Israel ports represent unjustified interference with the rights of nations to navigate the seas and to trade freely with one another, including the Arab States and Israel.[90]

Controversy about secondary boycotting by the Arab countries intensified sharply during the 1970s, in the wake of the steep rise in oil prices and the corresponding explosion in opportunities for Western companies to do business in the Arab world. The Arab countries were subjected to sharp criticism for blacklisting Western companies doing business with Israel (although there was clearly much inconsistency in the actual practices of the Arab states in this regard). Resentment against this practice led two countries, the United States and France, to adopt legislation to counter it.[91] The American law, enacted in 1977, was essentially designed to thwart the secondary aspect of the Arab boycott by forbidding American nationals from complying with boycott-related requests. The permissibility of primary boycotting, however, was recognized in the provision of the law allowing American companies to adhere to boycott policies of foreign host countries when they were actually operating in the territories of such states.[92] The EEC has followed a broadly similar policy, by entering into a series of economic cooperation agreements with Arab states in 1976–77, which (in the view of the EEC Commission, at least) prohibit the Arab countries from subjecting EEC companies to secondary boycotting.[93]

Another economic-warfare campaign in which secondary tactics have given rise to resentment is the one waged by the United States against Cuba since the early 1960s.[94] Here, the United States has been the perpetrator of the secondary action, rather than the champion of its victims.[95] Until 1975, it blacklisted all ships calling at Cuban ports, whatever the state of registry of the vessels. Blacklisted vessels were then denied access to American port facilities. Another method of secondary economic warfare employed by the United States was the policy of halting foreign aid to countries that permitted their nationals to trade with Cuba. Reductions of small amounts of aid were imposed against Britain, France and Yugoslavia in 1964 on this ground, together with rather larger cuts against Spain and Morocco.[96] Rather more serious was the U.S. delay in providing food assistance to Bangladesh in a period of famine in 1974, on the ground that that country had sold jute to Cuba.[97] This aid reduction policy, like the blacklisting of ships, was finally discontinued in 1975, having produced more resentment against the United States than injury to Cuba.[98]

Some of the most bitter disputes about secondary economic warfare have arisen in the context of the American export-control laws. Even after the formation of CoCom and the instituting of a multilateral strategic-embargo program, the United States continued to operate an embargo effort of its own which swept more broadly than the CoCom one. Over the years, this program has become more and more sophisticated in its administrative controls of U.S. exports—and, correspondingly, more and more intrusive into the economic affairs of foreign companies and states. The United States export-control program has become immensely complex. For present purposes, it will suffice to note that it involves a heady combination of secondary economic-warfare tactics, with a de facto (if not de jure) extension of American law into the affairs of the transnational "mercantile republick" at large. The United States policy, broadly speaking, requires American exporters of strategic goods or technology to obtain certain contractual commitments from their foreign customers. These contractual commitments are to the effect that, in dealing with the goods or technology in question, the foreign customers will abide by the United States export-control laws as they may happen to be from time to time, i.e., that they will act in accordance even with *future* U.S. export-control rules. The effect is to subject the foreign business interests to U.S. law, through the medium of these private contracts. The penalty for the foreign party's transgression of the American rules is secondary boycotting, in the form of exclusion from the United States market—a potentially crippling penalty for a foreign business.[99]

Strictly speaking, this exclusion, like any refusal to trade, could be legally justified as an exercise by the United States of its inherent sovereign right for which it is answerable to no one. Foreign businesses and their governments, however, have not seen the matter in that light. This became sharply evident in 1982, in the most controversial case to date involving this American export-control policy. The controversy arose when, in the aftermath of the martial-law crisis in Poland in December 1981, the United States government attempted to stop various Western European companies from assisting the Soviet Union in the construction of a gas pipeline from Siberia to Western Europe. To perform the necessary work, the European companies acquired American goods and technology and accordingly entered into the contractual commitments just outlined. At the time that these firms signed their contracts with the Soviet Union, the American export laws permitted the use of goods and technology of U.S. origin for that purpose. The change of rules by the United States in December 1981, however, reversed the position and forbade compliance.[100] The European companies were thereby landed in an impossible dilemma: either they had to breach their contracts with the Soviets, and thereby expose themselves to damages; or else they had to disobey the United States export laws and thereby risk exclusion from American markets.

A storm of protest arose, in which the companies were firmly supported by their home governments. The British, Italian and French governments showed their resentment against this interference by the United States in the commercial activities of their companies, by taking steps to ensure that the pipeline contracts were fulfilled. Britain promulgated legal regulations directly forbidding their firms from complying with the American rules.[101] France took a slightly different approach. It requisitioned one of its companies, Dresser France (a subsidiary of the American Dresser Industries), to ensure that the pipeline contract was fulfilled as promised. In the case of Dresser, the United States acted upon its export-control policy and excluded it from American markets.[102]

The legal intricacies of this affair need not be explored for present purposes.[103] It is sufficient to note that, according to the traditional law, the United States was probably acting within its rights. But it was also engaging in the nefarious practice of secondary boycotting— a practice which is increasingly felt to be unjustifiable. In the event, the international legal issues in this crisis were not forced. In the face of the storm of protest over its policy, the United States gave in and withdrew the offending regulations.[104] The incident was, however, a dramatic demonstration of the depth of feeling that can arise in the international community over the practice of secondary boycotting.[105]

It is probably reasonable to conclude that a legal rule prohibiting secondary boycotting is in the process of emergence. Whether it is actually in existence at the present time cannot be stated with certainty. (The point, unfortunately, did not arise in the *Nicaragua v. United States* case, which involved a complaint by the main target of the boycott, and not by an innocent third party.) In any event, the significance of secondary boycotting, for present purposes, is not its precise current legal status, but rather its clear analogy to the law of neutrality in armed conflict. The function of that law, it will be recalled, is to confine the effects of hostilities to the belligerents themselves and thereby to leave the rest of the world undisturbed. Putting the matter in rather broader terms, it may be said that the law of neutrality is based on the premise that the interests of those at peace should prevail over the interests of those at war and that, for the good of the world community as a whole, it is desirable to confine the effects of armed conflict within as narrow an ambit as possible. It is then no large jump to say that, in a truly ideal world, there would be no war at all; and that all nations would be "neutral."

It is very easy—if, admittedly, speculative—to see precisely the same chain of reasoning at work in the economic sphere as in the political one. The widespread resentment against secondary forms of economic warfare (or the law against it, if there is one) surely reflects the premise that the interests of those who trade in the ordinary way should prevail over the interests of those who impose boycotts and embargoes and the like. Such a belief must be based in turn on the thesis that, in the interest of the world community as a whole, it is desirable that trading be as free as possible and that, correspondingly, measures which disrupt or inhibit trade be kept to a minimum. It is also no large jump to conclude that, in a truly ideal world, there would be no economic warfare or disruption at all, that all nations here too would be "neutral." All of mankind, as Mirabeau had dreamed, would then have friends but no allies; and peace would reign throughout the great "mercantile republick" (if not in the whole of international affairs).[106]

That the world appears to be evolving in the direction of increasingly restricting the waging of economic warfare is the single most concrete indication that the dream of Mirabeau and his followers may likewise be evolving—or rather, inching—toward realisation. Excessive optimism, however, is not in order. There is no evidence that any iron laws are at work here. There is no guarantee that this law of economic neutrality—even assuming it to be the law—will necessarily evolve into a full-blooded general prohibition against economic warfare. It must further be recalled that economic warfare in any event is only the most marginal and extreme manifestation of a force, or a mentality, which is far more general and far-reaching: economic nationalism. Unless serious progress is made against this practice on a broad range of fronts, the dream of an economic world order will remain in the realm of utopia. We will, accordingly, turn our attention to this wider struggle.

SIX

CAPITALISM'S POLICEMEN: The Struggle Against Third-world Economic Nationalism

Economic warfare is only the most extreme and aggressive form of the more general phenomenon of economic nationalism. A single basic idea lies at the heart of each: the belief that states have the right (if not the duty) to use their sovereign powers to regulate their own economies in their own overall national interest. That fundamental idea is the principal target of the crusaders for a liberal economic world order—a fact recognized by the advocates of a new international law of "solidarity" in the early twentieth century.[1] From the standpoint of classical liberalism, then, policies of *national* economic development are every bit as reprehensible as economic warfare, and for precisely the same reason: both entail an interference with the integration of the world into a single economic community.

The vision of a liberal economic world order is, therefore, directly and fundamentally at odds with the kind of economic development policies expounded in the nineteenth century by Friedrich List and implemented by Chancellor Bismarck. These same policies have been widely adopted throughout the twentieth century by third-world states seeking to promote industrialization. Economic nationalist practices are, of course, no monopoly of the developing countries. No industrial state is free (or even very nearly free) from the taint of protectionism.[2] Nevertheless, there is an important difference between developed and developing states in this regard. The industrialized countries readily accept that, in principle, economic nationalism is an evil and that any interference with freedom of trade (however common it might be) calls for justification. The typical national development policies of the third-world countries, in contrast, are intrinsically antithetical to the ways of classical liberalism. The campaign against economic nationalism is therefore inevitably a struggle against some of the most deeply felt aspirations of the developing world.

One of the principal innovations of the post-World War II "mercantile republick" was the creation of international institutions explicitly designed to lead the crusade against economic nationalism. The three principal agencies—GATT, the World Bank, and the IMF—all have their allotted roles in the struggle, although pride of place must surely go to the IMF. It is, accordingly, hardly a coincidence that, of the three agencies, it has had the rockiest relations with the developing countries. Especially with the economic dislocations of the 1970s and 1980s—the collapse of the fixed-exchange-rate system, the oil price shocks, the most serious global recession since the 1930s and the international debt crisis—the IMF has increasingly assumed the role of chief disciplinarian of an ever-more-restive group of wards.

It should not be supposed, however, that individual states have been altogether precluded from acting as enforcers of the norms of the liberal international economic order. The developed Western countries remain active in this process, if less spectacularly than in the days of nineteenth-century gunboat diplomacy. It is easy to see why: the advanced capitalist countries have an obvious vested interest in a liberal economic order. Most notably, the major capital-exporting states have an interest in safeguarding the rights of property and of contract. It is therefore hardly surprising that the two most active protectors of the rights of foreign investors have been Britain and the United States. These countries have not hesitated to use the standard weapons of the economic warrior—boycotts and capital embargoes—in the neatly combined causes of global liberalism and material self-interest.

It certainly has not escaped the attention of the third-world countries that the principles of a liberal economic order are, to a remarkable degree, coextensive with the interests of the developed capitalist states. Or that a crusade against economic nationalism amounts, in effect, to a systematic attempt to undermine and sabotage programs of national economic development. It is hardly surprising, then, that efforts to stamp out economic nationalism, however well-intentioned, have generated the bitterness and rancor characteristic of class warfare.[3]

THE LEGACY OF FRIEDRICH LIST: INWARD-LOOKING DEVELOPMENT STRATEGIES

There has been no fundamental innovation in third-world economic nationalism since the nineteenth century. Now, as then, the precepts of Friedrich List hold sway through much of the developing world. The leading intellectual theorist of economic development since World War II, the Argentinian economist Raúl Prebisch, has acknowledged the influence of List on his views.[4] Prebisch, like his predecessor, had a historicist outlook. Also like his predecessor, he was concerned with promoting economic development *within* the various countries of the third world. For him, as for List, that meant, above all else, industrialization. This drive to lessen the dependence of poor-country economies on raw-material production was underpinned by a theory that, over the long run, there is a tendency for the terms of international trade to shift in favor of manufactured goods and against primary products.

The political and economic atmosphere at the conclusion of the Second World War certainly lent support to this belief. The prices of raw-material exports had plunged disastrously during the Great Depression of the 1930s. Wartime demand brought a sharp upturn, but the fear was that it would prove only temporary—a concern shared by postwar planners in the United States Department of State. In his basic reading of the postwar economic situation, Prebisch therefore did not differ very radically from the founders of the postwar "mercantile republick."

Where Prebisch parted company with the planners of the postwar order was in his assessment of the nature and magnitude of the problem. In his view, it was not a matter of a one-off adjustment from war to peace. He believed that the tendency for the terms of trade to incline in favor of manufactured goods was an intrinsic property of economic evolution. This theory was essentially a variant of Sombart's "law of declining exports" of the late nineteenth century. Prebisch's thesis, like Sombart's, was based on the idea that, with advancing industrialization, an ever higher proportion of the value of finished goods would be accounted for by industrial processing and an ever smaller share by the raw materials themselves. He claimed to have empirical proof for this proposition, in the form of a study of raw-material price trends for the period 1870–1938.[5] The policy implications of the Prebisch view were clear. A country that specializes, whether by choice or necessity, in primary production is doomed to perpetual and ever worsening impoverishment. The way to escape is to develop an industrial base.

To achieve this goal, two alternate strategies are available: an outward-looking one, entailing production for the world markets generally; and an inward-looking one, involving production for the home market in substitution for goods traditionally imported. The advantages and risks associated with these two strategies are apparent. The advantage of the export-oriented option is that it entails producing for the largest possible market—that of the entire world—but, by the same token, it means facing the largest possible array of competitors as well. This strategy is, therefore, not for the faint-hearted or the indolent. Inefficient producers risk being outdone by foreign competitors. A fairly high degree of specialization is therefore almost inevitable. Japan is the archetypal illustration of a nation that has developed industrially by this kind of strategy, with other countries such as South Korea and Taiwan following in its wake. The import-substitution strategy, in contrast, is more modest in its ambitions, but also less risky. If production is primarily for the home market, then there is necessarily a limit to how large a market one will have. At the same time, however, it is far easier to shield oneself against bruising competition from foreigners. One has merely to erect tariff barriers or quotas in order to exclude foreign competitors. Germany and the United States during the nineteenth century are prime examples of states which industrialized by this means.

It is easy to see that these two basic strategies appeal to two quite distinct kinds of political-economic mentality. The export-oriented strategy appeals to those who believe in free enterprise, in the dismantling of barriers to trade and the creation of integrated global markets. In short, it is wholly within the spirit of a liberal world economic order. Import substitution, in contrast, is the very embodiment of economic nationalism, in that it seeks the development of a balanced economy within the confines of a single country, along the lines advocated by Hamilton and List and followed so single-mindedly by Bismarck. It is also the policy endorsed by Prebisch and followed, for the most part, by the third-world countries since the Second World War.[6]

Some developing countries have taken inward-looking development to its extremes and adopted radical autarkist programs. The Soviet Union did so, with remarkable thoroughness, in the 1930s. Since World War II, Burma provides probably the best example of a country taking this path. Communist China, for a time, followed suit. Also, Tanzania's Arusha Declaration, its charter of "African socialism," is strongly autarkist in principle.[7] Most developing countries, however, have not taken this radical path, accepting instead that a certain degree of involvement with the outside world is inevitable and even—if skillfully managed—desirable. Most third-world states following inward-looking policies, then, have chosen not to cut their links with the wider "mercantile republick," but rather to police them carefully so as to ensure that the general goal of national economic development is always being served. Certain imports, of course, should be excluded, such as luxuries which drain away precious hard currency, together with any products that compete with developing local industries. But certain others are essential. Foodstuffs are one common example, since most third-world states are not self-sufficient in food. Modern armaments, regrettably, are often seen as essential too. So are capital goods for the furthering of the industrialization effort. Far from seeking to exclude goods of these favored categories, a typical import-substitution developing state will positively seek to promote their import. It may even follow what is, in effect, a medieval-style "policy of provision" for these select categories of goods, while at the same time taking care to restrict the entry of goods of the non-favored sort.

A policy of promoting the import of certain goods, while at the same time restricting that of others, requires a fair degree of steady watchfulness and administrative sophistication. It requires, in other words, scientific economic management of the sort pioneered by the nineteenth-century economic nationalists. In the area of international trade, the measures that might typically be adopted are obvious. Protective tariffs and quota arrangements are the key devices—but carefully structured so as to ensure that the appropriate goods are admitted into or excluded from the country, as the case may be. In addition, imaginative currency arrangements of various sorts can play an important role. For a state following a "policy of provision," the deliberate overvaluation of the currency is an obvious tactic for facilitating essential imports. The difficulty, of course, is that such a policy also facilitates nonessential imports. A state can counteract this undesirable effect in various ways. It can erect trade barriers (either tariffs or quotas) against goods that are deemed to be non-essential. It can also restrict access by its citizens to foreign exchange through a rationing arrangement or similar administrative device. Or it might establish a government monopoly over foreign trade so as to ensure that only the "right" materials are imported. Another possibility is a multi-tier exchange rate—with a higher rate applicable to purchases of favored imports, and a lower rate to non-favored ones. In this case, too, ancillary administrative arrangements will be required, to ensure that currency obtained by traders at the more favorable rate is actually used for the purposes intended.[8]

Finally, it may be noted that a state following a "policy of provision" with respect to capital and capital goods can extract various involuntary contributions from foreign investors. High taxes are the most obvious device. Another is the restricting of the repatriation of profits, so as to compel the foreign party to increase its investment.[9] More robust and confrontational methods are sometimes employed as well. Deliberately defaulting on debt repayments, a strategy employed by Peru and Brazil in the 1980s, is one example. In addition, there is the outright nationalization of foreign investments.[10] In such a case, it is generally accepted that compensation must be paid by the nationalizing state, although there is considerable controversy as to the amount. It is, of course, in the interest of the nationalizing state to pay as little as possible. A payment of the full value of the property taken—the standard supported, naturally, by the investors themselves—clearly would leave the nationalizing country no better off in terms of net national wealth. From its standpoint, nationalization makes little sense unless it entails a net transfer of real wealth.[11]

It is easy to see why all of these measures are opposed by liberal economists, who tend to favor market-based, export-oriented strategies of development, as do the principal institutions of the international economic system—GATT, the World Bank and the IMF—and the principal capital-exporting countries (especially the United States). Any development strategy that entails the raising of tariffs or the imposing of quotas on imports or exports is likely to fall foul of GATT rules. Similarly, any policy of deliberate overvaluation of a currency (including a multi-tier currency system) is likely to be deemed by the IMF to be a "manipulative" arrangement, designed to secure unfair trade advantages. In addition, the World Bank, the institutional patron saint of foreign investment, disapproves of defaulting on debts and nationalizing foreign-owned property without the payment of full compensation, on the ground that such policies undermine the general confidence of foreign investors and inhibit the free movement of capital. More generally, the belief among liberals is that development strategies that involve significant government intervention in foreign trade and the administrative allocation of foreign exchange are inefficient because they distort the working of free-market processes. The substitution of the dictates of government administrators for the impersonal demands of the marketplace is seen as inviting corruption, because of the high premium that it places on access to government favors rather than on the creation of real wealth.[12]

For a very long time, there has been guerrilla warfare and skirmishing between the economic nationalists and the liberals. As early as the sixteenth century, Vitoria revealed himself to be as keen to extirpate economic nationalist heresy as his fellow Dominicans were to root out the religious variety. He maintained that, if the native rulers of the New World persisted in refusing entry into their kingdoms to Spanish traders, then the aggrieved Spaniards could put their cities to the torch and even enslave their populations.[13] We have observed La Pradelle's impatience with China's concern to safeguard its civilization from the inroads of barbarians (although he, unlike Vitoria, stopped short of condoning the use of armed force).[14] During the 1920s, the American international lawyer and world-government advocate Clyde Eagleton echoed these views, when he stressed that the "backward" countries of the world should not be allowed to stand in the way of progress toward the progressive unification of international society. "The backward state," he contended, "cannot be allowed to stand as an obstacle in the path of ... development of an effective system of world law; and if it be argued that such an attitude lends itself to imperialistic purposes, the reply is that regression is impossible."[15]

Whether "regression" is truly impossible or not may be the subject of some debate. Shortly after Eagleton wrote these words, it might be noted, some considerable regression did take place, in the form of the economic-nationalist surge of the 1930s. Since the 1940s, however, the world has possessed some stern guardians against regression, in the form of the principal institutions of the international economic system.

THE "OFFICIAL" CAMPAIGN AGAINST ECONOMIC NATIONALISM: GATT, THE WORLD BANK AND THE IMF

The original intention of the founders of the post-World War II "mercantile republick" had been that economic law enforcement would be entirely centralized in the ITO, just as the use of military force was, in principle, centralized in the UN Security Council. Article 86(2) of the ill-fated Havana Charter stipulated that the individual states members of the organization were to forgo unilateral economic measures.[16] Since that provision never took effect, the individual states have retained their freedom of action. Nevertheless, the three principal multilateral bodies maintain the leading, if not the exclusive, role as the scourges of economic nationalism. The weapons available to them are not novel. They are chiefly the standard tools of the economic warrior: capital embargoes and trade restrictions. In principle, as we have seen, the use of such devices in the sphere of international economic relations is disfavored. There is, however, one important difference between the cases to be considered here, and those discussed in the previous chapter: here, the various economic weapons are being used not to further the self-interest (political or economic) of any particular state, but rather to enforce the norms of the system as a whole. The tools of the economic warrior are, therefore, being put to use as constables' truncheons. We shall survey the activities of each of the three economic agencies in turn, and then proceed to consider the "unofficial" enforcement activities of individual states.

The GATT does not, strictly speaking, possess enforcement powers of its own, since it is not an organization. Instead, it provides criteria for determining when the individual states parties are permitted to act against violators of the agreement. In other words, it provides a licensing mechanism, enabling states to undertake, in the name of the GATT system as a whole, measures of economic pressure which ordinarily would be forbidden. Against two specific forms of economic delinquency, the GATT permits direct economic retaliation by injured states: the subsidizing of exports, and dumping (i.e., selling goods in foreign markets at less than their "normal" price). Against these two nefarious distortions of free-market principles, Article 6 of the GATT authorizes injured parties to impose countervailing duties (in the case of export subsidies) or anti-dumping duties (in the case of dumping). The principles governing these actions are essentially those of the United States's "scientific" tariff of the 1920s. That is, the counter-vailing or anti-dumping duties (as the case may be) must be designed solely to counteract the adverse effects suffered, and not to gain an unfair trading advantage. They must be tools strictly of self-defense and not of aggression.[17]

The nearest thing that the GATT possesses to a true enforcement mechanism is its dispute-settlement system, which functions largely to identify violators of the agreement and to shame them into compli-ance. Under this procedure, a party to the GATT is entitled to bring a complaint against another and to request the formation of a panel of neutral persons to hear the dispute and to decide whether or not there is a violation of the agreement. When a complainant state requests the formation of a panel, it is the "customary practice" within GATT for the respondant country not to object. The disputing parties gener-ally determine the identity of the panel members between themselves. (Exceptionally, however, the director-general of GATT can appoint the panel members from a list of agreed parties.) Strictly speaking, the panel reports are only recommendations, which the GATT council can then adopt as official rulings on behalf of the contracting parties as a whole. Adoption of the reports is on the basis of consensus. Consequently, a party to the dispute, by withholding its agreement to the panel report, can prevent its adoption. Alternatively, it can permit the adoption of the report, but express reservations to it. The general expectation is that, once violations have been officially identified, the miscreants will proceed to mend their ways. The only instrument of coercion possessed by the GATT council is the power to authorize retaliation by victim states against wrongdoers. As this power has been used only one time (in 1952), it is more of a theoretical than an actual threat.[18]

In the first forty years of the GATT's existence, approximately one hundred complaints led to the formation of dispute panels. Some nine-tenths of these were resolved satisfactorily, either through agreed settlements by the parties or else through implementation of the panel's recommendations.[19] (One panel report that was *not* imple-mented, it will be recalled, was the one in 1984 on the Nicaraguan sugar-quota complaint against the United States). For substantial periods of time, the dispute-settlement procedure was relatively little used. In the face of the protectionist pressures of the 1970s and 1980s, it experienced something of a renaissance. Even so, the developing countries have played relatively little role in it, either as complainants or as respondants. From 1947 to 1987, only some fifteen complaints were lodged by third-world states. In general, the interest of developing countries has been to secure preferential treatment in the trade area, rather than to press for strict compliance with the normal rules of the GATT. (It may also be that the third-world states are fearful of economic retaliation by their developed counterparts.)[20] Conversely, there have been relatively few claims by developed countries against developing ones. (During one ten-year period, beginning in the late 1950s, there were none at all.) Two factors probably account for this situation. One is that individual developing-state markets are usually too tiny to warrant the effort of pursuing a complaint. The other is that compliance of the third-world states with GATT reports tends to be more formalistic than substantive. As one practice is condemned, another often appears in its place.[21]

The GATT, then, plays only a relatively peripheral role in the campaign against third-world economic nationalism. The same cannot be said of the World Bank and the IMF. As lending bodies—or, as the case may be, non-lending bodies—these two organizations naturally have a significant economic leverage over the policies of states which beseech their support. It must be recalled, in this connection, that the World Bank and the IMF are not development agencies per se. Rather, they are guardians and stabilizers of the international economy generally. Their mission, therefore, is not simply (or perhaps even primarily) to supply much-needed hard currency to the poor countries. It is also to ensure that the policies which those countries adopt are correct from the technical economic standpoint—i.e., from the basic free-market perspective to which both agencies are clearly committed. In the eyes of these organizations, development, over the long term, is more a matter of right conduct on the part of the borrowers than of material support on the part of the lenders.

The early experience of the World Bank aptly illustrates these points. It expressed the view in one of its early annual reports that "the real measurement of the Bank's effectiveness will be, not so much the number and amount of its loans and guarantees, significant as they may be, but rather its success in influencing attitudes—in promoting a realistic constructive approach to development problems on the part of its members and in fostering a greater degree of confidence among investors."[22] The Bank was quite definite that the bulk of the capital for the development of the poor countries of the world must come from private sources.[23] An important part of its function, therefore, is to ensure that those countries present themselves as attractively as possible to potential private investors.

To this end, it is essential, in the eyes of the World Bank, that developing countries adopt orthodox free-market economic policies; that they scrupulously respect the rights of property and of contract; and, in general, that they shun the wicked ways of economic nationalism. The Bank, in an account of its early years, confirmed that one of its important tasks is to counteract the temptation of governments to stray from the path of liberal righteousness:

> It must be remembered [the Bank pointed out] that governments, however conscientious, are apt to be subject to political pressure to emphasize short-run objectives which promise immediate advantage rather than policies designed primarily for the long-run development of their countries, particularly where long-range policies entail some sacrifice of immediate benefits or adversely affect important local interests. In this type of situation, the Bank's insistence upon appropriate economic and financial measures to create a favorable environment for development over the long term has not infrequently provided a countervailing influence of some considerable significance.[24]

The World Bank has consistently shown itself to be opposed to policies involving unilateral appropriations by countries of the wealth of foreign investors, whether in the form of nonpayment of debts or of nationalization of property without full compensation. In the early period of its operation, the Bank made it clear that potential borrowers, in order to qualify for loans, would have to resume payment on debts which had gone into default during the Great Depression.[25] Similarly, countries that nationalize foreign-owned property are required to reach satisfactory compensation arrangements before the World Bank will lend to them.[26] On several occasions, this policy has led to an actual withholding of loans. Perhaps the most notable involved Egypt after the nationalization of the Suez Canal in 1956. Only after Egypt reached a compensation agreement with the Suez Canal Company in 1959 did it receive World-Bank support for the Aswan High Dam project. The Bank even played an important role in negotiating the settlement.[27]

In one instructive respect, the World Bank has proved itself to be even stricter than Western countries in its approach to nationalization. It has insisted that nationalizations undertaken for political, rather than for bona fide economic, purposes are impermissible, even if full compensation is paid.[28] This position is, of course, a reflection of the basic dualistic structure of the international system generally, with its insistence on the exclusion of political factors from the sphere of economic relations.

Finally, we should note the measures that the Bank takes against states which violate obligations owed directly to it. It may suspend any member state which violates any of the duties set forth in the Articles of Agreement. If the state does not mend its ways after one year, then the suspension ripens into expulsion.[29] The only country, so far, to suffer this ignominious fate is Czechoslovakia, which was suspended in 1953 for failure to pay its subscription. At the end of 1954, it was duly expelled.[30] In addition, the Bank, as a matter of operational practice, takes certain steps against borrowers that default on their loan repayments. It is a sternly inflexible lender, resolutely refusing to reschedule past loans (so as to protect its own credit rating as a borrower on the international capital markets). If a borrowing country falls into arrears on scheduled repayments for seventy-five days, the Bank halts further disbursements to it, although it refrains from publicly identifying the delinquent. Once the arrearages have extended for six months, however, the Bank does make a public pronouncement. For a very long time, it had no occasion to make use of these devices. Chile fell into default briefly during the early 1970s. But it was only in the 1980s, with the general global recession, the steep fall in commodity prices and the intensification of the international debt crisis, that defaulting occurred on any scale. By the middle of 1988, eight countries had been identified by the Bank as being six months in arrears: Nicaragua, Guyana, Syria, Liberia, Peru, Sierra Leone, Zambia and Panama.[31]

Of the three principal international economic organizations, the IMF has the greatest role to play as an upholder of free-market economic orthodoxy and nemesis of economic nationalism.[32] It was noted above that the Fund is a dedicated foe of the various exchange-rate management devices that commonly accompany import-substitution development programs—multi-tier exchange rates, the administrative rationing of foreign currency, and the deliberate overvaluation of exchange rates. Most egregious of these manifold sins is probably the maintenance of an overvalued currency—that essential component of the "policy of provision" which third-world countries often follow in selected economic sectors. The IMF's stoutly negative attitude toward this practice emerges clearly from the text of the Second Amendment of the Fund's Articles of Agreement, adopted in 1976 and in force in 1978.[33] The amendment permits states parties to adopt policies of flexible, rather than fixed, exchange rates. At the same time, it imposes a general requirement that countries "avoid manipulating exchange rates . . . to gain an unfair competitive advantage over other members." To ensure that this command is being observed, the Second Amendment entrusts the IMF with the task of exercising continuous surveillance over the exchange-rate policies of its members. The agency's "Principles of Surveillance over Exchange Rate Policies," adopted in 1977, identify some of the things that would alert it to possible misconduct by a member: "protracted large-scale intervention in one direction in the exchange market"; excessive borrowing for balance-of-payments (as opposed to investment) purposes; the pursuit of policies that provide "abnormal encouragement or discouragement to capital flows"; and, more generally, any exchange-rate behavior "that appears to be unrelated to underlying economic and financial conditions."[34] The general thrust of these concerns is clear. Exchange rates should be a fair reflection of basic economic realities and should not function as a means for manipulating or distorting the economy.

The IMF has three principal enforcement techniques at its disposal, two of which are explicitly spelled out in its Articles of Agreement. The lesser of these two sanctions is a declaration by the IMF that a member state is ineligible to use its resources. Such declarations may be made on several grounds: an unauthorized change by a state in the par value of its currency; the use of borrowed resources contrary to the purposes of the Fund; the use of borrowed funds to meet "a large and sustained capital outflow"; or, more generally, any failure on the part of a state to fulfill its obligations under the Articles of Agreement.[35] Early declarations of ineligibility were made against France in 1948 and Czechoslovakia in 1953, in both cases for unauthorized changes in par values. (France was restored to grace in 1954.)[36] More recently, this penalty has been invoked in cases where states have defaulted on the repayment of sums borrowed from the Fund. Cuba, in 1964, was on the brink of being declared ineligible on this ground, when it forestalled matters by withdrawing from the IMF.[37] It was only in the 1980s, however, that arrearages on repayments to the Fund led to the use of this sanction on a significant scale. By the middle of 1989, nine countries were in the ineligibility category: Vietnam, Guyana, Liberia, Sudan, Peru, Zambia, Sierra Leone, Somalia and Panama.[38]

The more severe sanction provided for in the IMF Articles of Agreement is outright expulsion from the organization. This may be the fate of a country that persists in a failure to fulfill its obligations to the Fund for an unreasonable period of time. This penalty has been inflicted only once, when Czechoslovakia was, in effect, expelled in 1954. (There remains some doubt about the legal technicalities in the matter. The IMF intimated to Czechoslovakia that, as a result of its unauthorized par-value change and its failure to make amends within a reasonable time, its membership in the Fund had lapsed as of the end of 1954. Czechoslovakia refused to accept this termination of its membership and purported instead, in May 1955, to withdraw from the organization voluntarily.)[39]

These two formal sanctions conferred onto the IMF by its Articles of Agreement have not been the source of any great controversy. The same cannot be said, however, of the other principal means at the IMF's disposal for the enforcement of liberal economic orthodoxy: the policy known as conditionality, i.e., of simply declining to lend to an applicant country that fails to adopt general economic policies which the IMF believes are necessary for the stabilization of its currency. As a variant of this policy, the Fund can discontinue disbursements previously arranged if the country fails to implement measures agreed upon. This policy of conditionality is not explicitly conferred by, or mentioned in, the Articles of Agreement. It has evolved over a number of years as a matter of organizational practice.[40] A crucial early step came in 1952, when the executive board decided that borrowers' general economic policies should be such as to enable them to cope with balance-of-payments problems over a three-to-five year period. After reviews of the conditionality policy in the late 1960s and again in the late 1970s, a set of guidelines on the subject was issued in 1979.[41] These guidelines provide for continuous consultation between the IMF and the borrowing country throughout the course of the loan, as well as for periodic reviews of programs by the IMF staff. Borrowing states are expected to meet various performance criteria, and their conduct in this regard is to be analyzed and assessed by the IMF staff. In order to avoid the appearance of dictation by the Fund to the member states—or, indeed, even the existence of formal agreements between the two—the practice is that the conditions for an IMF loan take the form of a unilateral commitment by the borrowing state, expressed in a "letter of intent," which it furnishes to the Fund at the outset of the arrangement. Failure to meet the conditions, therefore, is not, strictly speaking, a breach of international law on the part of the state. It is, however, grounds for a suspension of support by the IMF.[42]

The details of the IMF's conditionality policy have been the subject of extensive study (and controversy) elsewhere.[43] Here, it is only necessary to make a few points about the general character of IMF adjustment programs.[44] Broadly speaking, they are likely to be incompatible with import-substitution development programs and, more generally, with economic nationalist policies. The IMF typically seeks to increase the export orientation of the economy in question, so as to raise general world demand for its currency. The most obvious single step in this direction is the devaluation of the borrowing country's currency, which increases foreign demand for its goods by the simple device of making them cheaper for foreigners. It is equally obvious, though, that devaluation undermines "policies of provision" of the kind described above, by making essential imports (and all other imports as well) more expensive from the standpoint of the developing state. In addition, devaluation policies produce their inhibiting effects on imports immediately, whereas their stimulatory effects upon exports are only realized in the longer term. For this reason, some developing countries tenaciously resist the harsh medicine of devaluation. Other parts of the typical IMF package are often equally unwelcome to developing countries. The Fund commonly presses for reductions in government spending, particularly on consumer subsidies (as opposed to investment). The sharp increases in consumer prices of basic commodities which this policy can entail raise the spectre of public unrest.

It is hardly to be wondered at, that practicing politicians in the third world commonly look upon IMF adjustment policies in much the same way that rulers of the eighteenth century looked upon the program of the physiocrats. The prescriptions of the IMF, like those of Quesnay and his fellow Confucian literati, are often condemned as too impractical, too "academic" or theoretical, too doctrinaire, too far divorced from harsh political reality. There is at least some truth in these contentions, just as there was in the eighteenth century. For societies that are continuously haunted by shortage and privation— as so much of the third world is—"policies of provision" can only be abandoned with considerable trepidation. As in the eighteenth century, the implementation of the free-market principles of the literati have sometimes led directly to social disturbances. During the 1970s and 1980s, "IMF riots" became a dispiritingly common feature of the third-world landscape—Egypt in 1977, Zambia in 1986–87, Algeria in 1988 and Jordan and Venezuela in 1989 provide ready illustrations.

The viewpoint of the beleaguered politicians of the developing world was articulated in 1989 by President Carlos Andres Perez of Venezuela. In the wake of the destructive outbreaks in his country that followed the implementation of an IMF-approved program, he wrote plaintively to the managing director of the IMF. Of the Fund's general approach, he commented:

> Its formulas are unobjectionable from the technical standpoint, and its aims are most surely sound. But they take no account at all of the . . . economic realities in the countries where they are implemented. This is tantamount to giving medicine to a patient without taking into account his physical condition or capacity to withstand it, and without taking other steps to strengthen his ability to tolerate the dose. . . . No consideration is given to the possibilities for economic growth or to halting the serious deterioration of the society's health provoked by the adjustment measures; there is thus a serious impact on the poorest sectors of our countries, which explode with despair, fostered by injustice, in the appalling violence we have seen unleashed in the streets of Caracas, and which we are sure to see and experience again in cities elsewhere in the developing world.[45]

Here, in poignant modern form, is the age-old concern of the economic nationalist for the overall health of society, rather than for the liberation of individual entrepreneurs.

However sad their plight, developing countries that are desperate for assistance are seldom able to resist the advice of the IMF for long. The main reason is that alternate forms of assistance, such as loans and loan reschedulings from both public and private sources, are frequently conditioned on the implementation of IMF-approved policies. One of the most stubborn, but ultimately unsuccessful, attempts to defy the Fund was made by Tanzania in the 1980s. That country's much-vaunted program of "African socialism" was dogmatically inward-looking, at least in principle, which hardly boded well for harmonious dealings with the IMF. In 1980, relations between the two turned sour, with the collapse of a standby arrangement because of Tanzania's failure to fulfill conditions set out in its letter of intent. Over a period of some six years, the two sides tenaciously held their ground, the IMF refusing to lend and the Tanzanian government refusing to alter its economic policies. In the course of the long contest of wills, President Julius Nyerere loudly excoriated the IMF as "capitalism's policeman" and denounced it as a colonialist power.[46] In the end, however, the country gave in. After a change of leadership in

1986, the new government consented to a 33 percent devaluation of the currency, an increase in consumer prices and the imposition of a ceiling on public-sector borrowing and credit expansion. The reward was a standby arrangement from the IMF for SDR 650 million, plus the opening of access to World Bank assistance. The price was the abandonment of "African socialism."[47]

THE "UNOFFICIAL" CRUSADE AGAINST ECONOMIC NATIONALISM: INDIVIDUAL STATES AS AUXILIARIES

Among the countries of the world, the foremost proponents of a liberal, open-door international economy are the developed Western states (plus Japan). In light of the obvious vested interest that those countries have in such a system, it may be surmised that self-interest plays a rather greater role than idealism. In any event, the developed countries, with their hunger for open export markets and their solicitude for protecting the rights and property of foreign investors, have sometimes proved to be willing—even eager—"takers of the cross" against the heresy of economic nationalism. From the standpoint of the third-world countries, the picture naturally appears somewhat different. To them, the activities of the developed states look rather more like vigilantism in the cause of material self-interest. In their view, the activities of the advanced states often amount to nothing more than a direct continuation of nineteenth-century gunboat diplomacy.

The more spectacular methods of the nineteenth century, however, have fallen largely, although not entirely, into disuse. On only one occasion since World War II, the Suez Canal nationalization of 1956, has military force been used for the protection of foreign investments —and then, only with much controversy.[48] For the most part, the modern-day gunboats are of a financial rather than a ferrugenous character.[49] The two main weapons available to states are those already identified: capital embargoes and trade restrictions (with some overlap between the two). These measures can be imposed by private-sector interests on their own initiative, as well as, or in coordination with, state governments, in the style of the associationalism of the 1920s. It happens, as will be observed presently, that action by the private sector has frequently been more effective than that of governments.

Capital embargoes can take the form, familiar from the nineteenth century and from the 1920s, of a choking off of private lending by state government action. Since this kind of measure can impair the ability of the target country to finance imports, it can also have a trade-restriction effect. In addition, capital embargoes come in more modern forms, such as a reduction of foreign aid. This, too, can have a trade-restriction component, since it can take the form of a revocation of the privilege of preferential trade treatment.

Boycotting is a familiar practice, but it too has some modern guises. The most notable is the phenomenon of the "hot commodity" campaign, which by its nature is a private-sector initiative. It is based on the thesis that a state which nationalizes property, say an oil concession, without paying full compensation thereby violates international law. As a consequence, it does not acquire good legal title to the property taken. The nationalizing state, in short, is a thief; and it is a general principle of law that thieves do not acquire legal title to things which they steal. On that assumption, no one who purchases from the nationalizing state can acquire valid title either. A nationalization victim waging a "hot commodity" campaign therefore gives general notice to the world that he will assert his rights as the true legal owner of the nationalized property, i.e., he will sue in the domestic courts of countries around the world to reclaim the property (or the fruits thereof) from anyone who purchases from the villainous state. Potential buyers are therefore put on notice that, as holders of stolen property, they stand to be divested of their title. The purpose of such a campaign is, of course, to discourage would-be purchasers from buying and thereby to prevent the state from marketing the nationalized goods. The result—if the campaign is successful—is a de facto boycott of the nationalizing state.[50]

In general, it cannot be said that either of these principal weapons —capital embargoes or boycotts—has been particularly successful in "persuading" refractory countries to alter or reverse their policies, although it is quite possible that they have had some *in terrorem* effect. Their real function, in fact if not by design, has probably been to define and delineate the frontiers of acceptable economic conduct —from the basic liberal capitalist standpoint, that is—and sternly to remind the developing countries of their obligations as good citizens of the global "mercantile republick." The various measures of economic reprisal have therefore functioned more as economic civics lessons than as effective police actions. A brief illustrative survey of this aspect of the campaign against economic nationalism is therefore all that is necessary here. We shall deal first with the responses to the problem of debt defaults and then turn our attention to the nationalization of foreign-owned property. The focus naturally will be on the activities of the developed state which has assumed the highest profile in both of these areas: the United States.[51]

Debt defaults by states had been one of the concerns of the American loan-supervision program of the 1920s. They have continued to be. In 1934, the United States reaffirmed its disapproval of debt defaulters by adopting the Johnson Debt Default Act, which was an attempt to choke off private lending to states which had failed to pay their debts to the United States government.[52] The law made such lending by American nationals a criminal offence. It has been almost completely ineffective, however, because of the large number of major exceptions made over the years. A statutory amendment of 1945, for example, removed states members of the IMF from its field of application.[53] In addition, the law has been held, by interpretation, not to prohibit the granting of routine trade credits, and also not to apply to the activities of Americans abroad (including overseas branches of American banks). In over half a century of the law's existence, there has not, as yet, been a single prosecution.[54]

In the early 1960s, the United States took some further steps against debt defaulters, by inaugurating a policy of cutting off foreign aid (including, since 1974, tariff preferences) to states that fall behind by more than six months in debt repayments to the United States government.[55] This policy, unlike the Johnson Act, has been acted upon. In 1988, for example, Zambia suffered a suspension of aid on this ground.[56] The United States has a similar policy of discontinuing foreign aid to states which default on debts to U.S. nationals.[57]

It would appear that aid reductions are, in general, not very effective as coercive devices.[58] The reason is simple enough. Foreign aid is usually modest in quantity, so that its loss has no serious impact. This is especially so, if (as is frequently the case) continuing aid programs are left in place when the sanction is imposed. It would appear that capital embargoes can probably only be truly effective when the private sector is highly mobilized. On one notable occasion when that was so, the target country did capitulate. This was Brazil, which brazenly instituted a unilateral moratorium on its interest payments to private banks in 1987. A painful year later, it confessed that the policy had been a mistake. Three forms of response by Western governments and private banks had cost it dearly. One was the cutting off of support from the Western governmental export-credit agencies, which virtually halted Brazil's imports of capital goods. In addition, private trade credits dwindled alarmingly, also with a serious effect on imports. Finally, Brazil missed the opportunity to negotiate lower interest rates on its loans from private banks. By the beginning of 1988, the country was sheepishly taking steps to restore its credit-worthiness.[59]

Against the most conspicuous form of economic nationalist wrong-doing—the nationalization of property without full compensation—developed countries have deployed both capital embargoes and various forms of boycotting. These measures have not been very successful in reversing nationalization policies of developing countries, or in obtaining compensation at a level wholly satisfactory to the companies involved. They may have been effective, however, in various other ways. For example, they have sometimes succeeded in inflicting genuine economic harm onto the nationalizing country, thereby (perhaps) adding to its inducement to negotiate an eventual settlement of the matter. In addition, the threat of retaliatory measures may have discouraged would-be nationalizers from taking to the path of plunder.

An instructive illustration of these various factors in operation is the first major third-world nationalization crisis, the expropriation by Mexico of foreign-owned oil interests in 1938—the occasion, incidentally, for Secretary of State Hull's famous articulation of the "adequate, prompt and effective" standard for compensation.[60] In this pre-foreign-aid era, there was no scope for a reduction in foreign assistance to Mexico. The United States, however, together with the oil companies, did adopt several types of boycott measure. One was to halt purchases (if only for a short time) of silver from Mexico. This proved to be little more than a symbolic gesture, since the United States merely shifted its purchasing to the spot market, where much of the silver was of Mexican origin in any event.[61]

In addition, there was a campaign to boycott Mexican oil. The Department of State publicly urged U.S. nationals not to purchase oil of Mexican origin. At the same time, the victim companies organized a "hot oil" campaign against Mexico, the earliest major instance of a "hot commodity" campaign of the kind described above.[62] It was largely unsuccessful, however, because of the reluctance of courts to hold that Mexico's legal title to the oil was invalid. Even courts in the United States declined to make rulings to that effect, on the principle (known as the foreign act of state doctrine) that the courts of one country should refrain from judging the legality of acts undertaken by a foreign state in its own territory.[63] This principle is the juridical rock upon which most "hot commodity" campaigns have foundered.[64]

The most damaging economic measure taken against Mexico, by a considerable margin, was the tanker boycott organized by the oil companies. In an impressive display of capitalist solidarity, the owners of some 90 percent of the world's tanker tonnage refused to lease vessels to Mexico and thereby seriously impeded its ability to market the newly nationalized oil. Oil sales in 1938 (in peso terms) declined by about 50 percent compared with the previous year. Even this measure, however, did not, on its own, force Mexico into a settlement. The United States government eventually decided that, in the face of the general crisis in world affairs, a mending of fences with its southern neighbor was appropriate. Accordingly, in 1941, a settlement agreement was arrived at between the two countries, in which the United States agreed to accept compensation that was significantly below what the oil companies had been demanding. The companies protested loudly but to no avail.[65]

A broadly similar series of boycott efforts were mounted against Iran, after its nationalization of the British-owned Anglo-Iranian Oil Company by a left-wing nationalist government in 1951. Because of Iran's membership in the Sterling Area, Britain was in a position to impose various currency regulations that had the effect of subjecting it to de facto trade embargoes. Requiring Iran to obtain the permission of the Bank of England before it could use sterling to pay for imports meant that it could be deprived of the ability to import goods from any Sterling-Area country. Similarly, requiring Iran to obtain the Bank of England's permission to exchange sterling for dollars hampered its ability to import goods from the rest of the world as well.[66] In addition, a "hot oil" campaign was mounted by a the victim company similar to the one against Mexico. As in the Mexican case, however, the foreign act of state doctrine meant that, for the most part, courts in various countries were reluctant to question Iran's legal title to the nationalized oil.[67]

Also as in the case of Mexico, the most damaging response was a boycott campaign mounted by the international oil companies. Unfortunately for Iran, the nationalization took place during a period of serious over-supply in the world oil markets. It was therefore relatively easy to induce potential purchasers to forego Iranian oil and to buy from other sources instead. The result was a catastrophic 95 percent decline in Iranian oil export revenues. Again as in the case of

Mexico, however, it was not the economic pressure alone that brought the crisis to an end. This time, a coup d'état within Iran brought a new government to power that was willing to reverse the nationalization measures.[68] Nationalization crises have been played out on several occasions along these same general lines. "Hot commodity" campaigns have continued to be waged, and have continued to be largely unsuccessful. "Hot sugar" and "hot tobacco" efforts by American companies against Cuba in the 1960s failed, again largely because of the foreign act of state doctrine.[69] Perhaps the most ambitious "hot commodity" campaign of all was by BP against Libya in the early 1970s, following the nationalization of its interests on political grounds (as a measure of reprisal against the United Kingdom for refusing to act against Iranian expansionism in the Persian Gulf). Again, however, the foreign act of state doctrine frustrated the effort.[70]

Aid reductions have also been invoked against states nationalizing foreign-owned property, but with little apparent effect. The most ambitious effort was the American policy, set out in the Hickenlooper Amendment of 1962, of automatically halting foreign aid to countries that nationalized American-owned property in violation of international law.[71] In later years, parallel measures of various kinds were enacted to supplement this policy. In 1972, the Gonzalez Amendment was adopted, compelling American directors in the World Bank and the various regional development banks to vote against all loans to countries nationalizing American-owned property without paying full compensation.[72] A similar threat was built into the tariff preferences for developing states which the United States instituted in 1974: any state nationalizing property without paying full compensation risks the loss of its preferential status.[73] None of these measures has ever amounted to much. The Hickenlooper Amendment has been invoked only once, against Ceylon in 1963–65, after it nationalized gasoline stations owned by American oil companies. It duly agreed to compensate the companies in exchange for a restoration of the aid.[74] The exclusion from the tariff-preference program was invoked against the Congo in 1977.[75]

Inflexible measures of this kind, however, can sometimes be more of a hindrance than a help in nationalization crises. That was the case in the affair of the nationalization by Peru in 1968 of the American-owned International Petroleum Company (I.P.C.). It is interesting to note that, while the Nixon administration did reduce foreign aid to Peru as a means of pressure, it shied away from formally invoking the

Hickenlooper Amendment. The (supposed) inflexibility of the amendment gave it an excessively dictatorial aura which, it was feared, would unduly sour the negotiating process. In all events, a negotiated settlement was eventually reached, in 1974, without a formal resort to the amendment.[76] In the course of this affair, the Hickenlooper Amendment was quietly relegated to oblivion by having the aid reduction made discretionary, rather than mandatory.[77] (The Gonzales Amendment, in contrast, has not been formally so relaxed, although the position de facto is that the discretionary approach is applied to American voting in the multilateral development banks as well.)[78]

On the whole, then, the function of both capital-embargo and boycott campaigns has been more to indicate disapproval of the conduct against which they are directed than actually to coerce the target countries. Aid cuts and "hot commodity" campaigns function as little more than standard dramatic devices in set-piece political-economy morality plays, which are usually preludes (after greater or lesser intervals) to serious negotiations. The fact remains that patient bargaining is generally more productive than confrontation in resolving nationalization disputes.

Even in the political-economy morality play *par excellence* of the post-World War II period—the confrontation between Chile and the United States in 1970–73—the U.S. economic reprisal measures had little material significance. This affair was a classic contest, pitting an American government (under President Richard Nixon) committed to the protection of U.S. business interests, against a third-world nationalist and socialist government (under President Salvador Allende) equally and oppositely committed to the struggle against economic imperialism.[79] The material spoils of the battle were the massive investments by American copper companies in Chile. More broadly, the issue was whether the advanced capitalist countries, when put to the test, did or did not possess the power to bring third-world economic nationalism to heel. With his aggressive posture and flair for publicity, Allende succeeded in making his nationalization effort into a *cause célèbre* throughout the third world.

Allende commenced the struggle on a defiant note. He contended that the past "excess profits" of the copper companies should be deducted from the compensation owing to them from the nationalization. The result, on the Chilean government's calculation, was that the companies owed money to it. The United States government, predictably, was outraged. It responded by organizing an economic campaign of the standard kind already described. It sharply reduced its bilateral aid commitments to Chile (although it did not disrupt continuing aid programs). It refused to reschedule intergovernmental debts owed to it by Chile (although it did not attempt to prevent other Western creditor governments from doing so). Loans to Chile from both private American banks and multilateral lending institutions dropped sharply. In the case of the Inter-American Development Bank, there is circumstantial evidence to suggest that American displeasure with Chile was a factor.[80] In addition, a "hot copper" campaign was launched to discourage potential purchasers from buying Chilean copper. Finally, the United States provided some financial assistance to opposition groups within Chile, most notably to striking transport workers and to opposition political parties.[81]

These measures, however, would appear to have had little effect on Chile, even in the aggregate. Other countries stepped readily into the foreign-assistance gap left by the United States, with the result that total foreign aid to Chile actually rose rather than declined during Allende's tenure. Also, other Western creditor states did reschedule Chilean loans. As a result, the financial pressure on the Allende government was not serious. Nor did the "hot copper" campaign meet with any greater success than such efforts generally have, for the reasons set out above. The foreign act of state doctrine, together with various other legal difficulties, meant that Chilean copper could be marketed without undue difficulty.[82] Finally, the American support for the opposition groups within Chile would appear not to have had a significant effect. The final—and abrupt—downfall of the Allende government came from quite another source: the Chilean military, which overthrew it in a bloody coup d'état in September 1973.

Ironically, it was in the interest of supporters of both Allende and the United States to exaggerate the material impact of the various American economic measures. From the standpoint of the United States, the *in terrorem* effect of the steps taken against Chile would be all the greater if its economic measures were widely (even if mistakenly) perceived to have been devastatingly effective. It was also to Allende's advantage to play up the significance of the measures, so as to lend greater credibility to claims that all of his difficulties were the fault of the vindictive giant to the north and generally to attract sympathy from the third world.

The real significance of the confrontation between Chile and the United States lay not in the material injury that either country inflicted upon the other, but rather in the way that it highlighted the alignment of vested interests of the various blocs of countries on the question of economic nationalism. One of the ambitions (if not the promises) of classical liberal economics is to show the way toward the maximization of the utility of the entire world considered as a single unit. Perhaps that claim is correct. Even assuming that it is, however, some will inevitably profit more than others from venture. There is little indication, so far, that the global "mercantile republick" will be a classless society. On the contrary, specialization, through the mechanism of the world-wide division of labor, is of the very essence of the liberal system. And that would appear to mean that some regions of the world would be fated to specialize for very long periods of time in such activities as agriculture or raw-material production. Given the immense prestige of industrialization, it is unreasonable to expect many countries passively to accept such a fate. As Edmund Burke shrewdly observed in another context, no one will be argued into slavery.

Many of the classical political economists of the nineteenth century, and of the interwar period, failed to appreciate this point. Particularly in the nineteenth century, there was a widespread assumption that opposition to the liberal program could only stem from ignorance of the newly revealed truths of political economy. There has been a tendency to portray the duel between economic liberalism and nationalism as a Manichaean struggle between enlightenment and superstition, between progress and reaction. Such a view is no longer tenable, and indeed never was. Economic nationalism is not, and never has been, a matter of mere obstinate provincialism (although there is no doubt that it has elements of that). It has far deeper roots both in human history and, quite probably, the human psyche as well. Economic nationalists have always perceived—and rightly so—that there is a certain abstract and doctrinaire spirit to liberalism. We have observed that the instinctive suspicion of practicing politicians toward the physiocrats in the eighteenth century and toward the IMF today are both based on this observation. The most perceptive liberal economists have readily conceded this point. Stanley Jevons, for example, candidly admitted that liberal economics had a natural appeal to persons "trustful in abstract principles."[83] Indeed, what is the concept of a global "mercantile republick" but an abstract principle on the very grandest of scales?

To the masses of mankind, the local community, the *polis* and the nation-state are more concrete and immediate entities than the terrestrial orb at large. The great religions may preach the unity of all mankind, but personal prayers are more commonly to local saints.

Economic nationalism reflects, as it always has, a deep-seated concern for the solidarity of the local community and the integrity of the social bonds that unite it. Ideas of social welfare and cooperation come naturally to it, as they do not to liberalism, with its atomistic and competitive ethos. It is hardly to be wondered at—save by those of an abstract turn of mind—that the masses of mankind (and their rulers) show an instinctive preference for the bonds of the family, community and nation over the prospect of arms-length contractual ties with total strangers from faraway parts of the globe. When the rootless entrepreneur comes into conflict with the home-grown patriot, there can be little doubt where the sympathies of the masses will lie. That is why Richard Nixon is so easily portrayed as an economic imperialist, and Salvador Allende as a patriotic martyr. Third-world economic nationalism, then, is unlikely to fade away even in the face of the most determined assaults by the literati of the World Bank and the IMF, or by the most aggressive pursuers of "hot commodities." On the contrary, the massive swelling in the ranks of third-world nations since 1945, and especially since 1960, has inevitably led to something of a resurgence of economic nationalism, in much the way that the advent of the new states onto the European scene after the Great War fuelled economic nationalism in the interwar years. By the 1960s, it was clear that the developing countries would constitute, for as far as anyone could foresee, a heavy majority of states on the international scene. Such a prospect could hardly fail to open up some interesting possibilities. One of these proved to be the development of —although it may sound paradoxical—a program of global economic nationalism, in conscious opposition to the liberal vision of a single integrated world economy.

SEVEN

GLOBAL ECONOMIC NATIONALISM:
Third-World Plans for a Social Democratic World Order

Economic nationalism is inward-looking in the sense that its primary, and ultimate, concern is with the development (economic and otherwise) of the nation-state as a collective unit. That is not to say, however, that economic nationalists favor cutting off all links with the outside world. Only the most extreme ones, such as Plato and Fichte, have taken such a line. The dominant, and more moderate, line of thought, in the tradition of List and Prebisch, has taken, on the contrary, a strong interest in relations with other states—and, more generally, with the question of the most appropriate system of international economic order. One of the earliest writers to speculate in this area was Friedrich Naumann, who, early in the twentieth century, posited the imminent passing away of the "commercial" (i.e., liberal) age of international economic relations, and the onset of a "social democratic" one.[1] At that time, the idea was little more than a suggestion. It was only during the post-World War II age, with the massive influx of new developing countries onto the world scene, that the notion could be spelled out in some detail. By the 1970s, it attained substantially canonical form, as the third-world program for a "new international economic order."

This proposed "new international economic order" is anything but new. From the economic standpoint, it is quite clearly rooted in nineteenth-century economic nationalism. From the legal standpoint, too, it is thoroughly traditional. The 1974 Declaration on the Establishment of a New International Economic Order, promulgated by the UN General Assembly, stated as the first of the principles on which the new order was based: "Sovereign equality of States, self-determination of all peoples, inadmissibility of the acquisition of territories by force, territorial integrity and non-interference in the internal affairs of other States."[2] This proposed world order, therefore, is essentially *political* in character rather than economic, in the sense that it is strongly oriented toward the interests of states rather than of peoples.

A social democratic system of world order envisages a world network of states on the model of Bismarckian Germany—i.e., a world of sovereign and independent countries, each engaged in developing a balanced economy within its own borders. International economic relations, on this model, are to be restructured with a view to facilitating this basic process. International arrangements, accordingly, should be designed not (as in the liberal system) to break down barriers between individual entrepreneurs, but rather to enhance the development prospects of the various nation-states as such. More specifically, the international economic system should be structured so as to enable the less developed states to "catch up" with their more advanced brethren by diversifying their national economies (i.e., by industrializing). International trade is to be governed not by the single sweeping principle of laissez-faire, but rather by "such rules as are consistent with the attainment of economic and social progress."[3] The fundamental goal of the "new international economic order," in sum, is to transform the liberal international economic system into a mechanism for promoting the *national* economic development of the countries of the world and, more specifically, to effect a redistribution of resources from the advanced nations to the poorer ones.

This emphasis on redistribution meant that one of the earliest and most prominent elements of the third-world program concerned the question of nationalization of foreign investment—under the rubric of "permanent sovereignty over natural resources." The concern in this regard was two-fold: first, to establish as clearly as possible the legal right of states to nationalize property (i.e., to reassert their inalienable sovereignty over their own resources); and second, to provide nationalizing countries with a measure of legal protection against the kind of retaliatory measures described in the previous chapter. From this second concern arose the third-world campaign to prohibit "economic coercion." Superficially, this campaign against economic coercion would appear to coincide with the general trend, discussed in Chapter 5, to restrict the waging of economic warfare. In fact, the differences between these two efforts are far more significant than the similarities. Where the liberal opposition to economic warfare is a function of the broader desire to promote freedom of trade for individuals and to integrate the entire world into a single global "mercantile republick," the third-world campaign against economic coercion is quite clearly economic nationalist in character. It is designed to safe-guard the traditional sovereign rights of states in the economic sphere, as they were laid down in the eighteenth century by Wolff and Vattel.[4]

The broader program for a "new international economic order" is of the same nature. It is forward-looking in its almost bewildering range of proposed reforms. At the same time, however, it is staunchly conservative in its fundamental legal principles. At its core is a dogmatic assertion of the traditional positivist principle of the sovereign equality of states. Ironically, this very conservatism is a factor which stands in the way of the realization of the third world's grand design for the creation of a transnational "welfare state."

FENDING OFF THE VIGILANTES: THE THIRD-WORLD EFFORT TO PROHIBIT "ECONOMIC COERCION"

The developing countries began their counter-attack against some of the more aggressive tendencies of the liberal "mercantile republick" during the nineteenth century. We have observed that the development of the Calvo doctrine dates to that period, with its reassertion of the traditional right to states to achieve "perfection" according to their own dictates, even if that entailed transgressing the norms of the wider "mercantile republick." Although the validity of the Calvo doctrine remains an open question to this day in international law, the developing countries did succeed in placing at least one mild restriction on the use of gunboat diplomacy in the cause of liberal economic orthodoxy. The Porter Convention of 1907 limited the use of armed reprisals in contractual disputes to cases in which the alleged delinquent state had refused arbitration or had failed to implement an arbitral award.[5]

After the Second World War, the focus of the battle shifted somewhat. The most contentious issue became nationalization of property by developing states, rather than denials of justice or breaches of contract; and the retaliation from the developed states now assumed more typically an economic than a military form. The developing countries, accordingly, sought to place legal limits on the kinds of economic retaliation described in the previous chapter. This was the impetus behind the formulation of the concept of permanent sovereignty over natural resources in the early 1950s. The very name of the doctrine has an obviously nationalistic ring to it.[6] Like the Calvo doctrine, it is an appeal to the norms of traditional international law in the field of economic relations. Its thrust is quite straightforward. It asserts that, as an intrinsic attribute of its sovereignty, a state is entitled to control the use and exploitation of any natural resource which the accidents of geography happen to place within its territory. This basic belief has several notable implications. One is that the territorial state is entitled, if it wishes, to withhold those resources from the stream of world commerce, as Wolff and Vattel vigorously asserted and as La Pradelle just as vigorously denied. Another implication is that the state has the right to reassert its sovereignty over such resources even after it has (supposedly) alienated them to foreign private investors.

That much of the doctrine is relatively uncontroversial, at least as a matter of general international law. What is decidedly more contentious are two other implications of this principle, as propounded by the developing states. One is that, if this right of nationalization is to be made effective in practice, then the developed countries whose interests are affected must be barred from taking retaliatory measures. The other is that it should be wholly within the province of the nationalizing state to determine what level of compensation would be appropriate for the interests affected. The basic principle of permanent sovereignty over natural resources has become accepted as a rule of customary international law[7]—but only at the expense of the careful concealment of the disagreement over these two points. A glance at the historical development of the concept will explain how this has occurred.

The most instructive discussion of permanent sovereignty over natural resources was the very first one, in 1952, when the idea was initially put forward in the UN General Assembly. The question of economic reprisals by developed states against developing ones was fresh on the delegates' minds because of two recent incidents. One was the Iranian oil nationalization discussed in the previous chapter. The other was the "tin buyers' strike" waged chiefly by the United States in response to alleged manipulation of the tin market by producing countries. The American government had formed the view that countries were holding tin off the world markets in order to drive prices upward in a time of shortages caused by the Korean War. It reacted by centralizing all American tin buying into government hands and then pointedly refusing to purchase on the world markets, so as to drive the price back downward. The policy was effective, but it caused resentment among tin-producing states (chiefly Bolivia).[8]

The initial debates at the UN over the principle of permanent sovereignty over natural resources reflected concerns arising from these incidents. The original draft resolution, submitted by Uruguay, would have had the General Assembly recognize "the right of each country to nationalize and freely exploit its natural wealth, as an essential factor of economic independence."[9] Bolivia then suggested that the resolution should also recommend that the developed countries not take retaliatory action when that right was exercised. Its proposal would have had the General Assembly recommend "that Member States, in deference to the right of each country to nationalize and exploit its natural wealth, should not use their governmental and administrative agencies as instruments of coercion or political or economic intervention."[10]

The developed Western countries lost no time in voicing their misgivings about this proposal. On the subject of permanent sovereignty over natural resources generally, the Netherlands expressed the view that the very concept was a reactionary one. It pointed out that the dominant trend in the world was in precisely the opposite direction, from "economic independence" as referred to in the Uruguayan draft, toward ever more comprehensive *interdependence*. It warned of the dangers involved if the "false doctrines" of economic nationalism, which had had such tragic results in Europe, should begin to spread elsewhere.[11]

In the event, the resolution adopted at that 1952 session was a compromise.[12] The emotive word "nationalize" was omitted, in favor of a less-threatening-sounding right of states "freely to use and exploit their natural wealth whenever deemed desirable by them for their own progress and economic development." In exercising this right, states were to have "due regard, consistently with their sovereignty, to the need for the maintenance of mutual confidence and economic co-operation among nations." This latter phrase could be interpreted, by those so inclined, to imply a requirement that nationalizing states pay full compensation for any property taken. Concerning responses to nationalizations, the resolution recommended that states "refrain from acts, direct or indirect, designed to impede the exercise of the sovereignty of any State over its natural resources."

During the years since the adoption of this leading resolution, the concept of permanent sovereignty over natural resources has undergone a certain evolution, but no real change of character. Its definitive formulation came in 1962, with the adoption by the UN General Assembly of the Declaration on Permanent Sovereignty over Natural Resources.[13] The unanimous support that it received was its passport into the realm of rules of general customary international law.[14] (As a general matter, UN General Assembly resolutions do not, in and of themselves, constitute rules of international law. Strictly speaking, they are only recommendations. What is required to make a principle into a rule of law is a high degree of consensus behind it. Voting in the General Assembly can constitute evidence of such a consensus. Some resolutions, like this 1962 declaration, are even carefully designed with a view to their being adopted by consensus—and, thereby, with a view to their being accepted as rules of law.)[15]

The consensus, however, came only at a price. The price was the deliberate papering over of the two controversial points: the level of compensation, and the right of affected states to take retaliatory measures. On the compensation question, the 1962 declaration delicately stated that "appropriate" compensation is owed to the former owners, in accordance with the rules of the state concerned and of international law (the contents of which were left tantalizingly unspecified).[16] On the question of retaliation, the 1962 declaration was equally delphic. It stated that violations of the right of permanent sovereignty over natural resources are contrary to the spirit and principles of the UN Charter. To the extent that the drafters of the declaration sought to avoid undue controversy, their efforts were a triumphant success. Even the United States, that most vigilant champion of the rights of foreign investors, has expressly conceded that the 1962 declaration expresses the concept of permanent sovereignty over natural resources "in a balanced way," even going so far as to declare the principle, as it was there set forth, to be "almost a sacred right." [17]

The contentious issues, however, could not be papered over forever. They came to a head in the early 1970s, largely as a consequence of the high-profile battle between Chile and the United States over the copper nationalizations. The developing states took up the cause of the Chilean David against the Yankee Goliath, in part by becoming bolder than ever before in their assertion of both the right of nationalization and the impermissibility of subsequent economic retaliation. A good illustration of this more confrontational trend is the Lima Declaration of 1971 by the nonaligned countries, which asserted that:

[E]very country has the sovereign right freely to dispose of its natural resources in the interests of the economic development and well-being of its own people; any external political or economic measures or pressures brought to bear on the exercise of this right is a flagrant violation of the principles of self-determination of peoples and of non-intervention, as set forth in the Charter of the United Nations and, if pursued, could constitute a threat to international peace and security.[18]

President Allende of Chile himself made a characteristically dramatic contribution to the debate when, in an appearance before the UN General Assembly in December 1972, he vigorously attacked both the United States and the various multinational companies which were hampering his program. He, too, expressly linked the concepts of nationalization and economic coercion, making "the categorical assertion that any action likely to hinder or curtail the exercise of a nation's sovereign right freely to dispose of its natural resources entails an act of economic aggression."[19]

Chilean affairs continued to occupy the attention of the UN the following year, when in March 1973, the UN Security Council decamped to Panama for discussions of relevant regional issues. One product of the sessions was the adoption of a resolution (on which the United States, Britain and France abstained) urging states to "refrain from using or encouraging the use of any type of coercive measures" against Latin American states.[20] The resolution did not name either the United States or Chile explicitly, but there was no doubt about what had inspired it.

The subject of economic coercion also played a role at the Conference of Nonaligned Countries of September 1973 (just as the Allende experiment in Chile was coming to its violent end). The conference's Economic Declaration noted the existence of the phenomenon of "overt and covert economic aggression," as exemplified by the activities of multinational companies. The nonaligned states further expressed "their ready and unreserved support to the developing countries . . . which are subject to boycott, economic aggression or political pressure" while struggling to regain control over their natural resources.[21]

The Political Declaration of that same conference called for an "economic dimension" of international security which would guarantee to all states "the right to implement their development programs free from economic aggression and any other form of pressure."[22] Another resolution envisaged the organization of an economic collective-security system for third world states. It stated that, whenever a nonaligned country deemed itself to be a victim of measures of economic coercion, it could request the convening of "a high-level consultative meeting" of such other nonaligned states as it might itself select, to devise a strategy of "collective action." More generally, the resolution envisaged that the nonaligned states should take "joint action" at the UN "with a view to extending the Organization's security system to include economic security."[23]

Plans (or rather hopes) for an economic collective-security arrangement for the Western Hemisphere surfaced soon afterward, in a protocol of amendment to the Rio Treaty, drafted in 1975.[24] Article 11 stated the view of the parties to be that "suitable mechanisms" for the guaranteeing of collective economic security should be provided for in a special treaty. President Ford of the United States, in transmitting the protocol to the Senate for its advice and consent, singled this provision out as "an unfortunate detraction from the Protocol's balance and good sense."[25] The United States's ratification duly contained a reservation on this point, to the effect that it regarded itself as under no obligation to enter into any such arrangement.[26] As of the end of 1989, the protocol to the Rio Treaty had not entered into force, nor had the envisaged special treaty emerged.

The definitive summary of the third-world view on these closely linked issues of nationalization and economic coercion appeared in the Charter of Economic Rights and Duties of States, adopted by the UN General Assembly—though with hardly any support from the developed Western countries—in 1974.[27] Article 2 of the charter, concerning permanent sovereignty over natural resources, explicitly affirmed the right of nationalization, with the payment of "appropriate" compensation (repeating the terminology of the 1962 declaration). It then went on to endorse the Calvo doctrine, by providing that the decision as to what compensation is "appropriate" should be resolved under the domestic law of the nationalizing state.[28] The charter also included an express provision, in Article 32, against "the use of economic, political or any other type of measures to coerce another State in order to obtain from it the subordination of the exercise of its sovereign rights." On this occasion, in marked contrast to the situation in 1962, broad-based consensus was conspicuously absent. Seventeen states (including all of the major developed countries) voted against the provision dealing with compensation. No state voted against Article 32, but most of the Western countries abstained.[29]

What was happening during this period, by degrees, was that the concept of a prohibition against economic coercion was coming to be seen, not merely as a defensive component of the right of permanent sovereignty over natural resources, but rather as an autonomous legal principle, providing *general* protection to developing states against acts of economic hostility by developed ones. It was becoming, in short, an attempt to reverse the failure of Brazil in 1945 to have a general ban on economic coercion written into the UN Charter.

Although the concept of a prohibition against economic coercion has been severed from its original link to the principle of permanent sovereignty over natural resources, it nevertheless has clearly retained its character as a specifically third-world concern. This fact became particularly evident during the 1980s, when a new third-world *cause célèbre* appeared: the struggle of Nicaragua against the United States. At the 1983 session of the UN Conference on Trade and Development (UNCTAD), the developing states successfully sponsored a resolution entitled "Rejection of Coercive Economic Measures," which stated that "all developed countries shall refrain from applying trade restrictions, blockades, embargoes and other economic sanctions incompatible with the provisions of the Charter of the UN . . . against developing countries as a form of political coercion which affects their economic, political and social development."[30] Ever since that time, the adoption of similar resolutions by the UN General Assembly has become an annual, and little-heeded, ritual.[31]

The patience of the Western countries, however, was wearing ever thinner. Most had abstained (as just observed) in the vote on Article 32 of the Charter of Economic Rights and Duties of States. At the 1983 UNCTAD conference, they voiced firmer opposition to the third-world position. No fewer than eighteen countries voted against the economic-coercion resolution, with a further seven abstaining. In the explanations of their votes, the Western countries frequently cited the explicitly one-sided nature of the UNCTAD resolution. Some, such as Greece (on behalf of the EEC states), explicitly objected to the intrusion of political considerations into a conference on economic affairs.[32]

Just how little consensus there was behind the third-world campaign for a prohibition against economic coercion became apparent in the debates in the UN Security Council in 1985, where Nicaragua brought a complaint against the United States trade boycott. A parade of developing countries leaped to Nicaragua's defense, condemning the boycott as illegal, citing such "authority" as Article 32 of the Charter of Economic Rights and Duties of States and the 1983 UNCTAD resolution. The United States dismissed all such contentions by bluntly asserting the sovereign right of states to decide for themselves whether or not to trade with others.[33] There was, not surprisingly, a heavily ritualistic aura to this debate, since the United States, in possession of the veto power, was able to ensure that the resolution adopted by the Council was acceptably innocuous.[34]

Only a brief comment is necessary on the evolution of these two originally correlative—but later disconnected—principles of permanent sovereignty over natural resources, and the prohibition of economic coercion. The outstanding point to note about both of these doctrines is that they are firmly political in character, rather than economic, in the sense that they are concerned with safeguarding the traditional sovereign rights of individual states rather than with promoting economic cooperation for the advancement of mankind as a whole. Therein lies the explanation for the reluctance of the Western countries to endorse an express rule against economic coercion of the kind that the developing states have promoted. It is not that the developed states are opposed to the restriction of economic hostility between countries. On the contrary, they designed the postwar world with just such a goal very firmly in mind. But their method of operation was very different. From the liberal standpoint, the prohibition against economic warfare has never been an autonomous principle. Rather, it has been a logical consequence of a much broader program —involving the integration of the entire world into a single economic community, the promotion of maximum freedom of trade for individuals and the elimination of economic nationalism. As those broader goals inch nearer to achievement, economic warfare will automatically be subjected to greater and greater legal constraint. The third-world concept of an express ban on economic coercion against developing states is entirely different. It is itself an essentially economic nationalist doctrine, designed not to promote the economic integration of mankind generally, but rather to safeguard the sovereign right of states to embark upon economic-development programs of their own choosing. It is a doctrine whose intellectual ancestors are Wolff and Calvo, rather than Mill or La Pradelle.[35]

The most striking illustration of the distinction between the liberal Western and the third-world views of the question of economic warfare is afforded by the Arab oil embargo of 1973–74, which has a very different character, depending upon whether it is viewed from an economic perspective (of the classical liberal kind), or a political one. The embargo was a flagrant violation of what we have termed the "common law" of international economic relations, since it was a blatant intrusion of political concerns into the normal economic relations of states. From the standpoint of the developing countries, however, as well as of traditional international law generally, precisely the opposite conclusion applies. The Arab oil exporters were simply exercising their general sovereign right to refuse to trade. They were also exercising their right of permanent sovereignty over natural resources (i.e., their oil wealth). Ironically, it happened that, during the very period that the embargo was in force, the developing countries were sponsoring another UN General Assembly resolution on permanent sovereignty over natural resources—this one including an explicit statement that states should refrain from using economic coercion against other states. The Arab oil embargoers cheerfully supported the measure, apparently with no wrenching sense of incongruity.[36]

The third-world campaign for a legal ban on economic coercion, then, is largely negative in character, in that it is a defensive measure for upholders of economic nationalism to use against liberal opponents. It is a weapon of international economic class warfare, designed to be a juridical counter to the capital embargoes and boycotts described in the previous chapter. The overall program of the "new international economic order," however, also contains many positive elements, designed to promote the economic welfare of the developing states, rather than merely to defend them from attack. Here, particularly, is where the social democratic aspect of the third-world system comes prominently into play, since the "new international economic order" is, in effect, a design for a transnational social welfare mechanism.

PLANS FOR A GLOBAL WELFARE STATE: THE "NEW INTERNATIONAL ECONOMIC ORDER"

The third-world program for a "new international economic order" is an interesting blend of the progressive and the traditional (if not, indeed, the reactionary). In its aggressively critical tone, and its ringing call for a wholesale transformation of the system of international economic relations, it is a kind of Futurist Manifesto of international political economy. On the progressive side as well is the concern for the disadvantaged and the desire to devise mechanisms for the transferring of resources from the rich to the poor. The UN General Assembly's 1974 Declaration on the New International Economic Order states the determination to "correct inequalities and redress existing injustices, . . . to eliminate the widening gap between the developed and the developing countries and ensure steadily accelerating economic and social development and peace and justice for present and future generations."[37] The zeal and idealism of the humanitarian reformer are everywhere evident in the program.

What is also everywhere evident, however, is a legalistic mentality of the most doggedly traditional sort. Even the most cursory glance at the principal documents of the "new international economic order" will bear this point out. Article 1 of the Charter of Economic Rights and Duties of States, for example, offers a clear insight into the general frame of mind behind the third-world proposals:

> Every State has the sovereign and inalienable right to choose its economic system as well as its political, social and cultural systems in accordance with the will of its people, without outside interference, coercion or threat in any form whatsoever.[38]

The "Fundamentals of international economic relations" set forth in the Charter are in the same vein. The majority are clearly state-centered and political in character, stressing such principles as the sovereign equality of states, non-aggression, non-intervention, peaceful coexistence, the peaceful settlement of disputes and the fulfilment in good faith of international obligations. There is no trace of a concern for the promotion of freedom of trade generally. The "new international economic order," then, is not primarily an economic program at all, in the sense in which a liberal economist would use that term. Rather, it is a political program which seeks to reorder international economic relations along politically determined lines.

The program has been the subject of study elsewhere and so need only be given in outline here.[39] Its overall thrust may be stated simply enough. It is a grand design for the redistribution of global wealth—not, however, from wealthy to poor individuals, but rather from wealthy to poor *states*.[40] It seeks to accomplish this basic goal by means of changes in the whole range of international economic practices and institutions together with the implementation of a number of new programs.[41] In the field of trade, for example, the basic GATT principle of nondiscrimination is to give way to one of "[p]referential and non-reciprocal treatment for developing countries."[42] In particular, the program favors the granting by the developed states of tariff preferences for the nontraditional (i.e., manufactured) exports of the developing countries. Regarding trade in raw materials, the program endorses the formulation of international commodity agreements to regulate and stabilize prices. It also supports the activities of producers' associations, including "joint marketing arrangements."[43] In a clear reference to Prebisch's theory of the declining terms of trade in primary commodities, the program endorses measures to reverse the trend of stagnation or decline in certain commodity prices. More generally, it favors the evolution of "a just and equitable relationship" between the prices of the exports and imports of the developing countries.[44]

Concerning the international monetary system, the goal is to ensure that one of its central purposes is "the promotion and development of the developing countries and the adequate flow of real resources to them."[45] Somewhat surprisingly, there is no overt reference to the IMF's conditionality policies in the detailed Program of Action of the "new international economic order."[46] The principal specific demands are two. One is for "[f]ull and effective participation of developing countries in all phases of decision-making" in the monetary sphere. This point reflects dissatisfaction with the IMF's weighted voting system. The other major demand is for the creation of additional liquidity through the issuing of special drawing rights (SDRs) and their distribution to the developing countries as a form of development assistance (rather than, as at present, distributing them to the entire IMF membership in proportion to their quotas in the Fund).[47]

Regarding the World Bank and the various international development institutions, the third-world program seeks a policy of "untied" assistance (i.e., assistance not confined to a specified project). In ad-

dition, these institutions should take into account "the special situation of each developing country" in deciding upon their lending
policies. The program of action also favors, rather delphically,
"improvement in practices" of these institutions with respect to development financing and international monetary problems.[48]

In addition to these changes in existing practices and institutions,
the program for the "new international economic order" envisages a
variety of other measures. It favors accelerating the transfer of technology to developing countries. It also stresses the right of third-world
states to regulate the activities of multinational companies operating
within their jurisdictions. It proposes an integrated program of commodities, financed by a common fund and covering some eighteen
commodities.[49] Most innovative of all are the proposals to ensure that
the deep sea-bed is administered as a part of the "common heritage
of mankind" and not simply left to the mercy of private capitalist
interests. The third-world proposal has been to establish an international regulatory body that would oversee (and sometimes restrict)
the exploitation of deep seabed resources. Most outstandingly, it would
assess a royalty on mineral production by developed-state enterprises
for the benefit of the developing countries. This arrangement, if it
becomes operative, will therefore be a true international taxation
mechanism.[50]

The program for a "new international economic order" is, in sum,
a grand manifesto for a social democratic system of world economic
order. Its contrast with the classical liberal program is obvious—
explaining why economists from the classical liberal tradition tend to
have only scant regard for it.[51] The liberal approach is libertarian in
character, with the individual entrepreneur or corporation as the
basic economic actor, and the private-law rules of property and contract as the basic norms of conduct. The task of states is to sweep
aside all barriers that lie in the path of private enterprise and to
construct a stable framework in which the forces of free competition
will be allowed the greatest possible scope. The third-world approach,
in contrast, is *dirigiste* in nature, with the nation-state as the primary
economic actor. In this view, the basic task of the international economic system is to promote the economic development (i.e., the industrialization) of the poorer states. The basic intention is to guide,
regulate or manipulate (as the case may be) the world economy, so as
to bring about a flow of real resources from the developed nations to
the developing ones. The intention, in other words, to transform the
liberal "mercantile republick" into a sort of global welfare state.

The goal is ambitious. The implementation remains, to put it mildly, a distant prospect. The nature of the international system is such that wholesale transformations of the kind envisaged here are not to be expected overnight. Change tends to occur incrementally, if at all. That is what has happened in this area. Over the years, more and more changes have been made in a variety of areas, for the benefit of the developing countries. Whether they amount, in the aggregate, to an advance installment on the "new international economic order" is, however, open to some considerable doubt.

In the field of trade, some amendments have been made to the GATT in the interest of the third-world states.[52] In 1955, the provision allowing the contracting parties to authorize the adoption of protective tariffs for infant industries was liberalized somewhat. (This was in response to public complaints by Ceylon about the strictness of the scrutiny applied to a number of its applications under the original provision.)[53] During the following decade, the developed states accepted the principle of nonreciprocity vis-à-vis the developing ones regarding tariff reductions and trade concessions. This decision was then incorporated into an additional protocol to the GATT, drafted in 1965 and in force the following year.[54] These preferences were duly authorized by GATT in 1971 (on a temporary basis, made permanent in 1979) and then implemented by the various GATT parties.[55]

In addition, the World Bank has been brought increasingly into the field of economic development over the years. An important step was taken in this direction in 1960, with the founding of the International Development Association, as an affiliate of the Bank. This new body, unlike the Bank itself, was designed specifically to provide lending on concessionary terms to the developing countries. Over the years, a number of regional development agencies have been established for the same purpose: the Inter-American Development Bank in 1959, the African Development Fund in 1964, the Asian Development Bank in 1966 and the Caribbean Development Bank in 1970. The World Bank itself made an important change in its lending policy in 1980 when it implemented a policy of structural adjustment lending, i.e., lending money for broad-ranging structural economic reforms, rather than merely for single specific projects.[56] In 1989, the Bank made the further step of announcing that it would begin providing support for the reduction of indebtedness as well.[57]

At the IMF, a variety of special funds and programs have been instituted for the purpose of assisting the developing countries. In 1963, the Fund established a Compensatory Financing Facility, to assist states suffering shortfalls in export earnings because of declines in world commodity prices. In 1969, it established a Buffer Stock Facility to assist in the financing of buffer stocks in connection with international commodity agreements. During the 1970s and 1980s, it established facilities to assist developing countries with the financing of certain essential imports—"policy of provision" facilities, as they might be termed. In the wake of the steep oil price rises of 1973–74 came a temporary Oil Facility. Then, in 1981, a facility was instituted to help developing states cope with fluctuations in the prices of cereal imports. (In 1988, this was combined with the Compensatory Financing Facility into a new Compensatory and Contingency Financing Facility.)[58] The creation of SDRs was made possible by an amendment of the Articles of Agreement in 1968.[59] One round of SDR distributions took place in 1970–72, and a second one in 1979–81.

With the passage of time, the IMF has strayed ever further from its original mission of providing support exclusively for balance-of-payments purposes. In 1976, for example, it began a policy of concessionary lending to developing countries, financed by a trust fund from the proceeds of the sale of part of its gold stock. In the late 1980s came some further initiatives. With the repayments from the trust-fund lending, the IMF set up a Structural Adjustment Facility in 1986, analogous to the World Bank program of that name, and for the same purpose. This was supplemented the following year by an Enhanced Structural Adjustment Facility, financed by special loans and contributions from IMF members. In 1989, the IMF, like the World Bank, announced that it would begin to make its resources available for the reduction of indebtedness by its members.[60] In the meantime, it had taken some account of the criticisms of its conditionality policy. Its 1979 guidelines on the subject included a statement that, in devising stabilization programs for its borrowers, the Fund would have "due regard to domestic social and political objectives" of the assisted state.[61]

The developing states also made progress in the creation of some of the new programs which they advocated. In 1980, agreement was reached on a common fund for an integrated program of commodities. It did not enter into force until 1989, however, because of the requirement that two-thirds of the necessary capital had to be committed first—a difficult feat because of the refusal of the United States to become a party.[62] In 1982, a Convention on the Law of the Sea provided for an International Sea-bed Authority that would issue licences for exploitation of the sea-bed and assess royalties on the proceeds, as favored by the developing countries.[63]

As impressive as these various measures might sound at first, they

hardly amount to an implementation of the "new international economic order." The changes have been, on the whole, marginal rather
than fundamental in character. In the area of trade, for example, the
changes to the GATT have amounted to very little in practice. The
provision on protection of infant industries, for example, has fallen
into total disuse. The 1965 amendments were, in reality, general statements of intention bringing little concrete change. Even the principal
achievement in this area, the granting of tariff preferences to developing states, has been of only limited value. One reason is that, as
general world tariff levels fall ever further with each successive GATT
tariff round, the value of the preferences declines correspondingly.
Also, it may be borne in mind that tariff preferences generally provide
the most assistance to the more advanced of the developing states
(such as Brazil or South Korea) rather than to the very poorest.[64]

The many changes in the IMF over the years have certainly not
satisfied the developing countries. Some of the various special facilities have been little used, such as the Compensatory Financing Facility and the Buffer Stock Facility. More to the point, there has been no
significant relaxing of the rigors of conditionality on the part of the
Fund. Managing Director Michel Camdessus, in 1988, firmly reasserted the traditional role of the IMF when he emphasized that its
essential task in the international debt crisis was not to minister
exclusively to the needs of the debtors, but rather to provide both the
debtor and the creditor countries with a general framework of confidence and stability. He explicitly rejected the relaxing of IMF conditionality as a solution to the debt crisis. "Debtors and creditors alike,"
he asserted, "need the Fund to remain as you presently know it—a
non-complaisant institution."[65]

Nor is the outlook at all promising for the integrated commodity
scheme. Commodity agreements have generally been unsuccessful in
attempting to counteract fundamental economic trends. Furthermore, even if successful, they have only a limited capacity for redistri-
buting resources from rich countries to poor ones. It has been estimated that some 75 percent, by value, of exports of commodities
covered by the integrated program go to other developing states rather
than to the developed world.[66] (This fact, incidentally, provides an
interesting insight into the nature of the "new international economic
order" as a political, rather than economic, program. When the oil-
producing states succeeded in effecting a stunning, four-fold increase
in the price of oil in 1973–74, their actions were loudly applauded by
their fellow developing countries. On narrowly economic grounds,

that made little sense, since the non-oil developing states were clearly the principal material victims. Apparently the spectacle of a third-world triumph of *any* nature was a welcome sight—at least to diplomats—even if the developing countries themselves bore the brunt of the material hardship.)

Finally, it may be noted that the deep sea-bed arrangements may have an undistinguished future. By the end of 1989, it was by no means certain that they would ever enter into force, since most of the developed countries were refraining from ratifying the 1982 Law of the Sea Convention. Even if the convention were to enter into force (with the obtaining of the necessary sixty ratifications), it is far from clear whether the deep sea-bed arrangements will be viable if the developed states persist in their refusal to participate.

The prospects of implementation of the "new international economic order" are, in a word, bleak.[67] In 1986, the developing countries themselves candidly acknowledged that virtually nothing had been done to implement the Charter of Economic Rights and Duties of States.[68] The reason is painfully apparent. The developed countries, which hold the world's real economic power, have declined to endorse the program. They have been willing to make limited changes, of the kind described above. But they show no sign of consenting to a fundamental alteration of the nature and purpose of the international economic system as a whole.

More generally, it may be said that, because of the very nature of the third-world program itself, it is extremely difficult (if not impossible) to envisage its being adopted. It requires purposeful action on the part of states, through the medium of public international law, to effect a conscious transfer of power and resources from one group of states to another. But, by the very nature of traditional international law—which, ironically, the third-world states so strongly endorse—new forms of cooperation of this kind, and new rules of customary law, can only evolve with the consent and the participation of the states themselves. In other words, the "new international economic order" cannot be implemented until and unless the developed countries consciously and deliberately agree to surrender an important share of their economic power and fundamentally to alter the character of institutions which they themselves devised and to which they remain committed. Seen in this light, the "new international economic order" becomes nothing less (or more) than a plea to the developed countries for an almost unimaginably heroic act of altruism.[69]

195

Both to its credit and its shame, the liberal system is considerably less utopian in this regard. It requires self-discipline on the part of states, to be sure, in the form of resisting the manifold temptations of protectionism and other forms of economic nationalism. But the real source of economic growth and progress is the dependable (if hardly praiseworthy) trait of individual human self-interest (or "utility maximization," in more polite terms). We have observed that, throughout history, moralists and economic nationalists—two far-from-distinct categories—have been distinctly uneasy at the idea of deliberately fashioning an entire social system based upon so unedifying a characteristic as naked greed. The contemporary call for a "new international economic order" is a modern expression, in the turgid prose of UN diplomacy, of this same age-old attitude. Whatever that program may lack in political realism or in technical feasibility, it makes up for in the general high moral tone that suffuses it. The call for justice, for concern for the downtrodden and for social solidarity will (it must be hoped) always strike at least some chord in the human heart.

Whether it will do much more than that may be doubted. It may be a sad comment upon human nature that greed appears to be a more powerful sentiment than self-sacrifice (at least in "normal" times). Liberals have never pretended otherwise. On the contrary, one of the most wondrous—if also somewhat suspicious—aspects of their system is the proposition that private vices can function as social virtues, that from the base metal of avarice can come the sparkling gold of world-wide peace and prosperity. That extraordinary claim, it must be confessed, still awaits its definitive empirical proof. There are, however, some straws in the wind, which are worthy of a brief notice.

EIGHT

OF COMMERCE AND DOMINION:
The Commerce of Peoples Amidst the Rivalry of Nations

The attainment of world peace, like any similarly ambitious enterprise, cannot be accomplished all at once. The theory behind the establishment of an economic system of world order envisages two basic steps, to be undertaken by different parties. First is the establishment of a general framework for the promotion of freedom of trade and the elimination of economic nationalism—a task entrusted to governments and, through their initiative, to international organizations. Then comes the substantive work of binding the peoples of the world together into an ever tighter web of economic interdependence. This is the task of individual and corporate entrepreneurs. This signal service to humanity, it will be recalled, is not, as such, consciously assumed by private parties. Instead, their sole immediate task is to make money (i.e., to maximize their utility). Peace between nations is to be the beneficent by-product of private free enterprise, rather than the conscious object of it. The thesis is that, by the natural course of economic evolution, private enterprise will constitute an ever stronger vested material interest in the cause of harmony between nations. By the end of the 1980s, when the third attempt at an economic world order had been in progress for some forty years, it was beginning to be possible to make a few tentative observations on how the great experiment was working.

It is impossible to deny that substantial progress has been made in the promotion of freedom of trade. As a result of the successive rounds of multilateral tariff reductions under the auspices of the GATT, average tariffs on industrial products have declined steeply from their post-World War II levels—from an average of approximately 40 percent, to less than 5 percent by the 1980s. World trade duly rose as a proportion of world economic output, from 7.7 percent in 1960, to 15.5 percent in 1980.[1] Of equal, or greater, importance than this lowering of tariff rates is the general character of the system of international trade. For the most part, it has been multilateral, rather than bilateral, in nature, so that traders are largely free to sell their wares anywhere in the global "mercantile republick" where the highest prices beckon. The stabilization of the major currencies has also been largely successful. By the late 1950s, the convertibility of the principal currencies was restored. The change-over in the early 1970s from a system of fixed exchange rates to one of floating rates added some elements of risk and uncertainty to transnational business dealings; but, for the most part, stability in this quarter has been achieved.

Our concern here is not with this general framework, but rather with the nature and significance of the "real" economic activities that have flourished within it. We shall therefore consider some of the more salient characteristics of the world of private international economic relations since 1945. In particular, we shall see how private economic interests have managed to divorce themselves, to a greater and greater extent, from ties with their own, or indeed any, state. The two outstanding illustrations of this phenomenon are the multinational companies and the international banks. As their material interests have become ever further flung, they have brought an ever more politically diverse array of countries within their ambit. The financial world especially has succeeded in attaining a significant degree of independence from the control of any one state—while, at the same time, continuing to deal impartially with all.

The crucial question, however, is whether this trend seems to be having the effect that the proponents of a system of economic world order predicted that it would. That is, does the increasing economic integration of peoples exert a dampening effect on political rivalry, and so promote the long-run cause of world peace? In a certain sense, there appears to be room for at least some optimism on this point. In a number of instances, the politicians of the world have shown themselves either unable or unwilling to disrupt transnational economic ties in the cause of political rivalry, even when no legal barriers stood in their way. On the broader question, of whether economic relations are displacing political relations in importance, the picture is (not surprisingly) far less certain.

TRANSNATIONAL ECONOMIC COMMUNITIES: FROM "SCARBOROUGH FAIR" TO "CASINO CAPITALISM"

As the distinctive unit of the political world is the nation-state, so the distinctive unit of the economic world is the multinational company.[2] Like practically every other basic element of international economic relations, this one is very far from new. Its ancestry, after a fashion, goes back to the great trading companies of the mercantilist era, from the sixteenth to the eighteenth centuries. In one crucially important respect, however, the present-day multinational company differs from its buccaneering forbears. That is, that the great mercantilist companies were intimately connected, in fact if not in law, with the governments that chartered them. The very nature of the powers conferred onto some of these old companies indicates their quasi-governmental character. The British East India Company, in the seventeenth century, for example, was granted the right, by royal charter, to coin money, equip armies and navies, conclude treaties with foreign rulers and maintain courts of admiralty. Even the twentieth-century "sovereign state" of ITT can boast of no privileges remotely resembling these. The powers of the modern-day multinational company are, in other words, truly *economic* in character in a way that those of the great mercantilist enterprises were not.

The latter-day multinational company is chiefly interested in promoting the interests of its shareholders and managers, rather than of the government that incorporated it. Its loyalty is to its own business prospects, which might lie far afield from its original home.[2] This modern breed of multinational enterprise only dates from the nineteenth century. A conventional starting date is sometimes given as 1867, when the Singer Sewing Machine Company of the United States established a factory in Glasgow. The years following the First World War witnessed important growth in the number, size and scope of such companies. The major oil companies, for example, established significant overseas operations in Latin America and the Middle East, stimulated by fears of a coming oil shortage in the United States. The presence of Firestone Rubber Company in Liberia and the large-scale operations of United Fruit Company in the banana-producing areas of Central America also date from the interwar period, as do the activities of ITT in a host of countries.

The explosive growth of the multinational company, however, came after the Second World War. So prodigious was their growth that, by the 1970s, as one academic writer truthfully noted, some firms were larger than most countries.[3] So significant had the scale of their transnational operations become that, by the end of the 1970s, it was estimated that intra-company transactions by the multinationals accounted for some 25 percent of total world trade.[4]

More important than their mere size, for present purposes, is the fact that they operate with comparative freedom across some of the major political fault lines of the world. The Central Selling Organization of de Beers, for example, a virtual monopolist of the world diamond-selling trade, deals (sometimes discreetly) with countries from all parts of the political and ideological spectrum: it markets diamonds for socialist Angola; also for that country's mortal enemy, the Republic of South Africa; and even for the Soviet Union. Armand Hammer's Occidental Petroleum Company has functioned, at times, as a kind of self-appointed corporate pioneer of U.S.-Soviet détente. American oil companies happily operate in and do business with Arab states, while their home government functions as the chief economic and political patron of Israel. Perhaps the most vivid single image of the political catholicity of the modern multinational company is Gulf Oil, whose installations in Angola were faithfully guarded by Cuban troops from potential sabotage—by dissident guerrilla forces supported by the United States government.

Speaking more broadly, it may be said that, in general, politics and business mix badly (contrary to the views of dogmatic conspiracy theorists). In a variety of areas, it may be seen that the very principle of state sovereignty is alien to the ways of the global "mercantile republick" in various respects. One illustration is the continued evolution of the law of state immunity. By the 1970s, all of the major Western states had accepted the restrictive viewpoint on this question, which had been evolving since the end of the nineteenth century.

Through most of the global "mercantile republick," therefore, the principle has been established that a state engaging in ordinary commercial activity is amenable to suit in the domestic courts of other states to the same extent as a private entrepreneur.[5]

Another illustration of this same general trend is the development of what are called "internationalized" contracts between states and private entities (typically, of course, multinational enterprises). Such a contract is not, strictly speaking, a treaty because of the fact that one party is not a state. But neither is it an ordinary contract, because it is not governed by the law of any particular state, but rather by public international law.[6] It is very difficult to say, in this arrangement, whether the company has been promoted to the status of a state, or whether the state has been reduced to the condition of a private party. More interesting yet is the phenomenon of "stabilization" clauses in contracts between states and private parties. The purpose of such clauses is to "freeze" the law of the state as of the time of conclusion of the agreement, so that any future changes will not affect the arrangement. Here, it is clear that the state, in effect, bargains away, to a private party, one of the most fundamental of sovereign rights—that of legislation.[7]

Not surprisingly, there is a wide diversity of views about these various trends. Perhaps no single issue so neatly separates the political from the economic frame of mind as the attitude toward multinational companies and their manifold works. The economic mentality tends to see them as the harbingers of the advancing trend of globalization, as the hardy pioneers of a unified world society. Persons of this persuasion, in their lyrical praise of multinational companies, can even faithfully recapture some of the evangelical zeal of the nineteenth-century political economists. Tom Clausen, for example, head of the Bank of America (and also president of the World Bank from 1981 to 1986), is a worthy successor of Passy or Cobden in his praise for the multinational company as the outward and visible sign of the "expansion of consciousness to the global level"—a development which, he averred, "offers mankind perhaps the last real chance to build a world order that is less coercive than that offered by the nation-state."[8] An important aspect of this great historical mission is the lack of strong ties of loyalty on the part of these enterprises to any particular country. Clausen eagerly looks forward to the evolution of a "supranational corporation which will not owe its charter to any nation-state and which will be equally resident—and equally nonresident—in any country in which it operates."[9]

The political mentality, in contrast, is inclined to see the multinational enterprise as a threatening, satanic force, insidiously subverting the foundations of civilized life. President Allende of Chile, appropriately, was an exemplar of this school of thought. In his speech to the UN General Assembly in 1972, he painted the struggle between sovereign states and multinationals in characteristically vivid terms:

> We are witnessing a pitched battle [he warned] between the great transnational corporations and sovereign States, for the latter's fundamental political, economic and military decisions are being interfered with by world-wide organizations which . . . are not accountable to or regulated by any parliament or institution representing the national interest. In a word, the entire structure of the world is being undermined. [10]

(Allende, it may be admitted, had greater reason than most to be wary of multinational companies. Upon his election as president in 1970, ITT attempted to "take out a contract" on his government, by financing a coup d'état by the United States. Henry Kissinger, who was something of a traditionalist in matters of this kind, turned this interesting offer down.)[11]

For all their differences of viewpoint, Clausen and Allende are in substantial agreement on one point: that the increasing power and influence of multinational companies in general bodes ill for such traditional ideas as state sovereignty. It is likely that the passion with which they hold their sharply opposing views has led them into some exaggeration of the power that these mysterious organizations actually possess. Be that as it may, both are clearly correct to perceive that important forces are loose in the world that do not fit within the received categories of the traditional law of nations.

The cosmopolitan character of the modern-day "mercantile republick" is illustrated even more strikingly by the world of international finance. Even more completely than the multinational companies, the major international banks have managed to slip the political moorings of the various nation-states and to conduct their affairs outside the sovereign controls of any ruler. The basic phenomenon is not at all new. During the Middle Ages, the sites of the major financial emporia, the great fairs, had been neutral ground, carefully shielded by various legal devices from the operation of the normal law of the territory in which they were held. These same considerations were very much present in the development of the Euro-currency market— the modern equivalent of the medieval fairs and exchanges—since

1945. This transnational and de-nationalized world of international finance had its origins in the outward flow of American dollars to Europe during the 1950s for the purchase of European goods and acquisition of investments. In a time of dollar shortage, demand for greenbacks was robust; and, as a consequence, interest rates were higher than in the United States (because of ceilings on interest rates imposed by the American Federal Reserve). Persons acquiring dollars naturally preferred to deposit them in European banks where they could earn the higher interest. Political factors played a part as well. The Soviet Union, for example, was reluctant to deposit dollars in the United States because of fears that the American government would freeze or confiscate them on political grounds.[12]

Dollars which flowed from the United States to Europe, therefore, tended not to flow back, but instead to be deposited in dollar accounts in banks in Europe (some of which were overseas branches of American banks). European governments, especially the British one, greatly assisted the process by refraining from imposing regulations on these deposits and confining their regulatory activity to dealings in their own currencies. London, accordingly, became the favored source of deposit of these "Euro-dollars," as they came to be called. With the passage of time, this pool of unregulated dollars swelled larger and larger.

It did not, of course, just sit there. It was put to a variety of creative uses. It was lent out to multinational companies, for example, and also to governments, which were duly and unsentimentally accorded credit ratings like any private borrower. (In 1988, it might be noted, *Euromoney* magazine awarded its highest credit rating to Japan, and its lowest to Lebanon.)[13] The Euro-currency deposits were also used for speculative purposes, for purchases and sales of various currencies in the hope of anticipating, and profiting from, changes in par values. By the early 1970s, the amounts of money involved in this kind of activity were so great as to enable speculators to do much to induce the very changes on which they were betting. So powerful had these forces of private finance become that, in 1971–1973, they definitively burst the bounds of the fixed-exchange-rate system established under the guidance of the IMF in the 1940s. The policy of fixed par values of currencies was abandoned, and the world was launched upon a new regime of continuously fluctuating exchange rates. The atmosphere of the medieval exchanges was, in a certain fashion, returning.

This Euro-currency system has become perhaps the archetypal institution of the post-World War II "mercantile republick," in the way that the gold standard had been of its nineteenth-century forbear. Like the gold-standard system, this Euro-currency world is highly decentralized. It possesses no single physical market place or trading floor comparable to a stock exchange or commodities exchange. It is a kind of "floating world," a more or less continuous system of negotiation and lending by any and all banks that possess currency deposits outside the territories of the issuing countries. This Euro-currency market is a continuous perpetual-motion churning of money through a largely unregulated network of banks. As a global hook-up of telexes and computers, this world of "casino capitalism" (as one observer has dubbed it) is a kind of etherealized and globalized avatar of the Antwerp exchange of the sixteenth century.[14]

This global casino is, from the political standpoint, the very broadest of churches. Ideology counts for nothing in this latter-day Antwerp, where governments of the most disparate persuasion—East and West, North and South, left and right, rich and poor—beseech the favors of the captains of world finance. Socialist countries have borrowed there, gaining valuable (if sometimes painful) insights into the ways of modern capitalists. During the 1970s, the oil-exporting countries became a substantial presence in the Euro-currency markets, as lenders, after the steep oil price rises of 1973–1974. The Euro-markets deftly assumed the task of recycling the petro-dollar surpluses, in substantial part to the governments of the non-oil developing states, whose catastrophic balance-of-payments problems were a direct counterpart of the good fortune of their oil-rich brethren. Thereby were sown the seeds of what, during the following decade, duly matured into the third-world debt crisis.[15]

As a result of this financial inter-meshing, countries from all corners of the geographical and ideological world have acquired a vested interest in the stability of the Euro-currency system. That stability, it should be noted, is the subject of some nervous speculation. The worries arise directly from the general cosmopolitan nature of this "floating world." On the one hand, the Euro-currency system is blissfully free from such humdrum inhibitions as reserve requirements, interest-rate ceilings or exchange controls. By the same token, however, it lacks the important safety net of a governmental lender of last resort in case of a crisis. There are, accordingly, fears that the Euro-currency markets might be disturbingly vulnerable to panic. It is further feared that, because of the high degree of integration of global financial markets, any loss of confidence, anywhere in the system, can have world-wide repercussions at lightning speed—a fact graphically demonstrated by the truly global stock-market crash of October 1987.

The chief source of concern is the potentially volatile nature of the Euro-currency markets. Much of the money there is on short-term deposit (of, say, thirty to sixty days). At the same time, many loans are made for durations of a number of years, with both the disbursements and the repayments coming in installments. Part of the skill of being a banker in this kind of world lies in making sure that, from day to day, inflows of cash are sufficient to cover the outflows to which one is committed. Ordinarily, modest shortages and surpluses present no problem, because the so-called inter-bank market exists to iron them out: banks borrow and lend needed funds to one another routinely, sometimes for extremely short periods of time, to smooth out such fluctuations. The question—as yet unanswered—is whether the market can stand up to a *general* shortage of funds induced by precipitate withdrawals of nervous investors from the entire Euro-currency system. It is even possible that quite modest actual shortfalls of cash can lead to panic and induce a desperate scramble for what remains. As the gigantic banks are driven desperately to compete with one another for a dwindling supply of funds, it is easy to imagine—though frightening to contemplate—that interest rates might be driven to alarming levels in extremely short periods of time, perhaps within hours or even minutes. It is far from clear what, if anything, the governments of the world could do to stave off an international banking crash—or what the consequences of such a crash might be.

The risks are compounded, ironically, by a common practice of the international banks themselves: the use of what are known as "cross-default clauses" in their syndicated loans. From the standpoint of each single lender, cross-default clauses are a form of insurance. In the event of a default crisis and a desperate scramble for scarce funds, no lender would wish to be the last one to call in its loans and pull its funds to safety out of the maelstrom. For that reason, lenders typically reserve for themselves the right to claim their money rapidly and withdraw at even the first sign of danger. Therefore, upon the occurrence of any defined "event of default" on the borrower's part, the lender reserves the right to "accelerate" the loan, i.e., to bring all future repayments under the agreement forward so as to make them due and payable immediately. Since this practice is designed for the benefit of the lender, to ensure that he can grab all of his money at the first hint of trouble, it is to his advantage to define an "event of default" as broadly as possible. Typically, it is defined to encompass a failure on the part of the borrower to honour *any* loan obligation to *any* party whatever.

From the perspective of the individual lender, cross-default clauses are rational, since they enable him to obtain his money as quickly as possible. From the standpoint of the system as a whole, however, the effect of cross-default clauses is worrisome in the extreme. They serve to chain the mass of lenders together, since a borrower's default against any one creditor immediately becomes, under these clauses, a default against all others as well. These clauses, then, operate rather like financial suicide pacts. They ensure that any instability anywhere instantaneously reverbrates around the entire system. The Euro-market system, therefore, operates on something akin to a hair trigger. (There was a nervous moment in 1979 when, in the course of the turmoil brought on by the Iranian revolution and the American hostages crisis, Chase Manhattan Bank formally called an Iranian loan in default. In the event, the other lenders to Iran held back from accelerating their loans, and so a general crisis was averted.)[16]

These various distinctive features of the modern transnational financial system—its strongly cosmopolitan nature, its substantial independence of the will of governments and its potential delicacy and vulnerability to panic—all combine to make it very risky to tamper with. Those who tend this wondrous machine are highly skilled lawyers, financiers, and accountants—latter-day Confucian literati, learned in the arcane and abstract wisdom of loan agreements and balance sheets, options and futures, spot markets and forward markets, and many other mysteries of modern financial alchemy. Moreover, these literati, like their ancient Confucian counterparts, are jealous guardians of their preserve. They do not welcome the interference of would-be emperors. Governments, to them, are clients or borrowers rather than masters.

In the financial field, then, as in international trade and investment generally, the ways of the sovereign are alien and suspect to the ways of the entrepreneur. Over the course of time, the politicians of the world have discovered on several occasions, to their chagrin, how difficult it is to manipulate the multifarious operations of the global "mercantile republick" to their own political advantage.

THE SILENT FORCES OF BUSINESS

As long ago as 1792, Thomas Paine was cautioning about the impossibility of "engross[ing] commerce by dominion,"[17] i.e., of successfully using the powers of government to manipulate the flow of commerce. History is full of demonstrations of the truth of Paine's contention—and never more so than during the post-World War II period. In the area of international trade, the difficulty of exerting effective political controls has been demonstrated over many centuries. Attempts to manipulate foreign investment have been rather more recent, though hardly more successful. Imposing effective controls over the activities either of multinational companies or of international banks in the Euro-currency markets has often proved beyond the power of even the most determined engrosser. A few concrete illustrations will reveal why.

Consider the field of international trade first. The earliest truly systematic attempt to exert political controls over trade was the ancient Chinese tribute system. Its purpose was to confine economic contact between the Chinese Empire and the surrounding barbarian tribes to carefully supervised channels—specifically, to official missions from the barbarian rulers who, as nominal subjects of the Chinese emperor, would periodically bring various goods as "tribute" to the Chinese court, and then receive "gifts" in return. One of the advantages for the barbarians of participating in this arrangement was the opportunity to trade illegally on the side with the Chinese people.[18] At about this same time, the Chinese government was attempting to police the trade with the barbarians along its borders, to prevent valuable materials from falling into the hands of the foreign tribes. Trade in metals, agricultural implements, and livestock was restricted in this fashion. Judging from the draconian penalties prescribed for engaging in this forbidden trade, it would appear that the controls were not very effective. We hear, for example, of the execution of some five hundred merchants in 121 B.C. for trading in illegal goods.[19]

Several centuries later, at the other end of Eurasia, the Roman imperial authorities had much the same difficulty policing the trade in strategic goods with the German tribes on their European frontiers. From the early third century A.D., it became a capital offence to export an ever-lengthening list of goods to the outside world—armour, weapons, horses, beasts of burden, specie, whetstones, iron, grain, salt, even wine. Controls on the export of technology were also imposed, to prevent knowledge of catapult construction from falling into potentially hostile hands.[20] During the Middle Ages, similar controls were imposed by the Roman Catholic popes on the exporting of strategic materials (such as iron and timber) to the Muslim lands. The use of ecclesiastical censures, including excommunication, signaled the formal enlisting of God in the war against Mammon. From the evidence, it would appear that Mammon managed at least to hold his own.[21]

President Thomas Jefferson of the United States later discovered, in a painful fashion, the strength of the human acquisitive instinct. The occasion was the imposition of a civil embargo in 1807, coupled with a general policy of non-exportation of goods from American territory. The purpose was to inflict economic injury upon Britain and thereby to extract concessions from it in various disputes over neutrality issues. Jefferson was dismayed to find that a major smuggling industry promptly arose on the United States-Canadian border which he was largely powerless to suppress. In ever more desperate attempts to stamp out the trade, he was compelled to resort to increasingly harsh methods, including the use of the army. By the end of the Jefferson presidency in 1809, the policy was thoroughly discredited and was discontinued, having done far more to embitter domestic American political life and to stimulate law-breaking than to intimidate the British.[22]

Similar lessons abound in modern life, though with one important difference. That is, that the modern international-trade system is, in effect, consciously designed to make political controls over international trade as difficult as possible. The reason, of course, is the multilateral character of the modern "mercantile republick," with its infinite pathways and multiple connections. Quite apart from any legal constraints on the waging of economic warfare per se (of the kind discussed in chapter 5), the sheer practical difficulties in effectively controlling international trade in this kind of system are immense. Suppose that some state wishes to curtail or control trade with some other. How can it ensure that exports do not eventually find their way to the embargoed state? Once exported goods are placed into the general stream of international commerce, it can be extremely difficult to say with any certainty where they will end up. The same considerations apply to restricting imports from a target country. One can, of course, refrain from importing directly; but how is one to ensure that goods bought from some third country did not originate, ultimately, in the target state?

The experience of many nations in trading with South Africa, knowingly or not, is an apt illustration. In the face of nominal trade boycotts against that outlaw nation by most of the third-world and socialist states, a thinly disguised clandestine trade continues to flourish. So does a thriving sanctions-busting industry in South Africa itself, whose principal function is to provide a more or less credible country-of-origin disguise for South African exports. The strategies used are not difficult to discern: transshipments through friendly states, false documentation and certifications, re-invoicing and the like.[23] Nor do imports appear to pose much difficulty. South Africa obtains oil supplies from countries that supposedly refuse to sell to it (although, to be sure, some rather imaginative devices need to be resorted to on occasion).[24]

Trade between Israel and the Arab states proceeds in much the same fashion, and in substantial quantity at that. It has been estimated that, in 1988, Israel sent some $900 million worth of goods to the Arab world—10 percent of its total exports. Since it imported virtually nothing from the Arabs, it thereby received a tidy sum of foreign exchange from its mortal enemies. As in the South African case, the essential requirement is to devise a respectable disguise of the origin of the goods, which often entails nothing more sophisticated than exporting at first instance to enterprising middlemen, who repackage and relabel the products.[25]

One of the most interesting illustrations of the limited control that politicians have over the working of the global economy was provided by the Arab oil embargo of 1973–1974. During the Middle East war of October 1973, the Arab oil-exporting states (with the exception of Iraq) attempted to impose a total oil embargo against the two most strongly pre-Israel states in the West, the United States and the Netherlands. Lesser reductions in supply were to be imposed against the other Western states, plus Japan. The embargo was bolstered by production cuts of approximately 14 percent, and by sharp price increases.

From the psychological standpoint, the effect was breathtaking. With astonishing rapidity, the Western countries relapsed into the mentality of medieval city-states in times of famine, as they desperately and competitively implemented what were, for all intents and purposes, "policies of provision" in the oil sector. To prevent the scarce oil supplies from slipping abroad, some states imposed export embargoes on the precious substance. Countries with significant oil refining capacities were well placed to steal a march on their rival consumers in this regard.[26] In addition, the old medieval economic vices of forestalling, regrating and engrossing came rapidly back into fashion, as the Western consumer countries engaged in an undignified competitive scramble for the apparently scarce resource. Western motorists engaged in regrating on the largest of scales, by attempting to ensure that their tanks of gasoline remained as full as possible at all times. The result was to aggravate the crisis considerably by immobilizing vast amounts of gasoline in millions of automobile tanks, in a process that modern economists have dubbed "invisible stockpiling."

These panic measures on the part of Western governments and consumers obscured the fact that the actual physical shortfall of oil was modest in the extreme. The reason is obvious. The non-Arab oil producers—notably Iran and the Soviet Union—with a conspicuous lack of remorse, stepped directly into the breach left by the production cuts of the Arab states and prospered mightily for their pains.[27] (The Soviet Union did so while giving noisy verbal support to the Arab states for the embargo—a most convenient coincidence of commercial advantage and political principle.)[28]

In addition, the Arab oil states found it impossible, as the more perceptive observers had predicted, to control the destination of their oil once it was sold into the general stream of international commerce. The real decision as to the allocation of oil supplies was made not by the Arab producers but rather by the middlemen—the international oil companies, which rapidly devised an allocation system for distributing the available oil among the consuming states. This distribution was made according to the companies' own criteria, which were largely commercial. Like good utility maximizers, they accorded a preference to the consumer states which imposed the fewest controls on their activities.[29] Not surprisingly, the age-old hostility of the patriot for the merchant immediately resurfaced during the crisis. The oil companies were widely condemned by the Western public for profiting from the crisis, to the point that one poll indicated that far more people blamed the companies for the crisis than the Arab governments.[30]

In any event, the actual material damage inflicted upon the consuming states by the cutbacks and delivery targeting was trivial. The total energy shortfall in the United States, for example, was approximately 2.4 percent. In Japan, which was particularly dependent upon Middle Eastern oil, it was only 2.8 percent. The corresponding figures for the Western European countries were similarly modest. Ironically, so small was the actual shortfall in oil supplies that those countries which were the most successful in their feverish quest for imports had difficulty in locating enough shipping and storage capacity to handle their supplies. The supposed total embargoes against the United States and the Netherlands were, for all intents and purposes, completely ineffective. Thanks to the efforts of the international oil companies, those two states fared no worse than others. (It was ironic that the most serious energy shortfall, though only by a trivial amount, was experienced by France, the most pro-Arab of the Western European countries.)[31]

All of this is not to say that the oil crisis of 1973–1974 was not real. It certainly was. What is important to grasp, however, is that the crisis was, in reality, psychological and political, rather than economic, in nature. One of the most valuable, and disturbing, lessons from the experience was the revelation of how near we still are to the mentality of the ancient and medieval worlds, with their fears of shortage and their defensive "policies of provision." Our fear of embargoes and "natural resource" weapons and the like is, however, largely a reflection of our ignorance of the nature of the economic system which we ourselves have created.

The story of the Afghanistan grain embargo of 1980–1981 holds many of the same lessons—though, significantly, without the crucial psychological element. In response to the entry of Soviet troops into Afghanistan in 1979, the United States suspended grain sales to the Soviet Union (except for sales provided for under a five-year treaty arrangement concluded in 1975).[32] Unlike the Arab countries, the United States did make an attempt to prevent potential alternative suppliers from simply stepping into its place. It obtained commitments from most—but, alas, not all—of the other major grain exporters to confine their sales to traditional levels. The significant exception was Argentina, which refused to cooperate in any way. As a result, the only effect of the supposed grain embargo was to redirect world commercial flows of grain, with scarcely any net change in the end. Argentina shifted its sales away from its traditional purchasers toward the Soviet market; while the United States in turn rechannelled its exports toward Argentina's former customers. There was, accordingly, no significant loss of exports to U.S. farmers (despite contentions to the contrary), and hardly any shortfall in supplies to the Soviet Union. Those who had urged the United States to emulate the mighty Arab oil suppliers by wielding the "food weapon" were thereby proved decisively wrong.[33]

In order for the political controlling of international trade to be even minimally effective, it is necessary that the policing state exert some kind of control over the activities of the global "mercantile republick" as a whole—no easy task. One strategy is to coordinate the policies of all states that deal in a particular good or class of goods, as the United States tried to do during the Afghanistan crisis.

The most notable attempt of this nature is the coordination, through CoCom, of the Western (plus Japanese and Australian) strategic embargo of the socialist states. Lists of materials to be controlled are agreed, on a basis of unanimity, at periodic CoCom sessions and then implemented by the various participating states through their domestic regulatory mechanisms.[34] Obviously, such an approach can only be effective if agreement can actually be reached, and if there are no possible alternate suppliers outside the group of coordinated states, and also if "legitimate" customers to whom the goods are sold can be dissuaded or prevented from re-exporting them to the target state. These are, to put it mildly, stringent conditions.

The alternative for a would-be engrosser of commerce by dominion is the use of more coercive methods, such as policies of secondary economic warfare directed against noncooperating parties. We have seen, in outline, how the United States employs such methods in the enforcement of its unilateral, stricter-than-CoCom embargo policy. We have also seen how the international community has become, over the years, progressively less tolerant of such practices, to the point that a good case can be made for their outright illegality. It is now possible to see the evolving legal rule against secondary boycotting in its most general context. It is a reinforcement, by legal means, of the essentially multilateral and integrated character of the system of international trade. It is, accordingly, a sort of customary-law analogue of the GATT. Its ultimate purpose, like that of the GATT, is to make the political manipulation of international trade as difficult as possible.

In the fields of foreign investment and finance, as in that of international trade, effective political manipulation of the affairs of the global "mercantile republick" has proved difficult in the extreme. The cosmopolitanism of the multinational companies plays an important part here. In the face of their myriad interests, even the apparently simple act of severing economic relations can become frustratingly complex. The experience of the United States and Libya in the 1980s is a case in point. In 1986, in the wake of a series of terrorist incidents in which the United States alleged Libyan involvement, the Americans imposed a range of economic sanctions (notably a total trade boycott and a freezing of Libyan government assets in U.S. banks).[35] Part of this package of measures was the supposedly mandatory departure of all U.S. nationals and companies from Libyan territory. American interests were a substantial presence in Libya. Five oil companies, employing some 1000 to 1500 American nationals, were involved in the production of some 45 percent of Libya's total oil output. In 1985, they had paid some $2 billion in taxes to the Libyan government (creditable against their American taxes under U.S. law).[36]

It soon became apparent that a rapid exit by the companies would not be possible without placing a large economic windfall in the hands of the Libyan government. The companies pointed out that the deadline for departure would compel them to dispose of their assets in a "fire sale." The Reagan administration relented and authorized them to continue their operations, with the proviso that they must wind them up as soon as possible (though with no particular deadline specified).[37] The five companies then reached a three-year "stand-still" agreement with the Libyan government. According to this arrangement, the operations of the oil companies were legally suspended, so as to protect them from possible breach-of-contract claims arising from their cessation of operations. The effect was to freeze the companies' Libyan assets for the duration of the agreement—but with the implicit suggestion that, if relations were not repaired by that time, the assets might be nationalized. With the impending expiry of the stand-still agreement, the United States held back from a damaging economic confrontation—damaging, that is, to the companies. On its last full day in office in January 1989, the Reagan administration formally relaxed the American measures against Libya, so as to allow the companies to resume operations. A White House statement candidly admitted that the purpose was to protect U.S. interests and to "eliminate the significant financial windfall" which Libya had been receiving since 1986 by itself marketing the companies' shares of Libyan oil production.[38]

This case is particularly interesting because it is so clear that the relaxation of the economic sanctions did not arise from any solicitude over the effect upon Libya. On the contrary, the Reagan administration proved its willingness to take the most drastic steps against that country in April 1986, when it sent its air force on a punitive bombing raid against Tripoli. It was clearly the presence of American interests that precluded comparably drastic action on the economic front.

It would appear that the most difficult economic links of all to sever are the financial ties created through the Euro-currency system. Difficulties in the way of political manipulation are manifold; but only the most important ones need be mentioned. One is the problem of controlling the activities of foreign branches of banks. International law does permit states to regulate the conduct of their nationals abroad. (Foreign branches of banks are typically nationals of the bank's home state and not of their host country.) The problem is that the territorial state also has a right to regulate the bank's conduct. As a result, foreign branches of banks can be subject to two different, and inconsistent, sets of instructions from two governments. An excellent illustration of this dilemma occurred after 1986, when the United States, as part of its program of economic sanctions against Libya, froze (or purported to freeze) all assets of Libyan government agencies in all American banks, both within and without the United States. Courts in Great Britain, however, ruled that the law governing the relationship between a depositor and his bank was the law of the territory in which the deposit was made. The effect was that British courts refused to enforce the American freeze orders and that American banks located there were compelled to permit Libyan withdrawals.[39]

The case of the Falklands conflict of 1982 between Britain and Argentina demonstrated some of the dilemmas that could arise when states that are linked together financially through the Euro-market system fall out with each other politically. Argentina and the United Kingdom imposed a number of economic measures against each other, principally trade boycotts and the freezing of the bank accounts of one another's nationals. It happened, however, that a number of British banks were creditors of Argentina, which was one of the third world's major debtor states. Both countries were reluctant to force a financial crisis. Argentina had no wish to commit an "event of default," since doing so could trigger large numbers of cross-default clauses and thus cause its monstrous debt burden to fall due and payable immediately, in the midst of a war. It therefore had every incentive to keep up its loan payments. At the same time, however, it was understandably reluctant to pay out public funds to the bankers of its enemy country while an armed conflict was in progress. Britain's main interest was in the stability of the Euro-currency system as a whole and in London's role as its major center. It therefore preferred to see financial business go on more or less as usual during the crisis.[40]

This common interest in financial tranquillity on the part of the two warring states ensured that only human, and not financial, blood was spilled. Britain, as the sovereign of the creditor banks, had the easier choice. It simply permitted its banks to receive and disburse loan repayments from Argentina as usual, if Argentina made them. New loan commitments were forbidden, however, as were disbursements pursuant to existing loan agreements (save with the consent of the Bank of England).[41] Argentina's solution was to continue payments on its loans, with the proviso that the share of any loan repayment that was attributable to a British bank would be separated from the main repayment and placed instead in an escrow account in Buenos Aires, for disbursement after the hostilities were over. Superficially, it seemed a neat solution. In reality, however, the creditor banks (to the knowledge of Argentina) were under a contractual obligation to share out any payments received among themselves on a *pro rata* basis according to the amount originally lent. It appears that most of the creditor banks adhered to this policy, with the result that, notwithstanding the escrow arrangement, Argentinian funds *did* flow to British banks even in the thick of the armed conflict.[42]

Another, and even more striking, illustration of how cautiously politicians have learned to tread in the financial minefields is afforded by the Polish marital-law crisis of 1981–1982. Here again, the prospect of igniting a chain reaction of cross-default clauses and provoking a general banking crisis led even superpowers to stay their hands. Even before the declaration of martial law in December 1981, Poland was on a financial cliff-edge, owing some $14 billion to approximately 450 Western banks. After martial law was declared, both the Soviet Union and Poland, on the one side, and the United States, on the other, found themselves in a position to wreak havoc upon the other —but possibly upon themselves as well.

Poland had the opportunity to make a dramatic repudiation of its debts to the Western banks—with the intriguing possibility of inducing a major financial panic on the Euro-currency markets. The prospect of throwing the capitalist financial system into chaos (and of saving itself the inconvenience of repaying its loans) must have seemed a tempting one. Similar considerations were on the mind of the United States. If an "event of default" on Poland's part were actually to occur, and if a sizeable number of creditor banks were to activate their cross-default clauses and accelerate their Polish loans, then that country— together with its larger patron to the east—would be landed with a most uncomfortable dilemma. In reality, the choice would be that of the Soviets, since Poland clearly could not pay its accelerated loans. The Soviet Union could bail Poland out—but only at a huge cost, and with the effect of shoring up the capitalist financial system. On the other hand, it could allow the accelerated loans to go unpaid and enjoy the spectacle of a possible banking panic—but only at the cost of the utter destruction of the credit ratings of the entire socialist bloc. The prospect of forcing the Soviet Union into such a choice must have seemed a delicious one to the United States—except for the worrying possibility that the Soviets would choose the default option and thereby set off the dreaded panic.

The United States soon found itself in possession of a lighted match for application to the financial powder keg. In January 1982, the Polish Bank Handlowy failed to pay $71 million which it owed to various American banks under some agricultural loans guaranteed by the United States government. Under the terms of the guarantee arrangement, the United States could pay the debt only if the banks supplied it with a written notice of default. There was some support within the Reagan administration for pressing ahead with this option, in the knowledge that the notice to the United States government would duly trigger the cross-default clauses in the other Polish loans.[43] The United States, however, backed down, so as to avoid setting off a general banking crisis. It decided, somewhat sheepishly, to pay Poland's debt for it, without requiring a formal notice of default—and without Poland's so much as troubling to request the favor. The effect was seriously to undermine the credibility of the Reagan administration's ostensible commitment to economic sanctions.[44]

These various illustrations of economic ties uniting political enemies afford a few general observations. There is nothing novel, or even particularly insightful, about the observation that economic sanctions are generally ineffective (in that they generally do not induce the changes of policy desired by the state imposing them). What is less often appreciated is the fact that the present system of international economic relations has been, in effect, deliberately structured with that very end in mind. This is so both in a negative and a positive way. The negative way consists of the various legal constraints against the waging of economic warfare—the explicit rules of the GATT and the IMF, together with the evolving customary-law prohibition against secondary economic warfare. The positive way consists of the phenomena under scrutiny here: the fact that economic integration through trade and investment has linked the countries of the world together so effectively through material ties, as to make the imposition of sanctions an unacceptably costly or risky business for the sanctioner himself. That this state of affairs exists may be awkward for politicians who seek to engross commerce by dominion; but it is entirely consistent with the philosophy behind the bifurcation of international relations into separate economic and political spheres. Indeed, the fact that the manipulation of the economic system for political ends has become so difficult is an accurate gauge of the success of that policy.

This basic idea is by no means novel. It is exactly what the advocates of an economic world order have had in mind since the eighteenth century. The conscious intention of the liberal political economists-*cum*-peace activists was to create as powerful a network as possible of vested private interests in support of closer contact between peoples, precisely with a view to frustrating and undermining the aggressive tendencies of politicians, with their petty obsessions with short-term national interests. As Norman Angell, writing in the early years of the twentieth century, had put it:

> While the statesman, the diplomat, the dilettante of high politics, imaging to themselves some dream world where nations are wild warring things living upon one another, to be thrown at one another in some grand series of Armageddons, go on repeating the aphorisms of Aristotle, Charlemagne, Machiavelli, the silent forces of . . . business . . . have been defeating their best-laid plans, reducing their machinations to naught, producing the very opposite result to that intended.[45]

It is clear that these "silent forces of business" are indeed at work in something like the way that Angell had in mind. It is much more difficult, however, to say with any certainty how powerful they really are. The extensive trade between South Africa and its various neighboring states, or between Israel and the Arab countries, would seem to have done little to promote the settlement of the political issues at stake in those conflicts. Similarly, the financial relations between Britain and Argentina may have survived relatively unscathed through the Falklands conflict; but they certainly did nothing to prevent or even mitigate the conflict itself. And economic relations have never played more than a very modest and subordinate role in détente between the United States and the Soviet Union. It would, in fact, be difficult to name even a single important instance in which an important political objective of a state was surrendered in the interest of retaining valued economic links.

One should also be cautious about attributing too great a significance to the cosmopolitan character of modern capitalism. The mere existence of international banks, multinational companies and far-flung trading networks does not, in and of itself, guarantee that the dream of a liberal economic world order is coming true. What is crucial is not the existence of economic interdependence, but rather the nature of attitudes toward it. Multinational companies may be immensely powerful—but if the politicians and the people of the world perceive them as intrinsically hostile forces, then the liberal cause is hardly being advanced. In this regard, as in so many others, the Arab oil crisis of the 1970s provides some revealing, and disturbing, insights into how little progress we have made since the age of Plato and Aristotle, rather than how much. We are still inclined, at the first hint of a real crisis, to see interdependence with the outside world as a threat rather than (as Libanius proclaimed) a gift from God. The urge toward self-reliance, the dark suspicion of cosmopolitan forces, the instinctive lunge toward the protection of the national interest—who would be so rash as to gamble that these tendencies are really in the process of fading into nothingness?

These factors highlight the need for caution when speculating in this area. We should always remember, when congratulating ourselves on how far we have come, that we are still perilously near the beginning of the journey which the physiocrats and the classical economists of the eighteenth and nineteenth centuries mapped out. Nation-states have certainly learned (or at least had occasion to learn) many much-needed lessons of humility in the sphere of economic affairs over the years, and particularly since the Second World War. In some measure, they have even been reduced to the juridical level of private parties in the economic sphere. And the severe limits on their ability to engross commerce by dominion have been exposed time and again. But nation-states are, as yet, very far from losing their grip upon human consciousness. In addition, the law governing the relationships between nation-states continues to prove stubbornly resistant to the siren call of a liberal economic world order. On this last point, some general concluding observations are in order.

CONCLUDING THOUGHTS

The cosmopolitan vision of an economic world order has been in existence in its modern form for something over two centuries, during which time there have been three concerted attempts to put it into practice. On the basis of the experience gained so far, it is possible to offer a few general thoughts on this great experiment in global social engineering.

Perhaps the most outstanding single feature of our story is the extraordinary constancy of the basic ideas involved. In terms of fundamental concepts, there has been little change since the days of the physiocrats in the eighteenth century and virtually none at all since the formative age of liberal political economy in the early nineteenth century. Almost as remarkable has been the persistence of optimism on the part of idealists that the dream is on the brink of realization. During the 1840s, for example, John Stuart Mill looked about him and confidently expressed the view that, even as he was writing, warfare was daily being rendered obsolete by the steady advance of international trade and world economic interdependence.[1] In the 1980s, Francis Fukuyama echoed him in foreseeing the imminent "end of History" and advent of "the universal homogenous state"—a time when the fiery clash of nations and ideologies "will be replaced by economic calculations, the endless solving of technical problems, environmental concerns and the satisfaction of consumer demands."[2]

And yet, great caution is in order. The demise of History—or of "politics" in the pejorative eighteenth-century sense of that term—has proved, time and again, to be greatly exaggerated. Another of the striking general lessons to be gleaned from this history is that there is no inevitability about the advance of freedom of trade, no iron law of progress in operation. On the contrary, great leaps forward have been interspersed with disastrous reversals. Until the 1940s (and possibly since then as well), the dream of an economic world order was largely in hock to the prevailing state of the global economy—in the face of serious economic recession, age-old economic nationalism reasserted itself. Since World War II, we have done much to insulate the system from such downturns. We have certainly not eliminated the business cycle—that great cosmic economic pulse-beat—but there are signs that we may have succeeded in moderating its most extreme effects, in part by devising various legal and institutional safeguards against the resort to economic nationalism.[3]

The taming of economic nationalism is indeed an important part of the struggle for a full-fledged system of economic world order—and one that remains very far from complete. But it is only the most superficial part of the struggle. The real battle is not so much against economic nationalism per se as against the more basic and visceral forces that sustain it. The enemy here is often identified as the sundry vested interests that will use any excuse to plead for protection by their governments against competition from foreigners. But vested interests of this kind, however powerful, are not, ultimately, the real problem. The most eloquent pleaders for the venerable cause of self-interest could not stand up to democratic masses who were truly committed to the principle of freedom of trade. The fact is that the masses are not so committed. Even in the late twentieth century, the feeling remains powerful on the part of common persons that local concerns mean more than faraway ones, that our neighbors whom we know should receive higher consideration than total strangers with whom we deal. The literati may well possess incontrovertible proof that the whole world is essentially one, and that the tumbling of share prices on Wall Street must inevitably have its effects on the miner in Bolivia and the weaver in Bombay. But their demonstrations, even now, have made no more than a superficial impression. It is striking how quickly their precepts are forgotten at the hint of danger. The energy crisis of the 1970s provided us with a graphic illustration of that point. The fact remains that a radically cosmopolitan program of the type put forward by the French physiocrats and their successors is too abstract and intellectual, too rationalistic to have a deep intuitive appeal.

Moreover, it should be conceded that there is even a certain speciousness about the apparently universalistic character of the vision of an economic world order. Like any other system of thought or of social relations ever devised, it holds out the prospect of more rewards for some than for others. The concern for open markets and freedom of trade is naturally far more acute to those who have much to produce and sell than to those who live on the margins of subsistence. Indeed, most powerful capitalist interests—the multinational companies and the international banks—far from standing in the way of a global, open-door "mercantile republick," are its most forceful proponents.

If intransigent vested interests must be sought who are impeding progress toward an economic world order, then we have not far to look. Nation-states—those quintessentially "political" creatures—present by far the most powerful resistance to the evolution of a single global society. No institution, public or private, is more directly and forthrightly threatened by this ideal than the traditional nation-state. The most radical champions of cosmopolitanism, such as St.-Simon, have made no secret of their wish to abolish states completely. Even the more moderate advocates of an economic world order, while conceding that states are here to stay, seek to transform them fundamentally. It is easy to see why. The single most stubborn barrier to the cosmopolitan vision is the permanent license that traditional public international law accords to states to seek their own "perfection," in preference to advancing the interests of humankind as a whole.

Even in the late twentieth century, international law remains stubbornly "mercantilist" in character—as obsessed by the dogma of state sovereignty as any finance minister ever was by the prospect of storehouses of precious metals. To this day, the basic positivist nature of international law has not been supplanted either by Kant's "cosmopolitical" law or by La Pradelle's law of "solidarity." That is, perhaps, not to be wondered at, since law is, after all, the most conservative of intellectual disciplines (and international law most of all). What is more worrisome, from the standpoint of the dream of an economic world order, is that the ideal itself may be in danger of being forgotten in the materialistic hurly-burly of the modern economic race.

In this regard, the decision made in the 1940s to effect a divorce between political and economic relations stands out as a crucial—and ambiguous—turning point. In certain respects, the decision was clearly a wise one. It made possible a more effective struggle against economic nationalism than had ever been mounted before. At the same time, however, it also made it possible—and therefore easy—to forget that the struggle against economic nationalism is not an end in itself, but a step in a far grander design. There is little sign today of the breadth of vision or the idealism of a La Pradelle or a Stowell. "Progressive" thinking (to use a rather loaded and misleading term) in the field of international law tends to concentrate on issues of third-world concern, such as colonialism and *apartheid*, economic development and the debt crisis. We have seen, however, that much of the third-world concern in the field of international law is essentially conservative, if not reactionary, from the standpoint of a holistic conception of world order. Whatever may be the fate of the economic elements of this third-world program, the juridical component is already in place—and indeed has been so for some two centuries.

It may be wondered whether we are not, in fact, further away from the realization of the dream of an economic world order today than we were a century ago.[4] As we have seen, the world was, in certain important respects, more open then than it is today (most outstandingly with respect to the free movement of peoples). Perhaps this means that the dream of an economic system of world order is fading, even in the face of advances in world prosperity (at least for the developed world).

That may be too pessimistic an interpretation, however. We know that in certain respects, most notably with regard to economic warfare, the law of nations does appear to be bending in the direction pointed by the liberal political economists. It may be that, as Friedrich List predicted, the world is simply evolving toward the ultimate goal of a unified global society by careful stages, rather than by a single mighty leap. There clearly is room for optimism that the day may yet arrive—if only distantly—when the states of the world will be reduced to the role of mere administrative agencies in the government of the human race, and when the law of nations will again become—as it once had been—a law of *peoples*. To those of an idealistic (and perhaps somewhat utopian) turn of mind, this prospect remains as tantalizing as when it was first articulated in the eighteenth century. To those with a historical sense, on the other hand, it is apparent that, even in the late twentieth century, the great experiment in economic world order has, in truth, barely begun.

Notes

Introduction

1. Paine, "Rights of Man," at 363. On the concept of an economic world order expressed in more modern terminology, see Röpke, "Economic Order"; Petersmann, "International Economic Theory"; and Ernst-Ulrich Petersmann, "International Economic Order," in Bernhardt, ed., *Encyclopedia of Public International Law*, 8:336–44.

2. Richard Gardner, "The Case for Practical Internationalism," *Foreign Affairs* (1988), 66:841.

3. Kant, *Perpetual Peace*, at 11, footnote.

1. From Polis to Cosmos

1. Roberto Ago, "Positivism," in Bernhardt, ed., *Encyclopedia of Public International Law*, 7:385–93.

2. Aristotle, *Nichomachean Ethics*, at 12.

3. Plato, *Laws*, at 499–500.

4. *Ibid.*, at 211–14.

5. On the trading policies of the ancient Greek city-states generally, see Hasebroek, *Trade and Politics*, at 117–30; and Finley, *Ancient Economy*, at 131–39. See also Wheeler, "Self-sufficiency"; and Heilperin, *Studies*, at 45–50. On the problem of famine in the ancient world, and ways of dealing with it, see Garnsey, *Famine and Food Supply*.

6. Finley, *Ancient Economy*, at 161–62. On Athenian food supply generally, see Garnsey, *Famine and Food Supply*, at 87–164.

7. See generally Rickman, *Corn Supply*; and Garnsey, *Famine and Food Supply*, at 165–268.

8. Lao Tse, *Tao Te Ching*, translated by D.C. Lau (Harmondsworth: Penguin, 1963), at 142.

9. Lord Shang, *Book of Lord Shang*, at 305–06.

10. For an excellent short description of the tribute system, see Yu, *Trade and Expansion*, at 135–50. On the system in later times, see Fairbank and Têng, "Ch'ing Tributary System."

11. Varma, *Political Philosophy of Aurobindo*, at 369–72.

12. Baldry, *Unity of Mankind*, at 151–66, and 177–94.

13. Gaius, *Institutes*, part 1, at 3. On the impact of Roman concepts of natural law, and in particular on the generalization of the Roman law of contract, see Bozeman, *Politics and Culture*, at 190–212. For perceptive remarks on the importance of Roman jurisprudence for the development of the later science of economics, see Alfred J. Marshall, *Principles of Economics*, 7th ed. (London: Macmillan, 1920), at 732–33.

14. Quoted in Heckscher, *Mercantilism*, 2:278–79.

15. Aquinas, *On Kingship*, at 74–78.

16. For excellent descriptions of this medieval food-supply policing, see Pirenne, *Economic and Social History*, at 171–76; and Heckscher, *Mercantilism*, 2:80–104.

17. Blackstone, *Commentaries*, 4:154–60.

18. Tawney, *Religion and the Rise of Capitalism*, at 36–55; Viner, "Economic Doctrines"; and Langholm, "Economic Freedom," at 273–83.

19. See Jarrett, *Social Theories*, at 161–62; Tawney, *Religion and the Rise of Capitalism*, at 30–36; and Baldwin, *Masters, Princes, and Merchants*, at 263–64.

20. See Pirenne, *Economic and Social History*, at 174–75; and McGovern, "Rise of New Economic Attitudes."

21. Wright, *Contribution of the Medieval Church*, at 32–33, and 185–86; and Baldwin, *Masters, Princes and Merchants*, at 240–41.

22. See, for example, Canon 11 of the Second Lateran Council of 1139, in Charles-Joseph Hefele, *Histoires des conciles d'après les documents originaux*, translated by H. Leclercq (Paris: Letouzey et Ané, 1913) 5:728. See also, to the same basic effect, Canon 11 of the Council of Rheims of 1148, *ibid.*, at 825; and Canon 22 of the Third Lateran Council of 1179, *ibid.*, at 1103.

23. Richard Perry, ed., *The Sources of Our Liberties* (New York: McGraw-Hill, 1959), at 17–18.

24. Beaumanoir, *Coûtumes de Beauvaisis,* at 129–34.

25. Richard B. Lillich, *The Human Rights of Aliens in Contemporary International Law* (Manchester: Manchester University Press, 1984), at 8–9.

26. Endre Ustor, "Most-Favoured-Nation Clause," UN Doc. A/CN.4/213 (1969), reprinted in *Year Book of the International Law Commission 1969,* UN Doc. A/CN.4/SER/A/1969/Add. 1 (1969), 2:159.

27. On the juridical aspects of the medieval fairs, see Pirenne, *Economic and Social History,* at 96–102.

28. On the law merchant, see Harold J. Berman, *Law and Revolution: The Formation of the Western Legal Tradition* (Cambridge, Mass.: Harvard University Press, 1983), at 333–56. The principal text setting forth the substantive principles of this body of law was Malynes, *Consuetudo.* On the medieval merchant community generally, see Bozeman, *Politics and Culture,* at 401–12. On various forms of medieval economic organization generally, see John H. Mundy, *Europe in the High Middle Ages 1150–1309* (London: Longman, 1973), at 153–73. For interesting illustrations of the phenomenon of "stateless trading" in Africa, see Curtin, *Crosscultural Trade,* at 46–49.

29. On medieval banking, see Pirenne, *Economic and Social History,* at 125–31; Edward P. Cheyney, *The Dawn of a New Era 1250–1453* (New York: Harper and Row, 1936), at 37–56; and Mundy, *Europe in the High Middle Ages,* at 167–73.

30. Tawney, *Religion and the Rise of Capitalism,* at 73.

31. On the early history of the exchanges, see Braudel, *Wheels of Commerce,* at 97–114. On Antwerp during its prime in the sixteenth century, see Tawney, *Religion and the Rise of Capitalism,* at 72–76.

32. Vitoria, "On the Indians," at 153.

33. *Ibid.,* at 154–56. On Vitoria's views on freedom of trade, see generally Barcia Trelles, "Vitoria," at 216–18; and Catry, "Liberté du commerce."

34. Crucé, *New Cyneas* at 25–35. On Crucé, see Souleyman, *Vision of World Peace,* at 9–20.

35. Sully, *Memoirs,* 4:244–45.

36. The classic work on mercantilism is Heckscher, *Mercantilism.* For an excellent short discussion of the basic ethos and ideas of mercantilism, see Crowley, *This Sheba Self,* at 34–49. For a useful collection of essays on the subject, see Coleman, ed., *Revisions in Mercantilism.* See also Viner, "Power Versus Plenty."

37. Michael Mann, *The Sources of Social Power, Volume 1: A History of Power from the Beginning to A.D. 1760* (Cambridge: Cambridge University Press, 1986), 1:474. On mercantilism as economic nationalism, see Heilperin, *Studies,* at 52–54.

38. Heckscher, *Mercantilism,* 2:104–11.

39. *Ibid.,* at 145–72.

40. On the crucial importance of foreign, as opposed to domestic trade in increasing the wealth of the nation, see Mun, *England's Treasure.* On the mercantilist attitude to foreign trade, see Gomes, *Foreign Trade,* at 38–93.

41. Gentili, *Law of War,* at 88.

42. *Ibid.,* at 101–2. On Gentili's view on freedom of commerce, see Cole-

man Phillipson, "Albericus Gentilis," in John MacDonell, ed., *Great Jurists of the World* (London: John Murray, 1913), at 121–24.

43. Grotius, *Law of Prize and Booty*, at 226–30, and 255–57.

44. Pufendorf, *Law of Nature and Nations*, at 368–71, and 393–96.

45. Wolff, *Law of Nations*, at 15–16. On the evolution of this concept to the middle of the eighteenth century, see Broms, *Doctrine of Equality*, at 27–39.

46. Wolff, *Law of Nations*, at 107.

47. *Ibid.*, at 20–27.

48. *Ibid.*, at 40–41.

49. *Ibid.*, at 45.

50. *Ibid.*, at 98.

51. Vattel, *Law of Nations*, at 6.

52. *Ibid.*, at 121–22.

53. *Ibid.*, at 15.

54. *Ibid.*, at 39.

55. *Ibid.*, at 43.

56. *Ibid.*, at 122.

57. *Ibid.*, at 41.

58. An excellent general account of the nature and history of the Continental System is Heckscher, *Continental System.*

59. House of Commons, April 28, 1812, 22 *Cobbett's Parliamentary Debates* (London: T. C. Hansard, 1812), at 1093.

60. For a general account of these policies, see Perkins, *Prologue to War*, at 226–60. On the U.S. non-importation policy specifically (as opposed to the more all-inclusive policy of nonintercourse), see Heaton, "Non-importation."

61. Wolff, *Law of Nations*, at 298–300.

62. Boedes Lust, 5 C. Rob. 233, 165 English Reports 759 (1804). See also Kent, *Commentary*, at 197–98.

63. Theodore Besterman, *Voltaire*, 3d ed. (Oxford: Basil Blackwell, 1976), at 243–44.

64. For an excellent short discussion of this point, see Appleby, *Capitalism*, at 29–34.

65. Paine, "Rights of Man," at 362.

66. Hume "Of Interest," in *Essays*, at 308.

67. See Hinsley, *Power*, at 82–83; Schlereth, *Cosmopolitan Ideal*, at 97–125; and Gomes, *Foreign Trade*, at 94–125.

68. Montesquieu, *Spirit of the Laws*, at 316.

69. *Ibid.*, at 321. On Montesquieu's views, see Hirschman, *Passions and Interests*, at 70–81.

70. Kant, *Perpetual Peace*, at 37.

71. Hume, "Jealousy of Trade," in *Essays*, at 334–38.

72. Paine, "Rights of Man," at 400.

73. Gilbert, " 'New Diplomacy.' "

74. The basic physiocratic text is Quesnay, *Physiocratie*. On the physiocrats, see generally Weulersse, *Le mouvement physiocratique*; and Fox-Genovese, *Origins of Physiocracy*. For good short accounts, see Gide and Rist, *History*, at 21–68; Leo Gershoy, *From Despotism to Revolution 1763–1789*

(New York: Harper and Row, 1944), at 67–72; Peter Gay, *The Enlightenment: An Interpretation,* 2: *The Science of Freedom* (New York: Vintage, 1969), at 347–53, and 493–96; Roll, *History,* at 128–37; and Routh, *Origin,* at 68–79. On the economic aspects of the movement specifically, see Ronald L. Meek, *The Economics of Physiocracy: Essays and Translations* (London: G. Allen & Unwin, 1962); and Gianni Vaggi, *The Economics of François Quesnay* (Basingstoke: Macmillan, 1987).

75. Quesnay, *Physiocratie,* at 43–98.

76. For the thirty maxims, see *ibid.,* at 99–122, with notes thereon at 123–72. The freedom of individuals to decide what to cultivate is the subject of maxim XIII, at 113–14, with notes at 144–54. Full liberty of commerce is the subject of maxim XXV, at 119. The freeing of the grain trade is the subject of maxim XVI, at 115, with notes at 158–61.

77. On property rights, see maxim IV, in *ibid.,* at 108.

78. See generally Mirabeau, *L'ami des hommes,* especially 3:1–72, and 259–90. On Mirabeau, see generally Fox-Genovese, *Origins of Physiocracy,* at 134–66.

79. Quoted in Gilbert, " 'New Diplomacy,' " at 20.

80. For a survey of the growing network of bilateral commercial agreements among the European states as of the mid-eighteenth century, see Hübner, *De la saisie,* 2:138–54.

81. See generally Philip C. Jessup and Francis Deak, *Neutrality: Its History, Economics and Law,* 1: *The Origins* (New York: Columbia University Press, 1935); and Carl J. Kulsrud, *Maritime Neutrality to 1800: A History of the Main Principles Governing Neutrality and Belligerency to 1780* (Boston: Little, Brown, 1936).

82. Britain, however, adhered to the traditional rule. See The Hoop, 1 C. Rob. 196, 165 English Reports 146 (1799), which relies on the authority of Bynkershoek; the United States, in turn, followed this British view. See The Rapid, 12 U.S. (8 Cranch) 155 (1814).

83. France-Great Britain, Treaty of Commerce and Navigation (Eden Treaty), Sep. 26, 1786, 50 Consolidated Treaty Series 71.

84. Bynkershoek, *Questions,* at 30.

85. Paine, "Rights of Man," at 403.

86. Hübner, *De la saisie,* 1:44–45.

87. Kant, *Perpetual Peace,* at 11, note.

88. *Ibid.,* at 35.

89. *Ibid.,* at 26–27.

90. On the Dutch policy, see generally de Witt, *True Interest and Political Maxims.* See also Alice Clare Carter, *Neutrality or Commitment: The Evolution of Dutch Foreign Policy 1667–1795* (London: Edwin Arnold, 1975).

91. Paul A. Varg, *Foreign Policies of the Founding Fathers* (Baltimore: Penguin, 1963), at 20. For the two treaties, see France-United States, Treaty of Alliance, Feb. 6, 1778, 46 Consolidated Treaty Series 447; and France-United States, Treaty of Amity and Commerce, Feb. 6, 1778, 46 Consolidated Treaty Series 417.

92. Convention of Mortefontaine, Sep. 30, 1800, France-U.S., 55 Consoli-

dated Treaty Series 343. On the preceding conflict between the two countries, see Albert Hall Bowman, *The Struggle for Neutrality: Franco-American Diplomacy during the Federalist Era* (Knoxville, Tenn.: University of Tennessee Press, 1974).

93. Gilbert, *To the Farewell Address,* at 49–54.

94. Netherlands-United States, Treaty of Amity and Commerce, Oct. 8, 1782, 48 Consolidated Treaty Series 137.

95. Sweden-United States, Treaty of Amity and Commerce, April 3, 1783, 48 Consolidated Treaty Series 269.

96. Prussia-United States, Treaty of Amity and Commerce, Sep. 10, 1785, 49 Consolidated Treaty Series 331.

97. Gerald Stourzh, *Benjamin Franklin and American Foreign Policy* (Chicago: University of Chicago Press, 1954), at 231. The treaty which replaced this one in 1799 did not contain such a provision. See Prussia-United States, Treaty of Amity and Commerce, July 11, 1799, 55 Consolidated Treaty Series 15.

98. Ruhl J. Bartlett, ed., *The Record of American Diplomacy: Documents and Readings in the History of American Foreign Relations,* 4th ed. (New York: Knopf, 1964), at 86. On the Farewell Address generally, see Gilbert, *To the Farewell Address,* at 115–36.

99. Bartlett, *supra* note 98, at 86.

100. *Ibid.,* at 87.

101. William Doyle, *The Old European Order 1660–1800* (Oxford: Oxford University Press, 1978), at 117–19. On the French experience in particular, see generally Kaplan, *Bread, Politics and Political Economy.*

2. Free Trade Is the International Law of God

1. Smith, *Wealth of Nations,* at 443. See also Miller, "Adam Smith."

2. See generally Langer, *Coming of Age.*

3. See generally D. P. O'Brien, *The Classical Economists* (Oxford: Oxford University Press, 1975).

4. Smith, *Wealth of Nations,* at 456–57. On the central role of the division of labor in Smith's theory, see Gide and Rist, *History,* at 73–85.

5. James Mill, "Commerce Defended," at 109–10.

6. Quoted in Silberner, *Problem of War,* at 105.

7. *Ibid.,* at 287; and Boulding, "Defense and Opulence," at 210–11.

8. Gomes, *Foreign Trade,* at 129–70.

9. Paine, "Rights of Man," at 400–401.

10. Quoted in Viner, "Intellectual History," at 61. See generally Dawson, *Cobden and Foreign Policy.* On Cobden's life and career generally, see Edsall, *Cobden: Independent Radical*; and Hinde, *Cobden: Victorian Outsider.*

11. Quoted in Silberner, *Problem of War,* at 105.

12. Mill, *Principles of Political Economy,* in *Collected Works,* 3:593–94.

13. Herbert Spencer, *Function and Evolution,* edited by Stanislav Andreski (London: Nelson, 1971), at 153–65. (1st ed. 1876).

14. On the connection between the peace movement and liberal political

economy in the nineteenth century, see generally Bosanquet, *Free Trade and Peace*; Silberner, *Problem of War*; Hinsley, *Power*, at 96–113, and Spall, "Free Trade."

15. Quoted in Frederick B. Artz, *Reaction and Revolution 1814–1832* (New York: Harper and Row, 1934), at 85–86.

16. Silberner, *Problem of War*, at 282–83.

17. See generally Kenwood and Lougheed, *International Economy*, at 105–15; Bordo and Schwartz, *Retrospective*; and de Cecco, *International Gold Standard*.

18. Cobden-Chevalier Treaty, Jan. 23, 1860, 121 Consolidated Treaty Series 243. See Iliasu, "Cobden-Chevalier Treaty."

19. Pollard, *Peaceful Conquest*, at 256–57.

20. Endre Ustor, "Most-favored-Nation Clause," in Bernhardt, ed., *Encyclopedia of Public International Law*, 8:411–16.

21. See Kindelberger, "Rise of Free Trade."

22. Articles Concerning the Navigation of the Rhine, Mar. 24, 1815, 64 Consolidated Treaty Series 16.

23. D. W. Bowett, *The Law of International Institutions*, 4th ed. (London: Stevens, 1982), at 6–7.

24. General Act of the Conference Respecting the Congo, Feb. 26, 1885, 165 Consolidated Treaty Series 485. For a later World Court case on this subject, see Oscar Chinn Case (United Kingdom v. Belgium), 1934 Permanent Court of International Justice Reports, ser. A/B, No. 63.

25. Convention Respecting Free Navigation of the Suez Canal (Constantinople Convention), Oct. 29, 1888, 171 Consolidated Treaty Series 241.

26. Nolde, "Droit et technique," at 373–90; and Nussbaum, *Concise History*, at 199–203. On FCN Treaties generally, see Dieter Blumenwitz, "Treaties of Friendship, Commerce and Navigation," in Bernhardt, ed., *Encyclopedia of Public International Law*, 7:484–90. On embargo provisions in these treaties, see Lindemeyer, *Schiffsembargo und Handelsembargo*, at 57–85.

27. Pollard, *Peaceful Conquest*, at 272–73; Kenwood and Lougheed, *International Economy* at 57–72; and Dowty, *Closed Borders*, at 42–47.

28. Waltz, "Myth of Interdependence," at 215. On foreign investment during this period, see generally Richardson, "British Emigration"; Cottrell, *British Overseas Investment*; and Kenwood and Lougheed, *International Economy*, at 38–56. See Röpke, "Economic Order," at 221, for a characterization of this period as "a secularized Res Publica Christiana." For perceptive general remarks about the nature of international economic interdependence in the nineteenth century, see Cooper, *Economics of Interdependence*, at 150–53.

29. Marx and Engels, *Communist Manifesto*, at 39.

30. See, for example, Martens, *Précis du droit*, at 256–65.

31. See Gamal Mourai Badr, *State Immunity: An Analytical and Prognostic View* (The Hague: Martinus Nijhoff, 1984), at 21–24.

32. The North Atlantic Fisheries Case (United Kingdom v. United States), 11 Reports of International Arbitral Awards 167 (1910), at 181.

33. See Wolff v. Oxholm, 6 M and S 92, 105 English Reports 1177 (1817); and Hangar v. Abbott, 73 U.S. (6 Wall.) 532 (1868).

34. See Project of an International Declaration Concerning the Laws and Customs of War, Aug. 27, 1874, art. 28, *American Journal of International Law,* Supp. (1907), 1:101. This provision was not a legally binding treaty, but rather an agreed statement of principle. For its incorporation into a binding treaty, see Hague Convention IV Respecting the Laws and Customs of Land Warfare, Annex: Regulations Concerning the Laws and Customs of Land Warfare ("Hague Rules"), Oct. 18, 1907, art. 46, 205 Consolidated Treaty Series 277.

35. Declaration Respecting Maritime Law (Declaration of Paris), April 16, 1856, 115 Consolidated Treaty Series 1. See generally Francis Piggott, *The Declaration of Paris 1856: A Study* (London: University of London Press, 1919).

36. Quoted in Moore, *Digest of International Law,* 7:781–82. Also opposed to commercial blockade was Hall, *International Law,* at 555–58. On commercial blockade generally, see Westlake, "Commercial Blockade."

37. Semmel, *Liberalism,* at 71. Palmerston, however, changed his mind on the subject. *Ibid.,* at 77–78.

38. Bluntschli, *Droit international,* at 393–94.

39. See generally Roth, *Minimum Standard.*

40. Michael Davitt, *The Fall of Feudalism in Ireland; or the Story of the Land League Revolution* (London: Harper and Brothers, 1904), at 274–79; and Joyce Marlow, *Captain Boycott and the Irish* (London: Deutsch, 1973).

41. Unfortunately, terminology in this area is not standard. There is a tendency among continental European writers to confine the term "boycott" to private, unofficial initiatives, and to refer to any and all government-directed trade restrictions as "embargoes." Hans G. Kausch, "Boycott," in Bernhardt, ed., *Encyclopedia of Public International Law,* 3:75. This practice seems to take the term "embargo" too far from its original meaning (of preventing ships from sailing from ports of the embargoing state), and also to conflate the rather different strategies of (a) refusing to export to a target state, (b) refusing to import from a target state and (c) refusing either to export to *or* to import from a target state. It is preferable, in my view, to refer to (a) as an embargo, (b) as non-importation and (c) as a boycott (formerly called "non-intercourse"). Unfortunately, the World Court adopted the continental approach, in Military and Paramilitary Activities in and Against Nicaragua (Nicaragua v. United States of America), 1986 I.C.J. Reports 14, referring to the U.S. total trade stoppage as an embargo. With apologies to the World Court, this text will adopt the preferred terminology suggested here.

42. See Ts'ai, "Reactions to Exclusion"; McKee, *Chinese Exclusion,* at 103–25; and McKee, "Chinese Boycott." For diplomatic correspondence relating to this incident, see [1905] *Foreign Relations of the United States,* at 204–34.

43. See generally Remer, *Study of Chinese Boycotts.*

44. Quataert, *Social Disintegration,* at 121–45.

45. Much of the debate—not directly germane to the present study—revolved around the question of the extent to which a state could be held responsible to another under international law for actions taken by its private citizens. See, for example, Dionisio Anzilotti, "La responsabilité internationale des États à raison des dommages soufferts par des étrangers," *Revue*

Générale de Droit International Public (1906), 13:5–34; and Laferrière, "Le boycott." For a perceptive analysis of the general issues underlying this legal question, see Pinon, "Forme nouvelle."

46. Baty, *International Law,* at 65–66.

47. Von Liszt, *Droit international,* at 74–75. See also, to this same general effect, Piédelièvre, *Précis,* 1:471–72; and Mérighnac, *Traité,* at 256–58. For a very clear delineation of the rival schools of thought on the question of the legality of boycotting, and of the different assumptions about the nature of international society underlying them, see Fauchille, *Traité,* 1(1):487–88.

48. Séfériadès, *Réflexions,* at 13–14.

49. *Ibid.,* at 5, note 2.

50. Hsu, *China's Entrance,* at 123–25.

51. Von Liszt, *Droit international,* at 74–75.

52. La Pradelle, "Question chinoise," at 338.

53. See, for example, Lambert, *Embargos,* at 65–66; and Myrdal, *International Economy,* at 41–42.

54. Myrdal, *International Economy,* at 41–42; and Carr, *Future of Nations,* at 41.

55. On U.S. protectionism in the late nineteenth century, see Hawke, "U.S. Tariff"; and Lake, *Power, Protection and Free Trade.*

56. La Pradelle, "Question chinoise," at 334–35.

57. *Ibid.,* at 333.

58. On the Don Pacifico incident, see Jaspar Ridley, *Lord Palmerston* (London: Book Club Associates, 1970), at 359–76. On various incidents of "gunboat diplomacy" for the protection of aliens during the nineteenth century, see Borchard, *Diplomatic Protection,* at 446–56.

59. See Landes, *Bankers and Pashas.*

60. On the experience of the Ottoman Empire, see Blaisdell, *European Financial Control.* On the experience of Greece, see Politis, "Contrôle international." On this phenomenon generally, see Andréadès, "Contrôle financière"; Strupp, "Intervention"; and McLean, "Finance and 'Informal Empire.'" On the juridical aspects of state loans and guarantees, see Politis, *Les emprunts d'État;* and Gaston Jèze, "La garantie des emprunts publics d'États," *Recueil des Cours* (Académie de Droit International) (1925), 7:151–236.

61. See generally M. F. Bleaney, *Underconsumption Theories: A History and Critical Analysis* (London: Lawrence and Wishart, 1976). On the development, for the first time in history, of export-oriented economies during the nineteenth century, see Kenwood and Lougheed, *International Economy,* at 144–59.

62. Marx and Engels, *Communist Manifesto,* at 40.

63. Carleton J. Hayes, *A Generation of Materialism 1871–1900* (New York: Harper and Row, 1941), at 104–9; Renouvin and Duroselle, *History of International Relations,* at 75–78; and Pollard, *Peaceful Conquest,* at 261–62.

64. Around the turn of the twentieth century, a considerable body of alarmist literature about the German trade menace appeared. See Hirschman, *National Power,* at 53–58.

65. On British-German economic rivalry at the end of the nineteenth and beginning of the twentieth centuries, see Hoffman, *Britain and German Trade*

Rivalry; and Kennedy, *Rise of Anglo-German Antagonism*, at 291–320. On the "fair trade" campaign in Britain, see Sykes, *Tariff Reform*.

66. On St.-Simonianism, see generally Charléty, *Histoire*; Manuel, *New World*; Iggers, *Cult of Authority*; and Carlisle, *Proferred Crown*.

67. Friedrich Engels, *Anti-Dühring: Herr Eugen Dühring's Revolution in Science* (Moscow: Progress Publishers, 1954), at 389. In this same work, at 359, Engels states that "in Saint-Simon we find a comprehensive breadth of view, by virtue of which almost all of the ideas of later socialists that are not strictly economic are found in him in embryo."

68. Steuart, *Inquiry*, 1:189–202. On Steuart, see Sen, *Economics of Steuart*; and Meek, "Rehabilitation of Steuart."

69. Rousseau, "Government of Poland," at 223–35; and "Project for Corsica." See Ann Tickner, "Rousseau's Concept of Self-reliance Compared with That of Some Contemporary Theorists," in Galtung, O'Brien and Preiswerk, eds., *Self-reliance*, at 58–79.

70. See E. A. J. Johnson, *The Foundations of American Economic Freedom: Government and Enterprise in the Age of Washington* (Minneapolis: University of Minnesota Press, 1973), at 121–51; and McCoy, *Elusive Republic*, at 146–61.

71. Clement Eaton, *Henry Clay and the Art of American Politics* (Boston: Little, Brown, 1957), at 43–46.

72. See Engelbrecht, *Fichte*; and Heilperin, *Studies*, at 82–96. On the influence of German romantic thinking on economic thought in the early nineteenth century, see Roll, *History of Economic Thought*, at 211–31.

73. On List, see generally Silberner, *Problem of War*, at 134–71; Lenz, *Lists Staats- und Gesellschaftslehre*; Henderson, *Friedrich List*; Gomes, *Foreign Trade*, at 262–77; and Szporluk, *Communism and Nationalism*, at 96–151.

74. List, *Natural System*, at 31. This work, written in 1837 but not published during List's lifetime, was in effect a "pilot project" for the major work of 1841.

75. *Ibid.*

76. List, *National System*, at 99–100.

77. On the German historical school of political economists, see generally Schumacher, "Historical School"; Silberner, *Problem of War*, at 172–92; Gide and Rist, *History*, at 383–409; and Roll, *History of Economic Thought*, at 303–11.

78. Schmoller, *Mercantilism*.

79. On Lassalle, see Gide and Rist, *History*, at 483–87.

80. On solidarism, see Theodore Zeldin, *France 1848–1945: Politics and Anger* (Oxford: Oxford University Press, 1979), at 290–97. See also Émile Durkheim, *The Division of Labor in Society*, translated by George Simpson (New York: Free Press, 1933) (1st ed. 1893).

81. For a very insightful analysis of this point, see Milward, "Tariffs as Constitutions."

82. T. O. Lloyd, *The British Empire 1558–1983* (Oxford: Oxford University Press, 1985), at 187–88.

83. See Golob, *Méline Tariff*. On French economic nationalist policies generally during this period, see Lebovics, *Alliance of Iron and Wheat*.

84. Gordon A. Craig, *Germany 1866–1945* (Oxford: Oxford University Press, 1981), at 85–100, and 150–52; and Webb, "Agricultural Protection."

85. Arno J. Mayer, *The Persistence of the Old Regime: Europe to the Great War* (New York: Pantheon, 1981), at 290–95.

86. On American dollar diplomacy, see Nearing and Freeman, *Dollar Diplomacy*; Munro, *Intervention and Dollar Diplomacy*; and Healy, *Hegemony in the Caribbean.*

87. On the French system of controls, see Becqué, *Internationalisation des capitaux*; and Feis, *Europe the World's Banker*, at 118–59. On the German system of controls, see Laves, "German Governmental Influence"; and Feis, *Europe the World's Banker*, at 163–74. On the British methods, see *ibid.*, at 84–95.

88. On the French policy generally, a most useful collection of primary-source materials is Poidevin, *Finances et relations internationales*. On the experience with Italy, see Feis, *Europe the World's Banker*, at 235–39.

89. Laves, "German Governmental Influence," at 500–2; and Viner, "International Finance," at 408–10.

90. Calvo, *Droit international*, 6:231. See also Shea, *Calvo Clause*; and F. W. Garcia-Amador, "Calvo Doctrine, Calvo Clause," in Bernhardt, ed., *Encyclopedia of Public International Law*, 8:62–64.

91. Convention Concerning the Rights of Aliens, Jan. 29, 1902, 190 Consolidated Treaty Series 445.

92. Hirschman, *National Power*, at 146–50.

93. Naumann, *Central Europe*, at 185–89. On Naumann's life and career generally, see Heuss, *Friedrich Naumann.*

3. Business, Not Politics

1. Quoted in Endre Ustor, "Most-favored-Nation Clause," UN Doc. A/CN.4/213 (1969), reprinted in *Year Book of the International Law Commission 1969*, UN Doc. A/CN.4/SER.A/1969/Add. 1 (1969), 2:162–63.

2. Pasvolsky, *Economic Nationalism*; and Mitrany, *Effect of the War*, at 184–205.

3. Hogan, *Informal Entente*, at 13–14.

4. Arthur Salter, "Economic Conflicts as the Causes of War," in Valentine Chirol et al., *The Reawakening of the Orient and Other Addresses* (New Haven: Yale University Press, 1925), at 157.

5. See generally Diamond, *Economic Thought*; and Link, *Woodrow Wilson*, at 72–103.

6. Link, *Woodrow Wilson*, at 76.

7. Ruhl J. Bartlett, ed., *The Record of American Diplomacy: Documents and Readings in the History of American Foreign Relations* 4th ed. (New York: Knopf, 1964), at 460.

8. Link, *Woodrow Wilson*, at 86, footnote.

9. For the text, see David Hunter Miller, *The Drafting of the Covenant* (New York: Putnam, 1928), 2:16–18. See also Bailey, "Political Aspect," at 109–12.

10. For the text of the Treaty of Versailles of June 28, 1919, see 225 Consol-

idated Treaty Ser. 188. The "war-guilt clause" was Article 231. For the various economic disabilities imposed on Germany, see Articles 45, 119–34, 156–58, 231–44, 248–79, 313–20, and 321–86. See generally Baruch, *Reparation and Economic Sections.*

11. For the text of the Covenant of the League of Nations of June 28, 1919, see 225 Consolidated Treaty Ser. 195, reprinted in Innis L. Claude, *Swords into Ploughshares: The Problems and Progress of International Organization,* 4th ed. (New York: Random House, 1971), at 453–62. For general histories of the League, see Walters, *History of the League*; and Northedge, *League of Nations.*

12. See generally Gerig, *Open Door.*

13. The "requirement" of member states of the League to provide "equitable treatment" for the commerce of other members was expressly stated to be "[s]ubject to and in accordance with the provisions of international Conventions existing or hereafter to be agreed upon." It was, accordingly, those other conventions which governed the actual rights and duties of states in this area, and not Article 23(e) itself. The World Court so held in Railway Traffic Between Lithuania and Poland, 1931 Permanent Court of International Justice Reports, ser. A/B, No. 42.

14. Culbertson, *Commercial Policy,* at 351.

15. *Ibid.,* at 308–10, and 336–37.

16. *Ibid.,* at 357–58.

17. *Ibid.,* at 351–52.

18. Viner, "National Monopolies," at 599–600.

19. Bailey, "Political Aspect," at 179. For other pleas against economic nationalism during this period, see Donaldson, *International Economic Relations*; and Salter, "Economic Organization."

20. Barcelona Convention on Freedom of International Transit, April 20, 1921, 7 League of Nations Treaty Series 11.

21. Convention and Statute on the Regime of Navigable Waterways of International Concern, April 20, 1921, *ibid.,* at 35.

22. Convention and Statute on the International Regime of Maritime Ports, Dec. 9, 1923, 58 League of Nations Treaty Series 285.

23. Convention on the International Regime of Railways, Dec. 9, 1923, 47 League of Nations Treaty Series 55.

24. Report by the Economic Committee of the Provisional Economic and Financial Committee, Submitted to the Council on May 13th, 1922, in *League of Nations Official Journal* (1922), 3:624–25.

25. League of Nations, *Commercial Policy,* at 33–35.

26. For the text, see *League of Nations Official Journal* (1930), 11:398–415. On this initiative, see Hill, *Economic and Financial Organization,* at 50–53; and Kindelberger, *World in Depression,* at 131–35. On activities of the League of Nations in the economic sphere, see generally Milhaud, "Organisation économique," at 281–304; Janne, "Règlementation"; Guillian, *Problèmes douaniers*; League of Nations, *Ten Years of World Co-operation* (Geneva: League of Nations, 1930), at 178–206; van Woerden, *Société des Nations*; Rappard, "Nationalisme économique"; Hill, *Economic and Financial Organization*; Wal-

ters, *History of the League*, at 175–94, 423–34, and 749–62; and Northedge, *League of Nations*, at 165–91.

27. On the associationalist philosophy and system generally, see Hawley, "Herbert Hoover"; Wilson, *Herbert Hoover*, at 31–53; Carl P. Parrini, "Hoover and International Economics," in Gelfand, ed. *Herbert Hoover*, at 182–206; and Hogan, "Revival and Reform"; and "Corporatism."

28. On Hoover generally, see Wilson, *Herbert Hoover*. On his activities as Secretary of Commerce (and general U.S. economic "tsar"), see Brandes, *Hoover and Economic Diplomacy*; and Hawley, ed., *Hoover as Secretary of Commerce*.

29. See generally Leffler, "Political Isolationism"; Hawley, *Great War*; Melvyn P. Leffler, "Herbert Hoover, the 'New Era,' and American Foreign Policy, 1921–1928," in Hawley, ed., *Hoover as Secretary of Commerce*, at 148–79; and Melvyn P. Leffler, "1921–1932: Expansionist Impulses and Domestic Constraints," in Becker and Wells, eds., *Economics and World Power*, at 227–37.

30. On the postwar fears of raw-material shortages in the United States, see Alfred E. Eckes, Jr., *The United States and the Global Struggle for Minerals* (Austin, Texas: University of Texas Press, 1979), at 3–55. On Hoover's efforts to promote and support foreign investment for the securing of rubber, see Brandes, *Hoover and Economic Diplomacy*, at 106–28. On the investment of Firestone Rubber Company in Liberia during this period, see Krasner, *Defending the National Interest*, at 98–106.

31. See Barber, *New Era to New Deal*, at 31–40.

32. On the reparations problem generally, see Kent, *Spoils of War*.

33. On the Ruhr occupation crisis, see Roosevelt, "Ruhr Occupation"; and Gordon A. Craig, *Germany 1866–1945* (Oxford: Oxford University Press, 1981), at 448–59.

34. Report of the Expert Committees Appointed by the Reparation Commission, Cmd. 2105 (1924), at 12.

35. *Ibid.* On the devising of the Dawes Plan, see generally Dawes, *Dawes Plan*; Schuker, *End of French Predominance*, at 169–93; and McNeil, *American Money*, at 24–34.

36. See Finch, "Dawes Report." For the text of the agreement implementing the recommendations of the Dawes Committee, see Agreement on the Experts' Plan of April 9, 1924, Aug. 30, 1924, 30 League of Nations Treaty Series 64.

37. On the massive American lending and its effects, see Sering, *Deutschland unter dem Dawes-Plan*; Wandel, *Bedeutung*; McNeil, *American Money*; and Schuker, *American 'Reparations.'*

38. See Wilson, *American Business*, at 123–56; and Costigliola, *Awkward Dominion*, at 114–39.

39. For the text of the press announcement outlining this arrangement, see [1922] *Foreign Relations of the United States*, 1:557. On the background to the formation of the policy, see Parrini, *Heir to Empire*, at 184–91.

40. There is a large body of literature on the loan-supervision program. See, for example, Williams, "Capital Embargoes"; Madden, Nadler and Sauvin, *America's Experience*, at 232–49; Feis, *Diplomacy of the Dollar*, at 7–77;

Brandes, *Hoover and Economic Diplomacy*, at 170–213; Parrini, *Heir to Empire*, at 184–211; Wilson, *American Business*, at 101–21; and Rosenberg, *Spreading the American Dream*, at 143–57. For Hoover's account of his own role in the program, see Hoover, *Memoirs*, 2:85–91.

41. United Kingdom-United States, Agreement on Debt Funding, June 18, 1923, *Treaties and Other International Agreements of the United States of America 1776–1949*, compiled by Charles I. Bevans (Washington, D.C.: GPO, 1968), 12:397.

42. Moulton and Pasvolsky, *World War Debt Settlements*; and Aldcroft, *Versailles to Wall Street*, at 92–96. On the war-debt question generally, see *ibid.*, at 239–67.

43. On the stabilization of currencies during the 1920s, see Aldcroft, *Versailles to Wall Street*, at 187–217.

44. *Ibid.*, at 187–217; and Buckingham, *International Normalcy*.

45. The S.S. 'Lotus' (France v. Turkey), 1927 Permanent Court of International Justice Reports, ser. A, No. 10, at 18.

46. Redslob, *Principes*, at 174–91.

47. Stowell, *International Law*, at 137–41. See also Brown, "Boycott in International Law."

48. For a discussion of this trend in the context of the rise of totalitarianism during this period, see Friedmann, "Growth of State Control."

49. Gamal Mourai Badr, *State Immunity: An Analytical and Prognostic View* (The Hague: Martinus Nijhoff, 1984), at 25–34, and 41–45.

50. Hyde, "Department of State," at 251.

51. Culbertson, *International Economic Policies*, at 383–85, and 389–90.

52. Dulles, "Foreign Loan Policy."

53. Angell, *Financial Foreign Policy*, at 111–13.

54. Ratner, *Tariff History*, at 48–49.

55. Scelle, "Phénomène juridique." See also Niemeyer, *Law Without Force*, at 229–33; and Hopkins, "International Role." For a vigorous argument against this idea, see Morgenthau, *Defense of the National Interest*, at 33–39.

56. Kelsen, "Rapports de système." See also J. G. Starke, "Monism and Dualism," *British Year Book of International Law* (1936), 17:66–81.

57. On economic warfare generally, see Greene, "Economic Sanctions"; and Michels, *Boycottage*. On the legal issues involved, see Lenz, *Wirtschaftskampf*; and Walz, *Nationalboykott und Völkerrecht*.

58. On this incident, see generally W. P. and Zelda K. Coates, *A History of Anglo-Soviet Relations* (London: Lawrence and Wishart, 1944), 1: 470–505. For the official correspondence relating to this matter, see Correspondence Relating to the Arrest of Employees of the Metropolitan-Vickers Company at Moscow, Cmd. 4286 (1933).

59. Lambert, *Les Embargos*, at 66.

60. Lambert, "Une fuite dans les institutions," at 49–59.

61. *League of Nations Official Journal* (1932), 13:1872.

62. *Ibid.*, at 1883.

63. Report Provided for in Article 15, Paragraph 4 of the Covenant, Submitted by the Special Committee of the Assembly in Execution of Part III (Paragraph 5) of the Resolution of March 11th, 1932, and Adopted by the

Assembly on February 24th, 1933, *League of Nations Official Journal,* Special Supp. No. 112 (1933), at 72. For an account of the League's consideration of the boycott aspects of the Manchurian crisis, see Willoughby, *Sino-Japanese Controversy,* at 604–22. For an analysis and discussion of many of the major issues, see M. Pelt, "Memorandum on Boycotts and Japanese Interests in China," in *Report of the Commission of Inquiry* (Lytton Commission), Annex, League of Nations Doc. C.663.M.320.VII (1932), at 208–50. On the effect of the boycott, see Remer, *Chinese Boycotts,* at 175–96.

For debates on various legal aspects of this boycott, and of boycotting generally, see Takayanagi, "Legality"; Hyde, "Boycott as a Sanction"; Hyde and Wehl, "Boycott in Foreign Affairs"; Lauterpacht, "Boycott in International Relations"; Wang, "International Law"; and Bouvé, "Boycott as Delinquency."

64. See generally Brandes, *Hoover and Economic Diplomacy,* at 61–147.

65. Aldcroft, *Versailles to Wall Street,* at 218–38.

66. See Silverman, *Reconstructing Europe,* at 242–70; and White, *Origins of Detente.*

67. Feis, *Diplomacy of the Dollar,* at 46–48.

68. See generally Wilson, *Ideology and Economics.*

69. Russia–United Kingdom, Trade Agreement, Mar. 16, 1921, art. 1, 4 League of Nations Treaty Series 127.

70. Turkey–U.S.S.R., Treaty of Friendship and Neutrality, Dec. 17, 1925, Protocol II, 157 League of Nations Treaty Series 353.

71. Germany–U.S.S.R., Treaty Signed at Berlin, April 24, 1926, art. 3, 53 League of Nations Treaty Series 387.

72. Lithuania–U.S.S.R., Treaty of Non-aggression, Sep. 28, 1926, art. 4, 60 League of Nations Treaty Series 145.

73. Persia–U.S.S.R., Treaty of Guarantee and Neutrality, Oct. 1, 1927, art. 3, 112 League of Nations Treaty Series 275.

74. Afghanistan–U.S.S.R., Treaty of Neutrality and Nonaggression, June 24, 1931, art. 2, 157 League of Nations Treaty Series 371.

75. Estonia–U.S.S.R., Treaty of Non-aggression and Peaceful Settlement of Disputes, May 4, 1932, art. 2, 131 League of Nations Treaty Series 297.

76. Latvia–U.S.S.R., Treaty of Non-aggression, April 4, 1934, art. 2, 148 League of Nations Treaty Series 113.

77. Germany–U.S.S.R., Treaty of Friendship, Oct. 12, 1925, art. 1, 122 *British and Foreign State Papers* 707.

78. Latvia–U.S.S.R., Treaty of Commerce, June 2, 1927, art. 1, 68 League of Nations Treaty Series 321.

79. Denmark–Russia, Preliminary Agreement, April 23, 1923, art. 2, 18 League of Nations Treaty Series 15.

80. Japan–U.S.S.R., Convention Embodying Basic Rules of Relations, Jan. 20, 1925, art. 4, 34 League of Nations Treaty Series 31.

81. Norway–U.S.S.R., Treaty of Commerce and Navigation, Dec. 15, 1925, art. 15, 47 League of Nations Treaty Series 9.

82. Estonia–U.S.S.R., Treaty of Commerce, May 17, 1929, art. 13, 94 League of Nations Treaty Series 323.

83. Turkey–U.S.S.R., Treaty of Commerce and Navigation, Mar. 16, 1931,

art. 16, in Jane Degras, ed., *Soviet Documents on Foreign Policy*, 2: *1925–32* (Oxford: Oxford University Press, 1952), at 479.

84. Ratner, *Tariff History*, at 49.

85. See [1923] *Foreign Relations of the United States*, 1:121–33.

86. "Unfavorable Attitude of the Department of State Toward American Loans to Foreign Enterprises Competing with American Enterprises in Third Countries," [1923] *Foreign Relations of the United States*, 2:503.

87. [1922] *Foreign Relations of the United States*, 2:455–57.

88. Wilson, *American Business*, at 118.

89. Barber, *From New Era to New Deal*, at 31–40.

90. See, for example, Denny, *America Conquers Britain*.

91. On the Great Depression generally, see Arndt, *Economic Lessons*; and Kindelberger, *World in Depression*.

92. See, for example, Feis, "After Tariffs"; Salter, "Future of Economic Nationalism"; Simonds and Emeny, *Great Powers*; Simonds and Emeny, *Price of Peace*; Sayre, "Menace of Economic Nationalism"; Rappard, *Common Menace*; and Fisher, *Economic Self-Sufficiency*.

93. Jones, Jr., *Tariff Retaliation*. See also Gordon, *Barriers to World Trade*.

94. See Drummond, *British Economic Policy*, at 170–338; Capie, *Depression and Protectionism*; and Boyce, *British Capitalism*.

95. See Harris, *Exchange Depreciation*.

96. On the policy of Germany, see Carroll, *Design for Total War*; Carr, *Arms and Autarky*; and Teichert, *Autarkie und Grossraumswirtschaft*.

97. Knickerbocker, *Red Trade Menace*.

98. Jonathon Haslam, *Soviet Foreign Policy 1930–1933: The Impact of the Depression* (London: Macmillan, 1983), at 51–52. For the text of the draft protocol, see Jane Degras, ed., *Soviet Documents on Foreign Policy, supra* note 83, at 499–500. For the discussion of the proposal by the League's Commission of Enquiry for European Union, see Minutes of the Session of Nov. 2–5, 1931, League of Nations Doc. C.910.M.478.1931.VII (1931). For the report of the special committee appointed to examine the proposed agreement, see Report by the Special Committee Appointed to Examine the Draft Pact of Economic Non-aggression, *League of Nations Official Journal* (1932), 13:152–54.

99. See generally Heuser, *Control of International Trade*. For a good short description of the "new protectionism" of the 1930s, see League of Nations, *Commercial Policy*, at 68–78.

100. For criticism of clearing arrangements, see League of Nations, *Enquiry into Clearing Agreements*; and Meade, *Economic Basis*, at 114–40.

101. See Kaiser, *Economic Diplomacy*; and Ranki, *Economy and Foreign Policy*.

102. Wiles, *Communist International Economics*, at 437. On the Stalinist program generally, see Day, *Leon Trotsky*; and Parrott, *Politics and Technology*, at 19–75.

103. On the economic nationalist character of centrally planned economies, see Bonn, "Paix économique"; Viner, *International Trade*, at 74–93; and Egon Neuberger, "Central Planning and Its Legacies: Implications for Foreign Trade," in Brown and Neuberger, eds., *International Trade*, at 349–77. See also

Holzman, *International Trade*. For a fascinating proposal for a similar autarkist-economic nationalist-central planning policy for the United States during the 1930s, see Beard, *Open Door at Home*.

104. On the economic nationalist character of the Roosevelt New Deal, see Dallek, *Franklin D. Roosevelt*, at 23–58.

105. Kindelberger, *World in Depression*, at 219–20. On the World Conference of 1933, see Walters, *History of the League*, at 517–23; and Kindelberger, *World in Depression*, at 204–24.

106. See Barnhart, "Japan's Economic Security"; and Barnhart, *Japan Prepares*.

107. See generally George W. Baer, *Test Case: Italy, Ethiopia and the League of Nations* (Stanford, Cal.: Hoover Institution Press, 1976).

108. Japan-United States, Treaty of Commerce and Navigation, Feb. 21, 1911, 213 Consolidated Treaty Series 98.

109. On U.S.-Japanese relations before the Second World War, see Feis, *Road to Pearl Harbor*; Lu, *Marco Polo Bridge*; Hosoya, "Miscalculations"; and Baldwin, *Economic Statecraft*, at 165–74.

4. Prosperity, Peace, and World Order

1. Allen, "International Trade Philosophy"; and Gaddis, *United States and Origins*, at 18–23.

2. See Pearson, *Reciprocal Trade Agreements Program*; Gardner, *Economic Aspects*, at 24–46; and Haggard, "Institutional Foundations." For Hull's own account of the program, see Hull, *Memoirs*, at 352–65, 518–30, and 746–50.

3. United Kingdom-United States, Atlantic Charter, Aug. 14, 1941, 55 U.S. Statutes at Large 1600; Cmd. 6321.

4. On the drafting of the economic provisions of the Atlantic Charter, see William L. Langer and S. Everett Gleason, *The Undeclared War 1940–1941* (New York: Harper, 1953), at 682–88; Dallek, *Franklin D. Roosevelt*, at 281–85; and Gardner, *Sterling-Dollar Diplomacy*, at 40–53. For notes by a participant in the discussions, see Memorandum of Conversation by the Under Secretary of State (Welles), Aug. 11, 1941, [1941] *Foreign Relations of the United States*, 1:361–63. On Hull's disappointment over the results, see Hull, *Memoirs*, at 975–76.

5. United Kingdom-United States, Lend-lease Agreement, Feb. 23, 1942, art. 7, 204 League of Nations Treaty Series 389. On the negotiation of the lend-lease agreement with Britain, which was the prototype for later such agreements, see Hull, *Memoirs*, at 1151–53; and Gardner, *Sterling-Dollar Diplomacy*, at 54–68.

6. For the definitive statement of the United States view on postwar international economic relations, see Department of State, *Proposals for Expansion*. On the planning for the postwar world generally, see Kolko, *Politics of War*, at 242–79; and Pollard, *Economic Security*, at 10–32.

7. On the prospects for Soviet-American economic cooperation during this period, see Paterson, *Soviet-American Confrontation*, at 57–62.

8. Department of State, *Proposals for Expansion*, at 20–23; and Knorr, "Problem of Cartels," at 1110–26.

9. Constance Howard, "Latin America During the Second World War," in Arnold and Veronica M. Toynbee, eds., *The War and the Neutrals* (London: Oxford University Press, 1956), at 152–57.

10. The Chargé in the United Kingdom (Matthews) to the Secretary of State, April 12, 1942, [1942] *Foreign Relations of the United States*, 1:163–64. See also W. Manning Dacey, "British Reconversion and Trade," *Foreign Affairs* (1945), 23:247–55.

11. Doc. No. 684, II/3/38, in *United Nations Conference on International Organization*, 10:127–30; Doc. No. 699, II/3/40, in *ibid.*, at 141–42; and Doc. No. 780, II/3/53, in *ibid.*, at 194–95. See also Russell, *History of the UN Charter*, at 788–89, and 802–3. For similar proposals, see Arndt, *Economic Lessons*, at 295–302. On the combined boards which the Allies formed during the war, see Rosen, *Combined Boards*.

12. On proposals of this kind, see Graham, *World Commodities*.

13. The Financial Adviser to the British Government (Keynes) to the Assistant Secretary of State (Acheson), June 4, 1941, [1941] *Foreign Relations of the United States*, 3:95–96.

14. United Kingdom-United States, Financial Agreement, Dec. 6, 1945, 126 UN Treaty Series 13. See also Polk and Patterson, "British Loan"; Paterson, *Soviet-American Confrontation*, at 159–73; Gardner, *Sterling-Dollar Diplomacy*, at 188–254; and Pollard, *Economic Security*, at 66–73.

15. See generally Milward, *Reconstruction*, at 421–61.

16. Charter for an International Trade Organization (Havana Charter), Mar. 21, 1948, UN Doc. E/CONF.2/78 (1948).

17. *Ibid.*, art. 29(1)(b).

18. On the debates which accompanied the drafting of the Havana Charter, see Feis, "Conflict over Trade Ideologies"; and Viner, "Conflicts of Principle."

19. See, for example, Philip Cortney, *The Economic Munich: The I.T.O. Charter, Inflation or Liberty, the 1929 Lesson* (New York: Philosophical Library, 1949).

20. See generally Diebold, *End of the ITO*; and Gardner, *Sterling-Dollar Diplomacy*, at 369–78.

21. General Agreement on Tariffs and Trade (GATT), Oct. 30, 1947, 55 UN Treaty Series 187.

22. Paterson, *Soviet-American Confrontation*, at 75–98.

23. George C. Herring, Jr., "Lend-lease to Russia and the Origins of the Cold War, 1944–1945," *Journal of American History* (1969), 56:93–114.

24. For good general accounts of the economic aspects of Soviet-U.S. relations at the onset of the Cold War, see Paterson, *Soviet-American Confrontation*; and Pollard, *Economic Security*.

25. See generally Pollard, *Economic Security*.

26. Kolko, *Limits of Power*, at 155–57; and Pollard, *Economic Security*, at 73–79. On U.S. policy vis-à-vis Italy, see John L. Harper, *America and the Reconstruction of Italy, 1945–1948* (Cambridge: Cambridge University Press, 1986).

27. Paterson, *Soviet-American Confrontation*, at 153–54; Pollard, *Economic Security*, at 162–63. On the attitude of McCloy, see Memorandum of Conversation by the Under Secretary of State (Lovett), Jan. 19, 1948, [1948] *Foreign Relations of the United States*, 4:514. See also The Under Secretary of State for Economic Affairs (Clayton) to the Under Secretary of State (Lovett), July 29, 1947, [1947] *Foreign Relations of the United States*, 4:435.

28. See, for example, the statement by Poland, in Summary Records of the 270th Meeting of the Economic and Social Council (ECOSOC) of the UN, in UN Economic and Social Council Official Records, 8th Sess., at 552; and the statement by the Soviet Union, in *Annual Report of the [Economic] Commission [for Europe] Covering the Period 9 May 1948 to 21 May 1949*, UN Economic and Social Council Official Records, 9th Sess., Supp. No. 12, UN Doc. E/1328–E/ECE104 (1949), at 34.

29. Quoted in Paterson, *Soviet-American Confrontation*, at 158.

30. IMF, *Annual Report 1950*, at 102. On Poland's experience as a World Bank member during this period, see Assetto, *Soviet Bloc*, at 69–75.

31. On Czechoslovakia's departure from the IMF, see de Vries and Horsefield, *IMF 1945–65*, 1:359–64. On its expulsion from the World Bank, see Mason and Asher, *World Bank*, at 171; and Assetto, *Soviet Bloc*, at 81–82.

32. Alexander Yanov, *Detente after Brezhnev* (Berkeley: Institute of International Studies, University of California, 1977), at 60–63.

33. Stalin, *Economic Problems*, at 18.

34. For examples of writers taking the threat of a "Communist economic offensive" seriously, see Thorp, "American Policy"; and Allen, *Soviet Economic Warfare*. For a more balanced view of Soviet international economic and political activity, see Kovner, *Challenge of Coexistence*. For a historical account of these fears and the policies to which they gave rise, see Kaufman, "U.S. Response."

35. Report of the Collective Measures Committee, UN General Assembly Official Records, 6th Sess., Supp. No. 13, UN Doc. A/1891 (1951), at 19.

36. Although the GATT is not, strictly speaking, an organization, the fact that it functions in practice as if it were one means that, for the purposes of this work, it may be so regarded. The GATT will, accordingly, occasionally be referred to as a "body" or "agency," substantially on a par with the IMF and World Bank. No important issue in this work hinges on this point.

37. On the GATT generally, see Curzon, *Multilateral Commercial Diplomacy*; Jackson, *World Trade*; Dam, *GATT*; Hudec, *GATT Legal System*; and Long, *Law and Its Limitations*.

38. GATT, art. 17.

39. *Ibid.*, art. 18.

40. Articles of Agreement of the International Bank for Reconstruction and Development (World Bank), Dec. 27, 1945, art. 3(5)(b), 2 UN Treaty Series 134. On the Bank's "project lending" policy, see Warren C. Baum and Stokes M. Tolbert, *Investing in Development: Lessons of World Bank Experience* (New York: Oxford University Press, 1985).

41. International Bank for Reconstruction and Development, *IBRD 1946–53*, at 4–7.

42. Articles of Agreement of the International Monetary Fund (IMF), Dec. 27, 1945, 2 UN Treaty Series 39.

43. On the operations and organization of the IMF, see A. W. Hooke, *International Monetary Fund: Its Evolution, Organization, and Activities* (Washington, D.C.: IMF, 1983); and Anand G. Chandavarkar, *The International Monetary Fund: Its Organization and Activities* (Washington, D.C.: IMF, 1984).

44. On international economic law, see Schwarzenberger, "Province and Standards"; Schwarzenberger, "Principes et normes"; Carreau, Juillard and Flory, *Droit international économique*; Laing, "International Economic Law"; John H. Jackson, "International Economic Law," in Bernhardt, ed., *Encyclopedia of Public International Law*, 8:149–61; Kohona, *Regulation*; and Seidl-Hohenveldern, "International Economic Law."

45. World Bank-United Nations, Agreement on Specialized Agency Status, Nov. 15, 1947, 16 UN Treaty Series 346.

46. See note 40 *supra*.

47. IMF-United Nations, Agreement on Specialized Agency Status, Nov. 15, 1947, 16 UN Treaty Series 328.

48. Joseph Gold, "Some Characteristics of Operation," in de Vries and Horsefield, *IMF 1945–65*, 2:589.

49. Havana Charter, art. 86(3).

50. UN General Assembly Res. 31/6H, UN General Assembly Official Records, 31st Sess., Supp. No. 38, UN Doc. A/31/38 (1976), at 14; and UN General Assembly Res. 37/2, UN General Assembly Official Records, 37th Sess., Supp. No. 51, UN Doc. A/36/51 (1982), at 14.

51. UN General Assembly Res. 2105 (XX), UN General Assembly Official Records, 20th Sess., Supp. No. 14, UN Doc. A/6014 (1965), at 3; and UN General Assembly Res. 2107 (XX), *ibid.*, at 62.

52. For the statement of the general counsel to the Fourth Committee of the UN General Assembly, see Summary Records of the 1645th Meeting of the Fourth Committee, UN General Assembly Official Records, 21st Sess., UN Doc. A/C.4/SR.1645 (1966), at 317–18. For the debate in the committee, see *ibid.*, at 318–25. For the statement of the Bank's position to the UN secretariat, see Secretary-General, "Consultation with the International Bank for Reconstruction and Development," UN General Assembly Official Records, 22d Sess., Annexes (Agenda item 66), at 2–9. (Hereinafter referred to as Secretary-General, "Consultation.")

53. Secretary-General, "Consultation," at 6–7.

54. *Ibid.*, at 9. On this incident, see Reisman, "Role of Economic Agencies"; Bleicher, "UN v. IBRD"; and Mason and Asher, *World Bank*, at 586–91. On the power of the World Bank to consider human-rights factors in its loan decisions, see Marmorstein, "World Bank Power."

5. Disarming Captain Boycott

1. On the subject of economic warfare and various aspects thereof, see generally Michels, *Boycottage*; Jack, *Studies in Economic Warfare*; Hirschman, *National Power*; Gordon and Dangerfield, *Hidden Weapon*; Wu, *Economic War-*

fare; Allen, "Economic Warfare"; Hasse, *Theorie und Politik*; Knorr, *Power and Wealth*; Knorr, *Power of Nations*; Lindemeyer, *Schiffsembargo und Handelsembargo*; Hasse, *Wirtschaftliche Sanktionen*; Losman, *International Economic Sanctions*; Barber, "Economic Sanctions"; Olson, "Economic Coercion"; Engels, *Zukunft des Embargos*; Seeler, "Wirtschaftssanktionen"; Daoudi and Dajani, *Economic Sanctions*; Ninic and Wallensteen, eds., *Dilemmas of Economic Coercion*; McCormick and Bissell, eds., *Strategic Dimensions*; Mayall, "Sanctions Problem"; Baldwin, *Economic Statecraft*; Daoudi and Dajani, *Economic Diplomacy*; Hufbauer and Schott, *Economic Sanctions*; Doxey, "International Sanctions"; and Leyton-Brown, ed., *Utility of Sanctions*.

2. Wolff, *Law of Nations*, at 298–300.

3. On the question of the legality of economic warfare, from various perspectives, see generally Lenz, *Wirtschaftskampf*; Brown, "Boycott in International Law"; Hyde and Wehl, "Boycott in Foreign Affairs"; Lauterpacht, "Boycott in International Relations"; Bouvé, "Boycott as Delinquency"; Rousseau, "Boycottage"; McDougal and Feliciano, *Law and Minimum Order*, at 193–96; Dubois, "Embargo"; Buchheit, "Use of Nonviolent Coercion"; Lillich, ed., *Economic Coercion*; Blum, "Economic Boycotts"; Neff, "Law of Economic Coercion"; Joyner, "Transnational Boycott"; Seidl-Hohenveldern, "UN and Economic Coercion"; Baldwin, *Economic Statecraft*, at 337–59; Farer, "Political and Economic Coercion"; Elagab, *Legality of Nonforcible Countermeasures*, at 190–213; Neff, "Boycott and the Law of Nations"; and Neff, "Economic Warfare."

4. Military and Paramilitary Activities in and Against Nicaragua (Nicaragua v. United States of America), 1986 International Court of Justice Reports 14. (Hereinafter cited as Nicaragua v. U.S.)

5. *Ibid.*, at 138, para. 276.

6. *Ibid.* See also Henderson, "Legality of Economic Sanctions."

7. On the American practice of economic warfare, see generally Williams, "Coming of Economic Sanctions"; Maw, "Historical Aspects"; Ayubi, Bissell, Korsah and Lerner, *Economic Sanctions*; Weintraub and Bertau, eds., *Economic Coercion*; Ellings, *Embargoes and World Power*; and Carter, *International Economic Sanctions*.

8. Mutual Defense Assistance Control Act of 1951 (Battle Act), 65 U.S. Statutes at Large 644, reprinted in Adler-Karlsson, *Western Economic Warfare*, at 28–30. This legislation was repealed in 1979.

9. Carter, *International Economic Sanctions*, at 40–61.

10. Wallerstein, *Food for War*, at 185–93; and Castore, "The United States and India: The Use of Food to Apply Economic Pressure — 1965–67," in Weintraub and Berteau, eds., *Economic Coercion*, at 129–53.

11. 22 U.S. Code §§ 2151n. See generally Cohen, "Conditioning U.S. Assistance."

12. 22 U.S. Code §§ 2291(h). See also Freedman, "U.S. Bilateral Aid."

13. 22 U.S. Code §§ 2371. On this legislation, see Richard B. Lillich and Thomas Carbonneau, "The 1976 Terrorism Amendment to the Foreign Assistance Act of 1961," *Journal of International Law and Economics* (1976), 11:223–36. See also 19 U.S. Code §§ 2462(b)(6), on the denial of preferential tariff

status to states supporting terrorism. See also 50 U.S. Code App. §§ 2405(j), on the application of export controls against states supporting terrorism. On this legislation, see David A. Flores, "Export Controls and the United States Effort to Combat International Terrorism," *Law and Policy in International Business* (1981), 13:521–90.

14. 22 U.S. Code §§ 2429 and 2429a.

15. 22 U.S. Code §§ 2370(e). See also 19 U.S. Code §§ 2462(b)(4), on the denial of preferential tariff status to states which nationalize American-owned property without paying legally required compensation.

16. On the use of foreign aid as a political instrument, see generally Liska, *New Statecraft*; Feis, *Foreign Aid*; Nelson, *Aid, Influence and Foreign Policy*; Knorr, *Power of Nations*, at 172–90; and Baldwin, *Economic Statecraft*, at 290–335.

17. "U.S.S.R. and Satellites Denied Import Tariff Concession," *Department of State Bulletin* (1951), 25:95.

18. 19 U.S. Code §§ 2432.

19. In January 1975, shortly after the adoption of this legislation, the Soviet Union suddenly announced that it would not accept a most-favored-nation status which was "discriminatory and subject to political conditions." See *Digest of U.S. Practice in International Law 1975*, at 536–39. It would appear that what actually caused this action by the Soviets was not the Jackson Amendment itself, but rather the unexpected imposition by the United States Congress of an extremely tight limit on credits which the United States Export-Import Bank would be permitted to grant in support of Soviet-American trade. See the Stevenson Amendment, 12 U.S. Code §§ 635(b)(3). See also William Korey, "Rescuing Soviet Jewry: Two Episodes Compared," *Soviet Jewish Affairs* (1975), 5 (Part 1):3–19. On the Jackson Amendment affair generally, see William W. Orbach, *The American Movement to Aid Soviet Jews* (Amherst, Mass.: University of Massachusetts Press, 1979); and Dan Caldwell, *American-Soviet Relations from 1947 to the Nixon-Kissinger Grand Design* (Westport, Conn.: Greenwood Press, 1981), at 190–98.

20. Nicaragua v. U.S., at 138–42, paras. 277–82. The treaty in question was an FCN treaty of Jan. 21, 1956, 367 UN Treaty Series 3.

21. Nicaragua v. U.S., at 128–29, para. 253.

22. See generally Colbert, *Retaliation*; Zoller, *Peacetime Unilateral Remedies*; Leben, "Contre-mesures"; and Elagab, *Legality of Non-forcible Countermeasures*.

23. Corfu Channel Case (United Kingdom v. Albania), 1949 International Court of Justice Reports 4.

24. On the United States sanctions against Iran during the hostages crisis, see generally Carswell, "Economic Sanctions"; Assersohn, *Biggest Deal*; Baldwin, *Economic Statecraft*, at 251–61; Robert Carswell and Richard J. Davis, "The Economic and Financial Pressures: Freeze and Sanctions," in Kreisberg, ed., *American Hostages*, at 173–200; and Cohen, *In Whose Interest*, at 147–76.

25. Bialos and Juster, "Libyan Sanctions," at 832–37.

26. "National Emergency in Panama," *Department of State Bulletin*, Dec. 1988, at 57.

27. On economic measures as reprisals, or counter-measures, see generally Hyde, "Boycott as Sanction"; Hyde and Wehl, "Boycott as Sanction"; Bowett, "Economic Coercion and Reprisals"; Leben, "Contre-mesures"; Dupuy, "Observations"; and Elagab, *Legality of Non-forcible Countermeasures*, at 190–213.

28. Heston, "Cuba, U.S. and Sugar Act."

29. See generally Muñoz Gonzalez, *Doctrina Grau.*

30. Inter-American Treaty of Reciprocal Assistance (Rio Treaty), Sep. 2, 1947, 21 UN Treaty Series 77.

31. The Chairman of the United States Delegation (Marshall) to the Acting Secretary of State, Aug. 19, 1947, [1947] *Foreign Relations of the United States,* 8:38; and The Chairman of the United States Delegation to the Acting Secretary of State, Aug. 23, 1947, *ibid.,* at 59.

32. Charter of the Organization of American States (OAS), April 30, 1948, 119 UN Treaty Series 3.

33. Declaration on the Inadmissibility of Intervention in the Domestic Affairs of States and the Protection of Their Independence and Sovereignty, UN General Assembly Res. 2131 (XX), UN General Assembly Official Records, 20th Sess., Supp. No. 14, UN Doc. A/6014 (1965), at 11.

34. Declaration on the Principles of International Law Concerning Friendly Relations and Co-operation among States, UN General Assembly Res. 2625 (XXV), UN General Assembly Official Records, 25th Sess., Supp. No. 28, UN Doc. A/8028 (1970), at 121.

35. Nicaragua v. U.S., at 106–10, and 125–26, paras. 202–9, and 244–45. On intervention by economic means in international law, see generally Dicke, *Intervention*; Bryde, "Intervention"; and Joyner, "Transnational Boycott," at 229–35.

36. For an informative summary of the various positions taken by various states in early UN debates on the question of including economic measures within the concept of aggression, see Report by the Secretary-General, UN Doc. A/2211 (1952), in UN General Assembly Official Records, 7th Sess., Annexes (Agenda item 54), at 74–75.

37. Consensus Definition of Aggression, UN General Assembly Res. 3314 (XXIX), UN General Assembly Official Records, 29th Sess., Supp. No. 31, UN Doc. A/9631 (1974), at 142. On the debates at the UN over the defining of aggression, see generally Ahmed M. Rifaat, *International Aggression: A Study of the Legal Concept* (Stockholm: Almqvist and Wiksell, 1979), at 222–80. See also Stone, *Conflict Through Consensus.*

38. See, for example, the accusation by Cuba against the United States, UN Doc. S/4378, in UN Security Council Official Records, 15th Year, Supp. for July-Sep. 1960, at 9; and the accusation by Argentina against the United Kingdom, UN Doc. S/14968, in UN Security Council Official Records, 37th Year, Supp. for April-June 1982, at 18.

39. Most writers have discussed this issue in terms of the prohibition by the UN Charter against the use of force, rather than by customary law, although the prevailing view is that the two prohibitions are identical. See, therefore, the references in note 47 *infra.*

40. Declaration on the Prohibition of Military, Political or Economic Coer-

cion in the Conclusion of Treaties, Final Act of the United Nations Conference on the Law of Treaties, UN Doc. A/CONF.39/26 (1969), in *United Nations Conference on the Law of Treaties, Official Records: Documents of the Conference*, UN Doc. A/CONF.39/11/Add. 2 (1971), at 285.

41. For the text of the Vienna Convention on the Law of Treaties, see 1155 UN Treaty Series 331. On this debate over economic pressure in the concluding of treaties, see Murphy, "Economic Duress"; Partridge, "Political and Economic Coercion"; and de Jong, "Coercion and the Conclusion."

42. See the references in note 48 *infra*.

43. See generally Singer, "Limits"; Feith, "Oil Weapon De-mystified"; and Hans W. Maull, "Oil and Influence: The Oil Weapon Examined," in Treverton, ed., *Energy and Security* at 3–39. For an almost comically apocalyptic view of the oil crisis, see Friedland, Seabury and Wildavsky, "Oil and Decline."

44. For various views on the legality of the Arab oil embargo, see Boorman, "Economic Coercion"; Paust and Blaustein, "Arab Oil Weapon — Threat"; Shihata, "Destination Embargo"; Paust and Blaustein, "Arab Oil Weapon — Reply"; and Paust, "International Law and Economic Coercion."

45. Doc. No. G/7(e)(4), in *United Nations Conference on International Organization*, 6:559.

46. Doc. No. 784, I/1/27, in *ibid.*, at 334–35. See Rifaat, *supra* note 37, at 120–22.

47. See, for example, Goodrich and Hambro, *Charter of the UN*, at 104; Humphrey Waldock, "The Regulation of the Use of Force by Individual States in International Law," *Recueil des Cours* (Académie de Droit International) (1952), 81:493–94; Bowett, *Self-defense*, at 148–49; Max Sorensen, "Principes de droit international public," *Recueil des Cours* (Académie de Droit International) (1960), 101:236–37; Ian Brownlie, *International Law and the Use of Force by States* (Oxford: Clarendon Press, 1963), at 361–62; Dubois, "Embargo," at 109–10; Lillich, "Status of Economic Coercion," at 18–19; Leben, "Contre-mesures," at 67; Seidl-Hohenveldern, "UN and Economic Coercion," at 10–11; Farer, "Political and Economic Coercion," at 408–10; and Michel Virally, "Article 2, paragraphe 4," in Jean-Pierre Cot and Alain Pellet, eds., *La Charte des Nations Unies: Commentaire article par article* (Paris: Economica, 1985), at 120–21.

For the minority view on the subject (i.e., that Article 2(4) of the UN Charter does constitute a general restriction on the resort of economic warfare), see Buchheit, "Use of Nonviolent Coercion"; Paust and Blaustein, "Arab Oil Weapon — Threat," at 415–19; and Zedalis, "Thoughts on the UN Charter," at 491–97.

48. Among writers endorsing this approach are McDougal and Feliciano, *Law and Minimum Order*, at 190–96; Brosche, "Arab Oil Embargo," at 34; Muir, "Boycott," at 202–4; Seidl-Hohenveldern, "UN and Economic Coercion," at 11–12; Farer, "Political and Economic Coercion," at 411–13; and Neff, "Economic Warfare," at 100–1. For case law from the United States which supports this reasoning by analogy (holding that economic measures can be of such a degree of severity as to amount to "persecution" for the

purposes of determination of refugee status), see Diminich v. Esperdy, 299 F. 2d 244 (2d Cir. 1961); Dunat v. Hurney, 297 F. 2d 289 (3d Cir. 1962); Soric v. Flagg, 303 F. 2d 289 (7th Cir. 1962); and Kovac v. I.N.S., 407 F. 2d 102 (9th Cir. 1969).

49. General Agreement on Tariffs and Trade (GATT), Oct. 30, 1947, 55 UN Treaty Series 187.

50. Articles of Agreement of the International Monetary Fund, Dec. 27, 1945, 2 UN Treaty Series 39.

51. Poland raised the matter at meetings of the GATT council for several years. See *GATT Activities 1982*, at 73–75; *GATT Activities 1983*, at 62–63; and *GATT Activities 1984*, at 53. It did not, however, call for the formation of a dispute panel for the making of a formal finding of illegality on the part of the United States.

52. GATT Basic Instruments and Selected Documents, 2:28. See Hudec, *GATT Legal System*, at 68; and Knoll, "Impact of Security Concerns," at 590–91.

53. Long, *Law and Its Limitations*, at 81–84.

54. *GATT Focus*, July-Aug., 1982, at 1. See also Dewost, "La Communauté"; and Kissler, *Zulassigkeit*.

55. GATT Basic Instruments and Selected Documents, Supp. No. 31, at 67–74.

56. GATT Doc. L/6053 (1986).

57. *GATT Activities in 1984*, at 39. See Knoll, "Impact of Security Concerns," at 598–99, and 603–6.

58. Strictly speaking, the position is that individual states are required, by Article 103 of the UN Charter, to accord the highest priority to their obligations under that instrument whenever there is a conflict of obligations. The UN Security Council does not, therefore, have the power to alter the law of the GATT or the IMF as such. On the sanctioning power of the UN, see generally Jean Combacau, *Le pouvoir de sanction de l'O.N.U.: Étude théorique de la coercition non militaire* (Paris: Pedone, 1974). See also Macdonald, "Resort to Economic Coercion."

59. See Jackson, *World Trade*, at 748–52; and Knoll, "Impact of Security Concerns," at 581–607.

60. GATT Doc. L/6053 (1986).

61. Nicaragua v. U.S., at 140–42, paras. 280–82.

62. On Article 35, see Jackson, *World Trade*, at 100–2.

63. Most of this information about the use of Article 35 is from the GATT Analytical Index of October 1985. On the invocation of Article 35 by Egypt against Israel, see 735 UN Treaty Series 294.

64. The Secretary of State to the Embassy in Czechoslovakia, July 18, 1951, [1951] *Foreign Relations of the United States*, 1:1381.

65. GATT Basic Instruments and Selected Documents, 2:36. Strictly speaking, this was not a waiver, but rather a "general declaration" by the contracting parties of the GATT. It may fairly be regarded as a de facto waiver, however. On this incident, see Curzon, *Multilateral Commercial Diplomacy*, at 298–300; Jackson, *World Trade*, at 749–50; and Knoll, "Impact of Security

Concerns," at 602–3. On the United States lobbying for the necessary support for this measure, see generally [1951] *Foreign Relations of the United States,* 1:1381–1424.

66. For the text, see de Vries and Horsefield, *IMF 1945–1965,* 3, at 257.

67. For a summary of the United States restrictions in force at the end of 1988, see IMF, *Annual Report on Exchange Restrictions 1989,* at 513. See also Lichtenstein, "Battle for Bank Accounts." For a description of the administration by the United States of its various sets of frozen assets, see Michael P. Malloy, "Embargo Programs of the United States Treasury Department," *Columbia Journal of Transnational Law* (1981), 20:485–516.

68. Jackson, *World Trade,* at 745.

69. GATT Basic Instruments and Selected Documents, Supp. No. 29, at 11.

70. *Ibid.,* Supp. No. 31, at 68–69.

71. GATT Doc. L/6053 (1986), at 18. See Whitt, "Politics and Procedure."

72. Government of the Republic of South Africa, *Commission of Inquiry into the Export Trade of the Republic of South Africa,* South African Gov. Doc. No. 69/72 (1972), at 68–79.

73. De Vries and Horsefield, *IMF 1945–1965,* 2:259–60.

74. On the Arab boycott of Israel, see generally Chill, *Arab Boycott;* Turck, "Arab Boycott"; Losman, *International Economic Sanctions,* at 47–79; Sarna, *Boycott and Blacklist;* and David B. Dewitt, "The Arab Boycott of Israel," in Leyton-Brown, ed., *Utility of Sanctions,* at 149–66.

75. See, for example, Iskander, *Arab Boycott,* at 14–21; Hassan A. Hassouna, *The League of Arab States and Regional Disputes: A Study of Middle East Conflicts* (Dobbs Ferry, N.Y.: Oceana, 1975), at 316–24; and M. Cherif Bassiouni, "The Arab Economic Boycott of Israel and U.S. Policy to Counteract It," in Bassiouni, Cleute and McCarthy, *Boycott and Anti-Boycott,* at 2–3. See also the statement by the commissioner-general of the Central Boycott Office of Damascus, of March 5, 1975, justifying the boycott as a self-defense measure, in Mersky, *Transnational Boycotts,* 2:114.

On the legality of the Arab boycott of Israel, see also Bilder, "Comments"; and Greene, Jr., "Arab Boycott."

76. See, to this effect, Paper Prepared by the Policy Planning Staff, Doc. PPS-17, Nov. 26, 1947, [1948] *Foreign Relations of the United States,* 4:489–98.

77. See, for example, the statement by the United States delegate at the 71st meeting of the Second Committee, UN General Assembly Official Records, 3d Sess., Summary Records of the Second Committee (1948), at 185–96.

78. *Ibid.,* at 157.

79. UN Doc. A/C.2/137 (1948).

80. Economic Cooperation Act of 1948, §§ 117(d), 62 U.S. Statutes at Large 154. This provision was known as the Mundt Amendment. The British government resented this legislation, but were advised by the legal adviser of the Foreign Office that it did not infringe international law. Memorandum by Gerald Fitzmaurice, Ministry of Supply Paper on "Implications of Section 117D of the Foreign Assistance Act," May 5, 1948, British Public Record Office, F.O. 371/71754, File No. UR 1318 (1948).

81. For the official British diplomatic protest lodged against the Battle

Act, see British Public Record Office, F.O. 371/94311, File No. M 3419/103 (1951).

82. The Secretary of State to the Embassy in France, Nov. 2, 1949, [1949] *Foreign Relations of the United States* 5:166.

83. On the formative period of the Western strategic embargo, see generally Adler-Karlsson, *Western Economic Warfare*, at 22–26; Paterson, *Soviet-American Confrontation*, at 66–74; Wolf, *U.S. East-West Trade*, at 47–51; Pollard, *Economic Security*, at 161–64; Stenger, "Development of Export Control"; and Mastanduno, "Trade as a Strategic Weapon."

84. On the general working of the CoCom system of multilateral export controls, see U.S. Office of Technology Assessment, *Technology and East-West Trade* (Washington, D.C.: GPO, 1981), at 153–70; Abraham S. Becker, *Economic Relations with the USSR: Issues for the Western Alliance* (Lexington, Mass.: Lexington, 1983), at 111–27; Hunt, "Multilateral Cooperation"; and Aeppel, "Evolution of Export Controls."

85. W. Allen Wallis, "Review of East-West Economic Relations," *Department of State Bulletin*, July 1984, at 60.

86. Robert Carswell and Richard J. Davis, "The Economic and Financial Pressures: Freeze and Sanctions," in Kreisberg, ed., *American Hostages*, at 175–77.

87. *GATT Activities in 1982*, at 73–75; *GATT Activities in 1983*, at 62–63; and *GATT Activities in 1984*, at 53.

88. For a strong condemnation of the practice by an international lawyer, see Moore, "U.S. Policy."

89. See Dinitz, "Legal Aspects"; Gross, "Passage through the Suez Canal"; and Bloomfield, *Egypt, Israel and the Gulf of Aqaba.*

90. UN Security Council Res. 95 (1951), UN Security Council Official Records, 6th Year, Resolutions and Decisions of the Security Council 1951, UN Doc. S/INF/6/Rev. 1 (1951), at 10.

91. For the United States law, see Export Administration Amendments of 1977, 50 U.S. Code App. §§ 2407. For the French law, see Article 32 of Law No. 77–574 of June 7, 1977, Making Various Dispositions of an Economic and Financial Order, 109 *Journal Officiel* 3151. On the French law generally, see Bismuth, *Boycottage.*

92. For descriptions of the American legislation and of the Department of Commerce regulations which implement it, see generally Paul McCarthy and John F. McKenzie, "Commerce Department Regulations Governing Participation by United States Persons in Foreign Boycotts," *Vanderbilt Journal of Transnational Law* (1978), 11:193–247; Williams, "U.S. Regulation"; A. A. Dubin, "Journey through the Antiboycott Laws," *Tulsa Law Journal*, 14:695–743; and Carter, *International Economic Sanctions*, at 175–80. On the background and drafting of the legislation, see Kennan Lee Teslik, *Congress, the Executive Branch, and Special Interests: The American Response to the Arab Boycott of Israel* (Westport, Conn.: Greenwood Press, 1982).

93. The provision in question, which is identically worded in bilateral economic cooperation agreements between the EEC and seven Arab states, stipulates that arrangements by the Arab state "shall not give rise to any

discrimination between the Member States of the EEC, their nationals, or their companies or firms." For the texts of these provisions, see the agreements between the EEC and Tunisia, April 25, 1976, art. 53, *Encyclopedia of European Community Law*, Section B-III, at B12–808; Algeria, April 26, 1976, art. 52, *ibid.*, at B12–760; Morocco, April 27, 1976, art. 54, *ibid.*, at B12–783; Egypt, Jan. 18, 1977, art. 45, *ibid.*, at B12–823; Jordan, Jan. 18, 1977, art. 42, *ibid.*, at B12–849; Syria, Jan. 18, 1977, art. 43, *ibid.*, at B12–860; and Lebanon, May 3, 1977, art. 43, *ibid.*, at B12–836. For the view of the EEC Commission that this rather tepidly-worded provision constitutes a prohibition against secondary boycotting, see Response by Claude Cheysson of April 9, 1985 to Written Question No. 1435/84 of Dec. 10, 1984 (by Gijsbert de Vries), 28 *Official Journal of the European Communities* (June 3, 1985), at C 135/17–18.

94. On U.S. economic warfare against Cuba, see generally Schreiber, "Economic Coercion," at 387–405; Bender, *Politics of Hostility*; Losman, *International Economic Sanctions*, at 20–46; Baldwin, *Economic Statecraft*, at 261–78; Sergio Roca, "Economic Sanctions Against Cuba," in Leyton-Brown, ed., *Utility of Sanctions*, at 87–104; and Morley, *Imperial State*, at 187–239. On the legality of this effort, see Shneyer and Barta, "Legality of Economic Blockade."

95. On secondary economic warfare against Cuba by the United States, see generally Morley, *Imperial State*, at 191–218.

96. *Ibid.*, at 216.

97. Donald F. McHenry and Kai Bird, "Food Bungle in Bangladesh," *Foreign Policy* (1977), 27:72–88; and Wallerstein, *Food for War*, at 161–62.

98. "U.S. Takes Steps to Conform with OAS Action on Cuba," *Department of State Bulletin* (1975), 73:404.

99. On U.S. export controls generally, see Luther Carl Branting, "Reconciliation of Conflicting Goals in the Export Administration Act of 1979—A Delicate Balance," *Law and Policy in International Business* (1980), 12:15–60; Abbott, "Linking Trade"; and Richard S. Elliott, "The Export Administration Act of 1979: Latest Statutory Resolution of the 'Right to Export' Versus National Security and Foreign Policy Controls," *Columbia Journal of Transnational Law* (1981), 19:255–99. On the problems that arise from the extraterritorial application of the United States laws, see Polier, "Western European Sovereignty."

100. "Export of Oil and Gas Equipment to the Soviet Union," *International Legal Materials* (1982), 21:864–66.

101. Britain invoked procedures available under its Protection of Trading Interests Act 1980, to forbid its companies from complying with the American regulations. On this legislation, see A. V. Lowe, "Blocking Extraterritorial Jurisdiction," *American Journal of International Law* (1981), 75:257–82.

102. See Dresser Industries v. Baldrige, 549 F. Supp. 1285 (D.D.C. 1982). See also James R. Atwood, "The Export Administration Act and the Dresser Industries Case," *Law and Policy in International Business* (1983), 15:1157–61. See also Eric Lebedoff and Caroline Raievski, "A French Perspective on the United States Ban on the Soviet Gas Pipeline Equipment," *Texas International Law Journal* (1983), 18:483–507.

103. For detailed explorations of the technical legal aspects of this incident, see generally A. V. Lowe, *Extraterritorial Jurisdiction: An Annotated Collection of Legal Materials* (Cambridge: Grotius, 1983), at 79–225; Duane D. Morse and Joan S. Powers, "U.S. Export Controls and Foreign Entities: The Unanswered Questions of Pipeline Diplomacy," *Virginia Journal of International Law* (1983), 23:537–67; Homer E. Moyer, Jr. and Linda A. Mabry, "Export Controls as Instruments of Foreign Policy: The History, Legal Issues and Policy Lessons of Three Recent Cases," *Law and Policy in International Business* (1983), 15:60–92; Jerome J. Zaucha, "The Soviet Pipeline Sanctions: The Extraterritorial Application of U.S. Export Controls," *Law and Policy in International Business* (1983), 15:1169–79; and A. V. Lowe, "Public International Law and the Conflict of Laws: The European Response to the United States Export Administration Regulations," *International and Comparative Law Quarterly* (1984), 33:515–30.

104. "East-West Trade Relations and the Soviet Pipeline Sanctions," *Department of State Bulletin*, Jan. 1983, at 28; and Department of Commerce, "Revision of Export Controls Affecting the U.S.S.R. and Poland," *International Legal Materials* (1983), 22:350–52.

105. For general accounts of the pipeline incident, see Stern, "Specters and Pipe Dreams"; Baldwin, *Economic Statecraft*, at 278–89; and Blinken, *Ally Versus Ally.*

106. See Neff, "Economic Warfare."

6. Capitalism's Policemen

1. Séfériadès, *Réflexions*, at 5, note 2.

2. See generally Shutt, *Myth of Free Trade.*

3. See Rothstein, *The Weak in the World of the Strong*, at 105, for the use of the expression "international class warfare" to describe this phenomenon.

4. Seers, *Political Economy*, at 52.

5. On this subject, see Bairoch, *Economic Development*, at 112–23.

6. On third-world economic nationalism generally, see Seers, *Political Economy*; Krasner, *Structural Conflict*; and Burnell, *Economic Nationalism.* For Prebisch's views on the appropriate trade policies for developing countries, see Prebisch, "Commercial Policy." For a bibliography of Prebisch's writings, see UNCTAD, "Raúl Prebisch: Thinker and Builder," UN Doc. TAD/INF/PUB/89/1 (1989), at 59–71.

7. On Tanzania, see Biersteker, "Self-Reliance"; and Okoko, *Socialism and Self-Reliance.*

8. For an excellent description of the practices employed, see Verbit, *International Monetary Reform*, at 45–92, and 211–49.

9. On various ways in which host countries restrict the freedom of action of foreign investors, see Burnell, *Economic Nationalism*, at 150–87. On ways in which host countries sometimes "persuade" investors to transfer their investments outright to the government, see Vagts, "Coercion." On foreign investment and economic nationalism generally, see Lipson, *Standing Guard*, at 178–86.

10. See Kobrin, "Expropriation as an Attempt."

11. On expropriation generally, see Wortley, *Expropriation*; Dolzer, "New Foundations"; Rosalyn Higgins, "The Taking of Property by the State: Some Recent Developments in International Law," *Recueil des Cours* (Académie de Droit International) (1982), 176:259–391; Rudolf Dolzer, "Expropriation and Nationalization," in Bernhardt, ed., *Encyclopedia of Public International Law*, 8:214–21; Sornarajah, *Pursuit*, at 167–237; and Samuel K. B. Asante, "International Law and Foreign Investment: A Reappraisal," *International and Comparative Law Quarterly* (1988), 37:588–628. On the compensation issue, see Daniel A. Lapres, "Principles of Compensation for Nationalised Property," *International and Comparative Law Quarterly* (1977), 26:97–109; Sornarajah, "Compensation"; and Pamela B. Gann, "Compensation Standard for Expropriation," *Columbia Journal of Transnational Law* (1985), 23:615–53.

12. See, for example, M. F. Scott, W. M. Corden and I. M. D. Little, *The Case Against Import Restrictions* (London: Trade Policy Research Centre, 1980). For a critique of Prebisch's view specifically, see Charles P. Kindelberger and Peter H. Lindert, *International Economics*, 6th ed. (Homewood, Ill.: R. D. Irwin, 1978), at 70–76; and Spraos, *Inequalising Trade*. On the preference of the World Bank for open trading regimes, see International Bank for Reconstruction and Development, *World Development Report 1987* (New York: Oxford University Press, 1987), at 78–112. On the preference of the IMF for open exchange-rate systems, see Peter J. Quirk, "The Case for Open Foreign Exchange Systems," *Finance and Development*, June 1989, at 30–33. On its opposition to over-valued exchange rates in particular, see Guy Pfefferman, "Over-valued Exchange Rates and Development," *Finance and Development*, Mar. 1985, at 17–19. For a classic illustration of the kind of corruption fostered by multi-tier exchange rates, see Joe Mann, "Tremors Over Foreign Exchange Probe," *Financial Times* (London), July 20, 1989, at 3, col. 4, concerning Venezuela.

13. Vitoria, "On the Indians," at 154–56.

14. La Pradelle, "Question chinoise," at 333.

15. Eagleton, *Responsibility of States*, at 228–29.

16. Charter for an International Trade Organization (Havana Charter), March 21, 1948, UN Doc. E/CONF.2/78 (1948).

17. General Agreement on Tariffs and Trade (GATT), Oct. 30, 1947, art. 6, 55 UN Treaty Series 187. The basic provisions of this article were supplemented (although not altered in character) in 1979, with the adoption of two additional codes under GATT auspices. For the subsidies code, see Agreement on the Interpretation and Application of Articles VI, XVI and XXIII of the GATT, April 12, 1979, in GATT Basic Instruments and Selected Documents, Supp. No. 26, at 56–83. For the anti-dumping code, see Agreement on the Implementation of Article VI of the GATT, April 12, 1979, in *ibid.*, at 171–88.

18. On the GATT dispute-settlement system, see Jackson, *World Trade*, at 171–87; Hudec, "GATT Dispute Settlement"; Long, *Law and Its Limitations* at 65–88; and von Bael, "GATT Dispute Settlement Procedure."

19. UN Press Release No. SI/50/87, Dec. 21, 1987, at 9–10. See also Hudec, *Developing Countries*, at 77–78.

20. Hudec, *Developing Countries*, at 48.

21. *Ibid.*, at 30–33. On the role of the developing countries in the GATT system generally, see Jackson, *World Trade*, at 625–72; Girling, *Multinational Institutions*, at 133–51; Hudec, *Developing Countries*; Long, *Law and Its Limitations*, at 89–106; and Tussie, *Less Developed Countries*.

22. World Bank, *Third Annual Report 1947–48*, at 21.

23. World Bank, *Fourth Annual Report 1948–49*, at 13.

24. International Bank for Reconstruction and Development, *IBRD, 1946–53*, at 55.

25. Mason and Asher, *World Bank*, at 155–58, and 336–37.

26. *Ibid.*, at 338–39.

27. *Ibid.*, at 628–42. For the text of the Agreement between the Government of the United Arab Republic and the Compagnie financière de Suez of July 13, 1958, see UN Doc. S/4089, in UN Security Council Official Records, 13th Year, Supp. for July-Sep. 1958, at 140.

28. International Bank for Reconstruction and Development, *IBRD, 1946–53*, at 54–55.

29. Articles of Agreement of the International Bank for Reconstruction and Development, Dec. 27, 1945, art. 6(2), 2 UN Treaty Series 134.

30. Mason and Asher, *World Bank*, at 171; and Assetto, *Soviet Bloc*, at 81–82.

31. "Arrears Force World Bank to Lift Reserves," *Financial Times* (London), July 12, 1988, at 4, col. 4. On the leverage possessed by the World Bank over its member states, see generally Mason and Asher, *World Bank*, at 424–34.

32. On the position of the developing countries in the international monetary system generally, see Verbit, *International Monetary Reform*; Bird, *Monetary System*; and Killick, ed., *Quest for Stabilization*.

33. Second Amendment to the Articles of Agreement of the International Monetary Fund, Mar. 24, 1976, 29 U.S. Treaty Series 2203, 1978 Great Britain Treaty Series No. 83 (Cmnd. 7331).

34. "Surveillance over Exchange Rate Policies," *IMF Annual Report 1977*, at 107–9.

35. Articles of Agreement of the IMF, arts. 4(6), 5(5), 6(1) and 15(2)(a) respectively, 2 UN Treaty Series 39.

36. De Vries and Horsefield, *IMF 1945–65*, 1:202, and 412.

37. *Ibid.*, at 548–50.

38. On the ineligibility of the first eight countries mentioned, see *IMF Annual Report 1988*, at 56–57. On the ineligibility of Panama, see "Panama: Ineligibility," *IMF Survey* (1989), 18:222.

39. De Vries and Horsefield, *IMF 1945–65*, 1:359–64. See Article 15(2)(b) of the IMF Articles of Agreement.

40. For a good historical survey of the evolution of IMF conditionality policy, see Ferguson, *Third World and Decision Making*, at 198–227. See also Dell, *On Being Grandmotherly*; and Guitian, *Fund Conditionality*.

41. For the text, see *IMF Annual Report 1979*, at 137–39, reprinted in Guitian, *Fund Conditionality*, at 45–46.

42. On the legal character of arrangements between the IMF and its borrowers, and of the measures which the Fund can take against such states, see Gold, " 'Sanctions.' "

43. For a general history of the IMF's experience with stabilization and adjustment programs, see de Vries, *Balance of Payments Adjustment*. See also Gerster, "IMF and Conditionality"; and Pirzio-Biroli, "Making Sense." For a third-world perspective on conditionality, see Saxena and Bakshi, "IMF Conditionality." For a useful short summary of the debate over the wisdom of the IMF approach to balance-of-payments adjustment, see Graham Bird, "Relationships, Resource Uses and the Conditionality Debate," in Killick, ed., *Quest for Stabilization*, at 145–82. See also Nowzad, *IMF and Its Critics*. Sharply critical of the IMF approach are Sidney Dell, "The Political Economy of Overkill," in Williamson, ed., *IMF Conditionality*, at 17–45; and Spraos, *IMF Conditionality*. More sympathetic to the IMF position is Raymond Mikesell, "Appraising IMF Conditionality: Too Loose, Too Tight, or Just Right?" in Williamson, ed., *IMF Conditionality*, at 47–62. For a popular presentation of the anti-IMF case, see Payer, *Debt Trap*.

44. For the view that the IMF adjustment programs are not the cause of social unrest, see Siddell, *IMF and Third World Instability*.

45. Carlos Andrés Perez, "World Economic System Is Unjust to Developing Countries," *IMF Survey* (1989), 18:82–83.

46. "Tanzania: The End of Ujamaa," *Economist*, Aug. 23, 1986, at 43, col. 1.

47. *Ibid.*; and Biermann and Wagao, "Quest for Adjustment." See also Trubitt, "IMF Conditionality."

48. For the contention that the military intervention in the Suez crisis was unlawful, see Quincy Wright, "Intervention 1956," *American Journal of International Law* (1957), 51:257–76. On the doubts within the British government over the legality of its own policy, see Geoffrey Marston, "Armed Intervention in the 1956 Suez Canal Crisis: The Legal Advice Tendered to the British Government," *International and Comparative Law Quarterly* (1988), 37:773–817.

49. See generally Olson, "Economic Coercion — North–South Relations."

50. On "hot-commodity" campaigns, see generally Sornarajah, *Pursuit*, at 239–311.

51. See generally Krasner, *Defending the National Interest*; and Rodman, *Sanctity Versus Sovereignty*.

52. 18 U.S. Code §§ 955. On the enactment of this legislation, see Vinson, "War Debts and Peace Legislation."

53. Bretton Woods Agreements Act of 1945, 59 U.S. Statutes at Large 512 (codified at 18 U.S. Code §§ 955).

54. Carter, *International Economic Sanctions*, at 148–49.

55. 22 U.S. Code §§ 2370(q). The president may waive this provision in the national interest.

56. "US to Stop New Aid to Zambia," *Financial Times* (London), Jan. 26, 1988, at 4, col. 1.

57. 22 U.S. Code §§ 2370(c). The president may waive this provision in the interest of national security.

58. On the ineffectiveness of foreign aid reductions as a coercive device, see Olmstead, "Foreign Aid"; and Knorr, *Power and Wealth*, at 172–90. For the opposing view (i.e., that aid reductions can be an effective tool of economic statecraft), see Baldwin, *Economic Statecraft*, at 290–335.

59. "Brazil: Better to Pay," *Economist*, Feb. 20, 1988, at 88, col. 1.

60. Hull to Castillo Najera, Aug. 22, 1938, [1938] *Foreign Relations of the United States*, 5:687. For a more recent pronouncement of the United States position on this issue, by President Nixon in 1972, see *American Journal of International Law* (1972), 66:620. See also American Law Institute, *Restatement of the Law Third: Restatement of the Foreign Relations Law of the United States*, 2 (St Paul, Minn.: ALI, 1987), §§ 712, at 196–97, which states that compensation for nationalized property must be "in an amount equivalent to the value of the property taken and be paid at the time of taking, or within a reasonable time thereafter with interest from the date of taking, and in a form economically usable by the foreign national." See also comment c, at 198–99.

61. Everest, *Morgenthau*, at 88–97.

62. The very earliest "hot commodity" effort was a "hot timber" action in Britain against purchasers of timber from the Bolshevik government of Russia after the revolution. It was a short-lived and unsystematic effort, and also was based upon a somewhat different legal theory from the "hot commodity" actions described in the text. See the British case of Luther v. Sagor, [1921] 3 K.B. 532. This action was based on the thesis that the nationalizing government was not recognized by the British government at the time of the litigation, and that consequently British courts could not give legal effect to any acts promulgated by the regime. The contention was correct. But the action failed because, in the course of the litigation, the British government extended recognition to the Soviet government. The British court then held that that recognition retroactively validated acts of the government.

63. Eastern States Petroleum Co. v. Asiatic Petroleum Co., 28 F. Supp. 279 (S.D.N.Y. 1939). For a Dutch case to this same general effect, see United States of Mexico v. Batsafasche Petroleum Maatschappij, 11 International Law Reports 16 (1938).

64. See Sornarajah, *Pursuit*, at 278–91.

65. For the settlement, see Mexico-United States, Agreement on Expropriation of Petroleum Properties, Nov. 19, 1941, 148 UN Treaty Series 367. On this affair generally, see Krasner, *Defending the National Interest*, at 181–85; Philip, *Oil and Politics*, at 201–26; Koppes, "Good Neighbor Policy"; and Chester, *U.S. Oil Policy*, at 123–32.

66. On the British measures against Iran, see Ford, *Anglo-Iranian Oil Dispute*, at 119–20; and Krasner, *Defending the National Interest*, at 119–21.

67. The record on the "hot-oil" campaign was mixed. Actions in the courts of Italy and Japan were unsuccessful. See, respectively, Anglo-Iranian Oil Co. Ltd v. S.U.P.O.R. Co. (The Miriella), 22 International Law Reports 19 (1953); and Anglo-Iranian Oil Co. Ltd v. Idemitsu Kosan Kabushiki Kaisha, 20 International Law Reports 305 (1953). An action in the Supreme Court of the colony of Aden, on the other hand, did succeed. Anglo-Iranian Co. Ltd v. Jaffrate (The Rose Mary), [1953] 1 Weekly Law Reports 246, 20 International Law Reports 316 (1953).

68. On this affair generally, see Ford, *Anglo-Iranian Oil Dispute.*

69. An unsuccessful "hot sugar" case was Banco Nacional de Cuba v. Sabbatino, 376 U.S. 398 (1964), which became the leading case in U.S. law on the foreign act of state doctrine. A largely unsuccessful attempt was made to prevent courts from applying the foreign act of state doctrine in disputes over title to property alleged to have been nationalized in violation of international law. 22 U.S. Code §§ 2370(e)(2). This legislation has proved to be of little real effect, because the courts have interpreted it as being inapplicable to cases in which the nationalized enterprise was incorporated under the law of the nationalizing state. Palicio y Compania, S.A. v. Brush, 256 F. Supp. 481 (S.D.N.Y. 1966), *aff'd* 375 F. 2d 1011 (2d Cir. 1967), *cert. denied* 389 U.S. 830 (1967).

70. BP v. SINCAT, 53 International Law Reports 297 (1973), reprinted in *International Legal Materials* (1974), 13:106–116. On the support of the British government for the campaign, see "Britain Calls for a Boycott of Oil from BP Wells in Libya," *Times* (London), Dec. 31, 1971, at 11, col. 1. For the American government's position on this question, see "Statement by the Department of State on 'Hot' Libyan Oil," *International Legal Materials* (1974), 13:767–82.

71. Foreign Assistance Act of 1962, 76 U.S. Statutes at Large 260. On the background to the amendment, see Lipson, "Corporate Preferences," at 399–405. The amendment was enlarged the following year, to cover breaches of contract on the part of states, as well as nationalizations. 77 U.S. Statutes at Large 386. See Stephen R. Luce, "Argentina and the Hickenlooper Amendment," *California Law Review* (1966), 54:2078–98.

72. 22 U.S. Code §§ 284j (concerning the World Bank); 22 U.S. Code §§ 283r (concerning the Inter-American Development Bank); and 22 U.S. Code §§ 285o (concerning the Asian Development Bank). See also 22 U.S. Code §§ 290g-8, enacted in 1976, imposing a similar requirement upon American directors on the African Development Fund. On the Gonzales Amendment, see Vandevelde, "Reassessing the Hickenlooper Amendment," at 134–38.

73. Trade Act of 1974, 19 U.S. Code §§ 2462(b)(4). See Vandevelde, "Reassessing the Hickenlooper Amendment," at 141–44.

74. See Olson, "Expropriation — Ceylon." For documentation relating to this affair, see *International Legal Materials* (1963), 2:386–87, and 393–94.

75. Department of State, *Digest of U.S. Practice in International Law 1977,* at 674.

76. On the reluctance of the Nixon administration to invoke the amendment, see Henry A. Kissinger, *The White House Years* (London: Weidenfeld and Nicholson, 1979), at 657; and Henry A. Kissinger, *Years of Upheaval* (London: Weidenfeld and Nicholson, 1982), at 376. For the settlement, see Peru-United States, Settlement of Certain Claims, Feb. 19, 1974, 944 UN Treaty Series 147. On this incident generally, see Jessica P. Einhorn, *Expropriation Politics* (Lexington, Mass.: Lexington, 1974); Ingram, *Expropriation,* at 33–69; and Krasner, *Defending the National Interest,* at 235–45.

77. Foreign Assistance Act of 1973, 87 U.S. Statutes at Large 722, codified at 22 U.S. Code §§ 2270(e)(1). See Richard B. Lillich, "Requiem for Hickenlooper," *American Journal of International Law* (1975), 69:97–100. On the U.S.

experience with the Hickenlooper Amendment generally, see Lillich, *Protection of Foreign Investment*, at 117–46; Lipson, *Standing Guard*, at 200–26; and Vandevelde, "Reassessing the Hickenlooper Amendment."

78. Lipson, "Corporate Preferences," at 398.

79. On the economic nationalist nature of the Allende program, see Dudley Seers, "Development Options: The Strengths and Weaknesses of Dependency Theories in Explaining a Government's Room to Manoeuvre," in Seers, ed., *Dependency Theory*, at 137.

80. Sanford, *U.S. Foreign Policy*, at 210–11; and Carter, *International Economic Sanctions*, at 169–71.

81. On the United States economic campaign against Chile, see generally Sigmund, " 'Invisible Blockade' "; and Krasner, *Defending the National Interest*, at 298–312. On the legality of these measures under international law, see Brosche, "Arab Oil Embargo."

82. On the "hot copper" campaign waged against Chile, see Prosper Weil and Patrick Rambaud, "Review by Courts of Third States of Chilean Copper Nationalization," in Bernhardt, ed., *Encyclopedia of Public International Law*, 8:76–78. See, in particular, the West German case of Sociedad Minera el Teniente S.A. v. Aktiengesellschaft Norddeutsche Affinerie, in *International Legal Materials* (1973), 12:251–89, and *ibid.*, 13:1115–25. On the "hot copper" cases in the West German courts, see I. Seidl-Hohenveldern, "Chilean Copper Nationalization Cases before German Courts," *American Journal of International Law* (1975), 69:110–19. See also the French case of Corporación del Cobre v. Société Braden Copper Corp. et Société le Groupement d'Importation des Métaux, in *International Legal Materials* (1973), 12:182–89.

83. Jevons, *Coal Question*, at xviii.

7. Global Economic Nationalism

1. Naumann, *Central Europe*, at 185–89.

2. UN General Assembly Res. 3201 (S-VI), UN General Assembly Official Records, 6th Special Sess., Supp. No. 1, UN Doc. A/9559 (1974), at 3.

3. General Principle Six, of UNCTAD General and Special Principles to Govern International Trade Relations and Trade Policies Conducive to Development, in *Proceedings of the United Nations Conference on Trade and Development, Geneva, 23 March–16 June 1964*, 1: *Final Act and Report*, UN Doc. E/CONF.46/141, I (1964), at 19.

4. See the discussion in Chapter 1.

5. Hague Convention II Respecting the Limitation of the Employment of Force for the Recovery of Contract Debts (Porter Convention), Oct. 13, 1907, 205 Consolidated Treaty Series 250.

6. On the early development of the principle, see Hyde, "Permanent Sovereignty." On the basically economic nationalist character of the concept, see Itagaki, "Economic Nationalism."

7. Texaco Overseas Petroleum Co. and California Asiatic Oil Co. v. Libya, 53 International Law Reports 389 (1977), at 487–88.

8. Fox, *Tin*, at 231–40. See the statement by Bolivia in the UN General

Assembly in 1952 criticizing the U.S. action in this affair as bearing "no relation to equity or to the spirit of co-operation." Verbatim Records of the 339th Plenary Meeting, UN General Assembly Official Records, 7th Sess., UN Doc. A/PV.339 (1952), at 54.

9. UN Doc. A/C.2/L.165 & Corr. 1 & 2 (1952), in UN General Assembly Official Records, 7th Sess. Second Committee, Annexes (Agenda Item 25), at 7.

10. UN Doc. A/C.2/L.166 (1952), in *ibid.*, at 7.

11. Summary Records of the 232d Meeting of the Second Committee, UN General Assembly Official Records, 7th Sess., Second Committee, at 259–60.

12. UN General Assembly Res. 626 (VII), UN General Assembly Official Records, 7th Sess., Supp. No. 20, UN Doc. A/2631 (1952), at 18.

13. UN General Assembly Res. 1803 (XVII), UN General Assembly Official Records, 17th Sess., Supp. No. 17, UN Doc. A/5217 (1962), at 15. See generally Rosenberg, *Principe de la souveraineté*; and Hossain and Chowdhury, eds., *Permanent Sovereignty*. On this doctrine as the cornerstone of the larger program for a "new international economic order," see de Waart, "Permanent Sovereignty."

14. See note 7 *supra.*

15. On the legal status of UN General Assembly resolutions, see generally Jorge Castañeda, "Valeur juridique des résolutions des Nations Unies," *Recueil des Cours* (Academie de Droit International) (1970), 129:205–331; Christopher C. Joyner, "UN General Assembly Résolutions and International Law: Rethinking the Contemporary Dynamics of Norm-Creation," *California Western International Law Journal* (1981), 11:445–78.

16. For an illustration of a case, from the United States, in which "appropriate" compensation was held, under the circumstances, to mean full compensation, see Banco Nacional de Cuba v. Chase Manhattan Bank, 658 F. 2d 875 (2d Cir. 1981).

17. Verbatim Records of the 2203d Meeting of the UN General Assembly, UN General Assembly Official Records, 28th Sess., Plenary Meetings, UN Doc. A/PV.2203 (1973), at 10.

18. The Declaration and Principles of the Action program of Lima, in *Proceedings of the United Nations Conference on Trade and Development, Third Session, Santiago de Chile, 13 April to 21 May 1972, 1: Report and Annexes*, UN Doc. TD/180, I (1973), at 376.

19. Verbatim Records of the 2096th Meeting of the UN General Assembly, UN General Assembly Official Records, 27th Sess., Plenary Meetings, UN Doc. A/PV.2096 (1972), at 8.

20. UN Security Council Res. 330 (1973), Security Council Official Records, 28th Year, Resolutions and Decisions of the Security Council 1973, UN Doc. S/INF/28 (1973), at 3.

21. UN Doc. A/9330 (1974), at 67.

22. *Ibid.*, at 9.

23. *Ibid.*, at 78. On the concept of collective economic security generally, see Nye, "Collective Economic Security."

24. Protocol of Amendment of the Inter-American Treaty of Reciprocal Assistance, July 26, 1975, art. 11, in *International Legal Materials* (1975), 14:1122–32.

25. "Protocol of Amendment to the Rio Treaty Transmitted to the Senate," *Department of State Bulletin* (1975), 73:903.
26. *Ibid.*, at 903, note 2.
27. UN General Assembly Res. 3281 (XXIX), UN General Assembly Official Records, 29th Sess., Supp. No. 31, UN Doc. A/9631 (1974), at 50.
28. See Weston, "Charter and Deprivation of Wealth."
29. UN Doc. A/9946 (1974), in UN General Assembly Official Records, 29th Sess., Annexes (Agenda Item 48), at 8.
30. UNCTAD Res. 152 (VI), in *Proceedings of the United Nations Conference on Trade and Development, Sixth Session, Belgrade, 6 June–2 July 1983*, 1, UN Doc. TD/326 (I) (1983), at 37.
31. UN General Assembly Res. 38/197, UN General Assembly Official Records, 38th Sess., Supp. No. 47, UN Doc. A/38/47 (1983), at 153; UN General Assembly Res. 39/210, UN General Assembly Official Records, 39th Sess., Supp. No. 51, UN Doc. A/39/51 (1984), at 160; UN General Assembly Res. A/40/185, UN General Assembly Official Records, 40th Sess., Supp. No. 53, UN Doc. A/40/53 (1985), at 146; UN General Assembly Res. 41/165, UN General Assembly Official Records, 41st Sess., Supp. No. 53, UN Doc. A/41/53 (1986), at 131; UN General Assembly Res. 42/173, UN General Assembly Official Records, 42d Sess., Supp. No. 49, UN Doc. A/42/49 (1987), at 130.
32. *Proceedings of the United Nations Conference on Trade and Development, Sixth Session, supra* note 30, at 84–89.
33. Verbatim Records of the 2578th Meeting of the Security Council, UN Security Council Official Records, 40th Year, UN Doc. S/PV.2578 (1985), at 26–30. This, incidentally, is an unusual example of a state's justifying a measure of economic warfare on the ground that it was simply acting within the scope of its general sovereign rights. More commonly, as observed in Chapter 5, states allege some kind of legally wrongful conduct on the part of their target country.
34. UN Security Council Res. 562 (1985), UN Security Council Official Records, 40th Year, Resolutions and Decisions of the Security Council 1985, UN Doc. S/INF/40 (1985), at 14. This resolution urged "all States to refrain from carrying out, supporting or promoting political, economic or military actions of any kind against any State in the [Central American] region which might impede the peace initiatives" then in progress. The United States had vetoed three other draft provisions of the resolution which would have condemned the boycott in more forthright terms. See Verbatim Records of the 2580th Meeting of the Security Council, UN Security Council Official Records, 40th Year, UN Doc. S/PV.2580 (1985), at 116–28.
35. Neff, "Boycott and the Law of Nations," at 135–45. On the concept of economic coercion in international law, see also Parry, "Defining Economic Coercion"; Farer, "Political and Economic Coercion"; and Detlev C. Dicke, "Economic Coercion," in Bernhardt, ed., *Encyclopedia of Public International Law*, 8:147–49.
36. UN General Assembly Res. 3171 (XXVIII), UN General Assembly Official Records, 28th Sess., Supp. No. 30, UN Doc. A/9030 (1973), at 52. On Arab oil policies in the 1970s and their relation to the "new international economic order," see Shihata, "Arab Oil Policies."

37. UN General Assembly Res. 3201 (S-VI), *supra* note 2.

38. UN General Assembly Res. 3281 (XXIX), *supra* note 27. On the charter, see generally Castañeda, "La Charte"; Tiewul, "UN Charter"; Meagher, *International Redistribution*; Stemberg, *Die Charta*; and Ernst-Ulrich Petersmann, "Charter of Economic Rights and Duties of States," in Bernhardt, ed., *Encyclopedia of Public International Law*, 8:71–76.

39. There is a vast literature on the "new international economic order." For a tiny sample of it, see Laszlo, Baker, Jr., Eisenberg and Raman, *Objectives*; Hossain, ed., *Legal Aspects*; Oswaldo de Rivero, *New Economic Order*; and Bulajic, *Principles of Development Law*.

40. See Meagher, *International Redistribution*.

41. See Krasner, "Transforming Regimes."

42. UN General Assembly Res. 3201 (S-VI), *supra* note 2.

43. Program of Action on the Establishment of a New International Economic Order, UN General Assembly Res. 3202 (S-VI), UN General Assembly Official Records, Sixth Special Sess., UN Doc. A/9559 (1974), at 5.

44. UN General Assembly Res. 3201 (S-VI), *supra* note 2.

45. *Ibid.*

46. The program instead states that "[i]nternational financial institutions should take into account the special situation of each developing country in reorienting their lending policies to suit these urgent needs." UN General Assembly Res. 3202 (S-VI), *supra* note 43.

47. *Ibid.* See Bird, *World Finance*, at 279–325; and Ferguson, *Third World and Decision Making*.

48. UN General Assembly Res. 3202 (S-VI), *supra* note 43.

49. For a thorough and lucid explanation of the proposal, see Secretary-General of UNCTAD, "An Integrated Program for Commodities: Trade Measures to Expand Processing of Primary Commodities in Developing Countries," UN Doc. TD/B/C.1/166 & Supps. 1–5 (1974).

50. See E.D. Brown, "Freedom of the High Seas Versus the Common Heritage of Mankind: Fundamental Principles in Conflict," *San Diego Law Review* (1983), 20:521–60.

51. See, for example, Corden, *NIEO Proposals*; and Kreinin and Finger, "Critical Survey." For a collection of essays on aspects of the "new international economic order" from the economic standpoint, see Cline, *Policy Alternatives*.

52. See Hudec, *Developing Countries*, at 56–59; and Tussie, *Less Developed Countries*, at 20–37.

53. Protocol Amending the Preamble and Parts II and III of the GATT, Mar. 10, 1955, 278 UN Treaty Series 168. See Jackson, *World Trade*, at 638–40. On the experience of Ceylon, see Hudec, *Developing Countries*, at 25.

54. Protocol Amending the GATT, Feb. 8, 1965, 572 UN Treaty Series 320. See Jackson, *World Trade*, at 645–48; and Hudec, *Developing Countries*, at 56–59.

55. GATT Basic Instruments and Selected Documents, Supp. No. 18, at 26; and *ibid.*, Supp. No. 26, at 203–4. See Takase, "Role of Concessions."

56. On the World Bank's experience with this policy, see William A. Mc-

Cleary, "Policy Implementation under Structural Adjustment Lending," *Finance and Development*, Mar. 1989, at 32–34.

57. "World Bank Adopts Guidelines for Debt and Debt-service Reduction," *IMF Survey* (1989), 18:188.

58. Roger Brownell and Brian Stuart, "The IMF's Compensatory and Contingency Financing Facility," *Finance and Development*, Dec. 1988, at 9–11.

59. Amendment to the Articles of Agreement of the IMF, May 31, 1968, 726 UN Treaty Series 266.

60. For a brief summary of these various changes, see "Fund's General Resources Available to Members under Various Policies," *IMF Survey (Supplement on the Fund)*, Sep. 1988, at 10–12. On the IMF's decision to permit borrowing for debt and debt-service reduction, see "Fund Acts to Strengthen Debt Strategy," *IMF Survey* (1989), 18:161.

61. *IMF Annual Report 1979*, at 137; and Guitian, *Fund Conditionality*, at 45.

62. Agreement Establishing the Common Fund for Commodities, June 27, 1980, UN Doc. TD/IPC/CF/CONF/24 (1980). See generally Amerasinghe, "Common Fund"; and Dell, "Politics of Commodity Trade."

63. United Nations Convention on the Law of the Sea, Dec. 10, 1982, UN Doc. A/CONF.61/122 AND Corr. 1–11 (1982), reprinted in Kenneth R. Simmonds, *UN Convention on the Law of the Sea 1982* (Dobbs Ferry, N.Y.: Oceana, 1983), at B1–B220.

64. Tracy Murray, "How Helpful Is the Generalized System of Preferences?" *Economic Journal* (1973), 83:449–55. This author finds the income transfers generated by the system to be "quite insignificant" compared to other types of aid (at 455). Also sceptical of the value of preferences are Kreinin and Finger, "Critical Survey," at 495–500; and R. Langhammer and A. Sapir, *Impact of Generalised Tariff Preferences* (Aldershot: Gower, 1987). On the other side of the debate is Craig R. MacPhee, "Evolution of the Trade Effects of the Generalized System of Preferences," UN Doc. TD/B/C.5/87 (1984).

65. Michel Camdessus, "Debt Strategy Needs Strengthening, But Basic Elements Remain Valid," *IMF Survey* (1988), 17:90. See also Klaus Didzsun, "The Debt Crisis and IMF Policy," *Intereconomics* (1988), 23:163–71.

66. Kreinin and Finger, "Critical Look," at 503–4.

67. See Boltho, "Is There a Future?"

68. Report of the Ad Hoc Committee to Review the Implementation of the Charter of Economic Rights and Duties of States, UN General Assembly Official Records, 40th Sess., Supp. No. 52, UN Doc. A/40/51 (1985), at 8.

69. See Bautista, "Christian Charity." See also Haq, "From Charity to Obligation."

8. Of Commerce and Dominion

1. Christian Tyler, "A Suitable Case for Salvage," *Financial Times* (London) June 23, 1986, at 24, col. 3.

2. See Miller, "Corporation as Private Government." For an infinitesimal

sample of the vast literature on multinational companies, see Vernon, *Sovereignty at Bay*; and Barnet and Müller, *Global Reach*.

3. Joseph L. Naar, "Some Firms Are Larger Than Most Countries," *American Journal of Economics and Sociology* (1981), 40:36.

4. Madsen, *Private Power*, at 140.

5. On the current law of state immunity, see generally Peter Trooboff, "Foreign State Immunity: Emerging Consensus on Principles," *Recueil des Cours* (Académie de Droit International) (1986), 200:235–431.

6. On internationalized contracts, see Sornarajah, *Pursuit*, at 79–166. For an interesting illustration of a private company which was granted a number of statelike privileges, including a measure of diplomatic-style immunities, see Practical Concepts, Inc. v. Republic of Bolivia, 811 F. 2d 1543 (D.C. Cir. 1987).

7. On stabilization clauses, see David Flint, "Foreign Investment and the New International Economic Order," in Hossain and Chowdhury, eds., *Permanent Sovereignty*, at 146–63; and Timothy A. Hansen, "The Legal Effect Given Stabilization Clauses in Economic Development Agreements," *Virginia Journal of International Law* (1988), 28:1015–41.

8. Barnet and Müller, *Global Reach*, at 56.

9. *Ibid.* For an example of a book which takes this evangelical, optimistic view of the role of multinational companies, see Madsen, *Private Power*.

10. Verbatim Records of the 2096th Plenary Meeting, UN General Assembly Official Records, 27th Sess., UN Doc. A/PV.2096 (1972), at 5–6.

11. Henry A. Kissinger, *Years of Upheaval* (London: Weidenfeld and Nicholson, 1982), at 389.

12. Kindelberger, *Power and Money*, at 172–74.

13. Matthew Barrett and Laura Irvine, "The Euromoney Country Risk Ratings," *Euromoney*, Sep. 1988, at 232–33.

14. Strange, *Casino Capitalism*. On the Euro-currency system, see generally Savona and Sutija, *Eurodollars*; and Mullineux, *International Money*. On London's role as the center of the system, see "London's Euroboom," *Economist*, Aug. 23, 1986, at 68–69.

15. See Gisselquist, *Political Economics*; Lomax, *Developing Country Debt Crisis*; Benjamin J. Cohen, *Banks and the Balance of Payments: Private Lending in the International Adjustment Process* (Montclair, N.J.: Allanheld, Osmun, 1981); and Holley, *Developing Country Debt*.

16. Robert Carswell and Richard J. Davis, "The Economic and Financial Pressures: Freeze and Sanctions," in Kreisberg, ed., *American Hostages*, at 193; and Cohen, *In Whose Interest*, at 171–72.

17. Paine, "Rights of Man," at 403.

18. Yu, *Trade and Expansion*, at 59–60.

19. *Ibid.*, at 117–32.

20. Thompson, *Romans and Barbarians*, at 10–15.

21. For the texts of the papal decrees of 1215 and 1245 forbidding the exporting to the Saracens of certain war-related supplies, see Charles-Joseph Hefele, *Histoires des conciles d'après les documents originaux*, translated by H. Leclercq (Paris: Letouzey et Ané, 1913), 5:1388–90, and 1655–57 respectively.

See also Palmer A. Throop, *Criticism of the Crusade: A Study of Public Opinion and Crusade Propaganda* (Amsterdam: N.V. Swets and Zeitlinger, 1940), at 244–46; and Maureen Purcell, *Papal Crusading Policy 1244–1291* (Leiden: Brill, 1975), at 179–80.

22. See generally Jennings, *American Embargo*; Sears, *Jefferson and the Embargo*; Perkins, *Prologue to War*, at 149–83; Levy, *Jefferson and Civil Liberties*; and Spivak, *Jefferson's English Crisis.*

23. Eric Marsden and Alexander MacLeod, "Sanctions. Pretoria: The Political Reality," *Sunday Times* (London), Aug. 3, 1986, at 25, col. 1.

24. For an instructive look at some of the techniques used by South Africa to obtain oil from countries which supposedly maintain embargoes against it, see Shell Int'l Petroleum Co. v. Gibbs (The Salem), 1982 Q.B. 946, at 950–58. See also the annual reports by the UN General Assembly's Intergovernmental Group to Monitor the Supply and Shipping of Oil and Petroleum Products to South Africa (the first of which was submitted in 1987).

25. Laura Blumenfeld, "Arab World Enjoys Forbidden Israeli Fruits," *Financial Times* (London), July 6, 1989, at 6, col. 4.

26. Romano Prodi and Alberto Clô, "Europe," in Vernon, ed., *Oil Crisis*, at 91–112. See also Norman Girvan, "Economic Nationalism," in *ibid.*, at 145–58.

27. See generally Singer, "Limits"; Hans Maull, "Oil and Influence: The Oil Weapon Examined," in Treverton, ed., *Energy and Security*, at 3–39; and Feith, "Oil Weapon De-mystified."

28. See Marshall I. Goldman, "The Soviet Union," in Vernon, ed., *Oil Crisis*, at 129–43; and Arthur Jay Klinghoffer, "The Soviet Union and the Arab Oil Embargo of 1973–74," *International Relations* (1976), 5:1011–23.

29. See Robert Stobaugh, "The Oil Companies in the Crisis," in Vernon, ed., *Oil Crisis*, at 179–202.

30. James W. McKie, "The United States," in Vernon, ed., *Oil Crisis*, at 85.

31. Perhaps the best single account of the crisis is Vernon, ed., *Oil Crisis.* See also Singer, "Limits"; Hans Maull, "Oil and Influence: The Oil Weapon Examined," in Treverton, ed., *Energy and Security*, at 3–39; and Feith, "Oil Weapon De-mystified."

32. U.S.S.R.-U.S., Grains Agreement, Oct. 20, 1975, 26 U.S. Treaty Series 2971.

33. See Hopkins, "How to Make Food Work." The majority of the more perceptive analysts of international political economy had grave doubts whether the "grain weapon" could be effectively wielded, even before the Afghanistan experience. See, for example, Schneider, *Can We Avert*; Maddock, "Economic and Political Characteristics"; Rothschild, "Food Politics"; Schneider, *Food*; and Batie and Healy, *Future of American Agriculture.*

On the Afghan grain embargo, see generally Paarlberg, "Lessons of the Grain Embargo"; Doxey, "Sanctions Against the Soviet Union"; Ghoshal, "Going Against the Grain"; Baldwin, *Economic Statecraft*, at 261–78; Lundborg, *Economics of Embargoes*; and Robert L. Paarlberg, "The 1980–81 Grain Embargo: Consequences for the Participants," in Leyton-Brown, ed., *Utility of Sanctions*, at 185–206.

34. On the CoCom mechanism, see generally U.S. Office of Technology Assessment, *Technology and East-West Trade* (Washington, D.C.: GPO, 1981), at 153–70; Abraham S. Becker, *Economic Relations with the USSR: Issues for the Western Alliance* (Lexington, Mass.: Lexington, 1983), at 111–27; John R. McIntyre and Richard T. Cupitt, "Multilateral Strategic Trade Controls within the Western Alliance," in Gary K. Bertsch and John R. McIntyre, eds., *National Security and Technology Transfer: The Strategic Dimensions of East-West Trade* (Boulder, Col.: Westview Press, 1983), at 140–58; Aeppel, "Evolution of Export Controls"; and Hunt, "Multilateral Cooperation." On the Western strategic embargo generally, see Adler-Karlsson, *Western Economic Warfare*; Wilczynski, "Strategic Embargo"; Baldwin, *Economic Statecraft*, at 235–51; and Hanson, *Western Economic Statecraft*.

35. "Libyan Sanctions," *Department of State Bulletin*, Mar. 1986, at 36–39.

36. "Libya: Where the Oil Men Still Operate," *Economist*, May 3, 1986, at 45, col. 1.

37. "Foreign Policy: Fits, Starts and Jerks," *Economist*, Feb. 8, 1986, at 34, col. 3.

38. "U.S. Oil Companies Authorized to Resume Operations in Libya," *Department of State Bulletin*, Mar. 1989, at 71.

39. See Libyan Arab Foreign Bank v. Bankers Trust Co. [1989] Q.B. 728; and Libyan Arab Foreign Bank v. Manufacturers Hanover Trust Co. (no. 2) [1989] 1 Lloyds Reports 608.

40. Peter Wilson-Smith, "Softer Line on Argentine Loans Likely," *Times* (London), April 10, 1982, at 13, col. 3.

41. Peter Wilson-Smith, "Bank Spells Out the Big Freeze," *Times* (London), April 14, 1982, at 11, col. 6; and William Hall, "Bank of England Clamp on Argentine Dealings," *Financial Times* (London), April 14, 1982, at 4, col. 6.

42. Peter Wilson-Smith, "Howe to Report on Argentine Sanctions," *Financial Times* (London), Aug. 23, 1982, at 2, col. 2.

43. "Weinberger Plan to Make Poles Default," *Financial Times* (London), Jan. 16, 1982, at 2, col. 2.

44. See Bjorklund, "Reprieve for Poland"; and Cohen, *In Whose Interest*, at 195–201. See also Victoria Bjorklund, "The Kasten-Moynihan Amendment and the Polish Debt Crisis," *Columbia Journal of Transnational Law* (1983), 21:394–409.

45. Angell, *Foundations*, at 125.

Concluding Thoughts

1. Mill, *Principles of Political Economy*, in *Collected Works*, 4:594.

2. Francis Fukuyama, "Marxism's Failure," *Independent* (London), Sep. 21, 1989, at 25, col. 4.

3. "The Business Cycle Gets a Puncture," *Economist*, Aug. 5, 1989, at 63, col. 1.

4. For a vigorous assertion of the claim that international interdependence is diminishing rather than increasing, see Northedge, "Transnationalism." In a similarly sceptical vein, see Waltz, "Myth of Intedependence"; Klaus Knorr,

"Economic Interdependence and National Security," in Knorr and Trager, eds., *Economic Issues,* at 1–18; Robert Gilpin, "Economic Interdependence and National Security in Historical Perspective," in *ibid.,* at 19–63; and Buzan, "Economic Structure." See also Lester Thurow, "A Time to Dismantle the World Economy," *Economist,* Nov. 9, 1985, at 21–26. For the opposing viewpoint, see Rosenau, *Study of Interdependence.*

Selected Bibliography

PRIMARY SOURCES

Aquinas, Thomas. *On Kingship to the King of Cyprus*. Translated by Gerard B. Phelan. Toronto: Pontifical Institute of Mediaeval Studies, 1949. (Drafted c. 1260–65)

Aristotle. *The Nicomachean Ethics*. Translated by David Ross. Oxford: Oxford University Press, 1980.

——*Politics*. Translated by Ernest Barker. Oxford: Clarendon Press, 1946.

Bastiat, Frédéric. *Economic Harmonics*. Translated by W. Hayden Boyers. Princeton, N.J.: Van Nostrand, 1964. (1st ed. Paris, 1850)

Blackstone, William. *Commentaries on the Laws of England*. 4 vols. Oxford: Clarendon Press, 1765–69.

Crucé, Éméric de. *The New Cyneas*. Edited by Thomas W. Balch. Philadelphia: Allen, Lane & Scott, 1909. (1st ed. Paris, 1623)

Fichte, Johann Gottlieb. *Der geschlossne Handelsstaat*. Tubingen: J.G. Cotta, 1800.

Hamilton, Alexander. "Report on the Subject of Manufactures." In *The Papers of Alexander Hamilton*, edited by Harold C. Syrett, 10:230–340. New York: Columbia University Press, 1966. (1st ed. Philadelphia, 1791)

Hume, David. *Essays Moral, Political and Literary*. London: Grant Richards, 1903. (1st ed. Edinburgh, 1741–42)

Jevons, Stanley W. *The Coal Question: An Inquiry Concerning the Progress of the Nation, and the Probable Exhaustion of Our Coal-mines*. London: Macmillan, 1865.

Kant, Immanuel. *Perpetual Peace*. New York: Columbia University Press, 1939. (1st ed. Konigsberg, 1795)

List, Friedrich. *The Natural System of Political Economy*. Edited and translated by W.O. Henderson. London: Cass, 1983. (Drafted 1837)

——*The National System of Political Economy*. Translated by Sampson S. Lloyd. London: Longman, 1916. (1st ed. Stuttgart, 1841)

McCullough, John Ramsay. *The Principles of Political Economy*. Edinburgh: W. & C. Tait, 1825.

Malynes, Gerard de. *Consuetudo, Vel Lex Mercatoria; or, The Ancient Law Merchant*. London: A. Islip, 1622.

Marx, Karl. *Capital: A Critique of Political Economy*. Translated by Samuel Moore and E. Aveling. New York: International Publishers, 1967. (1st ed. London, 1867)

Marx, Karl, and Friedrich Engels. "The Manifesto of the Communist Party." In *Selected Works*, at 31–63. London: Lawrence and Wishart, 1970. (1st ed. London, 1848)

Mill, James. "Commerce Defended." In *James Mill: Selected Economic Writings*, edited by Donald N. Winch, at 85–159. Edinburgh: Oliver & Boyd, 1966. (1st ed. London, 1807)

Mill, John Stuart. "Essays on Some Unsettled Questions of Political Economy." In *Collected Works of John Stuart Mill*, edited by John M. Robson, 4:229–339. Toronto: University of Toronto Press, 1967. (1st ed. London, 1844)

——"Principles of Political Economy, With Some of Their Applications to Social Philosophy." In *Collected Works of John Stuart Mill*, vols. 2–3, edited by John M. Robson. Toronto: University of Toronto Press, 1965. (1st ed. London, 1848)

Mirabeau, Victor Riqueti, Marquis de. *L'ami des hommes; ou, Traité de la population*. 6 vols. The Hague: Benjamin Gilbert, 1759–62. (1st ed. Avignon, 1756–57)

Montesquieu, Charles de Secondat, Baron de. *The Spirit of the Laws*. Translated by Thomas Nugent. New York: Hafner, 1949. (1st ed. Paris, 1748)

Mun, Thomas. *England's Treasure by Foreign Trade*. Glasgow: R. & A. Foulis, 1755. (1st ed. London, 1664)

Naumann, Friedrich. *Central Europe*. Translated by C.M. Meredith. London: P.S. King, 1916.

Paine, Thomas. "The Rights of Man" (Part Two). In *The Complete Writings of Thomas Paine*, edited by Philip S. Foner, at 345–458. New York: Citadel Press, 1945. (1st ed. London, 1792)

Plato. *The Laws.* Translated by Trevor J. Saunders. Harmondsworth: Penguin, 1970.

Quesnay, François. *Physiocratie; ou, Constitution naturelle du gouvernement le plus avantageux au genre humain.* Edited by Pierre Samuel Du Pont de Nemours. Leyden, 1768.

Rousseau, Jean-Jacques. "Constitutional Project for Corsica." In *Political Writings*, edited and translated by Frederick Watts, at 275–330. Edinburgh: Thomas Nelson, 1953. (Drafted 1765)

——"Considerations on the Government of Poland, and on Its Proposed Reformation." In *Political Writings*, edited and translated by Frederick Watts, at 157–274. Edinburgh: Thomas Nelson, 1953. (Drafted 1772)

Saint-Simon, Henri de. *Selected Writings on Science, Industry and Social Organisation.* Edited and translated by Keith Taylor. London: Croom Helm, 1975.

——*The Political Thought of Saint-Simon.* Edited by Ghita Ionescu. London: Oxford University Press, 1976.

Shang, Lord. *The Book of Lord Shang: A Classic of the Chinese School of Law.* Translated by J.J. Duyvendak. London: Arthur Probsthain, 1928.

Smith, Adam. *An Inquiry into the Nature and Causes of the Wealth of Nations.* Edited by R.H. Campbell and Andrew S. Skinner. Oxford: Oxford University Press, 1976. (1st ed. London, 1776)

Steuart, James. *An Inquiry into the Principles of Political Oeconomy.* Edited by Andrew S. Skinner. 2 vols. Edinburgh: Oliver & Boyd, 1966. (1st ed. London, 1767)

Sully, Maximilian de Béthune, Duc de. *Memoirs.* Translated by Charlotte Lennox. 4 vols. London: Henry G. Bohn, 1856. (1st ed. Amsterdam and Paris, 1640–62).

Witt, John de. *The True Interest and Political Maxims of the Republic of Holland and West-Friesland.* London: 1702.

OFFICIAL PUBLICATIONS

General Agreement on Tariffs and Trade (GATT):

Basic Instruments and Selected Documents, vols. 1–4, and Supplements No. 1–34 (1950–87).
GATT Activities, 1959/60–1989.

International Bank for Reconstruction and Development (IBRD, World Bank):

Annual Reports 1946/47–89.

International Monetary Fund (IMF):

Annual Reports 1946–1989.
Annual Reports on Exchange Arrangements and Exchange Restrictions 1950–1989.

League of Nations:

Commercial Policy in the Interwar Period: International Policies (1942).
Enquiry into Clearing Agreements, L.N. Doc. C.153.M.83.1935.II.B (1935).
League of Nations Treaty Series, vols. 1–204.
Official Journal, vols. 1–21 (1920–1940).
Permanent Court of International Justice Reports 1921–1940.
Report of the Commission of Inquiry (Lytton Commission), and Annexes, L.N. Doc. C.663.M.320.1932.VII (1932).

United Kingdom:

British and Foreign State Papers, vols. 1–170 (London: HMSO, 1841–1977).
Report of the Expert Committee Appointed by the Reparation Commission ("Dawes Committee"), Cmd. 2105 (1924).
Great Britain Treaty Series 1883–1989.

United Nations:

Documents of the United Nations Conference on International Organization, San Francisco, 1945. 10 vols. London: United Nations Information Organizations, 1945.
General Assembly Official Records, 1st Session (1945) — 43d Session (1988).
International Court of Justice Reports, 1946–1988.
Reports of International Arbitral Awards, vols. 1–17.
Security Council Official Records, 1st Year (1946) — 43d Year (1988).
United Nations Conference on Trade and Development (UNCTAD), *Proceedings*, 1st Session (1964) — 6th Session (1983).
United Nations Treaty Series, vols. 1–1235.

United States:

Department of State, *Department of State Bulletin* (1939–1989).
——*Digest of United States Practice in International Law* 1973–1979.
——*Foreign Relations of the United States* [1870]-[1958–60], vol. 1.
——*Proposals for Expansion of World Trade and Employment*, Publication No. 2411 (1945).
——*Treaties and Other International Agreements of the United States*, 1776–1949, compiled by Charles I. Bevans, vols. 1–12 (1968–74).
——United States Treaty Series, vols. 1–41 (1949–89).
Statutes at Large, vols. 1–202.

Hackworth, Green Hayward. *Digest of International Law.* 8 vols. Washington, D.C.: GPO, 1940–44.
Moore, John Bassett. *A Digest of International Law.* 8 vols. Washington, D.C.: GPO, 1906.
Whiteman, Marjorie M. *Digest of International Law.* 15 vols. Washington, D.C.: GPO, 1963–73.

INTERNATIONAL LAW TREATISES

Baty, Thomas. *International Law.* London: John Murray, 1909..
Beaumanoir, Philippe de. *Coûtumes de Beauvaisis.* Bourges: Francois Tubeau, 1690. (1st ed. 1283).
Bernhardt, Rudolf, ed. *Encyclopedia of Public International Law.* vols 1–10. Amsterdam: North-Holland, 1981–87.
Bluntschli, Johann K. *Le droit international codifié.* Translated by C. Lardy. 3d ed. Paris: Guillaumin, 1881.
Borchard, Edwin M. *The Diplomatic Protection of Citizens Abroad; or The Law of International Claims.* New York: Banks Law Publishing, 1915.
Bowett, Derek. *Self-defence in International Law.* Manchester: Manchester University Press, 1958.
Broms, Bengt. *The Doctrine of Equality of States as Applied in International Organizations.* Vammala: Vammalan Kirjapaino Oy., 1959.
Bynkershoek, Cornelius van. *Questions of Public Law.* Translated by Tenney Frank. Oxford: Clarendon Press (Carnegie Institute), 1930. (1st ed. Leyden, 1737)
Calvo, Carlos. *Le droit international théorique et pratique.* 5th ed. Paris: Rousseau, 1896.
Carreau, Dominique, Patrick Juillard and Thiebaut Flory. *Droit international économique.* 2d ed. Paris: Librairie Générale de Droit et de Jurisprudence, 1980.
Colbert, Evelyn. *Retaliation in International Law.* New York: King's Crown Press, 1948.
Dickinson, Edwin De Witt. *The Equality of States in International Law.* Cambridge: Harvard University Press, 1918.
Eagleton, Clyde. *The Responsibility of States in International Law.* New York: New York University Press, 1928.
——*International Government.* 3d ed. New York: Ronald Press, 1957.
Elagab, Omer Yousif. *The Legality of Non-forcible Countermeasures in International Law.* Oxford: Clarendon Press, 1988.
Fauchille, Paul. *Traité de droit international public.* 2 vols. Paris: Rousseau, 1922.
Friedmann, Wolfgang G. *The Changing Structure of International Law.* London: Stevens, 1964.
Gaius. *The Institutes.* Translated by Francis de Zulueta. 2 parts. Oxford: Clarendon Press, 1946–53. (Drafted c. A.D. 138–80).

Gentili, Alberico. *On the Law of War*. Translated by John C. Rolfe. Oxford: Clarendon Press (Carnegie Institute), 1933. (1st ed. Hanau, 1598)

Goodrich, Leland M. and Edward Hambro. *Charter of the United Nations: Commentary and Documents*. 2d ed. Boston: World Peace Foundation, 1949.

Grotius, Hugo. *Commentary on the Law of Prize and Booty*. Translated by Gwladys Williams. Oxford: Clarendon Press (Carnegie Institute), 1950. (Drafted 1604–05)

——*On the Law of War and Peace*. Translated by Francis W. Kelsey. Oxford: Oxford University Press (Carnegie Institute), 1925. (1st ed. Paris, 1625)

Hall, William Edward. *International Law*. Oxford: Clarendon Press, 1880.

Heffter, August W. *Le droit international de l'Europe*. Translated by Jules Bergson. Berlin: Schroeder, 1873.

Hindmarsh, Albert E. *Force in Peace: Force Short of War in International Relations*. Cambridge: Harvard University Press, 1933.

Hübner, Martin. *De la saisie des bâtiments neutres, ou Du droit qu'ont les nations belligérantes d'arrêter les navires des peuples amis*. 2 vols. The Hague: 1759.

Kent, James. *Commentary on International Law*. Edited by John T. Abdy. Cambridge: Deighton, Bell, 1866.

Kohona, Palitha T.B. *The Regulation of International Economic Relations through Law*. Dordrecht: Martinus Nijhoff, 1985.

Liszt, Franz von. *Le droit international: Exposé systématique*. Translated by Gilbert Gidel from the 9th German ed. Paris: Pedone, 1927.

McDougal, Myres S. and Florentino P. Feliciano. *Law and Minimum World Public Order: The Legal Regulation of International Coercion*. New Haven, Conn.: Yale University Press, 1961.

Mably, Abbé de. *Le droit public de l'Europe, fondé sur les traités*. 2 vols. Amsterdam: Uytwerf, 1748.

Martens, Georg Friedrich de. *Précis de droit des gens moderne de l'Europe fondé sur les traités et l'usage*. 3d ed. Göttingen: Librairie de Dieterich, 1821.

Mérignhac, Alexandre G.H.A. de. *Traité de droit public international*. Paris: Pichon et Durand-Auzias, 1905.

Möller, Axel. *International Law in Peace and War*. Translated by H.M. Pratt. 2 vols. London: Stevens, 1931–35.

Niemeyer, Gerhart. *Law Without Force*. London: Oxford University Press, 1941.

Nys, Ernest. *Le droit international: Les principes, les théories, les faits*. 3 vols. 2d ed. Brussels: Castaigne, 1904–08.

Oppenheim, L. *International Law: A Treatise*. Edited by Hersch Lauterpacht. 2 vols. 7th and 8th eds. London: Longman, 1952–55.

Piédelièvre, Robert. *Précis de droit international public; ou, Droit des gens*. 2 vols. Paris: Pichon, 1894–95.

Pradelle, Albert Geouffre de La. *Maîtres et doctrines du droit des gens*. 2d ed. Paris: Éditions Internationales, 1950.

Pufendorf, Samuel. *On the Law of Nature and Nations*. Translated by C.H. and W.A. Oldfather. Oxford: Oxford University Press (Carnegie Institute), 1934. (1st ed. Lund, 1672)

Redslob, Robert. *Histoire des grand principes du droit des gens depuis l'antiquité jusqu'à la veille de la Grande Guerre*. Paris: Rousseau, 1923.

——*Les principes du droit des gens moderne.* Paris: Rousseau, 1937.

Rivier, Alphonse P.O. *Principes du droit des gens.* Paris: Rousseau, 1896.

Scelle, Georges. *Précis de droit des gens: Principes et systématique.* 2 vols. Paris: Sirey, 1932–34.

Sibert, Marcel. *Traité de droit international public: Le droit de la paix.* Paris: Dalloz, 1951.

Stone, Julius. *Of Law and Nations: Between Power Politics and Human Hopes.* Buffalo, N.Y.: W.S. Hein, 1974.

——*Conflict Through Consensus: United Nations Approaches to Aggression.* Baltimore: Johns Hopkins University Press, 1977.

Stowell, Ellery C. *International Law: A Restatement of Principles in Conformity with Actual Practice.* New York: Holt, 1931.

Strupp, Karl. *Éléments du droit international public universel, européen et américain.* 2d ed. Paris: Éditions Internationales, 1930.

Themaat, Pieter Verloren van. *The Changing Structure of International Economic Law.* The Hague: Martinus Nijhoff, 1981.

Vattel, Emmerich de. *The Law of Nations; or, The Principles of Natural Law Applied to the Conduct and the Affairs of Nations and of Sovereigns.* Translated by Charles G. Fenwick. Washington, D.C.: Carnegie Institution, 1916. (1st ed. London, 1758)

Vitoria, Francisco de. "On the Indians Lately Discovered." In *De Indis et de Ivre Belli Reflectiones,* at 115–62. Translated by John Pawley Bate. Washington, D.C.: Carnegie Institution, 1917. (Drafted 1532; 1st ed. Lyon, 1557)

Wolff, Christian. *The Law of Nations Treated According to a Scientific Method.* Translated by Joseph H. Drake. Oxford: Clarendon Press (Carnegie Institute), 1934. (1st ed. Halle, 1749)

Woolsey, Theodore D. *Introduction to the Study of International Law.* 5th ed. New York: Scribner, 1879.

Zoller, Elizabeth. *Peacetime Unilateral Remedies: An Analysis of Countermeasures.* Dobbs Ferry, N.Y.: Transnational, 1984.

BOOKS AND ARTICLES

Abbott, Kenneth W. "Linking Trade to Political Goals: Foreign Policy Export Controls in the 1970s and the 1980s." *Minnesota Law Review* (1981), 65:739–889.

Abrahams, Paul P. *The Foreign Expansion of American Finance and Its Relationship to the Foreign Economic Policies of the United States, 1907–1921.* Salem, N. H.: Ayer, 1976.

Acheson, Dean. *Present at the Creation: My Years in the State Department.* New York: Norton, 1969.

Adams, Brooks. "The Commercial Future: The New Struggle for Life Among Nations." *Fortnightly Review* (1899), 65:274–83.

Adler-Karlsson, Gunnar. *Western Economic Warfare 1947–1967: A Case Study in Foreign Economic Policy.* Stockholm: Almqvist & Wiskell, 1968.

Aeppel, Timothy. "The Evolution of Multilateral Export Controls: A Critical Study of the CoCom Regime." *Fletcher Forum* (1985), 9:105–24.

Akinsanya, Adeoye A. *The Expropriation of Multinational Property in the Third World*. New York: Praeger, 1980.

Aldcroft, Derek H. *From Versailles to Wall Street 1919–1929*. London: Allen Lane, 1977.

Allen, Robert L. *Soviet Economic Warfare*. Washington D.C.: Public Affairs Press, 1960.

——"Economic Warfare." In *International Encyclopedia of the Social Sciences*, edited by David L. Sills, 4:467–71. London: Collier-Macmillan, 1968.

Allen, William R. "The International Trade Philosophy of Cordell Hull, 1907–1933." *American Economic Review* (1953), 43:101–16.

Amerasinghe, C. F. "The Common Fund for Commodities." *George Washington Journal of International Law and Economics* (1983), 7:231–80.

Anand, Ram Prakash. "Sovereign Equality of States in International Law." *Recueil des Cours* (Académie de Droit International) (1986), 197:9–228.

Andréadès, Andreas M. "Les contrôles financières internationaux." *Recueil des Cours* (Académie de Droit International) (1924), 5:1–108.

Angell, James Waterhouse. *Financial Foreign Policy of the United States*. New York: Institute of Pacific Relations, 1933.

Angell, Norman. *The Foundations of International Polity*. London: Heinemann, 1914.

Appleby, Joyce. *Capitalism and a New Social Order: The Republican Vision of the 1790s*. New York: New York University Press, 1984.

Arndt, Heinz W. *The Economic Lessons of the Nineteen-Thirties*. London: Oxford University Press, 1944.

Ashley, Percy W. L. *Modern Tariff History: Germany—United States—France*. 3d ed. London: John Murray, 1920.

Assersohn, Roy. *The Biggest Deal: Bankers, Politics and the Hostages of Iran*. London: Methuen, 1982.

Assetto, Valerie J. *The Soviet Bloc in the IMF and the IBRD*. London: Westview Press, 1987.

Ayubi, Shaheen, Richard E. Bissell, N. Korsah and L. Lerner. *Economic Sanctions in U.S. Foreign Policy*. New York: Foreign Policy Research, 1982.

Bael, Ivo van. "The GATT Dispute Settlement Procedure." *Journal of World Trade* (1988), 22(4):67–77.

Bailey, Stephen H. "The Political Aspect of Discrimination in International Economic Relations." *Economica* (1932), 12:89–115, and 160–79.

Bairoch, Paul. *The Economic Development of the Third World Since 1900*. Translated by Cynthia Postan. London: Methuen, 1975.

Baker, Ray Stannard. *Woodrow Wilson and World Settlement*. Garden City, N.Y.: Doubleday, Page, 1923.

Baldry, Harold C. *The Unity of Mankind in Greek Thought*. Cambridge: Cambridge University Press, 1965.

Baldwin, David A. "The International Bank in Political Perspective." *World Politics* (1965), 18:68–81.

——"Economic Power." In *Perspectives on Social Power*, edited by James T. Tedeschi, at 395–413. Chicago: Aldine, 1974.

——*Economic Statecraft*. Princeton: Princeton University Press, 1985.

Baldwin, John W. *Masters, Princes and Merchants: The Social Views of Peter the Chanter and his Circle*. Princeton: Princeton University Press, 1970.

Barber, James. "Economic Sanctions as a Policy Instrument." *International Affairs* (1979), 55:367–84.

Barber, William J. *From New Era to New Deal: Herbert Hoover, the Economists, and American Economic Policy, 1921–33*. Cambridge: Cambridge University Press, 1985.

Barcia Trelles, Camilo. "Francisco de Vitoria et l'école moderne du droit international." *Recueil des Cours* (Académie de Droit International) (1927), 19:109–342.

Barnet, Richard J. and Ronald E. Müller, *Global Reach: The Power of the Multinational Corporations*. London: Jonathon Cape, 1974.

Barnhart, Michael A. "Japan's Economic Security and the Origins of the Pacific War." *Journal of Strategic Studies* (1981), 4:105–25.

——*Japan Prepares for Total War: The Search for Economic Security, 1919– 1941*. Ithaca, N.Y.: Cornell University Press, 1987.

Baruch, Bernard M. *The Making of the Reparation and Economic Sections of the Treaty*. London: Harper, 1920.

Basch, Antonin. *The Danube Basin and the German Economic Sphere*. London: K. Paul, Trench, Trubner, 1944.

Bassiouni, M. Cherif., Norman V. Cleute and Paul McCarthy. *Boycott and Anti-Boycott: Implications in Arab-U.S. Relations*. Chicago: Mid-America Arab Chamber of Commerce, 1986.

Batie, Sandra S. and R. Healy, eds. *The Future of American Agriculture as a Strategic Resource*. Washington, D.C.: Conservation Foundation, 1980.

Bauer, Robert A., ed. *The Interaction of Economics and Foreign Policy*. Charlottesville: University Press of Virginia, 1975.

Bautista, Lilia R. "The New International Economic Order and Christian Charity." *Catholic Lawyer* (1980), 25:171–86.

Beard, Charles A. *The Open Door at Home: A Trial Philosophy of National Interest*. New York: Macmillan, 1935.

Becker, William H. and Samuel F. Wells, Jr., eds. *Economics and World Power: An Assessment of American Diplomacy Since 1789*. New York: Columbia University Press, 1984.

Becqué, Émile. *L'internationalisation des capitaux: Étude économique, financière et politique*. Montpellier: Imprimerie Générale du Midi, 1912.

Bender, Lynn D. *The Politics of Hostility: Castro's Revolution and United States Policy*. San German, P.R.: Inter American University Press, 1974.

Bennett, Edward W. *Germany and the Diplomacy of the Financial Crisis*. Cambridge: Harvard University Press, 1931.

Bergsten, C. Fred, Robert O. Keohane and Joseph S. Nye. "International Economics and International Politics: A Framework for Analysis." *International Organization* (1975), 29:3–36.

Bergsten, C. Fred and Lawrence B. Krause, eds. *World Politics and International Economics*. Washington, D.C.: Brookings Institution, 1975.

Bernholz, Peter. *Aussenpolitik und Internationale Wirtschaftsbeziehungen*. Frankfurt: Klostermann, 1966.

Bewes, Wyndham A. *The Romance of the Law Merchant.* London: Sweet & Maxwell, 1923.

Bialos, Jeffrey P. and Kenneth I. Juster. "The Libyan Sanctions: A Rational Response to State-Sponsored Terrorism?" *Virginia Journal of International Law* (1986), 26:799–855.

Biermann, W. and J. Wagao. "The Quest for Adjustment: Tanzania and the IMF." *African Studies Review* (1986), 29:89–103.

Biersteker, Thomas J. "Self-Reliance in Theory and Practice in Tanzanian Trade Relations." *International Organization* (1980), 34:229–64.

Bilder, Richard E. "Comments on the Legality of the Arab Oil Boycott." *Texas International Law Journal* (1977), 12:41–46.

Bird, Graham R. *The International Monetary System and the Less Developed Countries.* 2d ed. London: Macmillan, 1982.

——*World Finance and Adjustment: An Agenda for Reform.* London: Macmillan, 1985.

Bismuth, Jean-Louis. *Le Boycottage dans les échanges économiques internationaux au regard du droit: Remarques autour et sur la loi française du 7 juin 1977.* Paris: Economica, 1980.

Bjorklund, Victoria. "Reprieve for Poland on Declaration of Default." *Columbia Journal of Transnational Law* (1981), 20:581–85.

Blaisdell, Donald C. *European Financial Control in the Ottoman Empire: A Study of the Establishment, Activities, and Significance of the Administration of the Ottoman Public Debt.* New York: AMS Press, 1966.

Blake, David H. and Robert S. Walters, *The Politics of Global Economic Relations.* 3d ed. Englewood Cliffs, N.J.: Prentice-Hall, 1987.

Bleicher, Samuel A. "UN v. IBRD: A Dilemma of Functionalism." *International Organization* (1970), 24:31–47.

Blinken, Antony J. *Ally Versus Ally: America, Europe, and the Siberian Pipeline Crisis.* New York: Praeger, 1987.

Bloomfield, Louis M. *Egypt, Israel and the Gulf of Aqaba in International Law.* Toronto: Carswell, 1957.

Blum, Yehuda Z. "Economic Boycotts in International Law." *Texas International Law Journal* (1977), 12:5–15.

Boltho, A. "Is There a Future for Resource Transfers to the LDCs?" *World Development* (1988), 16:1159–66.

Bonn, Moritz J. "La paix économique: Dans quelle mesure les régimes autarciques sont-ils conciliables avec le maintien de la paix?" *Esprit International* (1938), 12:238–55.

Boorman, James A. III. "Economic Coercion in International Law: The Arab Oil Weapon and the Ensuing Juridical Issues." *Journal of International Law and Economics* (1974), 9:205–31.

Bordo, Michael D. and Anna J. Schwartz, eds. *A Retrospective on the Classical Gold Standard, 1821–1931.* Chicago: University of Chicago Press, 1984.

Born, Karl E. *International Banking in the 19th and 20th Centuries.* Leamington Spa: Berg, 1983.

Bosanquet, Helen. *Free Trade and Peace in the Nineteenth Century.* New York: G.P. Putnam and Sons, 1924.

Boulding, Kenneth E. "Defense and Opulence: The Ethics of International Economics." *American Economic Review* (Papers and Proceedings) (1951), 41:210–20.

Bouvé, C.L. "The National Boycott as an International Delinquency." *American Journal of International Law* (1934), 28:19–42.

Bowett, Derek W. "Economic Coercion and Reprisals by States." *Virginia Journal of International Law* (1972), 13:1–12.

Boyce, Robert W. D. *British Capitalism at the Crossroads: A Study in Politics, Economics, and International Relations.* Cambridge: Cambridge University Press, 1987.

Bozeman, Adda B. *Politics and Culture in International History.* Princeton: Princeton University Press, 1960.

Brandes, Joseph. *Herbert Hoover and Economic Diplomacy: Department of Commerce Policy, 1921–28.* Pittsburgh: University of Pittsburgh Press, 1962.

Braudel, Fernand. *The Wheels of Commerce.* Translated by Sîan Reynolds. London: Collins, 1982.

Bridbury, A. R. "Markets and Freedom in the Middle Ages." In *The Market in History,* edited by B.L. Anderson and A.J.H. Latham, at 79–119. London: Croom Helm, 1986.

Brosche, Hartmut. "The Arab Oil Embargo and United States Pressure Against Chile: Economic and Political Coercion and the Charter of the United Nations." *Case Western Reserve Journal of International Law* (1974), 7:3–35.

Brown, Alan A. and Egon Neuberger, eds. *International Trade and Central Planning: An Analysis of Economic Interactions.* Berkeley: University of California Press, 1968.

Brown, E. A. "The Boycott in International Law." *Canadian Bar Review* (1933), 11:325–32.

Brown, Philip Marshall. "Economic Warfare." *American Journal of International Law* (1917), 11:847–50.

Brown, William A. *The United States and the Restoration of World Trade: An Analysis and Appraisal of the ITO Charter and the General Agreement on Tariffs and Trade.* Washington: Brookings Institution, 1950.

Bryde, B. O. "Die Intervention mit wirtschaftlichen Mitteln." In *Staatsrecht—Völkerrecht—Europarecht, (Festschrift für Hans-Jürgen Schlochauer zum 75. Geburstag am 28 Marz 1981),* edited by Ingo von Munch, at 227–45. Berlin: Walter de Gruyter, 1981.

Buchanan, James M. *Market and State: Political Economy in the 1980s.* Brighton: Wheatsheaf, 1986.

Buchheit, Lee C. "The Use of Nonviolent Coercion: A Study in Legality under Article 2(4) of the Charter of the United Nations." *University of Pennsylvania Law Review* (1974), 122:983–1011.

Buckingham, Peter H. *International Normalcy: The Open Door Peace with the Former Central Powers 1921–29.* Wilmington, Del.: Scholarly Resources, 1983.

Bulajic, Milan. *Principles of International Development Law: Progressive Development of the Principles of International Law Relating to the New International Economic Order.* The Hague: Martinus Nijhoff, 1986.

Burnell, Peter J. *Economic Nationalism in the Third World*. Brighton: Wheatsheaf, 1986.

Butler, Nick. "The United States Grain Weapon: Could It Boomerang?" *World Today* (1983), 39:52–59.

Buzan, Barry. "Economic Structure and International Security: The Limits of the Liberal Case." *International Organization* (1984), 38:597–624.

Capie, Forrest. *Depression and Protectionism: Britain Between the Wars*. London: Allen & Unwin, 1983.

Carlisle, Robert B. *The Proferred Crown: Saint Simonianism and the Doctrine of Hope*. Baltimore: Johns Hopkins University Press, 1988.

Carr, E. H. *The Future of Nations: Independence or Interdependence?* London: K. Paul, Trench, Trubner, 1941.

Carr, William. *Arms, Autarky and Aggression: A Study in German Foreign Policy, 1933–39*. London: Edwin Arnold, 1972.

Carroll, Berenice A. *Design for Total War: Arms and Economics in the Third Reich*. The Hague: Mouton, 1968.

Carswell, Robert. "Economic Sanctions and the Iran Experience." *Foreign Affairs* (1981/82), 60:247–65.

Carter, Barry E. *International Economic Sanctions: Improving the Haphazard U.S. Legal Regime*. Cambridge: Cambridge University Press, 1988.

Castañeda, Jorge. "La Charte des droits et devoirs économiques des États." *Annuaire Français de Droit International* (1974) 20: 31–77.

Catry, Joseph. "La liberté du commerce international d'après Vitoria, Suarez et les scolastiques." *Revue Générale de Droit International Public* (1932), 39: 193–218.

Cecco, Marcello de. *The International Gold Standard: Money and Empire*. London: Frances Pinter, 1984.

Chamberlain, Joseph P. "Embargoes as a Sanction of International Law." *Proceedings of the American Society of International Law* (1933), 27:66–78.

Charléty, Sebastien C. G. *Histoire du Saint-Simonisme 1825–1864*. Paris: P. Hartmann, 1931.

Chester, Edward W. *United States Oil Policy and Diplomacy: A Twentieth Century Overview*. Westport, Conn.: Greenwood Press, 1983.

Chill, Dan S. *The Arab Boycott of Israel: Economic Aggression and World Reaction*. New York: Praeger, 1976.

Cilliers, A. "Economic Coercion and South Africa, Part III: The Legality of International Economic Coercion." *South African Year Book of International Law* (1977), 3:126–35.

Clark, Evans. *Boycotts and Peace: A Report by the Committee on Economic Sanctions*. New York: Harper, 1932.

Claudon, Michael P., ed. *International Lending on Trial*. Cambridge, Mass.: Ballinger, 1986.

Clémentel, Étienne. *La France et la politique économique interallié*. Paris: Presses Universitaires de France, 1931.

Cline, William R. *Policy Alternatives for a New International Economic Order*. New York: Praeger, 1979.

Cohen, Benjamin J. *In Whose Interest? International Banking and American Foreign Policy*. New Haven: Yale University Press, 1986.

Cohen, Stephen B. "Conditioning U.S. Security Assistance on Human Rights Practices." *American Journal of International Law* (1982), 76:246–79.

Coleman, Donald C., ed. *Revisions in Mercantilism.* London: Methuen, 1969.

Condliffe, John B. *The Reconstruction of World Trade.* New York: Norton, 1940.

——"Economic Power as an Instrument of National Policy." *American Economic Review* (Papers and Proceedings) (1944), 34:305–14.

——*The Commerce of Nations.* London: Allen & Unwin, 1951.

Cooper, Richard N. *The Economics of Interdependence: Economic Policy in the Atlantic Community.* New York: McGraw-Hill, 1968.

——"Economic Interdependence and Foreign Policy in the Seventies." *World Politics* (1972), 24:159–81.

Corden, Warner Max. *The NIEO Proposals: A Cool Look.* London: Trade Policy Research Centre, 1979.

Costigliola, Frank. *Awkward Dominion: American Political, Economic, and Cultural Relations with Europe, 1919–1933.* Ithaca, N.Y.: Cornell University Press, 1984.

Cottrell, P. L. *British Overseas Investment in the Nineteenth Century.* London: Macmillan, 1975.

Crowley, John E. *This Sheba, Self: The Conceptualization of Economic Life in Eighteenth-Century America.* Baltimore: Johns Hopkins University Press, 1974.

Culbertson, William S. *Commercial Policy in Wartime and After: A Study of the Application of Democratic Ideas to International Commercial Relations.* New York: Appleton, 1919.

——*International Economic Policies: A Survey of the Economics of Diplomacy.* New York: Appleton, 1925.

Curtin, Philip D. *Cross-Cultural Trade in World History.* Cambridge: Cambridge University Press, 1984.

Curzon, Gerard. *Multilateral Commercial Diplomacy: The General Agreement on Tariffs and Trade and Its Impact on National Commercial Policies and Techniques.* London: Michael Joseph, 1965.

Cynkin, Thomas M. *Soviet and American Signalling in the Polish Crisis.* Basingstoke: Macmillan, 1988.

Dallek, Robert. *Franklin D. Roosevelt and American Foreign Policy, 1932–1945.* New York: Oxford University Press, 1979.

Dam, Kenneth. *The GATT: Law and International Economic Organization.* Chicago: University of Chicago Press, 1970.

Daoudi, M. S. and M. S. Dajani. *Economic Sanctions: Ideals and Experience.* London: Routledge & Kegan Paul, 1983.

——"Sanctions: The Falklands Episode." *World Today* (1983), 39:150–60.

——*Economic Diplomacy: Embargo Leverage and World Politics.* Boulder, Col.: Westview Press, 1985.

Darvall, Frank O. *The Price of European Peace.* London: Hodge, 1927.

Dawes, Rufus C. *The Dawes Plan in the Making.* Indianapolis: Bobbs-Merrill, 1925.

Dawson, William H. *Richard Cobden and Foreign Policy: A Critical Exposition, with Special Reference to Our Day and Its Problems.* London: Allen & Unwin, 1926.

Day, Richard B. *Leon Trotsky and the Politics of Economic Isolation.* Cambridge: Cambridge University Press, 1973.

Dean, Robert W. *West German Trade with the East: The Political Dimension.* New York: Praeger, 1974.

Deese, David A. and Joseph S. Nye, eds. *Energy and Security.* Cambridge: Ballinger, 1981.

Delaisi, Francis. *Political Myths and Economic Realities.* London: Douglas, 1925.

Delanis, James A. " 'Force' under Art 2(4) of the United Nations Charter: The Question of Economic and Political Coercion." *Vanderbilt Journal of Transnational Law* (1979), 12:101–31.

Dell, Sidney. *On Being Grandmotherly: The Evolution of IMF Conditionality.* Princeton: Department of Economics, Princeton University, 1981.

——"Free Trade and Reciprocity." *World Economy* (1986), 9:125–39.

——"The Politics of International Commodity Trade: The Common Fund." *International Affairs* (1986/87), 63:21–38.

——*The Politics of Economic Interdependence.* Basingstoke: Macmillan, 1987.

Denny, Ludwell. *America Conquers Britain: A Record of Economic War.* London: Knopf, 1930.

Dewost, Jean-Louis, "La Communauté, Les Dix et les 'sanctions' économiques: De la crise iranienne à la crise des Malouines." *Annuaire Français de Droit International* (1982), 28:215–32.

Diamond, William. *The Economic Thought of Woodrow Wilson.* Baltimore: Johns Hopkins University Press, 1943.

Dicke, Detlev C. *Die Intervention mit Wirtschaftlichen Mitteln im Völkerrecht.* Baden-Baden: Nomos, 1978.

Diebold, William. *The End of the International Trade Organization.* Princeton: International Finance Section, Department of Economics and Social Institutions, Princeton University, 1952.

Dinitz, Simcha, "The Legal Aspects of the Egyptian Blockade of the Suez Canal." *Georgetown Law Journal* (1957), 45:169–99.

Diumulen, I. I. "Boycott." In *Great Soviet Encyclopedia,* edited by Aleksandr M. Prokhorov, translated by Diana G. Nakeeb, 3d ed., 3:512–13. New York: Macmillan, 1970.

Dolman, Antony J. *Resources, Regimes, World Order.* New York: Pergamon, 1981.

Dolzer, Rudolf. "New Foundations of the Law of Expropriation of Alien Property." *American Journal of International Law* (1981), 75:553–89.

Domb, Martin. "Defining Economic Aggression in International Law: The Possibility of Regional Action by the Organization of American States." *Cornell International Law Journal* (1978), 11:85–105.

Donaldson, John. *International Economic Relations: A Treatise on World Economy and World Politics.* New York: Longman, 1928.

Dormael, Armand van. *Bretton Woods: Birth of a Monetary System.* London: Macmillan, 1978.

Douglas, Henry Hulbert. "A Bit of American History—Successful Embargo Against Japan in 1918." *Amerasia* (1940), 4:258–60.

Dowty, Alan. *Closed Borders: The Contemporary Assault on Freedom of Movement.* New Haven: Yale University Press, 1987.

Doxey, Margaret P. "Sanctions Revisited." *International Journal* (1975), 30:53–78.

——"Oil and Food as International Sanctions." *International Journal* (1981), 36:311–34.

——"Sanctions Against the Soviet Union: The Afghan Experience." *Year Book of World Affairs* (1983), 37:63–80.

——"International Sanctions in Theory and Practice." *Case Western Reserve Journal of International Law* (1983), 15:273–88.

Drummond, Ian M. *British Economic Policy and the Empire, 1919–1939.* London: Allen & Unwin, 1972.

Dubois, Louis. "L'embargo dans la pratique contemporaine." *Annuaire Français de Droit International* (1967), 13:99–152.

Dulles, John Foster. "Our Foreign Loan Policy." *Foreign Affairs* (1926), 5:33–48.

——*War, Peace and Change.* New York: Harper, 1939.

Dupuy, Pierre-Marie. "Observations sur la pratique récente des 'sanctions' de l'illicité." *Revue Générale de Droit International Public* (1983), 87:505–48.

Eckalbar, John C. "The Saint-Simonians in Industry and Economic Development." *American Journal of Economics and Sociology* (1979), 38:83–96.

Eckes, Alfred E. Jr. "Open Door Expansionism Reconsidered: The World War II Experience." *Journal of American History* (1973), 59:909–24.

Edsall, Nicholas C. *Richard Cobden: Independent Radical.* Cambridge: Harvard University Press, 1986.

Einzig, Paul. *Behind the Scenes of International Finance.* London: Macmillan, 1932.

Ellings, Richard. *Embargoes and World Power: Lessons from American Foreign Policy.* Boulder, Col.: Westview Press, 1985.

Emmanuel, Arghiri. *Unequal Exchange: A Study of the Imperialism of Trade.* London: NLB, 1972.

Engelbrecht, Helmuth C. *Johann Gottlieb Fichte: A Study of His Political Writings with Special Reference to His Nationalism.* New York: Columbia University Press, 1933.

Engels, Benno. *Die Zukunft des Embargos in den Internationalen Beziehungen.* Hamburg: Dt. Ubersee Inst., 1981.

Everest, Allan A. *Morgenthau, the New Deal and Silver: A Story of Pressure Politics.* New York: Da Capo Press, 1950.

Fairbank, J. K. and J. Y. Têng. "On the Ch'ing Tributary System." *Harvard Journal of Asiatic Studies* (1941), 6:135–246.

Falk, Richard A. *The Promise of World Order: Essays in Normative International Relations.* Brighton: Wheatsheaf, 1987.

Farer, Tom J. "Political and Economic Coercion in Contemporary International Law." *American Journal of International Law* (1985), 79:405–13.

Feinberg, Kenneth R. "Economic Coercion and Economic Sanctions: The Expansion of United States Extraterritorial Jurisdiction." *American University Law Review* (1981), 30:323–48.

283

Feis, Herbert. *Europe the World's Banker 1870–1914: An Account of European Foreign Investment and the Connection of World Finance with Diplomacy before the War.* New York: Keiley, 1930.

——"After Tariffs, Embargoes." *Foreign Affairs* (1931), 9:398–408.

——"The Conflict over Trade Ideologies." *Foreign Affairs* (1947), 25:217–28.

——*The Diplomacy of the Dollar: First Era 1919–1932.* Baltimore: Johns Hopkins University Press, 1950.

——*The Road to Pearl Harbor: The Coming of the War Between the United States and Japan.* Princeton: Princeton University Press, 1950.

——*Foreign Aid and Foreign Policy.* London: Macmillan, 1964.

Feith, Douglas J. "Oil Weapon De-mystified." *Policy Review* (1981), 15:19–39.

Ferguson, Tyrone. *The Third World and Decision Making in the International Monetary Fund: The Quest for Full and Effective Participation.* London: Pinter, 1988.

Finch, George A. "The Dawes Report on German Reparation Payment." *American Journal of International Law* (1924), 18:419–35.

Finley, Moses I. *The Ancient Economy.* London: Chatto & Windus, 1973.

Fischer, Louis. *Oil Imperialism: The International Struggle for Petroleum.* New York: International Publishers, 1926.

Fisher, Allan G. B. *Economic Self-Sufficiency.* Oxford: Clarendon Press, 1939.

Fishlow, Albert. *Lessons from the Debt Crisis.* New York: Basil Blackwell, 1987.

Fishlow, Albert, Carlos F. Diaz-Alejandro, R. Fagen and R. Hansen, eds. *Rich and Poor Nations in the World Economy.* New York: McGraw-Hill, 1978.

Ford, Alan W. *The Anglo-Iranian Oil Dispute of 1951–1952: A Study of the Role of Law in the Relations of States.* Berkeley: University of California Press, 1954.

Fox, William. *Tin: The Working of a Commodity Agreement.* London: Mining Journal Books, 1974.

Fox-Genovese, Elizabeth. *The Origins of Physiocracy: Economic Revolution and Social Order in Eighteenth-Century France.* Ithaca, N.Y.: Cornell University Press, 1976.

Frankel, P. H. "Oil Supplies During the Suez Crisis—On Meeting a Political Emergency." *Journal of Industry and Economics* (1958), 6:85–100.

Fredman, Steven J. "U.S. Trade Sanctions Against Uganda: Legality Under International Law." *Law and Policy in International Business* (1979), 11:1149–91.

Freedman, Eric. "U.S. Bilateral and Multilateral Aid to Nations Which Do Not Cooperate with the United States to Combat International Drug Traffic." *New York University Journal of International Law and Politics* (1974), 7:361–82.

Freeman, Christopher and Marie Jahoda, eds. *World Futures: The Great Debate.* London: Martin Robertson, 1978.

Frey, Bruno S. *International Political Economics.* Oxford: Basil Blackwell, 1984.

Friedland, Edward, Paul Seabury and Aaron Wildavsky. "Oil and the Decline of Western Power." *Political Science Quarterly* (1975), 90:437–50.

Friedmann, Wolfgang. "The Growth of State Control Over the Individual, and Its Effect Upon the Rules of International State Responsibility." *British Year Book of International Law* (1938), 19:118–50.

Friessen, Connie M. *The Political Economy of East-West Trade.* New York: Praeger, 1976.

Gaddis, John L. *The United States and the Origins of the Cold War 1941–1947.* New York: Columbia University Press, 1972.

Gal, Imre. "The Commercial Law of Nations and the Law of International Trade." *Cornell International Law Journal* (1972), 6:55–75.

Gallagher, John and Ronald Robinson. "The Imperialism of Free Trade." *Economic History Review* (1953), 6:1–15.

Galtung, Johan, Peter O'Brien and Roy Preiswerk, eds. *Self-Reliance: A Strategy for Development.* London: Institute for Development Studies, 1980.

Gantenbein, James W. *Financial Questions in United States Foreign Policy.* New York: Columbia University Press, 1939.

Gardner, Lloyd C. *Economic Aspects of New Deal Diplomacy.* Madison, Wis.: University of Wisconsin Press, 1964.

——"Economic Foreign Policy and the Quest for Security." In *The National Security: Its Theory and Practice, 1945–1960,* edited by Norman A. Graebner, at 76–102. New York: Oxford University Press, 1986.

Gardner, Richard N. *Sterling-Dollar Diplomacy in Current Perspective: The Origins and Prospects of our International Economic Order.* 3d ed. New York: Columbia University Press, 1980.

Garnsey, Peter. *Famine and Food Supply in the Graeco-Roman World: Responses to Risk and Crisis.* Cambridge: Cambridge University Press, 1988.

Garnsey, Peter, Keith Hopkins and C. R. Whittaker, eds. *Trade in the Ancient Economy.* London: Chatto & Windus, 1983.

Garson, Robert. "The Role of Eastern Europe in America's Containment Policy, 1945–1948," *Journal of American Studies* (1979), 13:73–92.

Gelfand, Lawrence E. *Herbert Hoover: The Great War and Its Aftermath, 1914–1923.* Iowa City: University of Iowa Press, 1979.

Gerig, Benjamin. *The Open Door and the Mandates System: A Study of Economic Equality Before and Since the Establishment of the Mandates System.* London: Allen & Unwin, 1930.

Gerster, Richard. "The IMF and Basic Needs Conditionality." *Journal of World Trade Law* (1982), 16:497–517.

Ghoshal, Animesh. "Going Against the Grain: Lessons of the 1980 Embargo." *World Economics* (1983), 6:183–93.

Gide, Charles and Charles Rist. *A History of Economic Doctrines from the Time of the Physiocrats to the Present Day.* Translated by R. Richards. 2d English ed. London: George P. Harrap, 1948.

Gierke, Otto F. von. *Natural Law and the Theory of Society 1500 to 1800.* Translated by Ernest Barker. Cambridge: Cambridge University Press, 1934.

Gilbert, Charles. *American Financing of World War I.* London: Greenwood Press, 1970.

Gilbert, Felix. "The 'New Diplomacy' of the Eighteenth Century." *World Politics* (1951), 4:1–38.

———*To the Farewell Address: Ideas of Early American Foreign Policy.* Princeton: Princeton University Press, 1961.

Girling, Robert Henriques. *Multinational Institutions and the Third World: Management, Debt, and Trade Conflicts in the International Economic Order.* New York: Praeger, 1985.

Gisselquist, David. *Political Economics of International Bank Lending.* New York: Praeger, 1981.

Gold, Joseph. "The 'Sanctions' of the International Monetary Fund." *American Journal of International Law* (1972), 66:737–62.

———*The Rule of Law in the International Monetary Fund.* Washington, D.C.: IMF, 1980.

Golob, Eugene O. *The Méline Tariff: French Agricultural and Nationalist Economic Policy.* New York: Columbia University Press, 1944.

Gomes, Leonard. *Foreign Trade and the National Economy: Mercantilist and Classical Perspectives.* Basingstoke: Macmillan, 1987.

Gong, Gerritt W. *The Standard of 'Civilisation' in International Society.* Oxford: Clarendon Press, 1984.

Goodman, Louis W. *Small Nations, Giant Firms.* New York: Holmes & Meier, 1987.

Gordon, David L. and Royden Dangerfield. *The Hidden Weapon: The Story of Economic Warfare.* New York: Harper, 1947.

Gordon, Margaret S. *Barriers to World Trade: A Study of Recent Commercial Policy.* New York: Macmillan, 1941.

Graham, Benjamin. *Storage and Stability: A Modern Ever-Normal Granary.* New York: McGraw-Hill, 1937.

———*World Commodities and World Currency.* New York: McGraw-Hill, 1944.

Greene, J. "Economic Sanctions as Instruments of National Policy." *Annals of the American Academy of Political and Social Science* (1932), 162:100–102.

Greene, Jr., Preston L. "The Arab Economic Boycott of Israel: The International Law Perspective." *Vanderbilt Journal of Transnational Law* (1978), 11:77–94.

Gross, Leo. "Passage through the Suez Canal of Israel-bound Cargo and Israel Ships." *American Journal of International Law* (1957), 51:530–68.

Guerrieri, Paolo and Pier Carlo Padoan. "Neomercantilism and International Economic Stability." *International Organization* (1986), 40:29–42.

Guillain, Robert. *Les problèmes douaniers internationaux et la Société des Nations.* Paris: Sirey, 1930.

Guitian, Manuel. *Fund Conditionality: Evolution of Principles and Practices.* Washington, D.C.: IMF, 1981.

Haas, Ernest B. *Beyond the Nation State.* Stanford: Stanford University Press, 1964.

———"Is There a Hole in the Whole? Knowledge, Technology, Interdependence, and the Construction of International Regimes." *International Organization* (1975), 29:827–76.

Hadas, Moses. "From Nationalism to Cosmopolitanism in the Greco-Roman World." *Journal of the History of Ideas* (1943), 4:105–11.

Haggard, Stephen. "The Institutional Foundations of Hegemony: Explaining the Reciprocal Trade Agreements Act of 1934." *International Organization* (1988), 42:91–119.

Hammond, Matthew B. "Economic Conflict as a Regulating Force in International Affairs." *American Economic Review* (1931), 21:1–9.

Hanson, Philip. *Western Economic Statecraft in East-West Relations: Embargoes, Sanctions, Linkage, Economic Warfare, and Detente.* London: Routledge & Kegan Paul, 1988.

Haq, Inamul. "From Charity to Obligation: A Third World Perspective on Concessional Resource Transfers." *Texas International Law Journal* (1979), 14:389–424.

Harris, Charles R.S. *Germany's Foreign Indebtedness.* London: Humphrey Milford, 1935.

Harris, Hugh Henry. "Greek Origins of the Idea of Cosmopolitanism." *International Journal of Ethics* (1927), 38:1–10.

Harris, Seymour E. *Exchange Depreciation: Its Theory and History, 1931–35, with Some Consideration of Related Domestic Policies.* Cambridge: Harvard University Press, 1936.

Hart, Jeffrey A. *The New International Economic Order: Conflict and Cooperation in North-South Economic Relations, 1974–77.* London: Macmillan, 1983.

Hasebroek, Johannes. *Trade and Politics in Ancient Greece.* London: G. Bell, 1933.

Hasse, Rolf. *Theorie und Politik des Embargos.* Cologne: Institute für Wirtschaftspolitik, 1973.

——*Wirtschaftliche Sanktionen als Mittel der Aussenpolitik.* Berlin: Duncker und Humblot, 1977.

Hawke, G. R. "The United States Tariff and Industrial Protection in the Late Nineteenth Century." *Economic History Review* (1975), 28:84–99.

Hawley, Ellis W. "Herbert Hoover, the Commerce Secretariat, and the Vision of an 'Associative State,' 1921–28." *Journal of American History* (1974), 61:116–40.

——*The Great War and the Search for a Modern Order: A History of the American People and Their Institutions, 1917–1933.* New York: St. Martin's Press, 1979.

Hawley, Ellis W., ed. *Herbert Hoover as Secretary of Commerce: Studies in New Era Thought and Practice.* Iowa City: University of Iowa Press, 1981.

Hawtrey, Ralph G. *Economic Aspects of Sovereignty.* 2d ed. London: Longman, 1952.

Healy, David F. *Drive to Hegemony: The United States in the Caribbean, 1898–1917.* Madison: University of Wisconsin Press, 1989.

Heaton, Herbert. "Non-Importation, 1806–1812." *Journal of Economic History* (1941), 1:178–98.

Heckscher, Eli F. *The Continental System: An Economic Interpretation.* Oxford: Clarendon Press, 1922.

——*Mercantilism.* Translated by M. Shapiro. 2 vols. London: Allen & Unwin, 1955.

Heilperin, Michael A. *Studies in Economic Nationalism.* Geneva: Droz, 1960.

Hein, Werner. "Economic Embargoes and Individual Rights Under German Law." *Law and Policy in International Business* (1983), 15:401–23.

Henderson, J. Curtis. "Legality of Economic Sanctions Under International Law: The Case of Nicaragua." *Washington and Lee Law Review* (1986), 43:167–96.

Henderson, William O. *Friedrich List: Economist and Visionary, 1789–1846.* London: Cass, 1982.

Hentenryk, Kurgan van, ed. *Les relations financières internationales, Facteurs de solidarité ou de rivalités.* Brussels: Centre d'Études Européennes de Waterloo, 1979.

Heston, Thomas J. "Cuba, The United States and the Sugar Act of 1948: The Failure of Economic Coercion." *Diplomatic History* (1982), 6:1–21.

Heuser, Heinrich. *Control of International Trade.* London: Routledge, 1939.

Heuss, Theodor, *Friedrich Naumann: Der Mann, Das Werk, Die Zeit.* 2d ed. Stuttgart: Wunderlich, 1949.

Hill, Martin. *The Economic and Financial Organization of the League of Nations: A Survey of Twenty-Five Years' Experience.* Washington, D.C.: Carnegie Endowment, 1946.

Hinde, Wendy. *Richard Cobden: A Victorian Outsider.* New Haven: Yale University Press, 1987.

Hinsley, F. H. *Power and the Pursuit of Peace: Theory and Practice in the History of Relations Between States.* Cambridge: Cambridge University Press, 1963.

Hirschman, Albert O. *National Power and the Structure of Foreign Trade.* Berkeley: University of California Press, 1945.

——*The Passions and the Interests: Political Arguments for Capitalism before Its Triumph.* Princeton: Princeton University Press, 1977.

Hoffman, F. "The Functions of Economic Sanctions: A Comparative Analysis." *Journal of Peace Research* (1967), 2:140–59.

Hoffman, Ross J. S. *Great Britain and the German Trade Rivalry 1875–1914.* Philadelphia: University of Pennsylvania Press, 1933.

Hoffman, Stanley. "Notes on the Elusiveness of Modern Power." *International Journal* (1975), 30:183–206.

Hogan, Michael J. *Informal Entente: The Private Structure of Cooperation in Anglo-American Economic Diplomacy, 1918–1928.* Columbia: University of Missouri Press, 1977.

——"Revival and Reform: America's Twentieth-Century Search for a New Economic Order Abroad." *Diplomatic History* (1984), 8:287–310.

——"Corporatism: A Positive Appraisal." *Diplomatic History* (1986), 10:363–72.

——*The Marshall Plan: America, Britain, and the Reconstruction of Western Europe, 1947–1952.* Cambridge: Cambridge University Press, 1987.

Holley, H. A. *Developing Country Debt: The Role of the Commercial Banks.* London: Routledge & Kegan Paul, 1987.

Holsti, Kal J. "Politics in Command: Foreign Trade as National Security Policy." *International Organization* (1986), 40:643–71.

Holzman, Franklyn D. *International Trade Under Communism: Politics and Economics.* London: Macmillan, 1976.

Hoover, Herbert C. *The Memoirs of Herbert Hoover: The Cabinet and the Presidency 1920–1933.* 2 vols. London: Hollis & Carter, 1952.
——*The Ordeal of Woodrow Wilson.* London: McGraw-Hill, 1958.
Hopkins, George W. "The Politics of Food: United States and Soviet Hungary, March-August 1919." *Mid-America* (1973), 55:245–70.
Hopkins, Raymond F. "The International Role of 'Domestic' Bureaucracy." *International Organization* (1976), 30:405–32.
——"How to Make Food Work." *Foreign Policy* (1977), 27:89–107.
Hosoya, C. "Miscalculations in Deterrent Policy: Japanese-U.S. Relations, 1938–1941." *Journal of Peace Research* (1968), 5:97–115.
Hossain, Kamal, ed. *Legal Aspects of the New International Economic Order.* London: Pinter, 1980.
Hossain, Kamal and Subrata Roy Chowdhury, eds. *Permanent Sovereignty Over Natural Resources in International Law: Principle and Practice.* London: Pinter, 1984.
Hsu, Immanuel C.Y. *China's Entrance into the Family of Nations: The Diplomatic Phase 1858–1880.* Cambridge: Harvard University Press, 1960.
Hudec, Robert E. *The GATT Legal System and World Trade Diplomacy.* New York: Praeger, 1975.
——"GATT Dispute Settlement after the Tokyo Round: An Unfinished Business." *Cornell International Law Journal* (1980), 13:145–203.
——*Developing Countries in the GATT Legal System.* London: Gower, 1987.
Hufbauer, Gary Clyde and Jeffrey J. Schott. *Economic Sanctions Reconsidered: History and Current Policy.* Washington, D.C.: Institute for International Economics, 1985.
Hull, Cordell. *The Memoirs of Cordell Hull.* London: Hodder & Stoughton, 1948.
Hunt, Cecil. "Multilateral Cooperation in Export Controls—The Role of CoCom." *University of Toledo Law Review* (1983), 14:1285–97.
Hyde, Charles Cheney. "The Department of State on the American Flotation of Foreign Public Loans." *American Journal of International Law* (1922), 16:251–54.
——"The Boycott as a Sanction of International Law." *Proceedings of the American Society of International Law* (1933), 27:34–40.
——"The Boycott as a Sanction of International Law." *Political Science Quarterly* (1933), 48:211–19.
Hyde, Charles Cheney and Louis B. Wehl. "The Boycott in Foreign Affairs." *American Journal of International Law* (1933), 27:1–10.
Hyde, James N. "Permanent Sovereignty Over Natural Wealth and Resources." *American Journal of International Law* (1956), 50:854–67.
Iggers, George C. *The Cult of Authority: The Political Philosophy of the Saint-Simonians: A Chapter in the Intellectual History of Totalitarianism.* The Hague: Martinus Nijhoff, 1958.
Iliasu, A. A. "The Cobden-Chevalier Commercial Treaty of 1860." *Historical Journal* (1971), 14:67–98.
Imlah, Albert H. *Economic Elements in the Pax Britannica: Studies in British*

Foreign Trade in the Nineteenth Century. Cambridge: Harvard University Press, 1958.

Ingram, George M. *Expropriation of U.S. Property in South America: Nationalization of Oil and Copper Companies in Peru, Bolivia and Chile*. New York: Praeger, 1974.

International Bank for Reconstruction and Development. *The International Bank for Reconstruction and Development 1946–1953*. Baltimore: Johns Hopkins University Press, 1954.

Iskander, Marwan. *The Arab Boycott of Israel*. Beirut: Palestine Liberation Organization Research Center, 1966.

Itagaki, Y. "Economic Nationalism and the Problem of Natural Resources." *Developing Economies* (1973), 11:219–30.

Jack, Daniel. *Studies in Economic Warfare*. London: P.S. King & Son, 1940.

Jackson, John H. *World Trade and the Law of GATT (A Legal Analysis of the General Agreement on Tariffs and Trade)*. Indianapolis: Bobbs-Merrill, 1969.

——"The Crumbling Institutions of the Liberal Trade System." *Journal of World Trade Law* (1978), 12:93–106.

Jaehne, G., ed. *Sowjetische Landwirtschaft und Embargo*. Berlin: Duncker und Humblot, 1980.

James, Harold. *The German Slump: Politics and Economics 1924–1936*. Oxford: Clarendon Press, 1986.

Janne, Xavier. "La règlementation internationale des restrictions douanières." *Recueil des Cours* (Académie de Droit International) (1928), 21:109–85.

Jarrett, Bede. *Social Theories of the Middle Ages 1200–1500*. London: Benn, 1926.

Jennings, Walter W. *The American Embargo, 1807–1809*. Iowa City: University of Iowa Press, 1921.

Johnson, Harry G. "A Theoretical Model of Economic Nationalism in New and Developing States." *Political Science Quarterly* (1965), 80:169–85.

——*Economic Nationalism in Old and New States*. Chicago: University of Chicago Press, 1967.

——"Mercantilism: Past, Present and Future." *Journal of World Trade Law* (1974), 8:1–16.

Jones, Joseph M. Jr. *Tariff Retaliation: Repercussions of the Hawley-Smoot Bill*. Philadelphia: University of Pennsylvania Press, 1934.

Jong, H. G. de. "Coercion in the Conclusion of Treaties: A Consideration of Articles 51 and 52 of the Convention on the Law of Treaties." *Netherlands Year Book of International Law* (1984), 15:209–47.

Joyner, Christopher. "The Transnational Boycott as Economic Coercion in International Law: Policy, Place, and Practice." *Vanderbilt Journal of Transnational Law* (1984), 17:205–86.

Kaiser, David E. *Economic Diplomacy and the Origins of the Second World War: Germany, Britain, France, and Eastern Europe, 1930–1939*. Princeton: Princeton University Press, 1980.

Kaplan, Steven L. *Bread, Politicis and Political Economy in the Reign of Louis XV*. The Hague: Martinus Nijhoff, 1976.

Katzenstein, Peter J. "International Interdependence: Some Long-Term Trends and Recent Changes." *International Organization* (1975), 29:1021–34.

Kaufman, Burton I. "The United States Response to the Soviet Economic Offensive of the 1950s." *Diplomatic History* (1978), 2:153–65.

Kelsen, Hans. "Les rapports de système entre le droit interne et le droit international public." *Recueil des Cours* (Académie de Droit International) (1926), 14:227–327.

Kennedy, Paul M. *The Rise of the Anglo-German Antagonism, 1860–1914.* London: Allen & Unwin, 1980.

Kent, Bruce. *The Spoils of War: The Politics, Economics, and Diplomacy of Reparations 1918–1932.* New York: Oxford University Press, 1989.

Kenwood, A. G. and A. L. Lougheed. *The Growth of the International Economy 1820–1980: An Introductory Text.* London: Allen & Unwin, 1983.

Keohane, Robert O. *After Hegemony: Cooperation and Discord in the World Political Economy.* Princeton: Princeton University Press, 1984.

——"Reciprocity in International Relations." *International Organization* (1986), 40:1–27.

Keohane, Robert O. and Joseph S. Nye. *Power and Interdependence: World Politics in Transition.* Boston: Little, Brown, 1977.

Keynes, John Maynard. *The Economic Consequences of the Peace.* London: Macmillan, 1920.

——"National Self-sufficiency." *Yale Review* (1933), 22:755–69.

Killick, Tony, *The Quest for Economic Stabilisation: IMF and Third World.* London: Heinemann, 1984.

Killick, Tony, ed. *Adjustment and Financing in the Developing World: The Role of the International Monetary Fund.* Washington, D.C.: IMF, 1982.

Kindelberger, Charles P. *Power and Money: The Economics of International Politics and the Politics of International Economics.* London: Macmillan, 1970.

——*The World in Depression 1929–1939.* London: Allen Lane, 1973.

——"The Rise of Free Trade in Western Europe 1820–1875." *Journal of Economic History* (1975), 35:20–55.

——*International Capital Movements.* Cambridge: Cambridge University Press, 1987.

Kissler, Klaus-Peter. *Die Zulassigkeit von Wirtschaftssanktionen der Europäischen Gemeinschaft Gegenüber Drittstaaten.* Frankfurt: Lang, 1984.

Kleen, Richard. *Lois et Usages de la Neutralité.* 2 vols. Paris: A. Chevalier-Marescq, 1898–1900.

Klein, Julius. "International Cartels." *Foreign Affairs* (1928), 6:448–58.

——*Frontiers of Trade.* New York: Century, 1929.

Knickerbocker, Hubert R. *Fighting the Red Trade Menace.* New York: Dodd, Mead, 1931.

Knoll, David D. "The Impact of Security Concerns Upon International Economic Law." *Syracuse Journal of International Law and Commerce* (1984), 11:567–624.

Knorr, Klaus E. "The Problem of International Cartels and Intergovernmental Commodity Agreements." *Yale Law Journal* (1945–46), 55:1097–1126.

——Power and Wealth: The Political Economy of International Power. London: Macmillan, 1973.

——The Power of Nations: The Political Economy of International Relations. New York: Basic Books, 1975.

——"The Limits of Economic and Military Power." Daedalus (1975), 104 (4): 229–43.

Knorr, Klaus E. and Frank N. Trager, eds. Economic Issues and National Security. Manhattan: University Press of Kansas, 1977.

Kobrin, Stephen J. "Expropriation as an Attempt to Control Foreign Firms in LDCs: Trends from 1960 to 1979." International Studies Quarterly (1984), 28:329–48.

Kolko, Gabriel. The Politics of War: The World and United States Foreign Policy, 1943–1945. New York: Random House, 1968.

Kolko, Joyce. Restructuring the World Economy. New York: Pantheon, 1988.

Kolko, Joyce and Gabriel. The Limits of Power: The World and United States Foreign Policy, 1945–1954. New York: Harper & Row, 1972.

Koppes, Clayton R. "The Good Neighbor Policy and the Nationalization of Mexican Oil: A Reinterpretation." Journal of American History (1982), 69:62–81.

Kovner, Milton. The Challenge of Coexistence: A Study of Soviet Economic Diplomacy. Washington, D.C.: Public Affairs Press, 1961.

Krasner, Stephen D. Defending the National Interest: Raw Materials Investments and U.S. Foreign Policy. Princeton: Princeton University Press, 1978.

——"Transforming International Regimes: What the Third World Wants and Why." International Studies Quarterly (1981), 25:119–48.

——Structural Conflict: The Third World Against Global Liberalism. Berkeley: University of California Press, 1985.

Kreinin, Mordechai E. and J. M. Finger. "A Critical Survey of the New International Economic Order." Journal of World Trade Law (1976), 10:493–512.

Kreisberg, Paul H., ed. American Hostages in Iran: The Conduct of a Crisis. New Haven: Yale University Press, 1985.

Laferrière, J. "Le boycott et le droit international." Revue Générale de Droit International Public (1910), 17:288–326.

Laing, Edward A. "International Economic Law and Public Order in the Age of Equality." Law and Policy in International Business (1980), 12:727–81.

Lake, David A. "International Economic Structures and American Foreign Economic Policy, 1887–1934." World Politics (1983), 35: 517–43.

——Power, Protection, and Free Trade: International Sources of U.S. Commercial Strategy, 1887–1939. Ithaca, N.Y.: Cornell University Press, 1988.

Lambert, Édouard. "Une fuite dans les institutions de paix: Le libre jeu des represailles et l'embargo punitif sur les marchandises." Revue de l'Universite de Lyon (1935), 1:471–90; and 5:21–67.

——Les embargos sur l'importation ou l'exportation des marchandises: Leur effets sur les contrats en cours, sanctions collectives et represailles individuelles. Paris: Librairie Générale de Droit and de Jurisprudence, 1936.

Landes, David S. Bankers and Pashas: International Finance and Economic Imperialism in Egypt. Cambridge: Harvard University Press, 1958.

Langer, Gary F. *The Coming of Age of Political Economy, 1815–1825*. Westport, Conn.: Greenwood Press, 1987.

Langholm, Odd. "Economic Freedom in Scholastic Thought." *History of Political Economy* (1982), 14:260–83.

Laszlo, Ervin, R. Baker, Jr., E. Eisenberg and V. Raman. *The Objectives of the New International Economic Order*. New York: Pergamon Press, 1978.

Lauterpacht, Hersch. "Boycott in International Relations." *British Year Book of International Law* (1933), 14:125–40.

Laves, Walter H. C. "German Governmental Influence on Foreign Investments, 1871–1915." *Political Science Quarterly* (1928), 43:498–519.

Laviec, Jean-Pierre. *Protection des investissements: Étude de droit international économique*. Paris: Presses Universitaires de France, 1985.

Leben, Charles. "Les contre-mesures inter-étatiques et les réactions a l'illicité dans la société internationale." *Annuaire Français de Droit International* (1982), 28:9–77.

Lebovics, Herman. *The Alliance of Iron and Wheat in the Third French Republic, 1860–1914: Origins of the New Conservatism*. Baton Rouge, La.: Greenwood Press, 1987.

Leffler, Melvyn P. "Political Isolationism, Economic Expansionism, or Diplomatic Realism: American Policy Toward Western Europe, 1921–1933." *Perspectives in American History* (1974), 8:413–61.

Lenz, Adolf. *Der Wirtschaftskampf der Völker und seine internationale Regelung*. Stuttgart: Enke, 1920.

Lenz, Friedrich. *Friedrich Lists Staats- und Gesellschaftslehre: eine Studie zur Politischen Soziologie*. Neuwied: Luchterhand, 1967.

Levy, Leonard W. *Jefferson and Civil Liberties: The Darker Side*. Cambridge: Harvard University Press, 1963.

Leyton-Brown, David, ed. *The Utility of International Economic Sanctions*. London: Croom Helm, 1987.

Lichtenstein, Cynthia C. "The Battle for International Bank Accounts: Restrictions on International Payments for Political Ends and Article VIII of the Fund Agreement." *New York University Journal of International Law and Politics* (1987), 19:981–92.

Licklider, Roy. *Political Power and the Arab Oil Weapon: the Experience of Five Industrial Nations*. Berkeley: University of California Press, 1988.

Lillich, Richard B. *The Protection of Foreign Investment: Six Procedural Studies*. Syracuse, N.Y.: Syracuse University Press, 1965.

——"Economic Coercion and the International Legal Order." *International Affairs* (1975), 51:358–71.

——"Economic Coercion and the 'New International Economic Order': A Second Look at Some First Impressions." *Virginia Journal of International Law* (1976), 16:233–44.

——"The Status of Economic Coercion Under International Law: United Nations Norms." *Texas International Law Journal* (1977), 12:17–23.

——"Duties of States Regarding the Civil Rights of Aliens." *Recueil des Cours* (Académie de Droit International) (1978), 161:329–442.

Lillich, Richard B. ed. *Economic Coercion and the New International Economic Order*. Charlottesville: Michie, 1976.

Lincoln, George Arthur. *The Economics of National Security: Managing America's Resources for Defense.* New York: Prentice-Hall, 1954.

Lindell, Erik. "U.S.-Soviet Grain Embargoes: Regulating the MNCs." *Food Policy* (1982), 7:240–46.

Lindemeyer, Bernd. *Schiffsembargo und Handelsembargo: Volkerrechtliche Praxis und Zulassigkeit.* Baden-Baden: Nomos, 1975.

Link, Arthur S. *Woodrow Wilson: Revolution, War, and Peace.* Arlington Heights, Ill.: AHM, 1979.

Lipsky, Sherrie. "The Legitimacy of Economic Coercion: The Carter Foreign Aid Policy and Nicaragua." *Loyola of Los Angeles International and Comparative Law Annual* (1982), 5:101–27.

Lipson, Charles H. "Corporate Preferences and Public Policies: Foreign Aid Sanctions and Investment Protection." *World Politics* (1976), 28:396–421.

——*Standing Guard: Protecting Foreign Capital in the Nineteenth and Twentieth Centuries.* Berkeley: University of California Press, 1985.

Liska, George. *The New Statecraft: Foreign Aid in American Foreign Policy.* Chicago: University of Chicago Press, 1960.

Littauer, Rudolf M. "Unfreezing of Foreign Funds." *Columbia Law Review* (1945), 45:132–74.

Lomax, David F. *The Developing Country Debt Crisis.* Basingstoke: Macmillan, 1986.

Long, Olivier. *Law and Its Limitations in the GATT Multilateral Trade System.* London: Graham & Trotman, 1987.

Losman, Donald L. *International Economic Sanctions: The Cases of Cuba, Israel, and Rhodesia.* Albuquerque, N.M.: University of New Mexico Press, 1979.

Lowenfeld, Andreas F. *International Economic Law: Trade Controls for Political Ends.* 2d ed. New York: Matthew Bender, 1983.

Lu, David J. *From the Marco Polo Bridge to Pearl Harbour: Japan's Entry into World War II.* Washington, D.C.: Public Affairs Press, 1961.

Luard, Evan. *Economic Relationships Among States.* London: Macmillan, 1984.

Lundborg, Per. *The Economics of Export Embargoes: The Case of the U.S.-Soviet Grain Suspension.* London: Croom Helm, 1987.

McCormick, Gordon H. and Richard E. Bissell, eds. *The Strategic Dimensions of Economic Behavior.* New York: Praeger, 1984.

McCoy, Drew R. *The Elusive Republic: Political Economy in Jeffersonian America.* Chapel Hill, N.C.: University of North Carolina Press, 1980.

Macdonald, Ronald St. J. "The Resort to Economic Coercion by International Political Organisations." *University of Toronto Law Journal* (1967), 17:86–169.

McGovern, John F. "The Rise of New Economic Attitudes—Economic Humanism, Economic Nationalism—During the Later Middle Ages and the Renaissance, A.D. 1200–1550." *Traditio* (1970), 26:217–53.

McKee, Delber L. *Chinese Exclusion versus the Open Door Policy 1900–1906: Clashes Over China Policy in the Roosevelt Era.* Detroit: Wayne State University Press, 1977.

——"The Chinese Boycott of 1905–1906 Reconsidered: The Role of the Chinese Americans." *Pacific History Review* (1986), 55:165–91.

McKinlay, Robert D. and Richard Little. *Global Problems and World Order.* London: Frances Pinter, 1986.

McLean, David. "Finance and 'Informal Empire' before the First World War." *Economic History Review* (1976), 29:291–305.

McNeil, William C. *American Money and the Weimar Republic: Economics and Politics on the Eve of the Great Depression.* New York: Columbia University Press, 1986.

Madden, John T., Marcus Nadler and Harry C. Sauvin. *America's Experience as a Creditor Nation.* New York: Prentice-Hall, 1937.

Maddock, R. T. "The Economic and Political Characteristics of Food as a Diplomatic Weapon." *Journal of Agricultural Economics* (1978), 29:31–41.

Madsen, Axel. *Private Power: Multinational Corporations and Their Role in the Survival of Our Planet.* London: Abacus, 1980.

Maier, Charles S. *In Search of Stability: Explorations in Historical Political Economy.* Cambridge: Cambridge University Press, 1987.

Mallery, Otto Tod. *More than Conquerors: Building Peace on Fair Trade.* New York: Harper, 1947.

Manuel, Frank E. *The New World of Henri Saint-Simon.* Cambridge: Harvard University Press, 1956.

Margold, Stella K. *Let's Do Business with Russia: Why We Should and How We Can.* New York: Harper, 1948.

Marmorstein, Victoria E. "World Bank Power To Consider Human Rights Factors in Loan Decisions." *Journal of International Law and Economics* (1978), 13:113–36.

Mason, Edward S. and Robert E. Asher. *The World Bank since Bretton Woods.* Washington, D.C.: Brookings Institution, 1973.

Mastanduno, Michael. "Trade as a Strategic Weapon: American and Alliance Export Control Policy in the Early Postwar Period." *International Organization* (1988), 42:121–50.

Maull, Hans W. *Raw Materials, Energy and Western Security: Studies in International Security.* London: Macmillan, 1984.

Maw, Carlyle E. "Historical Aspects and the United States Involvement in Boycotts." *Proceedings of the American Society of International Law* (1977), 71:170–74.

Mayall, James. "The Sanctions Problem in International Economic Relations: Reflections in the Light of Recent Experience." *International Affairs* (1984), 60:631–42.

——"The Institutional Basis of Post-War Economic Cooperation." In *International Institutions at Work,* edited by Paul Taylor and A. J. R. Groom, at 53–74. London: Frances Pinter, 1988.

Meade, James. *The Economic Basis of a Durable Peace.* London: Allen & Unwin, 1940.

Meagher, Robert F. *An International Redistribution of Wealth and Power: A Study of the Charter of Economic Rights and Duties of States.* New York: Pergamon, 1979.

Meek, Ronald L. "The Rehabilitation of Sir James Steuart." In *Economics and Ideology and Other Essays: Studies in the Development of Economic Thought,* at 3–17. London: Chapman & Hall, 1967.

Mersky, Roy, ed. *Conference on Transnational Economic Boycotts and Coercion: Papers Presented at the Conference.* 2 vols. Dobbs Ferry, N.Y.: Oceana, 1978.

Michels, Robert. *Le boycottage international.* Paris: Payot, 1936.

Midgley, E. B. F. *The Natural Law Tradition and the Theory of International Relations.* London: Elek, 1975.

Mikesell, Raymond. *United States Economic Policy and International Relations.* New York: McGraw-Hill, 1952.

Milhaud, Edgar. "L'organisation économique de la paix." *Recueil des Cours* (Académie de Droit International) (1926), 15:277–431.

Miller, Arthur S. "Foreign Trade and the 'Security State': A Study in Conflicting National Policies." *Journal of Public Law* (1958), 7:36–96.

——"The Corporation as a Private Government in the World Community." *Virginia Law Review* (1960), 46:1539–72.

Miller, Judith. "When Sanctions Worked." *Foreign Policy* (1980), 39:118–29.

Miller, Stephen. "Adam Smith and the Commercial Republic." *Public Interest* (1980), 61:106–22.

Milward, Alan S. "Tariffs as Constitutions." In *The International Politics of Surplus Capacity: Competition for Market Shares in the World Recession,* edited by Susan Strange and Roger Tooze, at 57–66. London: Allen & Unwin, 1981.

——*The Reconstruction of Western Europe 1945–51.* London: Methuen, 1984.

Mintz, Ilse. *Deterioration in the Quality of Foreign Bonds Issued in the United States, 1920–1930.* New York: National Bureau of Economic Research, 1951.

Mitrany, David. *The Effect of the War in Southeastern Europe.* New Haven: Yale University Press, 1936.

——*The Functional Theory of Politics.* London: Robertson, 1975.

Moore, John Norton. "United States Policy and the Arab Boycott." *Proceedings of the American Society of International Law* (1977), 71:174–82.

Morgenthau, Hans J. *In Defense of the National Interest: A Critical Examination of American Foreign Policy.* New York: Knopf, 1951.

Morley, Morris H. "The United States and the Global Economic Blockade of Cuba: A Study in Political Pressure on America's Allies." *Canadian Journal of Political Science* (1984), 17:25–48.

——*Imperial State and Revolution: The United States and Cuba, 1952–1986.* Cambridge: Cambridge University Press, 1987.

Morris, Cynthia Taft and Irma Adelman. *Comparative Patterns of Economic Development, 1850–1914.* Baltimore: Johns Hopkins University Press, 1988.

Morse, Edward L. *Modernization and the Transformation of International Relations.* New York: Free Press, 1976.

Moulton, Harold G. and Leo Pasvolsky. *World War Debt Settlements.* New York: Brookings Institution, 1926.

Muir, J. Dapray. "The Boycott in International Law." *Journal of International Law and Economics* (1974), 9:187–204.

Mullineux, Andrew W. *International Money and Banking: The Creation of a New Order.* Brighton: Wheatsheaf, 1987.

Muñoz González, Rafael Perez. *Doctrina Grau.*Havana: Ministerio de Estado, 1948.

Munro, Dana Gardner. *Intervention and Dollar Diplomacy in the Caribbean, 1900–1921.* Princeton: Princeton University Press, 1964.

Murphy, Cornelius. "Economic Duress and Unequal Treaties." *Virginia Journal of International Law* (1970), 11:51–69.

Myrdal, Gunnar. *An International Economy: Problems and Prospects.* London: Routledge & Kegan Paul, 1956.

Nappi, Carmine. *Commodity Market Controls: A Historical Review.* Lexington, Mass.: Heath, 1979.

Nearing, Scott and Joseph Freeman. *Dollar Diplomacy: A Study in American Imperialism.* New York: Viking Press, 1926.

Neff, Stephen C. "The Law of Economic Coercion: Lessons from the Past and Indications of the Future." *Columbia Journal of Transnational Law* (1981), 20:411–37.

——"Boycott and the Law of Nations: Economic Warfare and Modern International Law in Historical Perspective." *British Year Book of International Law* (1988), 59:113–49.

——"Economic Warfare in Contemporary International Law: The Rival Schools of Thought, Evaluated According to a Historical Method." *Stanford Journal of International Law* (1990), 26:67–92.

Nelson, Joan M. *Aid, Influence, and Foreign Policy.* New York: Macmillan, 1968.

Nincic, Miroslav and Peter Wallensteen, eds. *Dilemmas of Economic Coercion: Sanctions in World Politics.* New York: Praeger, 1983.

Nolde, Boris. "Droit et technique des traités de commerce." *Recueil des Cours* (Académie de Droit International) (1924), 3:291–462.

Northedge, F. S. "Transnationalism: The American Illusion." *Journal of International Studies* (1976), 5:21–27.

——*The League of Nations: Its Life and Times.* Leicester: Leicester University Press, 1986.

Novogrod, A. "Collective Security Under the Rio Treaty: The Problem of Indirect Aggression." *JAG Journal* (1969–70), 24:99–110.

Nowzad, Bahram. *The IMF and Its Critics.* Princeton: International Finance Section, Department of Economics, Princeton University, 1981.

Nussbaum, Arthur. *A Concise History of the Law of Nations.* New York: Macmillan, 1947.

Nye, Joseph S. "Collective Economic Security." *International Affairs* (1974), 50:584–98.

Nys, Ernest. *Researches in the History of Economics.* Translated by N. F. and A. R. Dryhurst. London: A. & C. Black, 1899.

Okoko, Kisme A. B. *Socialism and Self-Reliance in Tanzania.* London: KPI, 1987.

Olmstead, Cecil J. "Foreign Aid as an Effective Means of Persuasion." *Proceedings of the American Society of International Law* (1964), 58:205–10.

Olson, Richard Stuart. "Economic Coercion in International Disputes: The United States and Peru in the IPC Expropriation Dispute of 1968–1971." *Journal of Developing Areas* (1975), 9:395–413.

——"Expropriation and International Economic Coercion: Ceylon and the 'West' 1961–1965." *Journal of Developing Areas* (1977), 11:205–25.

——"Economic Coercion in World Politics: With a Focus on North- South Relations." *World Politics* (1979), 31:471–94.

——"Expropriation and Economic Coercion in World Politics: A Retrospective Look at Brazil in the 1960's." *Journal of Developing Areas* (1979), 13:247–62.

Orchard, Dorothy J. "China's Use of the Boycott as a Political Weapon." *Annals of the American Academy of Political and Social Science* (1930), 152:252–61.

Ozawa, Terutomo. *Multinationalism, Japanese Style: The Political Economy of Outward Dependency*. Princeton: Princeton University Press, 1979.

Paarlberg, Robert L. "Lessons of the Grain Embargo." *Foreign Affairs* (1980), 59:144–62.

Padoan, Pier Carlo. *The Political Economy of International Financial Instability*. London: Croom Helm, 1986.

Parrini, Carl P. *Heir to Empire: United States Economic Diplomacy, 1916–1923*. Pittsburgh: University of Pittsburgh Press, 1969.

Parrott, Bruce. *Politics and Technology in the Soviet Union*. Cambridge: MIT Press, 1983.

Parry, Clive. "Defining Economic Coercion in International Law." *Texas International Law Journal* (1977), 12:1–4.

Partridge, Charles E. Jr., "Political and Economic Coercion: Within the Ambit of Art 52 of the Vienna Convention on the Law of Treaties?" *International Lawyer* (1971), 5:755–69.

Pasvolsky, Leo. *Economic Nationalism of the Danubian States*. New York: Macmillan, 1928.

Paterson, Thomas G. *Soviet-American Confrontation: Postwar Reconstruction and the Origins of the Cold War*. Baltimore: Johns Hopkins University Press, 1973.

Patterson, Ernest Minor. "Les Bases économiques de la paix." *Recueil des Cours* (Académie de Droit International) (1931), 37:413–525.

——*The Economic Bases of Peace*. New York: McGraw-Hill, 1939.

Paust, Jordan J. "International Law and Economic Coercion: 'Force,' the Oil Weapon and Effects Upon Prices." *Yale Studies in World Public Order* (1976), 3:213–27.

Paust, Jordan J. and Albert P. Blaustein. "The Arab Oil Weapon—A Threat to International Peace." *American Journal of International Law* (1974), 68:410–39.

——"The Arab Oil Weapon: A Reply and Reaffirmation of Illegality." *Columbia Journal of Transnational Law* (1976), 15:57–73.

——*The Arab Oil Weapon*. Dobbs Ferry, N.Y.: Oceana, 1977.

Payer, Cheryl. *The Debt Trap: The IMF and the Third World*. Harmondsworth: Penguin, 1974.

Pearson, James Constantine. *The Reciprocal Trade Agreements Program: The Policy of the United States and Its Effectiveness*. Washington, D.C.: Catholic University of America Press, 1942.

Penrose, Ernest Francis. *Economic Planning for the Peace*. Princeton: Princeton University Press, 1953.

Perkins, Bradford. *Prologue to War: England and the United States 1805–1812*. Berkeley: University of California Press, 1961.

Petersmann, Ernst-Ulrich. "International Economic Theory and International Economic Law: On the Tasks of a Legal Theory of International Economic Order." In *The Structure and Process of International Law: Essays in Legal Philosophy, Doctrine and Theory*, edited by R. St. J. Macdonald and Douglas M. Johnston, at 227–61. The Hague: Martinus Nijhoff, 1983.

Petras, James F. and Morris Morley. *The United States and Chile: Imperialism and the Overthrow of the Allende Government*. New York: Monthly Review Press, 1975.

Phelps, Clyde W. *The Foreign Expansion of American Banks*. New York: Ronald Press, 1927.

Philip, George D. E. *Oil and Politics in Latin America: Nationalist Movements and State Companies*. Cambridge: Cambridge University Press, 1982.

Pinon, René. "Une forme nouvelle des luttes internationales: Le boycottage." *Revue des Deux Mondes* (1909), 51:199–228.

Pirenne, Henri. *Economic and Social History of Medieval Europe*. Translated by Ivy E. Clegg. London: K. Paul, Trench, Trubner, 1936.

Pirzio-Biroli, Corrado. "Making Sense of the IMF Conditionality Debate." *Journal of World Trade Law* (1983), 17:115–53.

Platt, D. C. M. *Finance, Trade, and Politics in British Foreign Policy 1815–1914*. Oxford: Clarendon Press, 1968.

Plummer, James L., ed. *Energy Vulnerability*. New York: Ballinger, 1982.

Poidevin, Raymond. *Finances et relations internationales 1887–1914*. Paris: Colin, 1970.

Polier, Jonathan Wise. "Western European Sovereignty and American Export and Trade Controls." *Columbia Journal of Transnational Law* (1970), 9:109–39.

Politis, Nicolas S. *Les emprunts d'État en droit international*. Paris: Pedone, 1894.

——"Le contrôle international sur les finances helleniques et ses prèmieres résultats (1898–1901)." *Revue Générale de Droit International Public* (1902), 9:5–41.

Polk, Judd. "Freezing Dollars Against the Axis." *Foreign Affairs* (1941) 20:113–30.

Polk, Judd and Gardner Patterson. "The British Loan." *Foreign Affairs* (1946), 24:429–40.

Pollard, Robert A. *Economic Security and the Origins of the Cold War, 1945–1950*. New York: Columbia University Press, 1985.

Pollard, Sidney. *Peaceful Conquest: The Industrialization of Europe 1760–1970*. Oxford: Oxford University Press, 1981.

Pradelle, Albert Geouffre de La. "La question chinoise." *Revue Générale de Droit International Public* (1900) 8:272–340.

Prebisch, Raúlo. *The Economic Development of Latin America and Its Principal Problems*. New York: U.N. Doc. E/CN.12/89 (1950).

——"Commercial Policy in the Underdeveloped Countries." *American Economic Review* (Papers and Proceedings) (1959), 49:251–74.

——"Towards a New Trade Policy for Development." In *Proceedings of the United Nations Conference on Trade and Development, Geneva, 23 March — 16 June 1964*, vol. 2: *Policy Statements*, at 5–64. New York: U.N. Doc. E/CONF.46/141, vol. 2 (1964).

Quataert, Donald. *Social Disintegration and Popular Resistance in the Ottoman Empire, 1881–1908: Reactions to European Economic Penetration*. New York: New York University Press, 1983.

Ranki, Gyorgy. *Economy and Foreign Policy: The Struggle of the Great Powers for Hegemony in the Danube Valley, 1919–1939*. New York: Columbia University Press, 1983.

Rappard, William E. *The Common Menace of Economic and Military Armaments*. London: Cobden-Sanderson, 1936.

——"Le nationalisme économique et la Société des Nations." *Recueil des Cours* (Académie de Droit International) (1937), 61:97–252.

——*Post-War Efforts for Freer Trade*. Geneva: Geneva Research Centre, 1938.

Ratner, Sidney. *The Tariff in American History*. New York: Van Nostrand, 1972.

Rawson, Elizabeth D. *The Spartan Tradition in European Thought*. Oxford: Clarendon Press, 1969.

Reisman, W. Michael. "The Role of the Economic Agencies in the Enforcement of International Judgments and Awards: A Functional Approach." *International Organization* (1965), 19:929–47.

Remer, Charles Frederick. *A Study of Chinese Boycotts, with Special Reference to Their Economic Effectiveness*. Baltimore: Johns Hopkins University Press, 1933.

Renouvin, Pierre and Jean-Baptiste Duroselle. *Introduction to the History of International Relations*. Translated by Mary Ilford. New York: Praeger, 1967.

Richardson, H. W. "British Emigration and Overseas Investment, 1870–1914." *Economic History Review* (1972), 25:99–113.

Richardson, John Henry. *Economic Disarmament: A Study on International Cooperation*. London: Allen & Unwin, 1931.

——*British Economic Foreign Policy*. London: Allen & Unwin, 1936.

Richardson, Neil R. "Political Compliance and U.S. Trade Dominance." *American Political Science Review* (1976), 70:1098–1109.

Rickman, Geoffrey. *The Corn Supply of Ancient Rome*. Oxford: Clarendon Press, 1980.

Rivero, Oswaldo B. de. *New Economic Order and International Development Law*. Oxford: Pergamon, 1980.

Robbins, Lionel C. *Economic Planning and International Order*. London: Macmillan, 1937.

——*The Theory of Economic Policy in English Classical Political Economy*. London: Macmillan, 1952.

Robinson, Joan. *Economic Philosophy*. London: Watts, 1962.

Rodman, Kenneth A. *Sanctity Versus Sovereignty: The United States and the*

Nationalization of Natural Resources Investments. New York: Columbia University Press, 1988.

Roessler, Frieder. "GATT and Access to Supplies." *Journal of World Trade Law* (1975), 9:25–40.

Roll, Eric. *A History of Economic Thought.* 4th ed. London: Faber, 1973.

Rom, Michael. "Export Controls in GATT." *Journal of World Trade Law* (1984), 18:125–54.

Roosevelt, Nicholas. "The Ruhr Occupation." *Foreign Affairs* (1925), 4:112–22.

Roover, Raymond Adrien de. "Scholastic Economics: Survival and Lasting Influence from the Sixteenth Century to Adam Smith." In *Business, Banking, and Economic Thought in Late Medieval and Early Modern Europe: Selected Studies of Raymond de Roover,* edited by Julius Kirshner, at 306–35. Chicago: University of Chicago Press, 1974.

Röpke, Wilhelm. "Economic Order and International Law." *Recueil des Cours* (Académie de Droit International) (1954), 86:207–73.

Rosecrance, Richard and Arthur Stein. "Interdependence: Myth or Reality." *World Politics* (1973), 26:1–27.

Rosen, S. McKee. *The Combined Boards of the Second World War: An Experiment in International Administration.* New York: Columbia University Press, 1951.

Rosenau, James N. *The Study of Global Interdependence: Essays on the Transnationalization of World Affairs.* New York: Nichols, 1982.

Rosenberg, Dominique. *Le principe de souveraineté des États sur leurs ressources naturelles.* Paris: Librairie Générale de Droit et de Jurisprudence, 1983.

Rosenberg, Emily. *Spreading the American Dream: American Economic and Cultural Expansion 1890–1945.* New York: Hill & Wang, 1982.

Rosenfeld, S. S. "The Politics of Food." *Foreign Policy* (1974), 14:17–29.

Roth, Andreas Hans. *The Minimum Standard of International Law applied to Aliens.* Leiden: A. W. Sijthoff, 1949.

Rothschild, Emma. "Food Politics." *Foreign Affairs* (1976), 54:285–307.

Rothstein, Robert L. *The Weak in the World of the Strong: The Developing Countries in the International System.* New York: Columbia University Press, 1977.

Rousseau, Charles. "Le boycottage dans les rapports internationaux." *Revue Générale de Droit International Public* (1958), 62:3–25.

Routh, Guy. *The Origin of Economic Ideas.* London: Macmillan, 1975.

Rubner, Alex. *The Export Cult: A Global Display of Economic Distortions.* Aldershot: Gower, 1987.

Russell, Ruth B. *A History of the United Nations Charter: The Role of the United States 1940–1945.* Washington D.C.: Brookings Institution, 1958.

Rustow, Dankwart A. "Who Won the Yom Kippur and Oil Wars?" *Foreign Policy* (1974–75), 17:166–75.

Safford, Jeffrey J. "Experiment in Containment: The United States Steel Embargo and Japan, 1917–1918." *Pacific History Review* (1970), 39:439–51.

Salin, Edgar. "Romantic and Universalist Economics." In *Encyclopedia of the*

Social Sciences, edited by Edwin R. A. Seligman, 5:385–87. London: Macmillan, 1931.

Salter, Arthur. "The Economic Organisation of Peace." *Foreign Affairs* (1930), 9:42–53.

——"The Future of Economic Nationalism." *Foreign Affairs* (1932), 11:8–20.

——*The Causes of War.* London: Macmillan, 1932.

Salter, Leonard M. "International Trade and World Order." *Commercial Law Journal* (1965), 70:236–38.

Sanford, Jonathan E. *U.S. Foreign Policy and the Multilateral Development Banks.* Boulder, Col.: Westview Press, 1982.

Sarna, Aaron J. *Boycott and Blacklist: A History of Arab Economic Warfare Against Israel.* Totowa, N.J.: Rowman & Littlefield, 1986.

Savona, Paolo and George Sutija, eds. *Eurodollars and International Banking.* Basingstoke: Macmillan, 1985.

Saxena, R. B. and Heena R. Bakshi. "IMF Conditionality—A Third World Perspective." *Journal of World Trade* (1988), 22 (5):67–79.

Sayre, Francis B. "The Menace of Economic Nationalism." *Proceedings of the Academy of Political Science* (1935), 16:206–14.

Scelle, Georges. "Le phénomène juridique du dédoublement fonctionnel." In *Rechtsfragen der Internationalen Organisation (Festschrift für Hans Wehberg),* edited by Walter Schätzel and Hans-Jürgen Schlochauer, at 324–46. Frankfurt: Klostermann, 1956.

Schlereth, Thomas J. *The Cosmopolitan Ideal in Enlightenment Thought: Its Form and Function in the Ideas of Franklin, Hume, and Voltaire, 1694–1790.* Notre Dame, Ind.: University of Notre Dame Press, 1977.

Schlesinger, James R. *The Political Economy of National Security: A Study of the Economic Aspects of the Contemporary Power Struggle.* New York: Praeger, 1960.

Schmoller, Gustav Friedrich von. *The Mercantile System and Its Historical Significance.* Translated by William James Ashley. New York: Macmillan, 1910.

Schneider, William. *Can We Avert Economic Warfare in Raw Materials? U.S. Agriculture as a Blue Chip.* New York: National Strategy Information Center, 1974.

——*Food, Foreign Policy, and Raw Materials Cartels.* New York: National Strategy Information Center, 1976.

Schoultz, Lars. "Politics, Economics, and U.S. Participation in Multilateral Development Banks." *International Organization* (1982), 36:537–74.

Schreiber, Anna P. "Economic Coercion as an Instrument of Foreign Policy: U.S. Economic Measures Against Cuba and the Dominican Republic." *World Politics* (1973), 25:387–413.

Schuker, Stephen A. *The End of French Predominance in Europe: The Financial Crisis of 1924 and the Adoption of the Dawes Plan.* Chapel Hill: University of North Carolina Press, 1976.

——*American 'Reparations' to Germany, 1919–1933: Implications for the Third World Debt Crisis.* Princeton: Princeton University Press, 1988.

Schultze, Charles L. "The Economic Content of National Security Policy." *Foreign Affairs* (1973), 51:522–40.

Schumacher, Hermann. "The Historical School." In *Encyclopaedia of the Social Sciences*, edited by Edwin R. A. Seligman, 5:371–77. London: Macmillan, 1931.

Schumpeter, Joseph A. "The Sociology of Imperialism." In *Imperialism and Social Classes*, translated by Heinz Norden, at 1–98. New York: Meridian Books, 1951.

Schwarzenberger, Georg. "Province and Standards of International Economic Law." *International Law Quarterly* (1948), 2:402–20.

——"Les principes et normes du droit économique international." *Recueil des Cours* (Académie de Droit International) (1966), 117:1–98.

Sears, Louis Martin. *Jefferson and the Embargo*. Durham, N.C.: Duke University Press, 1927.

Seeler, Hans-Joachim von. "Wirtschaftssanktionen als zweifelhaftes Instrument der Aussenpolitik." *Europa-Archiv* (1982), 20:611–20.

Seers, Dudley. *The Political Economy of Nationalism*. Oxford: Oxford University Press, 1983.

Seers, Dudley, ed. *Dependency Theory: A Critical Reassessment*. London: Frances Pinter, 1981.

Séfériadès, Stylianos P. *Réflexions sur le boycottage en droit international*. Paris: Rousseau, 1912.

Seidl-Hohenveldern, I. "The United Nations and Economic Coercion." *Revue Belge de Droit International* (1984–85), 18:9–19.

——"International Economic Law." *Recueil des Cours* (Académie de Droit International) (1986), 198:9–264.

Semmel, Bernard. *The Rise of Free Trade Imperialism: Classical Political Economy and the Empire of Free Trade and Imperialism, 1750–1850*. Cambridge: Cambridge University Press, 1970.

——*Liberalism and Naval Strategy: Ideology, Interest, and Sea Power During the Pax Britannica*. London: Allen & Unwin, 1986.

Sen, Amartya. *On Ethics and Economics*. Oxford: Basil Blackwell, 1987.

Sen, S. R. *The Economics of Sir James Steuart*. London: London School of Economics and Political Science, 1957.

Sering, Max. *Deutschland unter dem Dawes-Plan*. Leipzig: de Gruyter, 1928.

Shafer, Michael. "Mineral Myths." *Foreign Policy* (1982), 47:154–71.

Shea, Donald Richard. *The Calvo Clause*. Minneapolis, Minn.: University of Minnesota Press, 1955.

Shihata, Ibrahim F. I. "Destination Embargo of Arab Oil: Its Legality Under International Law." *American Journal of International Law* (1974), 68:591–627.

——"Arab Oil Policies and the New International Economic Order." *Virginia Journal of International Law* (1976), 16:261–88.

Shneyer, Paul A. and Virginia Barta. "The Legality of the United States Economic Blockade of Cuba Under International Law." *Case Western Reserve Journal of International Law* (1982), 13:451–82.

Shutt, Henry. *The Myth of Free Trade: Patterns of Protectionism since 1945*. Oxford: Basil Blackwell, 1985.

Sidell, Scott R. *The IMF and Third-World Instability: Is There a Connection?* Basingstoke: Macmillan, 1988.

Sigmund, Paul E. "The 'Invisible Blockade' and the Overthrow of Allende." *Foreign Affairs* (1974), 52:322–40.

——*The Overthrow of Allende and the Politics of Chile 1964–1976.* Pittsburgh: University of Pittsburgh Press, 1977.

Silberner, Edmund. *The Problem of War in Nineteenth Century Economic Thought.* Translated by Alexander H. Krappe. Princeton: Princeton University Press, 1946.

Silverman, Dan P. *Reconstructing Europe After the Great War.* Cambridge: Harvard University Press, 1982.

Simonds, Frank H. and Brooks Emeny. *The Great Powers in World Politics: International Relations and Economic Nationalism.* New York: American Book Co., 1935.

——*The Price of Peace: The Challenge of Economic Nationalism.* New York: Harper, 1935.

Singer, Fred S. "Limits to Arab Oil Power." *Foreign Policy* (1978), 30:53–67.

Smith, J. G. "Economic Nationalism and International Trade." *Economic Journal* (1935), 45:619–48.

Smith, Richard Norton. *An Uncommon Man: The Triumph of Herbert Hoover.* New York: Simon & Schuster, 1984.

Sombart, Werner. *Die Deutsche Völkswirtschaft im Neunzehnten Jahrhundert.* Berlin: G. Bondi, 1903.

Sono, K. "Sovereignty, THis Strange Thing: Its Impact on the General Economic Order." *Georgia Journal of International and Comparative Law* (1979), 9:549–57.

Sornarajah, M. "Compensation for Expropriation: The Emergence of New Standards." *Journal of World Trade Law* (1979), 13:108–31.

——*The Pursuit of Nationalized Property.* Dordrecht: Martinus Nijhoff, 1986.

Souleyman, Elizabeth V. *The Vision of World Peace in Seventeenth and Eighteenth Century France.* Port Washington, N.Y.: Kennikat Press, 1941.

Spall, Francis, Jr. "Free Trade, Foreign Relations, and the Anti-Corn-Law League." *Review of International History* (1988), 10:405–32.

Spero, Joan Edelman. *The Politics of International Economic Relations.* New York: St. Martin's Press, 1977.

Spivak, Burton. *Jefferson's English Crisis: Commerce, Embargo, and the Republican Revolution.* Charlottesville: University Press of Virginia, 1979.

Spraos, John. *Inequalising Trade? A Study of Traditional North/South Specialisation in the Context of Terms of Trade Concepts.* Oxford: Clarendon Press, 1983.

——*IMF Conditionality: Ineffectual, Inefficient, Mistargeted.* Princeton: International Finance Section, Department of Economics, Princeton University, 1986.

Stagg, J. C. A. *Mr. Madison's War: Politics, Diplomacy, and Warfare in the Early American Republic, 1783–1830.* Princeton: Princeton University Press, 1983.

Stalin, Josef. *Economic Problems of Socialism in the U.S.S.R..* New York: International Publishers, 1952.

Stemberg, Harald. *Die Charta der Wirtschaftlichten Rechte und Pflichten der Staaten.* Berlin: Duncker und Humblot, 1983.

Stenger, Gernot. "The Development of American Export Control Legislation after World War II." *Wisconsin International Law Journal* (1987), 6:1–42.

Stent, Angela. *From Embargo to Ostpolitik: The Political Economy of West German-Soviet Relations 1955–1980.* Cambridge: Cambridge University Press, 1981.

Stern, Jonathan P. "Specters and Pipe Dreams." *Foreign Policy* (1982), 48:21–36.

Strange, Susan. "The Strategic Trade Embargoes: Sense or Nonsense?" *Year Book of World Affairs* (1958), 12:55–73.

——*The Soviet Trade Weapon.* London: Phoenix House, 1959.

——"What is Economic Power and Who Has It?" *International Journal* (1975), 30:207–224.

——*Casino Capitalism.* Oxford: Basil Blackwell, 1986.

——*States and Markets: An Introduction to International Political Economy.* London: Frances Pinter, 1988.

Strange, Susan, ed. *Paths to International Political Economy.* London: Allen & Unwin, 1984.

Street, James H. "Raúl Prebisch, 1901–1986: An Appreciation." *Journal of Economic Issues* (1987), 21:649–59.

Strupp, Karl. "Intervention en matière financière." *Recueil des Cours* (Académie de Droit International) (1925), 8:1–124.

Sykes, Alan. *Tariff Reform in British Politics 1903–1913.* New York: Oxford University Press, 1979.

Szporluk, Roman. *Communism and Nationalism: Karl Marx versus Friedrich List.* New York: Oxford University Press, 1988.

Szuprowicz, Bohdan O. *How to Avoid Strategic Materials Shortages: Dealing with Cartels, Embargoes, and Supply Disruptions.* New York: Wiley, 1981.

Takase, Tamotsu. "The Role of Concessions in the GATT Trading System and Their Implications for Developing Countries." *Journal of World Trade Law* (1987), 21(5):67–89.

Takayanagi, Kenzo. "On the Legality of the Chinese Boycott." *Pacific Affairs* (1932), 5:855–62.

——*Comparative Study of Boycotts.* Tokyo: Institute of Pacific Relations, 1933.

Tarullo, Daniel K. "Logic, Myth, and the International Economic Order." *Harvard International Law Journal* (1985), 26:533–52.

Tawney, R. H. *Religion and the Rise of Capitalism: A Historical Survey.* London: John Murray, 1926.

Teichert, Eckart. *Autarkie und Grossraumswirtschaft in Deutschland 1930–1939: Aussenwirtschaftspolitische Konzeptionen zwischen wirtschaftskrise und zweiten Weltkrieg.* Munich: Oldenbourg, 1984.

Thompson, E. A. *Romans and Barbarians: The Decline of the Western Empire.* Madison, Wis.: University of Wisconsin Press, 1982.

Thorp, Willard L. "American Policy and the Soviet Economic Offensive." *Foreign Affairs* (1957), 35:271–82.

Tiewul, S. Azadon. "The United Nations Charter of Economic Rights and Duties of States." *Journal of International Law and Economics* (1975), 10:645–88.

Tigar, Michael E. *Law and the Rise of Capitalism.* New York: Monthly Review Press, 1977.

Tolley, George S. and John D. Wilman. "The Foreign Dependence Question." *Journal of Political Economy* (1977), 85:323–47.

Trachtenberg, Marc. *Reparation in World Politics: France and European Economic Diplomacy, 1916–1923.* New York: Columbia University Press, 1980.

Treverton, Gregory, ed. *Energy and Security.* Farnborough: Gower, 1980.

Trubitt, Brian. "International Monetary Fund Conditionality and Options for Aggrieved Fund Members." *Vanderbilt Journal of Transnational Law* (1987), 20:665–97.

Ts'ai, Shih-Shan H. "Reactions to Exclusion: The Boycott of 1905 and Chinese National Awakening." *Historian* (1976), 39:95–110.

Tucker, Robert W. *The Inequality of Nations.* New York: Basic Books, 1977.

Turck, Nancy. "The Arab Boycott of Israel." *Foreign Affairs* (1977), 55:472–93.

Tussie, Diane. *The Less Developed Countries and the World Trading System: A Challenge to the GATT.* New York: St. Martin's Press, 1987.

Ullman, Richard H. "At War with Nicaragua." *Foreign Affairs* (1983), 62:39–58.

Vagts, Detlev F. "Coercion and Foreign Investment Rearrangements." *American Journal of International Law* (1978), 72:17–36.

Vandevelde, Kenneth J. "Reassessing the Hickenlooper Amendment." *Virginia Journal of International Law* (1988), 29:115–67.

Varma, Vishwanath Prasad. *The Political Philosophy of Sri Aurobindo.* Bombay: Asia Publishing House, 1960.

Veiga Simoes, A. da. "Les nouvelles orientations de la politique économique internationale." *Recueil des Cours* (Académie de Droit International) (1931), 35:233–351.

Verbit, Gilbert P. *International Monetary Reform and the Developing Countries: The Rule of Law Problem.* New York: Columbia University Press, 1975.

Vernon, Raymond. "Foreign Trade and National Defense." *Foreign Affairs* (1955), 34:77–88.

——*Sovereignty at Bay.* New York: Basic Books, 1971.

Vernon, Raymond, ed. *The Oil Crisis.* New York: Norton, 1976.

Viallate, Achille. *Economic Imperialism and International Relations During the last Fifty Years.* New York: Macmillan, 1923.

Viner, Jacob. "National Monopolies of Raw Materials." *Foreign Affairs* (1926), 4:585–600.

——"International Finance and Balance of Power Diplomacy, 1880–1914." *Political and Social Science Quarterly* (1929), 9:407–51.

——"Conflicts of Principle in Drafting a Trade Charter." *Foreign Affairs* (1947), 25:612–28.

——"Power Versus Plenty as Objectives of Foreign Policy in the Seventeenth and Eighteenth Centuries." *World Politics* (1948), 1:1–29.

——*International Trade and Economic Development.* Oxford: Clarendon Press, 1953.

——"The Intellectual History of Laissez Faire." *Journal of Law and Economics* (1960), 3:45–69.

——"The Economic Doctrines of the Christian Fathers." *History of Political Economy* (1978), 10:9–45.

Vinson, J. C. "War Debts and Peace Legislation: The Johnson Act of 1934." *Mid-America* (1968), 50:206–22.

Vries, Margaret Garritsen de. *Balance of Payments Adjustment, 1945 to 1986: The IMF Experience.* Washington: IMF, 1987.

Vries, Margaret Garritsen de and J. Keith Horsefield. *The International Monetary Fund 1945–1965: Twenty Years of Monetary Cooperation.* 3 vols. Washington, D.C.: IMF, 1969.

Waart, P.J.I.M. de. "Permanent Sovereignty Over Natural Resources as a Cornerstone for International Economic Rights and Duties." *Netherlands International Law Review* (1977), 24:304–22.

Wagner, R. Harrison. "Dissolving the State: Three Recent Perspectives on International Relations." *International Organization* (1974), 28:435–66.

Walker, Herman Jr. "Modern Treaties of Friendship, Commerce and Navigation." *Minnesota Law Review* (1958), 42:805–24.

Wallensteen, Peter. "Scarce Goods as Political Weapons: The Case of Food." *Journal of Peace Research* (1976), 13:277–98.

Wallerstein, Mitchel B. *Food for War—Food for Peace: United States Food Aid in a Global Context.* Cambridge, Mass.: MIT Press, 1980.

Wallman, Kathleen M. H. "The Politics of Default: Politically Motivated Sovereign Debt Default and Repudiation." *Texas International Law Journal* (1985), 20:475–515.

Walters, F.P. *A History of the League of Nations.* London: Oxford University Press, 1952.

Waltz, Kenneth N. "The Myth of National Interdependence." In *The International Corporation,* edited by Charles P. Kindelberger, at 205–23. Cambridge, Mass.: MIT Press, 1970.

Walz, Gustav. *Nationalboykott und Völkerrecht.* Berlin: Duncker & Humblot, 1939.

Wandel, Eckhard. *Die Bedeutung der Vereinigten Staaten von Amerika für das deutsche Reparationsproblem, 1924–9.* Tübingen: Mohr (Siebeck), 1971.

Wang, H.C. "International Law and Anti-Japanese Boycott." *Pacific Affairs* (1933), 6:373–81.

Webb, Steven B. "Agricultural Protection in Wilhelminian Germany: Forging an Empire with Pork and Rye." *Journal of Economic History* (1982), 42:309–26.

Weintraub, Sidney, and David Berteau, eds. *Economic Coercion and U.S. Foreign Policy: Implications of Case Studies from the Johnson Administration.* Boulder, Col.: Westview Press, 1982.

Westlake, John. "Commercial Blockade." In *The Collected Papers of John Westlake on Public International Law,* edited by L. Oppenheim, at 312–61. Cambridge: Cambridge University Press, 1914.

Weston, Burns. "The Charter of Economic Rights and Duties of States and the Deprivation of Foreign-Owned Wealth." *American Journal of International Law* (1981), 75:437–75.

Weulersse, Georges. *Le movement physiocratique en France (de 1756 à 1770).* 2 vols. Paris: F. Alcan, 1910.

Wheeler, A. "Self-Sufficiency and the Greek City." *Journal of the History of Ideas* (1955), 16:416–20.

Whitt, Richard Sutherland. "The Politics of Procedure: An Examination of the GATT Dispute Settlement Panel and the Article XXI Defense in the Context of the U.S. Embargo of Nicaragua." *Law and Policy in International Business* (1987), 19:603–31.

Wilczynski, J. "Strategic Embargo in Perspective." *Soviet Studies* (1967), 19:74–86.

——*The Economics and Politics of East-West Trade: A Study of Trade Between Developed Market Economies and Centrally Planned Economies in a Changing World.* London: Macmillan, 1969.

Wiles, Peter D. *Communist International Economics.* Oxford: Blackwell, 1968.

Williams, Benjamin H. "Capital Embargoes." *Political Science Quarterly* (1928), 43:229–48.

——*Economic Foreign Policy of the United States.* New York: McGraw-Hill, 1929.

——"The Coming of Economic Sanctions Into American Practice." *American Journal of International Law* (1943), 37:386–96.

Williams, Julie L. "U.S. Regulation of Arab Boycott Practices." *Law and Policy in International Business* (1978), 10:815–86.

Williamson, John, ed. *IMF Conditionality.* Washington, D.C.: Brookings Institution, 1983.

Williams, Walter L. Jr. "Nonmilitary Strategies and Competition for Power: The Need for Expanded Regulation of Coercion." *Proceedings of the American Society of International Law* (1976), 70:165–69.

Wilson, Joan Hoff. *American Business & Foreign Policy, 1920–1933.* Boston: Beacon Press, 1973.

——*Ideology and Economics: U.S. Relations with the Soviet Union 1918–1933.* Columbia: University of Missouri Press, 1974.

——*Herbert Hoover: Forgotten Progressive.* Boston: Little, Brown, 1975.

Wilson, Robert Renbert. *United States Commercial Treaties and International Law.* New Orleans: Hauser Press, 1960.

Woerden, F. van. *La Société des Nations et le rapprochement économique international.* The Hague: Martinus Nijhoff, 1932.

Wolf, Thomas A. *U.S. East-West Trade Policy: Economic Warfare versus Economic Welfare.* Lexington, Mass.: Lexington, 1973.

Woodbridge, George, ed. *UNRRA: The History of the United Nations Relief and Rehabilitation Administration.* 3 vols. New York: Columbia University Press, 1950.

Woolf, Leonard S. *Economic Imperialism.* London: Swarthmore Press, 1920.

Wortley, B. A. *Expropriation in Public International Law.* Manchester: Manchester University Press, 1959.

Wright, Robert Francis. *Medieval Internationalism: The Contribution of the Medieval Church to International Law and Peace.* London: Williams & Norgate, 1930.

Wu, Yuan-Li. *Economic Warfare*. New York: Prentice-Hall, 1952.

——*Japan's Search for Oil: A Case Study on Economic Nationalism and International Security*. Stanford: Hoover Institution Press, 1977.

Yorke, Valerie. "Oil, the Middle East and Japan's Search for Security." *International Affairs* (1981), 57:428–48.

Young, Carl Walter. *Japan's Special Position in Manchuria: Its Assertion, Legal Interpretation and Present Meaning*. Baltimore: Johns Hopkins University Press, 1931.

Yu, Ying-Shih. *Trade and Expansion in Han China: A Study in the Structure of Sino-Barbarian Economic Relations*. Berkeley: University of California Press, 1967.

Zedalis, Rex J. "Some Thoughts on the United Nations Charter and the Use of Military Force Against Economic Coercion." *Tulsa Law Journal* (1982), 17:487–506.

Cases

Treaties

Multilateral

Bilateral

Principal Treaty Series

British and Foreign State Papers, vols. 1-170.

Consolidated Treaty Series, edited by Clive Parry, vols. 1-231. Dobbs Ferry, N.Y.: Oceana, 1969-81.

Encyclopedia of European Community Law, Part B12. London: Sweet and Maxwell.

Great Britain Treay Series, 1883- .

League of Nations Treaty Series, vols 1-204.

Treaties and Other International Agreements of the United States of America, 1776-1949, compiled by Charles I. Bevans, vols. 1-12. Washington, D.C.: GPO, 1968-74.

United Nations Treaty Series, vols. 1- .

United States Treaty Series, vols. 1- .

Index

Belgium: commercial-treaty practice
of, 45; law of state immunity in,
49; and Ruhr occupation crisis,
79
"Belligerent commerce," right of,
35-36, 50
Belligerent rights, 3, 20; boycotting
as, 144; *see also* War, laws of;
Blockade; Contraband; Neutrality, law of
Berlin West Africa Conference, 46
Bilaterization, 94, 101, 113, 114,
116; *see also* Clearing agreements
Bismarck, Otto von (1815-98), 67,
153, 156, 179
Blacklisting: by Egypt, 147; by Arab
states, 147-48; by U.S., 148-50;
see also "Economic neutrality;"
Secondary economic warfare
Blackstone, William (1723-80), 16
Blockade, 33; commercial, 50; economic, 89-90; *see also* Economic
warfare; War, laws of
Bluntschli, Johann Kaspar (1808-
81), 50
Bolivia, 182, 221
Bolshevism, 73, 89; *see also* Communism; Soviet Union
Book of Lord Shang, The, 13-14
Bosnia-Herzegovina, 52
Boycott, Charles Cunningham (1832-
97), 51-52
Boycotting, 85, 89, 110, 138, 143,
185, 188; origin and definition,
51-52; and economic isolationism, 53-54, 125; primary and secondary distinguished, 146; in
nineteenth century, 52; in interwar period, 85-86, 144; legality
of, under traditional international law, 52, 127-28; opposition
to, by liberals, 52-53, 86, 126;
ambiguous legal status of, 86; Soviet treaties prohibiting, 89-90;
and FCN treaties, 129; and GATT,
7, 135-36, 139-40, 141-42; legality
of secondary, 146-51, 212; by

Arab states against Israel, 144,
147-48; by U.S. against Cuba,
148; by U.S. against Nicaragua,
127-28, 139, 141-42; by oil companies against Mexico, 172; by oil
companies against Iran, 172-73;
Nicaraguan complaints concern-
ing, 127-28, 129-30, 136, 141-42,
187; as enforcement technique,
153, 187; *see also* Economic war-
fare; "Economic neutrality;"
"Hot commodities" campaigns;
Non-intercourse; Secondary eco-
nomic warfare
BP, 131; *see also* Anglo-Iranian Oil
Company
Brazil, 194; proposed amendment to
UN Charter, 133-34, 186; debt de-
fault by, 157, 170-71; *see also* São
Paulo, Brazilian state of
Brentano, Lujo (1844-1931), 66
Bretton Woods Conference, 108-9
British East India Company, 21, 199
British Empire, 96
Buffer Stock Facility (IMF), 193, 194
Buonsignori, banking family of, 18
Burke, Edmund (1729-97), 176
Burma, 111; inward-looking devel-
opment policy of, 156
Bynkershoek, Cornelius van (1673-
1743), 34
Byzantine Empire, 17

Calvo, Carlos (1824-1903), 69, 188;
see also Calvo doctrine
Calvo doctrine, 69-70, 180-81, 185;
see also Aliens, rights of; International minimum standard
Cambodia: assets frozen by U.S.,
140
Camdessus, Michel (1933-), 194
Cameralism, 22
Canon law, 17
Capital embargoes, 84, 169; in nineteenth century, 51, 68-69; by U.S.
in 1920s, 81, 84, 91; modern
forms of, 169; as enforcement

Capital embargoes (*continued*)
technique, 153, 159, 168, 188; by
World Bank, 162-63; by IMF, 164-
68; *see also* Conditionality, IMF;
Foreign aid, reductions of; Loan-
supervision program
Capitalism, 4, 7, 43, 57, 59-60, 88,
153, 154, 169, 204, 215, 217; *see
also* Economic liberalism; Foreign investment; International
banks and banking; Multinational companies; Private enterprise
"Capitalist encirclement" of Soviet
Union, 102
Caribbean, 59, 68; Caribbean Development Bank, 192
Cartels, 88; *see also* Monopolies; Producers' associations
Cass, Lewis (1782-1866), 50
Catholic Church: support for "poli-
cies of provision," 16; and promotion of freedom of trade, 16-17
Central America, 59, 68, 200
Central Europe, 71, 73, 75, 94, 102
Central Selling Organization, 200
Cereal imports, IMF assistance for,
193
Ceylon: and Hickenlooper Amendment, 173; and GATT infant-
industries provision, 192
Charlemagne (c. 782-814), 217
Charter of Economic Rights and Duties of States, 185-86, 187, 189,
195
Chase Manhattan Bank, 206
Chevalier, Michel (1816-1879), 45
Chile, 202; in default to World Bank,
163; conflict with U.S., 174-76,
184-85; *see also* Allende y Gos-
sens, Salvador
China, 96; ancient, autarkist outlook
of, 13-14; tribute system, 14, 207;
economic isolationism of, 25, 26,
53-54, 58, 125, 158; physiocrats'
fascination with, 31; Opium War,
53, 59; boycotting by, 52, 53, 85,

86; assets frozen by U.S. and
Cuba, 142; inward-looking devel-
opment policy of, 156; *see also*
Sino-Japanese crisis
Christianity, universalistic ethos of,
2, 14; *see also* Catholic Church;
Papacy
City-states: ancient, 11-12, 15, 20,
93; medieval, 15-16, 19, 20, 93
Clausen, Alden W. (Tom) (1923-),
202, 203
Clay, Henry (1777-1852), 64, 65
Clayton, William L. (1880-1966), 100
Clémentel, Étienne (1864-1936), 72
Clearing agreements, 94, 116
Closed Commercial State, The, 64
Cobden-Chevalier Treaty, 45
Cobden, Richard (1804-65) 42, 45,
73, 78, 99, 109, 110, 201
CoCom, *see* Coordinating Committee
Code of Trade Liberalization, 105
Coffee, 28, 88
Colbert, Jean-Baptiste (1619-83), 22,
91
Cold War, 107, 108-11, 128, 144,
145; *see also* Communism
Colonies and colonialism, 122, 139,
167, 222; as raw-material
sources, 22, 70-71
"Commercial" era of international
relations, 70, 178
"Commercial" policies, 96; *see also*
"Territorial" policies
Commodities, raw-material: sur-
pluses in inter-war period, 88-89,
92, 94; post-World War II surplus
fears, 103-4, 154-55; proposals for
monetization of, 104; *see also*
Commodity agreements; Common Fund for Commodities; Integrated Program for Commodities;
Producers' associations; Raw-
material-producing countries;
Raw materials; Terms of trade;
"Tin buyers' strike"
Commodity agreements, 103, 194;
and Havana Charter, 107; and

Czechoslovakia (*continued*)
deprived of most-favored-nation
status by U.S., 129, 140; U.S. GATT
waiver against, 140; complaint
against U.S. in GATT, 135, 144

Danube River, tolls on, 46
Dawes, Charles G. (1865-1951), 79
Dawes Plan, 79-81, 87, 88, 89, 115
Debt crisis, third-world, 153, 163,
222; origin of, 204; World Bank
role, 192; IMF role, 193, 194
Debts, interstate: 1931 moratorium,
92; U.S. capital embargo against
defaulters, 170; Chilean, 175; *see
also* War debts, inter-Allied
Debts, private: exemption from sei-
zure, 49-50
Debts, sovereign, to private banks:
and World Bank lending, 162; of
Chile, 163, 175; of Brazil, 170-71;
of Argentina, 214-25; of Poland,
215-16; *see also* Defaults on debts
by states; Debt crisis, third-world
Declaration of Paris, 50
Declaration on Equality of Trade,
draft, 74-75
Declaration on Friendly Relations,
UN General Assembly, 132, 133
Declaration on Non-Intervention,
UN General Assembly, 132
Declaration on Permanent Sover-
eignty over Natural Resources,
UN General Assembly, 183; *see
also* Permanent sovereignty over
natural resources
Declarations of UN General Assem-
bly, legal status of, 183
Dédoublement fonctionnel, concept
of, 85, 99
Deep sea-bed, 191, 193, 195
Defaults on debts by states: in
Middle Ages, 18; in nineteenth
century, 59; in Great Depression,
92, 162; as a form of wealth
transfer, 157; owed to World
Bank, 163; owed to IMF, 164-65;

sanctions of private creditors,
171; and foreign-aid reduction,
170; case of Brazil, 170-171; *see
also* "Event of default;" Falklands
conflict, financial aspects; Iran,
Teheran hostages crisis; Poland,
martial-law crisis
Deflationary policies: and IMF, 117-
18, 166-67
Denmark, 90
Department of State, U.S., 81, 88,
89, 91, 100, 154
Depressions, economic, 39, 114; of
late nineteenth century, 5-6, 40,
60-61, 71, 114; of early 1980s,
153, 163; and economic nationalism, 21; *see also* Abundance,
crises of; Great Depression
Détente, U.S.-Soviet, 200, 217
Devaluation of currencies: during
Great Depression, 93, 116; competitive, 116, 117; IMF and, 166;
see also Exchange rates
Developed countries, 8, 58, 70, 133,
153, 154, 161, 182, 185, 191, 194,
222; *see also* Industrialized countries; Western countries
Developing countries, 7, 39-40, 59,
70, 88-89, 102, 114, 132, 133, 153,
161, 171, 180, 190, 191, 194-95;
see also Development, economic;
Raw-material-producing countries; Third-world countries
Development, economic, 89, 222;
liberalism and, 41, 57, 152-53,
155-56; and economic nationalism, 7, 63-67, 152-53; outward-
looking, 155; inward-looking, 155,
156-58; and "new international
economic order," 189-91; *see also*
Economic nationalism; Industrialization
Diplomatic relations, 1; breaking of,
as retorsion, 144
Division of labor, 4, 40-41, 42, 52,
54, 57, 88, 176; *see also* Economic
liberalism; Freedom of trade

Division of Labor in Society, The, 66
Dollar diplomacy, 68
Dominican order, 19, 158
Don Pacifico affair, 59
Douceur de commerce, 29
Douro River, tolls on, 46
Dresser Industries, Inc., 149-50; and
    Dresser (France), 149-50
Dulles, John Foster (1888-1959), 84, 91
Dualistic world order, post-World
    War II, 6-7, 99-100, 105-6, 119-20,
    124-25, 163, 216, 222
Dumping, 101, 107; in Great Depres-
    sion, 93-94; GATT and, 113, 159-
    60
Durkheim, Émile (1858-1917), 66
Dutch East India Company, 21
Duty to trade, natural-law, 19-20,
    25, 55; as imperfect obligation,
    21, 48; World Court rejection of,
    128; *see also* Freedom of trade,
    natural-law doctrine of; "Law of
    trade;" "Sociability" of states;
    "Solidarity," principle of

Eagleton, Clyde (1891-1958), 158
East-West trade, decline in Cold
    War, 110-11
Eastern Europe, 73, 75, 111, 128
Economic aggression, 102, 132, 184-
    85; *see also* Economic imperial-
    ism
Economic coercion, third-world
    campaign against, 180, 182, 184-
    88; economic nationalist charac-
    ter of, 180, 187-88; *see also*
    Aggression; Force, use of; Non-in-
    tervention; Permanent sover-
    eignty over natural resources; Re-
    taliation, economic
"Economic disarmament," 74-77
Economic imperialism, 91, 108, 174,
    177
Economic isolationism: of Sparta,
    11; of China, 25, 26, 48, 51; and
    economic warfare, 51-55, 125; le-
    gality of 53-55; *see also* Autarky;

Duty to trade, natural-law; Self-
    sufficiency
Economic liberalism, 7-8, 63, 152,
    153, 155, 217-18; and classical
    political economy, 7-8, 40-44; in
    nineteenth century, 44-48, 100; in
    1920s, 74-83; in post-World War
    II period, 100-107; significance
    for international law, 28, 33-34,
    39, 48-56, 83-87, 118-20, 126-27,
    134-51; "common law" of, 54-56;
    and peace movement, 41-43, 96,
    100, 196, 197-98, 217; and eco-
    nomic warfare, 51-53, 85-86, 125-
    26, 143-51; and economic isola-
    tionism, 53-55; enforcement of
    rules of, 58-59, 152-54, 159-77;
    importance of atmosphere of
    prosperity, 28, 38, 106, 114, 115,
    220; and industrialization, 56-57,
    88-89, 114, 154; and economic de-
    velopment, 152-53, 155-56; *see
    also* Capitalism; "Economic"
    world order; Freedom of trade;
    Freedom of trade, natural-law
    doctrine of; Individuals, role of;
    Interdependence, economic; In-
    ternational economic law; Inter-
    vention; Laissez-faire; Multilat-
    eral trade system; Open door
    principle; Physiocrats and physi-
    ocracy; Private enterprise; Pri-
    vate-law rights; "Sociability" of
    states; "Solidarity," principle of;
    States, role of in a liberal order;
    Utility maximization
Economic nationalism, 5, 6, 7, 104,
    119, 153, 154, 159, 161, 163, 168,
    169, 174, 182, 187, 196, 197, 200,
    222; main characteristics of, 12-
    13, 175-77, 196; moral element of,
    11, 13, 15, 95, 196; collectivist
    character of, 13, 21, 95, 167; in
    ancient civilizations, 9-10, 11-14;
    in Middle Ages, 15-16; mercantil-
    ism as, 20-22; in nineteenth cen-
    tury, 7, 39-40, 44, 61, 63-69, 71,

International banks (*continued*)
asset freeze, 213-14; and Falklands conflict, 214-15; and Polish martial-law crisis, 215-16; *see also* Capital embargoes; Dawes Plan; Debts, sovereign; Defaults on debts by states; Euro-currency markets

International Civil Aviation Organization (ICAO), 107

International Convention on Export and Import Prohibitions and Restrictions, 77

International Court of Justice, *see* World Court

International Development Association (IDA), 192

International economic law, 49; definition, 118; conservative character of, 6-7; contrasted with principle of "solidarity," 118-20; and economic warfare, 126-27, 134-37; question of "political exception" to, 126, 137-38, 140-43; *see also* Freedom of trade, natural-law doctrine of; General Agreement on Tariffs and Trade; International Monetary Fund; "Sociability" of states; "Solidarity," principle of; World Bank

International law, 1, 3, 6, 7, 36, 43, 52, 69, 74, 99, 126, 127, 147, 165-66, 169, 181, 202; political character of, 3-4; conservatism of, 48, 50, 69; and economic nationalism, 5, 8, 23-26, 27, 39, 69, 119-20, 222; and economic warfare, 125, 126, 127-34, 143, 222; implications of economic liberalism for, 33-34, 39, 48-56, 69, 83-87; *see also* Calvo doctrine; Duty to trade; Force, use of; Foreign act of state doctrine; Freedom of trade, natural-law doctrine of; International economic law; "Law of trade;" Neutrality; *Nicaragua v. U.S.* case; Non-intervention;

Permanent sovereignty over natural resources; Positivist conception of international law; "Solidarity," principle of; Sovereign rights of states; State immunity; World Court

International minimum standard, 51, 58, 69; *see also* Aliens, rights of; Calvo doctrine; Free movement of labor; Treaties of friendship, commerce and navigation (FCN)

International Monetary Fund (IMF), 6, 7, 107, 108, 110, 120, 170, 177; Articles of Agreement of, 116, 121, 134, 136, 138, 140, 163-64, 193; technocratic character of, 112, 113, 121, 166-67, 176; function of 116-18, 161; specialized-agency agreement with UN, 121; and freezing of assets, 130, 136-37, 140; national-security provision of, 139, 140; question of "political exception" to rules of, 126, 142; support for South Africa, 122; socialist countries and, 108-10; preference for outward-looking development policies, 157-58; and campaign against third-world economic nationalism, 153, 163-68; enforcement techniques, 164-66; general character of adjustment programs, 166-67; "IMF riots," 7, 166-67; clash with Tanzania, 167-68; third-world demands concerning, 190; special facilities of, 192-93, 194; role in third world-debt crisis, 193, 194; amendments to Articles of Agreement, 163-64, 193; *see also* Conditionality, IMF; Exchange rates, IMF surveillance of

International organizations, liberal hostility toward, 44

International Petroleum Company, 173-74

tawa agreements; Porter Convention; Specialized-agency agreements; Transport, freedom of; United Nations Charter; Versailles, treaty of; Vienna Convention on the Law of Treaties; World Bank, Articles of Agreement

Tribute system, ancient Chinese, 14, 207

"True" policies, 30

Truman administration, 104-5, 108

Tunisia, indebtedness of, 59

Turkey, 90; *see also* Ottoman Empire

Tuscany, physiocratic experiment in, 37

UNCTAD, *see* United Nations Conference on Trade and Development

Union of Soviet Socialist Republics, *see* Soviet Union

United Fruit Company, 200

United Kingdom, 82, 89, 104, 105, 130, 136, 214; *see also* England; Great Britain

United Nations (UN), 112, 121; political character of, 6, 99-100, 105; specialized-agency agreement with World Bank, 120-21; specialized-agency agreement with IMF, 121; and IMF support for South Africa, 122; dispute with World Bank over South African and Portuguese lending, 122; economic sanctions by, 138; socialist countries' attack on strategic embargo in, 144-45; Nicaraguan complaint against U.S. in, 187; General Assembly, 106, 122, 132, 179, 182, 183, 184, 185, 188, 189; Security Council, 134, 138-39, 147, 159, 184, 187; *see also* United Nations Charter; United Nations Conference on Trade and Development.

United Nations Charter, 6, 99-100, 120, 126, 127, 134, 138, 142, 143, 186; drafting of, 104, 133-34; Article 2(4), 132-33

United Nations Conference on Trade and Development (UNCTAD), 114, 186-87

United Nations Relief and Rehabilitation Administration (UNRRA), 108, 128

United States, 58, 60, 65, 74, 78, 92, 109, 170, 199, 217; as pioneer of liberal economic order, 35-36, 50; economic nationalism of, in nineteenth century, 57, 64, 155; boycotted by Chinese, 52; role in associationalist system, 6, 77-83, 87-88, 90-92; as foreign investor, 68, 78-79, 131, 153, 157, 200; as creditor, 79, 81, 82, 170; relations with Soviet Union in 1920s, 82, 89; tariff policy in 1920s, 85, 90, 93, 160; and nondiscrimination, 90, 100; most-favored-nation policy of, 91; economic nationalism of, in 1930s, 93, 95; relations with Japan in 1930s, 96-97; conversion to free-trade cause, 100; reciprocal trade agreements program, 101; Atlantic Charter, 101; plans for post-World War II liberal order, 100-105; failure to ratify Havana Charter, 108; Cold-War concerns of, 108, 109, 110, 128, 129, 139, 140; and strategic embargo of socialist states, 109-10, 144-46; Czechoslovakia complaint in GATT, 135; dominance of World Bank and IMF, 109-10; foreign-assistance policy of, 128-29, 145, 148, 170, 173, 174; freezing of foreign assets by, 96, 130, 140, 142; export-control program of, 110, 148-49, 212; economic warfare against Nicaragua, 127, 129-30, 136, 139, 141-42, 160, 187; economic warfare against Cuba, 131,